Institutions and Sustaina

Institutions and Sustainability

Political Economy of Agriculture
and the Environment - Essays in Honour
of Konrad Hagedorn

Edited by

Volker Beckmann
Humboldt Universität zu Berlin, Germany

and

Martina Padmanabhan
Humboldt Universität zu Berlin, Germany

 Springer

Editors

Volker Beckmann
Humboldt Universität zu Berlin
Philippstraße 13
10099 Berlin
Germany
v.beckmann@agrar.hu-berlin.de

Martina Padmanabhan
Humboldt Universität zu Berlin
Philippstraße 13
10099 Berlin
Germany
Martina.padmanabhan@agrar.hu-berlin.de

e-ISBN: 978-1-4020-9690-7

DOI 10.1007/978-1-4020-9690-7

Printed on acid-free paper

9 8 7 6 5 4 3 2 1

springer.com

Preface

From the first vague idea to use Konrad Hagedorn's 60th birthday as an inspiration for taking stock of his vibrant academic contributions, this joint book project has been a great pleasure for us in many ways. Pursuing Hagedorn's intellectual development, we have tried to reflect on the core questions of humanity according to Ernst Bloch "Who are we?", "Where do we come from?" and "Where are we heading?" In this way, and without knowing it, Konrad Hagedorn initiated a collective action process he would have very much enjoyed ... if he had been allowed to take part in it. But it was our aim and constant motivation to surprise him with this collection of essays in his honour.

Konrad Hagedorn was reared as the youngest child of a peasant family on a small farm in the remote moorland of East Frisia, Germany. During his childhood in the poverty-ridden years after the Second World War, he faced a life where humans were heavily dependent on using nature around them for their livelihoods; meanwhile, he learned about the fragility of the environment. As a boy, he attended a one-room schoolhouse, where his great intellectual talents were first recognised and used for co-teaching his schoolmates. These early teaching experiences might have laid the foundations for his later becoming a dedicated lecturer and mentor.

Between 1968 and 1979, Hagedorn attended the University of Göttingen, undertaking an intellectual apprenticeship in the field of agricultural economics and beyond as well as acquiring a command of the analytical and methodological tools that would later help him to improve the investigation and understanding of complex real-world problems. As a student, he soon attracted the attention of Günther Schmitt, Professor of Agricultural Policy, who subsequently became his Ph.D. advisor and intellectual mentor. Schmitt, who passed away in 2005, was one of the leading agricultural economists in Germany and a pioneer in applying theories and methods of New Political Economy and New Institutional Economics to agricultural economics. Schmitt's strong sense for the importance of theory in practical policy analysis had a long-lasting influence on Hagedorn, who achieved his first notoriety as a Ph.D. student when his comments on social policy in agriculture shocked the establishment of agricultural politics and lobbyists. Without claiming any biographic authority or completeness in this brief encapsulation of Hagedorn's development, we think it is safe to say that the learning environment fostered by Günther Schmitt is primarily where he acquired his skills for engaging in intellectual battles as well as his passion for stimulating provocation and debates with sparring partners from the international agricultural economics community. Leaving Göttingen, he spent 1980 as a Visiting Scholar of the German Research Foundation (DFG) at the University of California, Berkeley, USA, to broaden his perspective.

Back in Europe, Hagedorn joined the Federal Agricultural Research Centre (FAL) in Braunschweig in 1981, rendering conceptually sound policy advice on agricultural issues. During his years as a research fellow at the FAL, he continued teaching, being a guest lecturer at the Universities of Hannover and Wageningen. Besides giving concrete policy advice, Hagedorn went on to dig deeper into the institutional foundations of agricultural policy. His habilitation thesis on "Institutions as a Research Problem in Agricultural Economics" was completed in 1989 and has been considered to be a landmark in institutional agricultural economics ever since.

The fall of the Berlin Wall and the subsequent transformation processes were unique historical moments and significant for Hagedorn's further career and intellectual development. Institutions at different levels changed rapidly and opened up new "windows of opportunity". After German reunification in 1990, the Humboldt-Universität zu Berlin announced the establishment of a professorship in resource economics at the again merged agricultural and horticultural faculty. It was Konrad Hagedorn who obtained the position in 1994, and almost simultaneously, he was given the position of executive director of the Institute of Co-operative Science at Humboldt-Universität zu Berlin. From that time on, he has built up an ever enlarging research network. Pushing the frontiers of institutional research soon took Hagedorn across the borders of the New Federal States of the former East Germany (GDR), as he gathered an international team of pioneers and enthusiasts to venture into the unknown territories of the transition states in Eastern Europe. Large international research projects, such as KATO, GRANO and CEESA, paved the way towards the analysis of institutional change in agricultural and natural resource management and the development of concepts like "Institutions of Sustainability" or "Integrative and Segregative Institutions". Since then, his endeavours to understand institutional change and the demands of a sustainable future have never ceased. In 2002, he commenced a fruitful and enduring co-operative relationship with Elinor Ostrom, of Indiana University, Bloomington, with whom he shares a deep humanity and a belief in the possibility of local people successfully attaining self-governance in managing common pool resources.

Celebrating the 60th birthday of a scholar always holds the promise that there should still be much to expect of him. Meeting the future challenges of sustainability – such as global climate change; increasing food, water and energy scarcity; civil wars, economic crises or natural disasters – requires sound theoretical and empirical research and wise policy advice. We hope – no, we are sure – that Konrad Hagedorn will continue to contribute towards this end. Likewise, the contributions to this volume take stock of and impressively reflect on Hagedorn's curiosity, ingenuity and scholarship.

Needless to say, without his inspiration as the thoughtful and farsighted helmsman of the Division of Resource Economics, which has at times had to sail through the troubled waters of internal and external higher-education reforms, we would not have had the opportunity to enjoy the Division's collective spirit, which has in large part made this book possible. In particular, we would like to thank:

- Renate Judis, for her full-fledged support for this project, her kind insistence and communicativeness, her driving force in keeping loose ends together as well as meeting deadlines, her editorial assistance, many cups of tea, friendship and hands-on support;
- Ines Jeworski, for brushing up the graphs and tables to unparalleled standards and Sigrid Heilmann for the discrete supply with vital information on whereabouts of Konrad Hagedorn and literature. We also relied on the valuable experience both of them have gained in previous publishing projects;
- Christopher Hank, for his professional, most friendly and dialogical language editing, at all times and places, and the enormous training effect it provides;
- Sylvia Sieber, for type-setting the manuscript and thus transforming raw material into a proper book;
- Anja Techem, for painstakingly sorting out the index;
- Fritz Schmuhl and Takeesha Moerland-Torpey, from Springer Academic Publishers, for making it possible for this *Festschrift* to be brought out in a smooth fashion;
- All contributors, who responded enthusiastically to our request for a contribution, for their dedication towards putting their thoughts and extensions concerning the work of their colleague, Konrad Hagedorn, onto paper and putting up with our wishes and demands;
- Last, but not least, the collective at the Division of Resource Economics, which makes work and life more enjoyable through a shared belief in intellectual exchange and mutual learning, as continually exemplified at research colloquiums (FoKo) after questions for clarification have been posed.

September 2008   Volker Beckmann and Martina Padmanabhan

Contents

Part II: Institutions, Governance and Sustainability

List of Contributors

Volker Beckmann – Institute of Agricultural Economics and Social Sciences, Humboldt-Universität zu Berlin, Germany.

Regina Birner – International Food and Policy Research Institute (IFPRI), Washington D.C., USA

William Blomquist – Department of Political Science, Indiana University, Purdue University, Indianapolis, USA

Markus Hanisch – Division of Cooperative Studies, Humboldt-Universität zu Berlin, Germany

Guido Van Huylenbroeck – Department of Agricultural Economics, Ghent University, Belgium

Benedikt Korf – Department of Geography, University of Zurich, Switzerland

Peter Mehl – Johann Heinrich von Thünen Institute (vTI), Braunschweig, Germany

Ruth Meinzen-Dick – International Food Policy Research Institute (IFPRI), Washington D.C., USA

Esther Mwangi – Kennedy School of Government and the University Center for Environment, Harvard University, Cambridge, USA

Elinor Ostrom – Workshop in Political Theory and Policy Analysis, Indiana University, Bloomington, USA

Martina Padmanabhan – Institute of Agricultural Economics and Social Sciences, Humboldt-Universität zu Berlin, Germany

Nico B.P. Polman – Agricultural Economics Research Institute (LEI), The Hague, The Netherlands

Scott Rozelle – University of California, Davis and Stanford University, USA

Achim Schlüter – Institute of Forestry Economics, Albert-Ludwigs-Universität Freiburg, Germany

Louis G.H. Slangen – Agricultural Economics and Rural Policy Group, Wageningen University, The Netherlands

Brent Swallow – World Agroforestry Centre (ICRAF), Nairobi, Kenya

Johan F.M. Swinnen – LICOS Centre for Institutions and Economic Performance, Katholieke Universiteit Leuven, Belgium

Insa Theesfeld – Leibniz Institute for Agricultural Development in Central and Eastern Europe (IAMO), Halle, Germany

Clem Tisdell – School of Economics, University of Queensland, St Lucia, Australia

Arild Vatn – Department of International Environment and Development Studies, Norwegian University of Life Sciences, Aas, Norway

Wim Verbeke – Department of Agricultural Economics, Ghent University, Belgium

Anne Vuylsteke – Department of Agricultural Economics, Ghent University, Belgium

Heidi Wittmer – Helmholtz Centre for Environmental Research (UFZ), Leipzig, Germany

1 Institutions and Sustainability: Introduction and Overview

Martina Padmanabhan and Volker Beckmann

Division of Resource Economics, Institute of Agricultural Economics and Social Science, Faculty of Agriculture and Horticulture, Humboldt-Universität zu Berlin, Philippstr. 13, 10099 Berlin, E-mail: martina.padmanabhan@agrar.hu-berlin.de, v.beckmann@agrar.hu-berlin.de

Abstract. The analysis of institutions in the field of nature-related human endeavours has always been the key element of Konrad Hagedorn's academic writing and teaching. Pushing the frontiers of institutional economics to integrate sustainability concerns, he pioneered the reflection on institutions, values and norms in agricultural economics. The aim of this introduction is to outline the main facets of his conceptual and applied work, show the impact and inspiration it has had on the work of other academics in the area of institutional analysis, introduce the papers collected in this volume, and look ahead to further challenges to come.

Keywords: Agriculture, Konrad Hagedorn, Natural resources, Institutions, Sustainability

1.1 Introduction

The present collection of papers takes an institutional perspective on the management of natural resources in light of Konrad Hagedorn's work as an agricultural economist and his special interest in the interdisciplinary debates on sustainability. The essays aim to describe the latest trends in combining institutions and sustainability, summarise new conceptual developments in environmental economics, outline new approaches towards the analysis of governance of natural resources and present findings on the political economy of agriculture.

The authors brought together in this volume discuss institutional analysis of agriculture and natural resources in honour of Konrad Hagedorn on the occasion of his 60th birthday. The contributors are scholars from different disciplines, reflecting Hagedorn's spirit of academic cooperation worldwide. These original papers are extensions and applications of the innovative concepts developed by Konrad Hagedorn, particularly drawing on his theoretical foundations for institutional analysis in the field of environmental sustainability. Part 1 focuses on the "Political

Economy of Economic Development and Agricultural Policy", highlighting the fundamental role of political institutions and some difficulties encountered in implementing reform towards sustainability. Part 2, "Institutions, Governance and Sustainability", outlines different approaches and frameworks for analysing management structures in various natural resource settings. Part 3, "Property Rights, Collective Action and Natural Resources", presents empirical studies and frameworks concerning the role of collective efforts for coping with environmental challenges. Part 4 outlines the "Challenges of Institutional Analysis for Sustainability" with regard to further theoretical and empirical research. Contributing to the interdisciplinary debate on sustainability in the field of institutional, agricultural and natural resource economics and management, the present volume responds to the prominent global-political issues of food and energy security. The state-of-the-art discussion taking place here among members of the agricultural economics community and beyond, draws from debates in political sciences, development studies, sociology and environmental and resource economics, thus resonating Konrad Hagedorn's continual openness to concepts from different social disciplines.

This introduction to the volume is structured as follows: First, we present the key ideas of Konrad Hagedorn's scholarly work on institutions and sustainability within the four subject areas just mentioned. Second, we present an overview of the papers presented in this volume, drawing linkages between them and Hagedorn's contributions. We close with a perspective on future developments.

1.2 Konrad Hagedorn's Contributions to Institutional Analysis

This introductory section aims to provide an overview of Hagedorn's oeuvre: which ranges from the political economy of agricultural and environmental relations, through conceptual work towards developing and identifying institutions to govern sustainability, to concrete and categorical questions on how to manage the commons. Last but not least, his intellectual programme is driven by a keen interest in methodological, epistemological and visionary considerations.

1.2.1 The politics of agricultural and environmental relations

Konrad Hagedorn has made seminal contributions to the political economy of economic development and agricultural policy. His application of political economy concepts in the field of agricultural economics consisted of a great expansion or rather connection of these obvious themes that remained hitherto outside the research focus of conventional agricultural economics (Hagedorn, 1993a, 1996a, 1998b). Hagedorn's major theoretical works elaborate on the importance of political institutions for understanding agricultural policy and the limits of policy reform (Hagedorn, 1985a, 1988, 1996a). Besides classical farm income policy (Hagedorn, 1981; Hagedorn & Schmitt, 1985), he has applied the political economy perspective to a broad range of policy arenas, such as social policy (e.g., Hagedorn, 1977, 1981, 1982, 1985b, 1991a; Hagedorn & Mehl, 2001), agri-environmental policy (e.g., Hagedorn, 1993c; Eggers & Hagedorn, 1998; Hagedorn & Eggers, 1998; Hagedorn, 1999a, 1999b, 2007) and transition policy (e.g., Hagedorn, 1991b, 1992b, 1993b, 1996b, 2004b; Beckmann & Hagedorn, 1995, 1997, 1999, 2007).

Since the 1980s Hagedorn has included political institutions in his studies of agricultural policy in order to consider the processes whereby political institutions change and the decision-making processes they govern. In doing so, he met a number of methodological obstacles, such as in agricultural economics, where the spheres of objectives and values had been considered to be outside of scientific bounds (1993a, p. 850). Similarly, moral institutions like ethics and norms were widely neglected in agricultural economics at that time. However, the existing "inadequate feasibility" of policy recommendations was a great shortcoming of agricultural economics as an applied science. Using the ideas of the "new political economy" and public and institutional choice theory, Hagedorn set out to make the domain of political choice a systematic element of agricultural economic theory, strictly sticking to his credo that only theoretical conceptions enable individuals to perceive the existence and structure of complex issues (1993a, p. 851). The encountered paradox appeared to Hagedorn as something like "policy advisors do not reflect on institutional and political issues", the solution of which he broke down into two tasks. First, he searched for reasons for the dire theory deficiency and the obstacles causing it. Second, he set out to push for theoretical advances and the conceptual integration of found solutions. Hagedorn's strong devotion to theory development, in combination with the declared intention to contribute to real world problem solving, is one of his unique qualities or, as his fellows at the *Deutsche Forschungsgemeinschaft* would acknowledge, his *Alleinstellungsmerkmal*, that is, his outstanding feature as a scholar.

Starting from the hypothesis that norms and expectations regulate the relationship between applied social sciences (among them agricultural economics) and practical politics, Hagedorn encountered a dual orientation within the discipline: A certain division of labour exists where, like in other theoretical disciplines, conceptual work is central, while at the same time there is a demand for practical policy advise. This results in a conflict of loyalties, with an attempt being made to neutralise contradicting claims by conceptually separating and building "firewalls" between different research aims. Economists mainly focus on instruments, while politicians have a major interest in institutions (1994a). Taking aim at this disintegrative model, Hagedorn has dissected the epistemological norms that exclude values and institutions from scientific study, suggesting the integrative concepts of public and institutional choice theory as one step to solve the either-or dilemma. His attempt to combine institutions and decision-making processes has raised new research questions about the costs and deficits of collective action in political decision-making processes, with the New Political Economy thus promoting the integration of economic and political concepts and interests as essential elements of analysis.

1.2.2 Developing institutions to govern sustainability

Analysing the role of political, economic and social institutions for sustainable development requires new analytical frameworks to understand and design rules for governing the increasing complex interaction between ecological and social systems of modern societies. Konrad Hagedorn has proposed such a framework, known as *Institutions of Sustainability (IoS)* (Hagedorn, Arzt, & Peters, 2002; Gatzweiler & Hagedorn, 2002a, 2002b, 2004a, 2004b; Hagedorn, 2002, 2003, 2004a, 2004c, 2005, 2007, 2008a, 2008b), which requires in-depth analysis of actors and transactions as well as institutions and governance structures from the perspective of institutional performance and institutional innovation. Regarding the topic of cooperative strategies to cope with agri-environmental problems, Hagedorn has developed an analytical framework to approach theoretical and methodological questions in a systematic way. The IoS framework serves as a tool and procedure to conceptualise and implement environmental cooperatives and cooperation in agriculture and rural areas.

This institutional approach towards agri-environmental coordination focuses on institutional change in property rights regimes and governance structures as a response to technological, biological and economic factors, on the one hand, and societal and political influences on the other. The IoS is an explorative concept to analyse relationships and their interplay, whereby it is useful to distinguish four groups of determinants: First, institutional arrangements depend on the biophysical features and implications of transactions. Second, institutional change relies on the characteristics and objectives of actors involved. Third, these changes affect the design and distribution of property rights and cost and benefit streams. Fourth, such changes are accompanied by changes in governance structures for supervision and sanctioning, with organisation and coordination being based on self-organisation and/or government regulations.

The properties of transactions affecting the natural environment and ecological systems, in other words the perceived types of interaction between actors having impacts on ecosystems, form the central units of analysis of the IoS framework. Environmental problems often arise around public goods, entailing difficulties with regard to legal transformations that regulate their transfer between different actors. The IoS identifies the main properties of transactions arising at the junction between private and public goods. Considering the features of a specific resource use in the context of different governance options is a central contribution to the debate on institutions. The excludability of actors, rivalry asset specificity, site specificity, capital specificity and the particular knowledge comprising group-specific human capital (Ostrom, 1998) – such characteristics frame the options of institutionalisation. A low degree of separability and overall frequency of transactions may induce learning processes and bring about economies of scale, whereas uncertainty causes transaction costs for measuring, monitoring and information. Moreover, the complexity of environmental processes may produce opportunistic behaviour, while the heterogeneity and variability of stochastic phenomena, like the weather, also shape the properties of transactions.

Taking into account the characteristics of actors involved in agri-environmental coordination and their differences and particularities as land users, regulators or coordinators enhances understanding in the search for sustainable institutions. Important attributes of actors are not only their values and beliefs, but also their reputations for reliability and trustworthiness. Resources for participation, such as time, capacities to collect information, access to networks and bargaining power, are instrumental in influencing policy implementation through the mechanisms of interest representation in agrarian policy networks (Hagedorn 1994a). Acquiring and processing, retaining and using knowledge is vital under conditions of often asymmetric information, as principal-agent theory informs us. An actor's method of action selection (Ostrom, 1998) is based on his or her ability to learn from mistakes. The social embeddedness of actors regulates behavioural norms, preferences and distribution of resources. Culture refers to a common set of values and rules which governs the interaction between nature and actors.

Institutions of environmental sustainability are guided by property rights over natural components and governance structures for agri-environmental relations. Right holders can be favoured by benefit streams or burdened by cost components. Nevertheless, the institutional design of a right or duty can differ. Defining, establishing, quantifying and supervising measures all lead to transaction costs. The latter may be lowered by bundling rights in the hand of one actor, though a higher degree of centralisation has social and political consequences, affects motivation and participation of land users, and may precipitate moral dilemmas and undermine identification processes. Agricultural production results in a variety of cost and benefit streams with positive and negative effects for the public to bear. Often, rights and duties are conditional on the fulfilment of other rights and duties.

To analyse governance structure for regional or local agri-environmental coordination, different categories have been distinguished. Williamson (1996) differentiates between markets as (1) voluntary bilateral agreements between individuals, (2) hierarchies compulsorily selected by an authority as in organisations and (3) hybrid forms of contractual relations that are voluntary prior to the contract and compulsory afterwards. The third means of cooperation thus emerges as a type of horizontal non-market coordination. These categories reflect the relationships between the actors involved and the role of action selection as a relevant subject in negotiating these relationships.

The institutional interpretation sees sustainable development as a comprehensive process of searching, learning and gaining experience with regard to organising principles and policy instruments. Hagedorn sees sustainable development as a regulative idea that requires adequate institutions to become effective. Basing himself on the Enquete Commission's "Protection of Man and the Environment" (Enquete-Kommission, 1998) Hagedorn formulates four basic strategies for achieving "Institutions of Sustainability" in the long run: (1) the call for *reflexivity* builds on the reinforcement of actors' sensitivity to push for institutional reforms; (2) *self-organisation* and *participation* in the political process has an integrative impact; (3) *Interest harmonisation* and *conflict regulation* is central to balancing power and control over resources, thus requiring an investment in the development of conflict-solving mechanisms; and (4) *institutional innovation* emerges as a creative process of searching and learning using a cooperative approach. In line with Haberer (1996), Hagedorn et al. (2002) call for transparency-creating institutional arrangements.

1.2.3 Managing common pool resources

Property rights over agricultural land and other natural resources has been a principal subject of the research by Konrad Hagedorn. He has contributed, in particular, to the theoretical and empirical analysis of the economic and ecological consequences of land privatisation in transition economies (Gatzweiler & Hagedorn, 2002a, 2002b, 2004a; Gatzweiler, Judis, & Hagedorn, 2002; Hagedorn, 1991b, 1992b, 1993b, 1994b, 1996b, 1997, 1998a, 1998b, 2003, 2004, 2004c; Lütteken & Hagedorn 1998). Furthermore, he has analysed the importance of property rights for contractual arrangements and collective action in order to effectively manage common pool resources (Hagedorn, 2000, 2002; Hagedorn et al., 2002). As the director of the Institute of Cooperative studies, he has studied extensively the role of self-organised cooperative structures in solving economic, social and environmental problems (Hagedorn, 1998c, 2000; Eisen & Hagedorn, 1998, 2000).

Hagedorn's interest in the governance of natural resource use, especially common pool resources, has guided his work on collective action and property rights (Di Gregorio et al., 2008). Besides sustainability outcomes, poverty has increasingly become a focus of this work. Inspired by the prospects of applying theoretical conceptions to real world phenomena within larger international empirical research projects, for example in Ethiopia (Beyene, 2008; Beyene & Korf, 2008; Hundie, 2008; Hundie & Padmanabhan, 2008) and India (Sreedevi, Suhas, Wani, Chennamaneni, & Chaliganti, 2007), he has contributed to extending the analytical lens for investigating collective action and property rights by focusing on specific outcomes in terms of poverty in the realm of managing natural resources.

As Di Gregorio et al. (2008) propose, the insights gained on the role of formal and informal property rights and collective action in improving natural resource management can inspire policies for poverty reduction. This is especially important, as an incomplete understanding of the complexity of property rights can lead to reduced tenure security for poor and marginalised groups by weakening customary rights or allowing for elite capture. Collective action is furthermore required in order to adopt many technologies and natural resource management practices at higher levels (Meinzen-Dick, Knox, Place, & Swallow, 2002). Poor people and women are often disadvantaged in collective action through social exclusion, lack of time to participate, lack of education and confidence to speak in meetings and domination by local elites.

Property rights are "the capacity to call upon the collective to stand behind one's claim to a benefit stream" (Bromley, 1991, p. 15), involving a relationship between a right holder, group members and institutions backing up a claim. Titles combine a bundle of rights, such as those to use (usus), appropriation (usus fructus), decision-making (abusus) and, finally, alienation (Pejovich, 1990). Supporting institutions provide recognition and legitimacy for property rights to be effective, enforcing rights and their corresponding duties.

Collective action can be understood as an action taken by a group of individuals to achieve common interests (Marshall, 1998). As with property rights, it is important to look at both the formal and informal institutions that govern collective action. In the action arena, the actors, their action resources and the existing rules define the parameter of choice and decision within which the actors cooperate, discuss, negotiate, etc. Over time these actions create certain patterns in the form of regularised and observable behavioural outcomes based on a certain set of rules. Existing institutions mark the rule-bound space within which actors can make their choices. In patriarchal society, for example, often rules and norms particularly constrain women's voice and their ability to assert claims. While institutions do constrain, allow and affect it, collective action can bring about institutional change, thus altering the initial conditions.

Collective action is affected by social bargaining over the distribution of benefits and costs. Three sets of rules have been identified by Ostrom (1992): *operational* rules regulate day-to-day decisions, *collective-choice* rules prescribe how and who can change such daily routines, while *constitutional-choice* rules are those which govern the crafting of these very rules. In interaction processes, actors reinforce existing institutions while creating new ones. These patterns of action gradually come to form social relationships and structures.

Norms, legal structures and power relations have strong impacts on the assignment of property rights and the scope for possible change; meanwhile, the negotiation of property rights affects collective action, income generation and participation. Legal and power structures differ between countries and between governance levels. Federalism ideally reduces local and central information costs, though uniformity and standardisation decreases the fit of institutions. Decentralisation can help to change power structures (see Birner and Wittmer in this volume) and improve participation by engaging local voices in the political process. However, any decentralisation of services critically depends on the accountability of decision-makers and their ability to impose sanctions following violations (Ackerman, 2004). Participation through self-help is often regarded as a solution to break the vicious cycle of power, marginalisation and poverty. But participation will remain weak as long as the right to form groups cannot be enforced.

Cognitive schemata or mental models define what is imaginable in terms of both our understanding and normative perspective. North (1990) uses the term *ideology* to capture both aspects. On the one hand, ideology offers a mental model or cognitive map of the world, while proposing a normative idea of how the world should be structured on the other. Cognitive dissonance arises when differences appear between existing mental models – or "half-baked theories" as Schlüter puts it convincingly in this volume – and events. The normative side of ideologies serves the important task of providing legitimation and, thus, group solidarity. Cognitive schemata influence actors concerning whether to participate in deliberation or whether they dare to speak in public – and what is appropriate to say if they do so. The habitus of an actor in the public and private spheres is essential for gaining recognition in public discourse and collective action. Social standing is furthermore contingent upon the degree of embeddedness in social networks, either formal or informal.

1.2.4 The future of institutional analysis

Although the institutional analysis of sustainability has progressed significantly during the last three decades, important challenges remain for further theoretical, empirical and practical research. Konrad Hagedorn has often critically examined the methodological basis of political economy (Hagedorn, 1983, 1985a, 1985c) as well as of institutional analysis (Hagedorn, 1993b, 2004c, 2008a). He has stressed the importance of "mental models" for explaining both policy choices and institutional changes (Hagedorn, 1992a, 1998b, 2004b).

A centrepiece of Hagedorn's academic interest is the sustainable handling of natural resources, ranging from pastures in the lowlands of Ethiopia to water regulation in East Germany and the transformation of whole agricultural systems in Central and Eastern Europe. In view of the long-term consequences of inadequate and simplistic institutional regulations over the environment, he has continuously pushed for the development of more adequate theory in this domain. Looking ahead from the current state of the art, Hagedorn always digs into remaining conceptual black boxes with such rigour and intellectual enthusiasm that it can be expected that he will produce many more insights and even more questions.

One of Hagedorn's long-standing topics of interest has been segregating and integrating institutions (Hagedorn, 2003, 2008b). With his writings on the particular properties of transactions concerning natural systems, he proposes a heuristic framework to analyse the processes involved in institutionalising nature-related transactions (Hagedorn, 2008a). The physical world is just as important for institutional analysis as the social world. The challenge is that the particular properties of human–nature transactions are shaped by the attributes of natural systems, which have not been designed by humans and are not fully comprehended. In his keynote address to European agro-economists, Hagedorn builds upon his IoS framework, with its focus on transactions as the main analytical unit, proposing that research-ers distinguish between the basic attributes of physical entities, the properties of transactions influenced by them and the derived need for institutional and organ-isational governance. As transaction cost economics and the old institutionalism share transactions as their central unit of analysis, both dwell on the principles of conflict, mutuality and order. However, Hagedorn points out that concepts devel-oped for industrial purposes cannot adequately fit attempts to explain human–nature relationships. In particular, he asks whether concepts from transaction cost economics that emerged from the analysis of industrial organisation are capable of grasping the complexity and interconnectedness of nature-related transactions, which from Hagedorn's perspective require polycentric and hybrid forms of gov-ernance structures.

As Beckmann (2002) notes, the impact of transaction cost economics on envi-ronmental and resource economics has been small because, he argues, the transac-tion as the unit of analysis and the scope of governance structures developed for analysing industrial organisation are not appropriate for the problem settings and solution sets discussed in environmental and natural resource economics. In order to fill this obvious gap and to make the analytical power of transactions available to institutionalists in the field of natural resources, Hagedorn (2008a) has devel-oped a typology of nature-related transactions, posing three questions to guide his enquiry: First, what are the basic attributes of the physical entities affected by the transactions in question? Second, which properties of these transactions result from these attributes? Finally, what do the attributes and properties imply for gov-erning these transactions? The dimensions of modularity and decomposability, on the one hand, and of functional interdependence of processes, on the other, pro-vide for a basic typology, upon which Hagedorn categorises all transactions along a continuum between "atomistic-isolated" and "complex-interconnected".

Ostrom's (2007a) call to do justice to the complex realities of the actual world by applying diagnostic methods that grasp actors' subjection to diverse govern-ance systems echoes Hagedorn's concerns. A key term to unpack the complexity of nature-related interactions is decomposability. Here, again, Hagedorn returns to the central topic of cognitive scripts in the making of institutions: What cannot be imagined cannot be institutionalised, even if relationships in the physical world do exist beyond the grasp of humans. As partial decomposability of nature-related in-teractions cannot be achieved at the physical level, the task of conceptualising needs to be taken to the analytical level; similarly, if functional interdependence cannot be grasped at the physical level, then interrelatedness can be made trans-parent at a conceptual level (Hagedorn, 2008a, pp. 371–377). Following these thought experiments, a transaction-interdependence cycle can be developed. In-stead of pondering over an institutional change that has already occurred, an ex-post institutional situation is imagined and subsequently broken into the possible stages through which a physical transaction could become an institutionalised transaction.

Building on this puzzle of increasing knowledge regarding ecological interconnectedness and the need for adequate institutional reflection of these circumstances in the light of sustainability concerns, Hagedorn sets out to decompose the process of discovery of nature-related transactions and their subsequent entry into the social world of institutions. Picking up the idea of discriminate alignment for governance requirements from Williamson (1996), he extends the scope of institutional analysis to investigating the particular properties of nature-related transactions. Matching transactions with governance structures has consequences for transaction costs. Continuing along this line of thought, Hagedorn proposes discriminating between integrative and segregative institutions: the former contain decision-makers liable for the transaction costs they cause, while the latter relieve decision-makers from transaction costs and place the burden partially on others. The discriminating alignment hypothesis regarding nature-related transactions invites empirical testing and further theoretical refinements. In this way, Hagedorn is continuing to explore the future of environmental institutionalism.

1.3 The Contributed Papers

The occasion for celebrating Konrad Hagedorn's contributions to institutional economics has inspired many scholars to reflect on a variety of current issues. The authors whose work is gathered in this volume come from Australia, the United States, Kenya, Norway, the Netherlands, Belgium, Switzerland and the East, West, North and South of Germany, working on problems in China, Russia, Bulgaria, Sri Lanka, Uganda, Guatemala and their respective home countries. Related to Konrad Hagedorn through research projects, professional cooperation or as his students, these scholars are now carrying forward the topic of institutions and sustainability, as summarised in the following sections.

1.3.1 Political economy of economic development and agricultural policy

Konrad Hagedorn's work on political economy has inspired work on economic development in a more general sense as well as on core issues of agricultural policy. The essays in this section give an idea of the variety of Hagedorn's manifold academic collaborations and his keen interest in areas ranging from problems in transition and war economies to social and agri-environmental concerns.

Scott Rozelle and Johan F. M. Swinnen compare agricultural reforms in China and the Soviet Union as two prominent cases of economic transition in the post-communist era, unravelling the political economy of these seemingly similar processes. From an institutional perspective, the authors analyse the conditions under which radical market reforms were introduced in both countries, with the less-mechanised agriculture in China and industrial farming structures in the Soviet Union emerging as key dimensions. They reveal a political paradox: The early institutionalisation of market mechanisms through the household responsibility system in China stabilised the communist regime in the long run, as it tremendously increased the well-being of peasants and the larger population alike. In contrast, the envisaged market reforms in the Soviet Union in the mid-eighties were initially heavily resisted by farmers and local officials, fearing decollectivisation and loss of power. Under the old system, farming was largely mechanised and structured by food supply chains, which smaller production units would put at risk. Using the tools of political economy to search for explanations of the transition paths taken has been a shared interest of Swinnen and Hagedorn, which brought them together in the KATO project (Comparative Analysis of the Transition Process in the Agricultural Sector of Selected Central and Eastern European Countries) (see Beckmann & Hagedorn, 2007).

Taking a core theme of political economy, namely that of institutional change during a period of civil war, Benedikt Korf shows how powerful different fields of inquiry like the New Institutional Economics and anthropology can be in explaining the political economy of violence and appropriation. Previous contributions on this topic have more or less explicitly assumed the state to be a strong actor in the development of policies, though confronted with problems of acceptability, equity and implementation or transaction costs. Posing the question of institutional change in a situation of civil war requires a conceptualisation of the emergence and logic of the intrinsic rules of intra-state conflict. The idea of contracting, as in warlord or bandit models, is placed at the centre of the new institutional analysis. The different models of grabbing, looting or exploitation are dismissed by Korf on empirical grounds, as they do not sufficiently explain the ambiguous relationship between the state of civil war and the existing laws. The actor conceptualisation of rational agents in an institutional vacuum hinders our ability to grasp the complexity of a situation in flux. On the contrary, the real world of civil war is better understood as a simultaneous making of both war and law. Based on his ethnographic fieldwork in Sri Lanka, Korf can shows how a hybrid set of overlapping and contradictory sets of rules on many different scales and between civil persons and combatants emerges. Besides rules of violence, new norms for appropriation emerge, strongly influenced by the properties of transactions (Hagedorn, 2003, p. 52), determined by the characteristics of a resource in time and space. Recognising that civil war is not beyond human attempts to order actors' relationships, but rather an equally institutionalised process, opens new analytical approaches to political economy and highlights the complexity of this violent order (Padmanabhan, 2008b). Though dynamic and shaped by conditions of fear, the mental models of all involved actors are based on norms formed under conditions of competitive social relationships.

Peter Mehl, a fellow researcher of Hagedorn at the Federal Agricultural Research centre in Braunschweig, picks up the notion of policy development as an institutionalised process and analyses the reform of the social insurance system for farmers' pensions in Germany that took place from the 1980s on. While assessing the success of the measures taken in terms of equity, efficiency and acceptability, he elucidates the political economy of this agricultural policy as actually being a social policy stretching over decades. Consequently, Mehl shows that the assessment of the success of policy reform and policy impact has to be separated analytically. Mehl's historical case study of this insurance reform concretely illustrates the factor of complexity in institutional change – an issue elaborated later on at the theoretical level by Clem Tisdell. Mehl's taking the aim of induced institutional change from the abstract level of agricultural externalities to the domain of political bargaining and implementation, often with unintended consequences in the field of social policy, reminds us of Hagedorn's concern with the situated, rationally bounded and institutionally furnished environment of policy making. It is not always the economically superior policy that proves to be the ecologically, socially and politically sustainable one.

The fact that some key conclusions from Hagedorn's 1982 doctoral thesis were not implemented by the farmers' pension-scheme reform until 1994 illustrates that institutional change can often be contingent upon shocks or historical events, such as in this case the end of the Cold War and the subsequent German reunification. Looking at the history of this reform process in terms of it goals and main components, Mehl shows how targets were reached and what kinds of intentional and unintentional impacts emerged. While the improvements concerning social security for farmers' spouses, the stabilisation of the pay-as-you-go pension system, the elimination of disparities between insured farmers and the development of compatibility with other pension systems illuminate the many political dimensions of the economics of old-age insurance, the integration of the agricultural sector into mainstream social policy reflects the changing position of farmers in a highly industrialised country.

Building on Hagedorn's institutional perspective on the political economy of policy choices, Tisdell illustrates it by dissecting agricultural and environmental externalities. He proposes that public policy making aiming at sustainability must not only take economic criteria into account, but also social and political reasoning. To assess policy choices with regard to agricultural externalities and their relationship to sustainability, the transaction costs for non-marginal alternatives, equity and political acceptability are key. Difficulties in selecting public policies for regulating externalities generated by agricultural activity arise from attempting to maintain a perspective of economic efficiency when the natural functions involved are actually irregular and erratic. Bounds on rational choice become apparent once more in examining the complexity of public decision-making. The distribution of rights affects what an efficient economic solution to resource allocation can be and inevitably necessitates equity considerations. Each policy option entails specific institutional structures and resulting administration and transaction costs. Existing social structures and cultural factors influence what a politically acceptable or feasible policy can be. The challenge of choosing policy options regarding agricultural externalities is vividly illustrated, for example, by the International Convention on Biological Diversity and its belief in the suitability of establishing private property rights over genetic material to achieve sustainability.

1.3.2 Institutions, governance and sustainability

The analytical framework of IoS, has inspired structured and theory-led research on interactions between actors and their transactions, property rights and governance structures, with a pronounced interest in institutional outcomes and institutional innovation. The essays in this section expand on this and other analytical frameworks to understand the challenges facing the attainment of sustainability.

In his theoretical overview article, William Blomquist reviews the literature on the conditions for the sustainable management of natural resources. In the spirit of "The Workshop in Political Theory and Policy Analysis" at Indiana University, with which Konrad Hagedorn established fruitful transatlantic cooperation on the promotion of institutions for natural resource and environmental management in Central and Eastern Europe, Blomquist sketches an interdisciplinary research agenda. Proceeding from multi-disciplinary findings, including some from resource economics, ecology, law, and political science, he discusses the conceptual obstacles for natural resource management. He concludes that highly differentiated socio-ecological systems require equally complex and diverse governance structures spread over many levels. Striving for sustainable management of natural resources, he deduces that multiple and polycentric arrangements appear to be favourable, as they have the capacity to process and collect information, to reflect and adapt.

Taking up the notion of polycentric governance as a panacea for the production of non-private goods without central coordination, Markus Hanisch puts the theoretical assumptions on the development of metropolitan areas to a test concerning whether they also apply to rural areas in the enlarged European Union (EU-27). He shows that polycentric governance may be difficult to implement in rural areas, despite the lip service paid in favour of self-organisation and subsidiarity by the official agenda of the EU-27. Hanisch draws a rather dismal picture of public services in the countryside: confronted with problems of rural poverty, local budget crises and often missing services. In a search for reliable provision of public goods, and based on a historical example, he proposes cooperative associations to fill the service gap in the EU-27's rural economy.

Echoing the search for viable governance structures to improve human well-being, Regina Birner and Heidi Wittmer take a close look at the requisite conditions for effective administration of environmental resources, focusing specifically on the setting and enforcement of environmental standards and regulations, management of publicly owned natural resources and provision of environmental advisory services. Applying analytical concepts from the New Institutional Economics, particularly transaction cost economics, they identify *degree of decentralisation, degree of autonomy* and *level of participation* as critical organisational dimensions. Their focus on environmental administration is a unique one within this collection of essays, taking into account the necessity to take decisions on the institutional design of organisations.

Furthermore, similar to Blomquist and van Huylenbroeck et al., Birner and Wittmer pose questions regarding how well transactions match with governance structures. It should be obvious that governance structures that do not get the chance to be implemented remain paper tigers. Yet the "implementation gap" in environmental policy is faced both by developing and industrialised countries. To understand the effects of institutional arrangements on the performance of environmental administration, such as in ministries, departments and other government agencies, Birner and Wittmer propose an analytical framework for creating a mental model mapping out the interplay of autonomy, decentralisation and interaction between actors, illustrating it with empirical results from Guatemala and Uganda.

Similarly to Hagedorn's typology of transactions to conceptualise segregative and integrative institutions, Birner and Wittmer work with Williamson's "discriminating alignment hypothesis" (1991) to identify transactions relevant to administrative performance. According to the attributes that they have derived, such transactions have to be aligned with governance structures to achieve effectiveness. The comparative cost-effectiveness of different governance structures depends on their attributes and the functions they have to perform, revealing that trade-offs have to be considered when choosing an institutional design. Linking their conceptual, analytical framework with a translation into policy advice based upon specific empirical needs – in the very sense of Hagedorn's insistence on conceptual integration – Birner and Wittmer show how plans for administrative reform can be drawn. For building institutions of sustainability, it is not only necessary to gain political support for environmental issues, but also to keep in mind the political economy of organisational reform.

Hybrid governance structures hold promise for institutions as a means for achieving sustainability. In their conceptual paper, Guido van Huylenbroeck, Anne Vuylsteke and Wim Verbeke remind us that markets are not naturally given, but rather socially constructed. With this awareness, the authors discuss the particularities of markets for public goods and take the first steps towards suggesting how to frame these markets under conditions of uncertainty. Van Huylenbroeck et al. argue that hybrid governance structures enable actors to transfer part of their property rights to transaction partners without giving over their complete bundle of rights. Referring to Hagedorn's (2003) observation that public goods are defined as non-private goods, the authors set out to theorise on hybrid governance structures for private goods. They see the chance that, for those aspects of the market that are socially constructed, hybrid governance structures can facilitate the allocation of public goods and their development, thus contributing to "institutions of sustainability". Their concern about the need and demand for public good markets is also shared by Swallow and Meinzen-Dick.

1.3 3 Property rights, collective action and natural resources

The management of common pool resources in the field of natural resources has always been a principal research focus for Konrad Hagedorn. In this domain, property rights over land and collective action for stewardship of the environment are of eminent scientific interest. The essays gathered in this section offer empirically grounded studies on property rights, collective action and contracting for land, water and carbon sequestration.

Esther Mwangi and Elinor Ostrom review a century of institutional change and its effects on the ecology of East Africa's Rangelands, with a focus on the linkage between institutional robustness and ecological resilience. Their contribution provides evidence of the methodological diversity of institutional analysis, as emphasised by Beckmann and Padmanabhan.

Mwangi and Ostrom meticulously demonstrate that nested governance structures for natural resource management can support social and ecological resilience, as in the case of pastoralist areas of Kenya's Maasailand. Presenting a detailed case study – which is outstanding for its ecological and economic data and spans a period of analysis from prior to British colonial rule until early in the present century – Mwangi and Ostrom investigate the interaction patterns of varying governance institutions and dynamic ecological phenomena. They arrive at a conclusion concerning human behaviour and incentives, proposing that the indigenous institutions of the Maasai people were not only the most robust set of institutions, but have also been associated with a more resilient ecology. These authors share with Vatn (this volume) a deep concern over contemporary resource use and stress that the boundaries between social and natural systems are artificial (Berkes & Folke, 1998), preferring the term social-ecological systems.

Digging even deeper into the mechanisms of collective action, Insa Theesfeld investigates the decline of trust brought about through abuse of power. For the irrigation sector of the transition country Bulgaria she demonstrates how power abuse of central actors may lead to increasing distrust, undermining the sustainability of self-governed water management systems. Analysing the interdependency between unclear property rights and the deterioration of irrigation infrastructure, Theesfeld produces new insights into the failures of collective action for sustainable resource use. Reputation, trust, and reciprocity are the core features affecting cooperation (Ostrom, 2007b, Padmanabhan, 2008a) and are influenced by structural variables like the heterogeneity of participants. The empirical evidence from Bulgaria reveals that the disparity of regulations invites opportunistic behaviour, the establishment of a water-user association has been undermined by the abuse of power, and that the level of trust in formal actors is extremely low. Focusing on the link between heterogeneity of participants and trust, it becomes evident how misuse of power and the concomitant loss in trust induces a downwards spiral of eroding engagement in collective action. Ambiguous formal and informal institutions support opportunistic behaviour and have adverse effects on the sustainability of resource management.

The already discussed papers on the management of common pool resources rather formulate lessons of determent: detecting severe mismatches between institutions and resources, based on fallible understanding of the social-ecological system or unclear rules and enforcement mechanisms. To avoid these pitfalls at the very beginning of the establishment of new institutions to govern payment for environmental services, Brent Swallow and Ruth Meinzen-Dick take the trouble to conceptualise interactions between property rights and collective action on emerging carbon markets. Unlike van Huylenbrock et al., who approach the search for possible markets for public goods from an outspoken governance perspective on polycentricity, their key concern in developing an analytical framework is the normative call to make markets for environmental services relevant for the poor. Similarly to Hanisch, they view the supply of (local) public goods as dependent on capabilities and conditions for cooperation.

Swallow and Meinzen-Dick picture smallholders as efficient producers of environmental services of value – if the entailed transaction costs can be reduced through collective action. To design payments for environmental services (PES) as incentives for sustainable land management, the conditions regarding property rights need to be understood as well. The authors place the welfare of smallholder land users at the centre of their conceptual framework to examine the possible rewards for environmental stewardship. Reflecting Hagedorn's work on agri-environmental schemes, which stresses the need to consider resource properties in order to develop adequate institutions, the conceptual framework is applied to carbon sequestration, biodiversity, and watershed functions. Linking PES to other rural institutions can foster equitable outcomes, especially through collective action for lowering transaction costs and pulling down participation barriers to smallholders. Swallow and Meinzen-Dick's pronounced emphasis on the intrinsic linkage between poverty and natural resource management also echoes Hagedorn's great concern for social and environmental justice.

Property rights often appear as one side of the coin of common pool resource management, with collective action being the other. While the previously discussed authors within this section have made largely conceptual contributions, disaggregating actors and resources in order to detect logical relations for crafting institutions, Nico Polman and Louis Slangen present a rigorous empirically focused analysis. In their institutional economics analysis of land-use contracting in the Netherlands, they seek to trace the causes of a situation of continuously declining land leases in spite of a liberalisation of land-lease regulations. The choice of contract form for a particular land lease arrangement can be explained both by the attributes of the transaction and the characteristics of the land owner and tenant. While public land owners mainly rely on formal contracts, the agreement of choice between farmers is predominantly informal. For devising policies to regulate land leasing, it is therefore important to recognise the characteristics of contractual arrangements and the parties involved to understand how and why contract choices are made. While contract theory assumes that the transfer of fewer property rights from a landowner to a tenant-farmer will lead to an institutional change for land leasing, the character traits of trust and reputation appear as decisive factors for the grey contract. In these less explicit contracts, the core values of collective action play an important role for coordination. The question of how property rights on land are assigned and regulated is of major importance for sustainable resource use.

1.3.4 Challenges to institutional analysis towards sustainability

Institutions and sustainability both pose an intellectual task to the researcher. While work on the intersection of both fields has multiplied progressively, new frontiers continually emerge for further theoretical, empirical and practical research. Acknowledging Konrad Hagedorn's concern about questions of methodology and the twilight zone of epistemology, the essays in this section reverberate some of the fundamental questions of scientific craftsmanship and self-conception.

One of the obstacles to achieving sustainability is the still unclear nexus between institutions and actual behaviour. Arild Vatn approaches this black box. Guided by literature from different social sciences, he looks at human motivation and the relationship between motivation and institutions. Building on his main hypothesis that institutions act as rationality contexts, he concludes that these very structures, evoking certain rationalities, have to undergo change in order to achieve sustainability. He identifies the need to facilitate more integrative institutions that build on principles of social rationality and take ecological dimensions into account. Correspondingly, the incentive structure that perpetuates segregative institutions has to be tamed through fundamentally democratic regulations to produce accountability regarding sustainability in all spheres of life. As prevailing institutions foster a certain logic or rationality that is largely alien to sustainability concerns, it is crucial to make a radical turnaround in the institutional structures governing economic activity. A utopia of alternatives to support cooperative rationality is outlined in accordance with Hagedorn's credo: Conceptualisation is the first step towards understanding, finally leading to change. Arild Vatn's visionary essay clearly stands in the tradition of exercise of the imagination as the first step towards a sustainable future.

Picking up the issue of how to explain actors' behaviour, Achim Schlüter jumps right into one of the core issues of institutional economics, arguing that taking consideration of the ideas of both New and Classical Institutional Economics on actors' decision-making and preference ordering will enrich ecological economics in terms of explaining choice situations. Bounded rationality, mental models and sufficient reasons are similar but also competing key concepts of institutional economics used for understanding the cognitive processes of decision-making in complex settings of institutional choice or change. His detailed weighing of arguments and conceptualisations from the different schools of institutionalism leads him to the well-grounded conclusion of finding surprising complementarities between North's notion of mental models and Bromley's understanding of sufficient reasoning to explain institutional change. Proceeding from this relatively pure debate within high theory, Schlüter steps down to the prickly lowlands of empirical application, facing complex realities with well-developed analytical tools. Here, he explores possible futures for institutional research, while putting forward the requirement of a case study method and qualitative data analysis for meaningful empirical studies of institutional change. For illustration of his conceptual discussion, Schlüter draws on material from sustainability deliberations by forest owners in Germany, reminding us of the importance of mental models in theory and ideology, both for governance and the governed.

The essay of Volker Beckmann and Martina Padmanabhan ties in with the earlier-mentioned challenges to institutional analysis of other contributors, specifically raising the question of appropriate methods to apply. As the empirical studies gathered in this volume suggest, the methodological approaches to problems of institutions cover a broad range. Spanning from comparative country studies covering decades to explain regime changes (Swinnen and Rozelle) to broad-scale surveys in the research on contracts (Slangen and Polman), from in-depth qualitative interviews and ethnographic approaches (Schlüter, Korf), through combinations of qualitative interviews and structured games (Theesfeld) to modelling of policy options (Mehl), a multitude of methods has been applied. Reflecting on this methodological pluralism, Beckmann and Padmanabhan set out to develop a systematic process for selecting appropriate methodological tools in relation to the research questions at hand. Referring to Williamson (2000), they propose level of analysis and time scale as the two axes of a matrix depicting appropriate theories for conceptualisation of a study. Categorising theoretical approaches as being cause-, consequence- or process-related, they apply Williamson's frame of aggregation levels and time horizons to place theories of institutional change within the range of causes, consequences and co-evolution (Hanisch, Beckmann, Boger, & Brem, 2007). Although Beckmann and Padmanabhan do not pretend to have found the philosopher's stone, their systemisation helps to consider the aims of analysis as criteria for selecting appropriate methods. Furthermore, the level of analysis has an impact on the choice of empirical methods, as complexity is diametric to the number of cases and the ability to identify causalities. The authors highlight possible trade-offs of experiments, agent-based modelling, case studies and econometrics in relation to considerations of time, measurability of institutions, and actors' conceptualisations.

1.4 Looking Ahead Towards Sustainable Futures

This introduction to the work of Konrad Hagedorn and the overview of the contributed articles in this volume dedicated to him both consolidate gains in knowledge while raising new questions regarding further development in the field of institutions and sustainability. Among the conceptual concerns, the definition of transaction in the realm of environmental issues remains a hot topic. The same holds true for the concept of integrative and segregative institutions and polycentric governance of natural resources. Theorising the different pathways of institutional change towards sustainability remains an additional open question, and adequate integration of values, norms and cultural elements into institutional analysis requires debate. To be sure, the frameworks and theories advocated here have to be empirically tested and further developed. As Beckmann and Padmanabhan argue here, there is a need for a plurality of methods in order to be able to pay adequate attention to long-term developments, the complexity of institutions and the crucial roles of actors at certain moments in time. The creative interaction of theoretical and empirical research will hopefully provide us with the knowledge that is needed to craft future institutions to meet the ongoing challenges of sustainability.

This collection in honour of Konrad Hagedorn resembles a snapshot at a family reunion, with the various family members and branches meeting and commemorating their mutual experiences and adventures and wondering what their further journeys along life's paths will bring. And, as often happens at such occasions, there is one with pioneering ideas who may provoke the majority of mainstreamers, but also commands the respect of many, acknowledging his daring thoughts. Celebrating the scholar, teacher and colleague Konrad Hagedorn, we look forward to new discoveries emanating from this intellectual master.

References

Ackerman, J. (2004). Co-governance for accountability: Beyond "exit" and "voice". *World Development, 32*, 447–463.
Beckmann, V. (2002, December). *Transaction cost and environmental economics: Towards a new approach.* Paper presented at the Workshop in Political Theory and Policy Analysis, Indiana University, Bloomington.
Beckmann, V., & Hagedorn, K. (1995). De-collectivisation policies and structural changes of agriculture in Eastern Germany. *MOCT-MOST, 5*, 133–152.

Beckmann, V., & Hagedorn, K. (1997). De-collectivisation and privatisation policies and resulting structural changes of agriculture in Eastern Germany. In J. F. M. Swinnen, A. Buckwell, & E. Mathijs (Eds.), *Agricultural privatisation, land reform and farm restructuring in Central and Eastern Europe* (pp. 105–160). Aldershot: Ashgate.

Beckmann, V., & Hagedorn, K. (1999). Comparative analysis of the process of transition in the agricultural sector of selected Central and Eastern European countries: The KATO research project. *Bulgarian Journal of Agricultural Sciences, 5*, 254–265.

Beckmann, V., & Hagedorn, K. (Eds.). (2007). *Understanding agricultural transition: Institutional change and economic performance in a comparative perspective: Vol. 26. Institutional change in agriculture and natural resources.* Aachen: Shaker.

Berkes, F., & Folke, C. (1998). Linking social and ecological systems for resilience and sustainability. In F. Berkes & C. Folke (Eds.), *Linking social and ecological systems: Management practices and social mechanisms for building resilience* (pp. 414–436). Cambridge: Cambridge University Press.

Beyene, F. (2008). Institutions, determinants and effects of collective action among (agro)pastoralists of Eastern Ethiopia. *Quarterly Journal of International Agriculture, 47*, 97–119.

Beyene, F., & Korf, B. (2008). *Unmaking the commons: Collective action, property rights and resource appropriation among (agro-) pastoralists in Eastern Ethiopia* (CAPRi Working Paper 88). Washington D.C.: IFPRI.

Bromley, D. W. (1991). *Environment and economy: Property rights and public policy.* Cambridge: Blackwell.

Di Gregorio, M., Hagedorn, K., Kirk, M., Korf, B., McCarthy, N., Meinzen-Dick, R., et al. (2008). *Property rights, collective action, and poverty: The role of institutions for poverty reduction* (CAPRi Working Paper No. 81).Washington D.C.: IFPRI.

Eggers, J., & Hagedorn, K, (1998). Umwelteffekte und agrarumweltpolitische Ansätze der "Agenda 2000". *Agrarwirtschaft, 47*, 482–491.

Eisen, A. & Hagedorn, K. (Eds.). (1998). *Co-operatives in Central and Eastern Europe: Self-help in Structural Change: Vol. 4. Berlin co-operative studies.* Berlin: Edition Sigma.

Eisen, A., & Hagedorn, K. (Eds.). (2000). *Lernstücke: Genossenschaften in Ostdeutschland* (Berliner Schriften zur Kooperationsforschung, Bd. 6). Berlin: Edition Sigma.

Enquete-Kommission. (1998). *"Schutz des Menschen und der Umwelt"* des 13., Deutschen Bundestages, Konzept Nachhaltigkeit: Leitbild zur Umsetzung (Abschlußbericht).

Gatzweiler, F., & Hagedorn, K. (2002a). The evolution of institutions of sustainability in transition. In F. Gatzweiler, R. Judis, & K. Hagedorn (Eds.), *Sustainable agriculture in Central and Eastern European countries: The environmental effects of transition and needs for change: Vol. 10. Institutional change in agriculture and natural resources* (pp. 3–16). Aachen: Shaker.

Gatzweiler, F., & Hagedorn, K. (2002b). The evolution of institutions in transition. *International Journal of Agricultural Resources, Governance and Ecology, 2*, 37–58.

Gatzweiler, F., & Hagedorn, K. (Eds.). (2004a). *Institutional change in Central and Eastern European agriculture and environment: Vol. 1–3. CEESA/FAO series.* Berlin: Humboldt-Universität zu Berlin.

Gatzweiler, F., & Hagedorn, K. (2004b). Synopsis of the CEESA project. In F. Gatzweiler & K. Hagedorn (Eds.), *Institutional change in Central and Eastern European agriculture and environment: Vol. 4. CEESA/FAO series.* Berlin: Humboldt-Universität zu Berlin.

Gatzweiler, F., & Hagedorn, K. (2004c). Policies and institutions for agriculture and environment in Central and Eastern European countries. In G. V. Huylenbroeck, W. Verbeke, & L. Lauwers (Eds.), *Role of institutions in rural policies and agricultural markets* (pp. 361–373). Amsterdam: Elsevier.

Gatzweiler, F., Judis, R., & Hagedorn, K. (Eds.). (2002). *Sustainable agriculture in Central and Eastern European countries: The environmental effects of transition and needs for change: Vol. 10. Institutional change in agriculture and natural resources.* Aachen: Shaker.

Haberer, A. F. (1996). *Umweltbezogene Informationsasymmetrien und transparenzschaffende Institutionen.* Marburg: Metropolis.

Hagedorn, K. (1977). Konzeptionelle Agrarsozialpolitik. Grundsätzliche Überlegungen zum agrarsozialen Alterssicherungsziel. *Vierteljahresschrift für Sozialrecht, 5,* 203–249.

Hagedorn, K. (1981). Intersektorale Einkommensübertragungen und intrasektorale Umverteilungen in der Agrarsozialpolitik. *Agrarwirtschaft, 30,* 172–180.

Hagedorn, K. (1982). *Agrarsozialpolitik in der Bundesrepublik Deutschland: Kritik und Alternativmodelle zur Alterssicherung in der Landwirtschaft: Bd. 1. Beiträge zur Sozialpolitik und zum Sozialrecht.* Berlin: Erich Schmidt

Hagedorn, K. (1983). Reflections on the methodology of agricultural policy research. *European Review of Agricultural Economics, 10,* 303–323.

Hagedorn, K. (1985a). Notizen zur Methodologie der wissenschaftlichen Agrarpolitik. *Jahrbuch für Sozialwissenschaft, 36,* 322–351.

Hagedorn, K. (1985b). Zum revidierten Entwurf eines Dritten Agrarsozialen Ergänzungsgesetzes. *Agrarwirtschaft, 34,* 213–214.

Hagedorn, K. (1985c). Agrarpolitische Innovationen und wissenschaftliche Methodologie. *Agrarwirtschaft, 34,* 238–248.

Hagedorn, K. (1988). Politische Institutionen und Entscheidungsprozesse in der agrarökonomischen Politikforschung. *Landbauforschung Völkenrode, 37,* 290–303.

Hagedorn, K. (1991a). Financing social security in agriculture: The case of the farmers' old-age pension scheme in the Federal Republic of Germany. *European Review of Agricultural Economics, 18,* 209–229.

Hagedorn, K. (1991b). Gedanken zur Transformation einer sozialistischen Agrarverfassung. *Agrarwirtschaft, 40,* 138–148.

Hagedorn, K. (1992a). Das Leitbild des bäuerlichen Familienbetriebes in der Agrarpolitik der 1970er und 1980er Jahre. *Zeitschrift für Agrargeschichte und Agrarsoziologie, 40,* 53–86.

Hagedorn, K. (1992b). Transformation of socialist agricultural systems. *JOICE – Journal of International and Comparative Economics, 1,* 103–124.

Hagedorn, K. (1993a). Institutions and agricultural economics. *Journal of Economic Issues, 27,* 849–886.

Hagedorn, K. (1993b). Transforming socialist agriculture: An institutional perspective. In L. Kabat, P. Fandel, D. Bartova, & P. Kapustik (Eds.), *Eastern European agriculture – problems, goals and perspectives* (pp. 50–63). Proceedings of the 27th Seminar of the European Association of Agricultural Economists, March 18–20, 1992, Nitra, Vysoke Tatry, Slovakia.

Hagedorn, K. (1993c). Umweltpolitische und sozialpolitische Reformen in der Agrarpolitik: Parallelen und Unterschiede zwischen phasenverschobenen Politikprozessen. *Zeitschrift für Umweltpolitik und Umweltrecht, 16,* 235–280.

Hagedorn, K. (1994a). Interest groups. In G. Hodgson, M. Tool, & W. J. Samuels (Eds.), *Handbook of institutional and evolutionary economics* (pp. 412–418). Cheltenham and Northampton: Edward Elgar.

Hagedorn, K. (1994b). Die Privatisierung volkseigenen landwirtschaftlichen Bodens in den neuen Bundesländern. *Kühn Archiv, 88,* 226–244.

Hagedorn, K. (1996a). *Das Institutionenproblem in der agrarökonomischen Politikforschung.* Tübingen: J.C.B. Mohr (Siebeck).

Hagedorn, K. (1996b). Politisch dirigierter institutioneller Wandel: Das Beispiel der Privatisierung volkseigenen Bodens. In K. Hagedorn (Ed.), *Institutioneller Wandel und Politische Ökonomie von Landwirtschaft und Agrarpolitik: Festschrift zum 65. Geburtstag von Prof. Dr. Günther Schmitt* (pp. 149–192). Frankfurt: Campus.

Hagedorn, K. (1997). The politics and policies of privatization of nationalized land in Eastern Germany. In J. F. M. Swinnen (Ed.), *Political economy of agrarian reform in Central and Eastern Europe* (pp. 197–236). Aldershot: Ashgate.

Hagedorn, K. (1998a). Concepts of institutional change for understanding privatisation and restructuring of agriculture in Central and East European countries. In K. Frohberg & W. R. Poganietz (Eds.), *The importance of institutions for the transition in Central and Eastern Europe: With emphasis on agriculture and food industry: Vol. 1. Studies on the agricultural and food sector in central and Eastern Europe* (pp. 51–64). Kiel: Vauk.

Hagedorn, K. (1998b). Reasons and options for analyzing political institutions and processes. In K. Frohberg & P. Weingarten (Eds.), *The significance of politics and institutions for the design and formation of agricultural policy: Vol. 2. Studies on the agricultural and food sector in central and Eastern Europe* (pp. 14–33). Kiel: Vauk.

Hagedorn, K. (Ed.) (1998c). *Agrargenossenschaften. Mitgliederinteressen und ökonomische Perspektiven: Bd. 39. Berliner Beiträge zum Genossenschaftswesen.* Berlin: Institut für Genossenschaftswesen.

Hagedorn, K. (1999a). Der Double Dividend-Ansatz als institutionelle Weichenstellung zur Ökologisierung der Agrarpolitik? In P. Mehl (Ed.), *Agrarstruktur und ländliche Räume: Rückblick und Ausblick: Festschrift zum 65. Geburtstag von Eckart Neander* (pp. 177–210). Braunschweig: FAL.

Hagedorn, K. (1999b). Die Ökologische Steuerreform: Eine umweltpolitische Innovation für die Landwirtschaft? *Agra-Europe*, 40, Sonderbeilage.

Hagedorn, K. (2000). Umweltgenossenschaften aus institutionenökonomischer Sicht. In M. Kirk, J. W. Kramer, & R. Steding (Eds.), *Genossenschaften und Kooperation in einer sich wandelnden Welt: Festschrift zum 65. Geburtstag von Prof. Dr. Hans-H. Münkner* (pp. 267–291). Münster: LIT.

Hagedorn, K. (Ed.) (2002). *Environmental cooperation and institutional change: Theories and policies for European agriculture.* Cheltenham and Northampton: Edward Elgar.

Hagedorn, K. (2003). Rethinking the theory of agricultural change in an institution of sustainability perspective. In G. van Huylenbroeck, W. Verbeke, L. Lauwers, I. Vanslembrouck, & M. D'Haese (Eds.), *Importance of policies and institutions for agriculture* (pp. 33–56). Gent: Academia Press.

Hagedorn, K. (2004a). Institutionen der Nachhaltigkeit. In I. Dombrowsky, H. Wittmer, & F. Rauschmayer (Eds.), *Institutionen in Naturschutz und Ressourcenmanagement: Beiträge der Neuen Institutionen-ökonomik* (pp. 7–26). UFZ-Bericht 7/2004. Leipzig, UFZ.

Hagedorn, K. (2004b). Property rights reform on agricultural land in Central and Eastern Europe. *Quarterly Journal of International Agriculture, 43*, 409–438.

Hagedorn, K. (2004c): Institutionen der Nachhaltigkeit: Eine Theorie der Umweltkoordination. In S. Dabbert, W. Grosskopf, F. Heidhues, & J. Zeddies, J. (Eds.), *Perspektiven in der Landnutzung: Regionen, Landschaften, Betriebe – Entscheidungsträger und Instrumente* (pp. 65–73). Münster-Hiltrup: Landwirtschaftsverlag.

Hagedorn, K. (2005). Balanceakt zwischen Ernährung und Naturschutz – die Landwirtschaft. *Informationen zur politischen Bildung. Umweltpolitik, 287*, 36–43.

Hagedorn, K. (2007). Towards an institutional theory of multifunctionality. In Ü. Mander, K. Helming, & H. Wiggering (Eds.), *Multifunctional land use: Meeting future demands for landscape goods and services* (pp. 105–124). Heidelberg, Berlin: Springer.

Hagedorn, K. (2008a). Particular requirements for institutional analysis in nature-related sectors. *European Review of Agricultural Economics, 35*, 357–384.

Hagedorn, K. (2008b). Integrative and segregative institutions: A dichotomy for understanding institutions of sustainability. Unpublished manuscript.

Hagedorn, K., Arzt, K., & Peters, U. (2002). Institutional arrangements for environmental co-operatives: A conceptual framework. In K. Hagedorn (Ed.), *Environmental cooperation and institutional change: Theories and policies for European agriculture.* (pp. 3–25). Cheltenham and Northampton: Edward Elgar.

Hagedorn, K., & Eggers, J. (1998): Ökologische und ökonomische Effekte alternativer Politikvarianten zur Weiterführung der EU-Agrarreform. *Zeitschrift für Umweltpolitik und Umweltrecht, 21*, 549–582.

Hagedorn, K., & Mehl, P. (2001). Social policy reforms for German agriculture: Challenges and recommendations. *International Social Security Review, 54*, 85–100.

Hagedorn, K., & Schmitt, G. (1985). Die politischen Gründe für eine wirtschaftspolitische Vorzugsbehandlung der Landwirtschaft. In E. Boettcher, P. Herder-Dorneich, & K. E. Schenk (Eds.), *Jahrbuch für Neue Politische Ökonomie, Bd. 4* (pp. 250–295). Tübingen: Mohr Siebeck.

Hanisch, M., Beckmann, V., Boger, S., & Brem, M. (2007). In search of the market: Lessons from analysing agricultural transition. In Beckmann, V. & Hagedorn, K. (Eds.), *Understanding agricultural transition. Institutional change and economic performance in a comparative perspective: Vol. 26. Institutional change in agriculture and natural resources* (pp. 25–44). Aachen: Shaker.

Hundie, B. (2008). Property rights changes among Afar pastoralists of Ethiopia: The role of the state. *Quarterly Journal of International Agriculture, 47*, 121–144.

Hundie, B., & Padmanabhan, M. (2008). *The transformation of the Afar commons in Ethiopia: State coercion, diversification and property rights change among pastoralists* (CAPRi Working Paper 87). Washington D.C.: IFPRI.

Lütteken, A., & Hagedorn, K. (1998). Transformation and environment: Perspectives for Central and Eastern European countries. In G. H. Peters, G. C. van Kooten, & G. A. A. Wossink (Eds.), *Economics of agro-chemicals* (pp. 347–358). Aldershot: Ashgate.

Marshall, G. (1998). *A dictionary of sociology*. New York: Oxford University Press.

Meinzen-Dick, R. S., Knox, A., Place, F., & Swallow, B. (Eds.). (2002). *Innovation in natural resource management: The role of property rights and collective action in developing countries*. Baltimore: John Hopkins University Press.

North, D. C. (1990). *Institutions, institutional change and economic performance*. Cambridge: Cambridge University Press.

Ostrom, E. (1992). *Crafting institutions for self-governing irrigation systems*. San Fransisco: ICS Press.

Ostrom, E. (1998). The institutional analysis and development approach. In E. T. Loehman & D. M. Kilgour (Eds.), *Designing institutions for environmental and resource management* (pp. 68–90). Cheltenham and Northampton: Edward Elgar.

Ostrom, E. (2007a). A diagnostic approach for going beyond panaceas. *Proceedings of the National Academy of Sciences of the United States of America, 104*, 15176–15178.

Ostrom, E. (2007b). Collective action theory. In C. Boix & S. C. Stokes (Eds.), *The Oxford handbook of comparative politics* (pp. 186–208). Oxford: Oxford University Press.

Padmanabhan, M. (2008a). Collective action in agrobiodiversity management: Gendered rules of reputation, trust and reciprocity in Kerala, India. *Journal of International Development, 20*, 83–97.

Padmanabhan, M. (2008b). Pastoral women as strategic and tactical agents in conflicts: Negotiating access to resources and gender relations in Afar, Ethiopia. *Quarterly Journal of International Agriculture, 47*, 239–266.

Pejovich, S. (1990). *The economics of property rights: Towards a theory of comparative systems*. Dordrecht: Kluwer Academic Publishers.

Sreedevi, T., Suhas, P., Wani, K., Chennamaneni, R., & Chaliganti, R. (2007). Clean Development Mechanism (CDM) in Action: Prospects for urban and peri-urban forestry in Greater Hyderabad. Megacity: Sustainable Hyderabad. Research Report 15. Humboldt University of Berlin.

Williamson, O. E. (1991). Comparative economic organization: The analysis of discrete structural alternatives. *Administrative Science Quarterly, 36*, 269–296.

Williamson, O. E. (1996). *The mechanisms of governance.* New York: Oxford University Press.

Williamson, O. E. (2000). The new institutional economics: Taking stock, looking ahead. *Journal of Economic Literature, 38*, 595–613.

Part I

Political Economy of Economic Development and Agricultural Policy

2 The Political Economy of Agricultural Reform in Transition Countries

Scott Rozelle[1] and Johan F. M. Swinnen[2]

[1] Stanford University, Encina Hall East, E301, Stanford, CA 94305-6055, USA, E-mail: rozelle@stanford.edu

[2] LICOS Centre for Institutions and Economic Performance, Katholieke Universiteit Leuven, Debériotstraat 34, 3000 Leuven, Belgium, E-mail: Jo.Swinnen@econ.kuleuven.be

Abstract. The dramatic transition from Communism to market economies across Asia and Europe started in the Chinese countryside in the 1970s. Since then, more than a billion people, many of them very poor, have been affected by radical reforms in agriculture. However, there are enormous differences in the reform strategies that countries have chosen. This paper presents a set of arguments to explain why countries have chosen different those reform policies.

Keywords: Agriculture, Asia, Europe, Political economy, Transition

2.1 Introduction

The emergence of China as a global economic powerhouse, the uncertain path of Russia towards a market economy, and the integration of ten Central and Eastern European countries into the European Union (EU) have been occupying the minds and agendas of many policy-makers, business leaders and scholars all over the globe since the end of the twentieth century. Two to three decades ago these developments were unimaginable. The leaders of the Soviet Block and China at that time were clearly committed to Socialist ideology and designed their economies to be insulated from the world. Since the 1980s, however, Russia, China, Vietnam, Hungary, Poland and more than 25 other nations have emerged from their Socialist cocoons. While not all have succeeded, many have transformed the fabric of their economies, with several having achieved high rates of growth. One of the most interesting observations is that the winners and the losers have all taken fairly distinct paths to where they are today. The path each country has taken, and the choices that put them on it, will likely have implications for where they will go in the coming years. In many senses, however, the developments have been so fast and the impact of the changes so vast that they have taken the world by surprise, and we do not fully understand them yet.

V. Beckmann, M. Padmanabhan (eds.), *Institutions and Sustainability*,
DOI 10.1007/978-1-4020-9690-7_2, © Springer Science+Business Media B.V. 2009

In brief, the developments we want to explain began in the countryside of China in the late 1970s. Until then, a large share of the globe, from the center of Europe to much of East Asia, was under Communist rule, controlling the lives of more than 1.5 billion people and affecting those of many more in other countries. In 1978, China embarked on its economic reform path by introducing the household responsibility system (HRS) in agriculture. A few years later, Vietnam followed. Both countries reduced price distortions and reallocated key land rights from collective farms to rural households. In the initial years, however, market forces played little role. Nevertheless, the impact was dramatic. Productivity and incomes in both countries soared, with the reforms lifting hundreds of millions of rural households out of dire poverty.

Other communist regimes could have followed this path in the wake of China's moves. However, they generally did not. While a series of more timid reforms were tried out in the Soviet Union during the late 1970s and early 1980s, nothing of the sort of changes made in China followed, either in terms of policy or implementation. In fact, if anything, Communist governments during the 1980s remained stubbornly committed to their decades-old Socialist prescriptions. Performance during the 1970s and 1980s continued to worsen.

Although reform outside of East Asia was slow in coming, when it did, change came in a hurry. Around 10 years after the start of China's reforms, leaders in many nations of Central and Eastern Europe (CEE) and the former Soviet Union (FSU) began to dismantle Socialism and liberalize their economies. After the reform movement started, however, leaders in many nations accelerated their activity, implementing a bold series of policies that sought to rationalize prices, increase incentives through various ways of restoring property rights and modifying the institutions of exchange within which residents lived and worked. In a few years, the reformers pushed a policy agenda that often went far beyond the reforms that had already been implemented in China and Vietnam. Although output and incomes in some of these nations collapsed in the first few years of reform, productivity often began to rise and, within three to five years, output and incomes in many nations began to grow.

In terms of their reform strategies, there were also major differences among the CEE and FSU nations. In fact, even though leaders of most nations announced wide-ranging changes, in many FSU nations in particular, reforms were implemented in a much more piecemeal fashion. Subsidies and price controls remained, assets were distributed in ways in which property rights were not clear, and there was little commitment to dismantling state-run distribution and processing channels. In most of these nations, the reforms were ultimately disappointing, with output falling and poverty increasing until the end of the 1990s.

While the record on what happened and the effects of those reforms are now fairly well understood (see, e.g., a review of these events in Rozelle and Swinnen (2004)), it is less clear *why the decisions were made in the ways that they were.* If price changes, rights reforms and market emergence led to growth, why did leaders in many transitioning nations not choose to follow such a comprehensive prescription? More explicitly, why was it that leaders in China decided to implement their reforms gradually, while those in CEE did so all at once? Why was it that leaders in CEE undertook a broad spectrum of reforms, while those in many nations of the FSU did not? And, even more fundamentally, why is it that the policies were implemented by the leaders of some Communist regimes, while in others it took a major regime shift for policies to gain momentum? More generally, there is much less of an understanding of why decisions were made in the way that they were. In our opinion, when thinking about what additional lessons need to be drawn from the experience of transitioning nations, we believe that these are among the most critical of questions.

The goal of this paper is to explore some of these questions. However, the brevity of a single paper precludes doing so in a comprehensive (and hence convincing) fashion. As it turns out, in our book *From Marx and Mao to the Market* (Swinnen & Rozelle, 2006), we explore in greater detail the political economy of agricultural reform policies in transition countries. Therefore, using the approaches and findings that are contained therein as support, in this paper, we summarize our conclusions and begin to provide answers to the questions about why leaders in one set of countries took one path, while those in another took a different road.

Because of the number of nations, the complexities of the policies and the timing of reforms differ so substantially, we must necessarily limit the scope of our inquiry even further, primarily restricting our attention to three broad questions: Why was the Communist government in China able to guide the reform process, while it took a regime change in Russia (and in most of CEE and the other Commonwealth of Independent States (CIS) nations) to start the reforms? Why did the market liberalization and other reforms happen so fast in some nations, but only gradually in others? Why did the choice of property rights reform in land and farm restructuring differ so dramatically from nation to nation?

Even restricting the analysis to address these three questions, however, is an ambitious task and needs to be narrowed further. While we recognize that there certainly are other factors that influenced the decisions involved in making these changes, we focus on four general categories of determinants:

1. initial technological differences in farming practices and the environments within which farming occurs;
2. differences in wealth and economic structures;
3. differences in governmental organization and structure, especially focusing on the degree of decentralization; and
4. the historical legacy of Socialism.

The analysis in this paper relates to earlier work on the political economy of agricultural reforms, such as those by Hagedorn (1992, 1997) and Swinnen (1996,

1999), as well as to important new developments on political economy in the economics profession, which have potentially important implications for the political economy of agricultural reform (see e.g. Anderson, 2009; Rausser, Swinnen, and Zusman, 2008; Roland, 2000; and Weingast and Wittman, 2006).

2.2 Why Did the Communist Party Reform in China, but not in the Soviet Union?

Radical reforms under the Communist regimes could only occur when there was, simultaneously, strong grassroots support for the reforms and support at the upper echelons of the Communist Party. If support from both above and below was not there, it is likely that the policy efforts would succumb to inertia, foot-dragging and resistance from those that were not in favor of reform. For example, reform failed in China in the 1960s because there was no support by the leadership for the radical decollectivization demanded by households at the grassroots level. Reform failed in Russia in the 1970s because there was neither grassroots nor leadership support for radical changes. Agricultural reform failed in the 1980s in Russia because the reform proposals from the top of the Communist leadership under Gorbachev were not supported at the farm level. Only in China at the end of the 1970s and the early 1980s was there a confluence of interests in favor of radical reforms at the top and at the grassroots, from both farm households and local officials.

One of the main points that we make in our book regarding the reform strategy of China is that decollectivization was not a fully top-down political decision. In fact, it should be seen as being the result of fairly continuous pressure by farm families to return to family-based production over the decades preceding the HRS reforms. The grassroots pressure was most intense at those times and in regions where households suffered most from collective farming. For example, the pressure to decollectivize was strongest in the aftermath of the famine created by the Great Leap Forward policy and in times of drought, when the problems of collective farming intensified. With such crises, the pressure to shift to household-based production systems was strong at the grassroots levels.

While pressure from below is an important part of the dynamic, it should also be noted that grassroots pressure by itself cannot explain why the reforms took place in the late 1970s. The same pressures existed in the 1960s, but at that time China failed to decollectivize. Earlier grassroots attempt to move to household-based production were resisted by the Communist regime under Mao. However, after Mao died in 1976, the balance of power changed and gradually support grew in upper-level government and party cells for more fundamental reform in agriculture. In 1978, Deng Xiaoping had returned to assume important roles in the government and party, and support for HRS grew at the top.

It is this line of thinking then that underlies our observations of the need for both top- and lower-level support in order to have successful change under Communisms. In the late 1970s, the changes at the top – that is the rise of the reformers – and the existence of grassroots support were mutually reinforcing in China. While support in Beijing helped spread the HRS reforms, the grassroots support also helped the pro-reform leadership win its case. Reform-minded Communist officials saw an opportunity to exploit the agricultural changes in order to oust the Maoists. The decision to reform was a delicate balance between pressure from the grassroots and preference towards reform from a growing segment of the top leadership. In the temporary leadership vacuum that existed after Mao's death, both reinforced each other. The success of the HRS reforms in increasing output, reducing poverty and maintaining social stability in China's countryside strengthened the positions of the pro-reform groups in Beijing. Inversely, the enhanced position of the pro-reform groups created the policy space that was necessary for the grassroots initiatives to spread across rural China. By the time the leadership of the party formally announced its support of decollectivization, the HRS had already spread to most of China.

The situation was very different in the Soviet Union, where pressure for reform came almost solely from the top. Mikhail Gorbachev, a strong proponent of agricultural reform, rose through the Soviet hierarchy to become in charge of agriculture in the late 1970s and the leader of the Soviet Union in the mid 1980s. He introduced several proposals to reform agriculture. Interestingly, several of the proposals were similar to those forwarded by the Chinese leadership in the 1970s. However, the reforms generally failed to achieve the desired productivity changes. Instead of creating an economic miracle as in China, most of the old problems continued to affect farming and the impact of the reforms was disappointing.

In the Soviet Union the demand for (some) reform came primarily from a Communist leadership that was unsatisfied with previous reform attempts. Unlike in China, however, the central leadership in the Soviet Union had little support from farmers or local officials or party leaders. Under the Gorbachev regime, reforms were driven from the top and had to be supported by large-scale propaganda schemes. However, the proposals met with resistance and lethargy rather than enthusiasm at the farm level.

2.3 Causes of Differences in Grassroots Support

Why were the attitudes towards decollectivization of farm workers and local officials in China and the Soviet Union so different? One factor sometimes suggested to explain the *difference in farmers' motivations* is the historical legacy of Socialism. Rural households in the Soviet Union had been working under the collective system for much longer than in China, and there was no memory of family farm-ing. While this factor no doubt affected the attitudes of rural households, this is unsatisfactory as an explanation, because it cannot indicate why attitudes in many rural households in CEE countries were equally unenthusiastic about decollectivi-zation.

A more convincing argument points to the differences in standard of living of-fered by pre-reform collective agriculture in China and the Soviet Union. In China, rural households had faced famine in the recent past, and more than 30 per cent of households lived in utmost poverty. In contrast, farm workers in CEE and the Soviet-Union benefited from large government subsidies, high wages and were covered by social welfare benefits. Despite low farm productivity, workers in the Soviet Union's state farms and collectives lived at standards of living far higher than those in China's rural sector. In several countries, rural incomes were actually higher than urban incomes. With reforms, wages could fall and both effort and risk would have risen. Moreover, with the overemployment and soft-budget con-straints existing at that time, agricultural reform would almost certainly have trig-gered significant lay-offs. Not surprisingly, many farm workers in the Soviet Un-ion and CEE resisted agricultural reforms.

Technological differences further reinforced these differences in attitudes. Farmers in China purchased few of their inputs. Supply channels were simple. They sold relatively little of their output to the market, and almost no farmers in-terfaced with processors. Most importantly, given the high labor-factor share, the potential for effort-efficiency-enhanced output would mean significantly higher incomes for farmers.

In contrast, farms in the Soviet Union and Eastern Europe were much more in-tegrated into an industrialized production system and a complex network of rela-tions with input suppliers and processors. Moreover, they were much more capital and land intensive. Under these conditions, farms were less likely to receive a lar-ge boost from incentive improvements and more likely to face serious disruptions.

Because of the differences in the benefits derived from reform, there were dif-ferences in support from lower-level officials. For example, in China local offi-cials in rural villages generally supported the reforms. Being close relatives, friends or acquaintances, the interests of local leaders were often closely aligned with those of farmers. Team and brigade leaders derived most of their income from their own farming activities, not from the salaries paid by the collective or government, especially in poorer areas. Hence, in the same way and for some of the same reasons that farmers wanted decollectivization, local leaders supported it as well.

Second, although it is possible that local leaders could earn some rents from their positions, when a leader's entire village was mired in poverty, such rents, if they existed, were by definition not large. The scope for rent collection would in-crease with the reforms, as the level of wealth in the local economy grew, but in the late 1970s most villages in China were fairly poor. Hence, while empirical evidence shows that local cadres benefited more from the HRS reforms than the average farmers, it was only moderately so.

Third, in the 1980s the support of officials support for reforms was sustained by reforms of the bureaucracy itself as well as by rural industrialization and fiscal reforms. Rural fiscal reforms and the creation of Township and Village Enterprises (TVEs) were implemented from 1983 onwards. These proved to be beneficial to local leaders and secured support for the overall reform agenda. In other words, the reforms that followed (and were made possible by the HRS) were in some cases instrumental in buying-off local leaders and bringing their interests into alignment with those of the national reformers.

Finally, the economic reforms were further complemented by reforms to the way officials – at all levels – were treated. For example, in the early years following the implementation of the HRS, top reformers initiated a massive, mandatory retirement program, effectively removing the old guard and moving up many younger and more pro-reform people in the bureaucracy. The bureaucracy changed dramatically in terms of its support for reforms and its competency. Another major change took place in the mid 1980s, when bureaucrats were allowed to quit their government positions to join the business community. This "bureaucratic revolution" had a positive impact on China's reform process in the second half of the 1980s and after, as it stimulated interest of bureaucrats in local economic growth and new enterprises.

In the Soviet Union, although the interests of local officials were also aligned with those of farm managers, the rational response of both was to resist, not support, reform. In other words, local leaders opposed reforms, partly for the same reason farm managers and many employees did. Breaking up the farms implied losses of scale economies and threatened their status and salaries, with few gains to be expected, because they benefited disproportionately from the subsidized farming system.

In addition, local officials were concerned about the wider effects of an aggressive reform policy on rural communities. The collective or state farm in the Soviet Union provided most rural social services. Reforms could result in declining social service provision and safety nets for many residents. Rent-seeking aside, these were real concerns for local leaders, since there were no alternative institutions available to provide local services, and there were few off-farm jobs to which laid-off farm workers could have gone to.

Possible disruptions and negative equity effects were also important concerns for the central leadership in China and the Soviet Union. The equality of benefits (or costs) of reforms was important for making them socially and politically sustainable or not. Income distributional effects were as important as ideological arguments in the reform debate in the Chinese Communist Party on the HRS. Another concern was the possible disruptions that could be caused by the reforms: which might have reduced the existing rents collected by Communist officials or have had important negative social effects, like unemployment or losses in income. As such, they also could have created strong political opposition and anti-reform backlashes.

Differences in the nature of wealth, subsidies, and technology between the two systems of farming made it such that these concerns were less problematic in China than in the Soviet Union. In the labor-intensive farming systems in China, reform policies that changed incentives could increase incomes with little danger of disruption to the rest of the economy. China's leaders also faced less of an equity trade-off. The distribution of land to all households (a characteristic of the HRS) induced significant welfare gains. With few scale effects and better incentives, increased efficiency raised incomes substantially. In addition, because China's farmers were so poor, the reforms also helped to improve equity. In China, because of the nature of the technology, the reforms were win–win.

In contrast, in the Soviet Union, the nature of pre-reform subsidies and technology would have meant that there were going to inevitably have been winners and losers from reforms, because the reforms demanded restructuring, restitution, layoffs and other changes. Efficiency could only come at the cost of equity. In a system like that in the Soviet Union, this would have caused tension with leaders who were willing to sacrifice efficiency for a relatively more fair distribution. Hence, the nexus of the nature of technology and the institutional basis in the pre-reform economies is another reason that leaders in China were more willing to push the agricultural reforms than their counterparts in Russia.

2.4 Experimentation and Reforms

Despite the arguments of certain scholars, we find little support for the idea that differences in the organizational and hierarchical structures of the central planning systems of China and Russia allowed for more reform experimentation by Communist leaders in China, thereby facilitating the initial agricultural reform process in China (i.e., the HRS in the late 1970s and early 1980s). First, the introduction of China's HRS reforms was regionally concentrated and not due to the design of planners, but rather arising out of grassroots initiatives. Second, the location of the start of the reforms was often determined by the relative absence of control of the planners. Third, the spread of the HRS system did not reflect the careful planning of experimental reflection.

Ironically, experimenting with agricultural reform appears to have been more pervasive in the pre-reform Soviet Union. In the 1970s and 1980s there was a significant degree of experimentation in reforming the agricultural system. For example, leaders tried to push new forms of brigade and team contracting and new types of agricultural management. The decentralized nature of China – which allowed for a number of natural, albeit uncoordinated, experiments – played a more important role in the years afterwards, for example, during the period of market liberalization, in the implementation of the fiscal reforms, and in the emergence of TVEs.

2.5 Why Were Agricultural Reforms Implemented Gradually in China, but Simultaneously in Many CEE and the CIS States?

One of the other fundamental differences between China and many CEE and CIS states was in the pace of market liberalization. In fact, we believe there are a number of systematic differences that influenced the alternative approaches. For example, once China had successfully implemented property rights reform and restructured its farms (as well as adjusted prices to reduce the implicit tax on farmers), liberalizing markets became less imperative. The early pricing reforms and HRS helped the reformers to meet their initial objectives of increased agricultural productivity, higher farm incomes and food output. The agricultural reforms fuelled China's first surge in economic growth and reduced the concerns about national food security. The legitimacy of leaders, now seen as being able to run a government that could raise the standard of living of its people, was at least temporarily improved.

In contrast, a new set of reforms might have exposed the leaders to new risks, in particular regarding the impact on the nation's food supply. Decollectivization had erased the worst inefficiencies. With the urgency for additional reforms dampened for both top leaders, since their goals had been met, and farmers, since their incomes and control over the means of production had both improved, there was less policy pressure from both the top and grassroots.

Hence, paradoxically and ironically, the radical, though partial, economic reforms in the Chinese countryside did much to reinforce the Communist Party's hold on power. But the complete opposite was true in the Soviet Union, where the lack of significant reforms ultimately contributed to the fall of the Communist leadership. While radical agricultural reforms in the CEE and Soviet-Union were only possible after major political reforms in the CEE and CIS countries at the end of the 1980s, the radical reforms in China, which looked like moves away from Socialism, probably did more to consolidate the rule of the Communist Party than any other measures taken during this period. Although it is well-documented that the decisive changes directly affected the incomes and livelihood of more than 70 per cent of the population in the rural population, the agricultural reform also had a tremendous impact on the urban economy. The rise in food production and increases of food supplies to cities took a lot of pressure off the government. Urban wages, when raised, became real gains to income, since food became relatively cheaper. In addition, the rise of rural incomes created an immediate surge in the demand for non-food products. Many of the same dynamics occurred in Vietnam (Pingali & Xuan, 1992).

Political changes in the Soviet Union and CEE states in the late 1980s caused widespread reforms, not only in agriculture, but in the entire economy. The anti-communist political forces that came to power were determined to get rid of the Communist system and to introduce democracy and a market economy. Reforms were launched despite resistance by farm managers, workers and local officials. Reformers chose to push through as much of the economic reform agenda as possible at the time that they were (still) in charge. Hence, for both political and economic reasons, a comprehensive set of radical reforms was pursued. Since the previous reforms had failed to result in efficiency improvements from marginal and slow policy shifts, in the view of the reformers a more radical and broad-based reform approach was necessary.

The same dynamics applied to the reform program in agriculture. The post-communist policy shifts needed to be sufficiently radical to have a significant impact on the productivity of the entire food system. This required a broad and encompassing reform strategy that needed to address several key issues. First, the more industrialized nature of the Soviet agricultural production system and the inefficiencies imbedded in the agro-food supply chain required an approach beyond the confines of the farming sector. The organizational inefficiencies in the supply chain were already an important cause of low agricultural efficiency and would have severely limited the potential impact of farm-level reforms in the Soviet Union. As a result, solving the problems of Soviet agriculture would require policy reforms beyond the farms.

Second, in terms of administrative feasibility, the more complicated technologies in Soviet agriculture and the CEE meant a more complex set of exchanges between a larger number and greater variety of firms. Whereas China's farming sector was largely based on small, mostly self-subsistence, farmers selling grain and oilseed commodities to a trading system that in turn only had to re-transfer the stocks to urban sales outlets or, at the most, to rudimentary processing firms (such as oil crushing mills), in the Soviet Union and the CEE the food economy was dominated by livestock, dairy and other more sophisticated products that required more processing. To design an optimal policy sequence for a gradual reform strategy, policy makers would have been required to have access to extensive information on a vast number of processes (McMillan, 2002). But such information had not even been available for planning purposes; there is no reason to believe it would have been available for a gradual reform program.

Third, the overall importance of agriculture in the economy (measured as the share of GDP or employment) was also an important feature that helped determine the pace of reform. Unlike in China, where agriculture made up such a huge share of the economy at the outset of reforms, agriculture in the Soviet Union and the CEE was much less important in the economy. Reformers made several decisions which had a major impact on agriculture and on the sequencing of the agricultural reforms as part of a broader reform agenda. Agriculture did not necessarily need to be singled out.

Hence, for all of these reasons, the same factors that kept reform from occurring in the Soviet Union and the CEE in the pre-reform era made it imperative that the reforms take place all at once, once the decision to reform was adopted. In this way, like the case of China, there is an element of path dependency. The factors that put the country in a situation which made it so difficult to reform were, in fact, the same factors that made it so difficult to reform during the Socialist era, and it was these factors that made reformers opt for "once and for all" policies when the opportunity came for them to try to change the policy direction of their country.

Finally, it should be emphasized that in several the CIS countries no leadership changes occurred. The lack of political reform in several countries, in particular in the least reformed countries such as Belarus, Turkmenistan and Uzbekistan, has been a major constraint on the progress of economic reforms there.

2.6 What Are the Causes for the Differences in Land and Farm Reform Strategies?

Of all of the policies that have characterized agricultural transition, the reform of the property rights of cultivated land was probably one of the most important. Interestingly, however, the array of policies across nations is probably broader than in any other policy reform initiative, often differing sharply from country to country. In this section, we argue that there are several reasons for this.

First, the *choice to privatize land or not* was affected by historical and legal legacies of land ownership. The hitherto present memory of their history of private land rights provided a strong incentive for CEE reformers to choose to privatize land. Households and individuals in regions in which there was a tradition of private farming before the period of Communist rule responded more favorably to reform policies based on privatization than those that lived in areas in which there had been less private farming. Proximity to the EU and the familiarity of the local population with the land systems in Western Europe might also have reinforced this preference for private land ownership.

In contrast, in Russia and Central Asia, where no such tradition existed, there was no privatization of land during the initial years of transition. In many regions, there was a popular preference that land should not be privately owned. There, the absence of a tradition in private farming was reinforced by the relatively great length of time since the onset of collectivization. After more than 60 years of collectivization, in many parts of the former Soviet Union the absence of the skills and farming practices necessary for private farming could dissuade a nation from choosing privatization. Although collective workers may have had experience with household plots connected to collective farms, for the previous five to six decades none had ever run larger, independent farms.

In China and Vietnam, ideology still played an important role. Unlike the CEE nations, private farming history did not induce the leaders to privatize land. Clearly, the continuation of the Communist regime and its ideology played an important role here. With land the most basic factor of production in agriculture in a Communist country, leaders have believed that the state, or its representative, the collective, should have control over land. Yet, in both nations reformers have provided (increasingly) well-defined control and income rights, and the de facto difference with actual ownership of land is decreasing.

Second, the *decision for land restitution* in a number of CEE countries was strongly influenced by another historic legacy: a nation's legal history. Restitution of farmland to former owners, many of whom were no longer active in agriculture, was vehemently opposed by collective farm managers. It was argued that the efficiency of farming would suffer, due to a high incidence of tenancy and excessive fragmentation. Many economists and policy advisors were also opposed to restitution.

Despite the objections, land restitution became the most common method of land reform in Central and Eastern Europe. The strongest determining factor appears to have been the pre-reform legal ownership structure. In China and in the Soviet-Union in 1978, all cultivated land in the nation was either owned by the state or by the collective. However, in most CEE nations, through the entire period of Communism, individuals were still the legal owners of most of the farm land. Although control rights and income rights had been usurped by the collective farms after collectivization, the land titles had never been taken away from the original owners. The historic legacy of the CEE made restitution the natural choice despite the economic counter-arguments.

Third, among those nations that did not restore land, why did some choose to give *land in specifically delineated plots (in-kind)* to rural households and others decided to distribute *land in shares* to groups of farmers? There is a strong empirical relationship between wealth, technology and a propensity to distribute land in kind to households. In poor nations with labor intensive technologies (for example China, Vietnam and Albania), almost all land was distributed in-kind to rural households. In the richer and more capital-intensive farming countries, such as Russia, Ukraine and Kazakhstan, all land was distributed as shares to groups of farmers. Also in poor and labor-intensive European and Transcaucasian countries, such as Albania, parts of Romania, Armenia, and Georgia, there was a rapid shift to household-based farms. These processes included in-kind distribution of land. The regions where this occurred were typically very poor, with relatively recent experiences of family farming and with high labor intensity in agriculture.

The distribution of land in specific and clearly delineated plots to farm workers or rural households made it easier for poor households and individuals to use that land for themselves and leave the large-scale farm to start one of their own if they wished to do so. Such direct access to land was particularly important for poor households to increase their food security, incomes, and assets. Poor households would therefore prefer in-kind distribution, ceteris paribus. These preferences were reinforced in labor-intensive farming systems – which are typical for the poorest countries. The benefits of farm individualization are higher and the costs lower with higher labor intensity. Hence, households would be more inclined to take their land and start producing on their own. Rural households would have strong preferences for in-kind distribution of land, since it would allow them to reap these gains.

Share distribution of land was more likely to stimulate the continuation of large farms and prevent fragmentation, as it made leaving the farms more difficult for households, especially with farm managers being hostile to the idea. In richer and more land – and capital-intensive systems, households were less inclined to leave the large farms and start farming on their own, because the economic incentives were less and because of the social benefits associated with the large farms. Farm managers and employees with specific skills that were more valuable to the large farm organizations generally opposed any policies that undermined the survival of the collective, and later corporate, farms. Farm managers therefore preferred share privatization over in-kind distribution, as it also offered additional benefits in accumulating shares, and thus wealth, for themselves.

The empirical observations suggest that these different structural conditions have been translated into different government choices. In the most extreme cases, these differences have played themselves out immediately (e.g., China and Albania); in other cases they have evolved gradually, with grassroots preferences and pressures gradually influencing new governments as they came to power (e.g., Azerbaijan).

2.7 Concluding Comments

In this brief and results-oriented paper, we have tried in outline form to address some of the most perplexing puzzles of the reform era. Although theorists and empiricists have concluded that successful agricultural reform in the (formerly) Socialist countries requires price reform, land rights restructuring and market liberalization, not all of the nations involved have pursued the same set of policies during their transitions. Instead, we see different combinations of policies, different sequences and different approaches to implementation We have tried here to use a policy economy viewpoint to explain difference across nations.

In doing so, we have identified four different sets of factors that we believe are responsible for the reform choices that we have observed reformers make. While we recognize that there certainly are other factors that have influenced the decisions made, we find four general categories of determinants repeatedly arise: initial technological differences in farming practices and the environments within which farming occurs; differences in wealth and the structures of the economies;

the ways the different governments are organized – especially focusing on the degree of decentralization; and the historical legacy of Socialism differ among nations. The variability of these factors, we believe, can account for many of the different ways that nations have approached transition. Since differences in approach have been demonstrated by us to cause differences in performance, ultimately, we believe we have also been able to contribute to the literature's understanding of why some nations succeeded and others did not.

Of course, the implications of the new understanding are subtle. In many cases, there is not much policy makers could have done (or could do in the future). If a nation's technology is labor intensive and another's is capital intensive, and if the nature of the technology is a key factor in the choice of reform strategy, there may not be many options. However, understanding the constraints and factors that facilitate change itself is important. In some ways it might help to eliminate false starts, as for example when leaders of the Soviet Union tried to proceed gradually.

The understanding of the determinants of transition may also have implications for understanding the process of development. In the same way that price reform, property rights restructuring and market liberalization were key for transition, we also believe that there are many lessons to be learned by those nations trying to develop now and in the future. If so, then the determinants of a development strategy will also likely be affected by factors of political economy. Hence, as leaders and advisors consider the road a nation should take, it is important to remember that the same factors that affected the ability of one nation to succeed in transition may affect adversely another nation's ability to develop.

References

Anderson, K. (Ed.), (2009) *The political economy of distortions to agricultural incentives.* Washington: World Bank Publications.

Hagedorn, K. (1992). Transformation of socialist agricultural systems. *JOICE – Journal of International and Comparative Economics, 1*, 103–124.

Hagedorn, K. (1997). The politics and policies of privatization of nationalized land in Eastern Germany. In: J. F. M. Swinnen (Ed.), *Political economy of agrarian reform in Central and Eastern Europe.* (pp. 197–236). Aldershot: Ashgate.

McMillan, J. (2002). *Reinventing the bazaar: The natural history of markets.* New York: W. W. Norton & Company.

Pingali, P. L., & Xuan, V. -T. (1992). Vietnam: Decollectivization and rice productivity growth. *Economic Development and Cultural Change, 40*, 697–718.

Rausser, G. C., Swinnen, J. F. M., & Zusman, P. (2008). *Political power and endogenous policy formation.* Berkeley: Mimeo.

Roland, G. (2000). *Transition and economics: Politics, markets, and firms.* Cambridge: MIT Press.

Rozelle, S., & Swinnen, J. F. M. (2004). Success and failure of reform: Insights from the transition of agriculture. *Journal of Economic Literature, 42*, 404–456.

Swinnen, J. F. M., & Rozelle, S. (2006). *From Marx and Mao to the market. The economics and politics of agricultural transition.* Oxford: Oxford University Press.

Swinnen, J. F. M. (Ed.). (1996). *Political economy of agrarian reform in Central and Eastern Europe.* Aldershot: Ashgate.

Swinnen, J. F. M. (1999). The political economy of land reform in Central and Eastern Europe. *The Economics of Transition, 7,* 637–664.

Weingast, B. R., & Wittman, D. A. (2006). *The Oxford handbook of political economy.* Oxford: Oxford University Press.

3 Make Law, Not War? On the Political Economy of Violence and Appropriation

Benedikt Korf

Division of Human Geography, Department of Geography, University of Zurich-Irchel, Winterthurerstr. 190, CH-8057 Zurich, Switzerland, E-mail: korf@geo.unizh.ch

Abstract. Economists have developed a number of theories based on warlord or bandit models to explain intra-state conflict and civil war. These models assume rational agents that agitate in a kind of institutional vacuum. This view is flawed. Ethnographic studies from civil wars suggest that livelihoods and institutions in the context of a war economy are very complex, more complex than those models suggest. We do not find an institutional vacuum – or anarchy – but a hybrid set of overlapping and contradictory sets of rules. This paper applies several concepts of institutions discussed in literature on new institutional economics and sociology to an analysis of the emergence and logic of the rules of the game in the political economy of civil wars. The analysis indicates that contracting in civil wars, whether complete or incomplete – and the opportunity to grab (Skaperdas), to loot (Collier) and to exploit others (Hirshleifer) – takes place on many different scales and between different agents, not only among combatants. This creates a complex, dynamic and hybrid institutional amalgam of coercively imposed rules, traditional norms and co-existing formal institutions.

Keywords: Civil war, Order, Political economy, Sri Lanka, Violence

3.1 Hobbes and the Political Economy of Violence

Konrad Hagedorn has often argued that economists tend to hold naïve views about a benevolent state (Hagedorn, 1996, 2004), believing similarly to Hobbes that a powerful ruler is needed to uphold the law – or, in the language of New Institutional Economics – to enforce rights. Thomas Hobbes argued in *Leviathan* that individual humans grant this authority to their king voluntarily, out of fear. Most economists writing on property rights firmly subscribe to this idea from the Hobbesian imaginary: law (and order) is the alternative to violence. Their vision is a society with clearly articulated (preferably private) property rights, enforced by a benevolent state which holds the monopoly on violence. Robert Bates, for example, writes that, "in the process of development, coercion alters in nature. Rather

V. Beckmann, M. Padmanabhan (eds.), *Institutions and Sustainability*,
DOI 10.1007/978-1-4020-9690-7_3, © Springer Science+Business Media B.V. 2009

than being privately provided, it instead becomes publicly provisioned" (2001, p. 50). If states fail or remain in a trap of underdevelopment, this is often attributed to a lack of secure property rights.

It is by means of a similar Hobbesian imagination that economists have conceptualized their studies on contemporary warfare. Political scientists Mary Kaldor (1999) and Herfried Münkler (2002) most famously suggested that we could observe the emergence of "new wars", mostly of the intra-state variety, where the state's monopoly on violence has been transformed into an oligopoly of violence shared by competing warlords. They contrast this with "old wars", where revolutionaries fought for political causes against an existing order to replace it with a new order. Economists have adopted this basic intuition and provided several models and econometric studies to substantiate the economics of resource appropriation that, in their view, underpin the causes of violent conflict. Most influential have been the studies of Paul Collier (2000), who has suggested that it is the opportunity to loot resources that provides the incentives for rebellion. Even before Collier popularized his economic theory of civil war, anthropologists contended that warlords were economically rational agents. These anthropologists studied "markets of violence" (Elwert, 1997) and explored the "economic incentives of war" (Keen, 1998). "Homo economicus goes to war", notes Christopher Cramer (2002, p. 1845) with a tone of irony, as this scholarship makes the disintegration of states and the persistence of warlordism in war-torn societies appear to be the outcome of the activities of entrepreneurial rational choice agents.

More problematic, however, is that this rational choice perspective on violent conflict implicitly celebrates the Hobbesian imagination, in which the notion of violence is inextricably counterposed to the idea of a social order. It is associated with unlawful behavior (Blok, 1988, p. 785). Civil war is modeled according to the intuition of Hobbes' understanding of the state of nature. Unrestrained – privately exerted – violence is placed in opposition to the normative ideal of a monopoly on violence vested in the legitimate ruler or the state. "Private" violence is, then, conceived as inflicting illegitimate, unacceptable physical harm. Law becomes an alternative to violence: the legal use of force is deemed socially authorized and, therefore, legitimate (Coutin, 1995, p. 517), with (unlawful) violence becoming something that has to be harnessed, controlled. The Hobbesian imagination thereby places all violence not exerted by the state outside the bounds of legitimate order.

The political economy of property relations, however, suggests otherwise. The existing "social order" is often inequitable, and conflict is intrinsic to social relations. Even if law does promote "order", this order may be regarded as unjust, and as itself "violent" by some members of a society (Coutin, 1995, p. 518). Law or property rights can themselves be used to repress, at times violently. Law and property rights often legitimize unjust power relations, as they are the outcome of social conflict, thereby reflecting the relative bargaining power of the different actors involved (Hagedorn, 2004; Hanisch, 2003; Knight, 1992; Theesfeld this volume). The legitimacy of the state's use of force and the legitimacy of others' use of force may be contested between different groups in society: "even if law does promote "order", "order" may be regarded as unjust, and as itself violence" (Coutin, 1995, p. 518).

The Hobbesian proposition to "make law, not war" is misleading. Indeed, I want to argue that the tactics pursued in civil war are rather to "make law *and* war", as new rules emerge in the political economy of violence and appropriation. This chapter, therefore, considers warfare to be a means to produce rules and order(s) – in a different sense, however, than the Hobbesian imagination purports. This argument is based on the proposition that, in many contemporary civil wars, violence produces multiple co-existing orders of rules.

The chapter proceeds as follows: It first reviews how economists and anthropologists have conceptualized the economic dynamics of warlordism and have thereby developed a "theory" regarding the causation and duration of civil wars. This discussion suggests that, while economic bandit models of the farmer-warlord linkage implicitly follow a kind of Hobbesian logic concerning a violence/order dichotomy, anthropologists have rather emphasized the embeddedness of warlords and markets of violence within social (and agrarian) relations. However, both views remain trapped in a predominant focus on warlords and their economic motivations, thereby leaving out a number of other actors present in the social arena of contemporary civil wars.

I sketch out a third way of reading the social figurations of violent conflict, emphasizing the ethnography of mundane practices of the different categories of actors who are embedded in the political economy of violence and appropriation, including combatants and non-combatants (although, admittedly, the boundary between these two categories has become blurred in many wars). In order to study these mundane practices, we need to rethink what "order", "rule" or "institution" means in the context of violent conflict. I illustrate these points through ethnographic examples from my own field research on the Sri Lankan civil war.

3.2 The Economics of Violence: How Order Emerges from Predation

When economists study phenomena of violent conflict, state failure and civil war, they do so through the analytical lens of dilemmas of collective action, which emerge from the rational choices that individual agents face in the making of society, order and the state. In this sense, they share a number of underlying propositions. *First*, individuals make decisions in the form of rational choices based on an ex-ante cost-benefit assessment. *Second*, as Hirshleifer (1994) has argued, cooperation occurs only in the shadow of conflict: when people cooperate, they do so out of a conspiracy against others (or as a response to the aggression of others). Cooperation, in Hirshleifer's view, is cooperation against somebody else. This anthropological model of human beings as aggressive creatures is similar to Hobbes' argument proposing a state of nature that results in anarchy, as each individual will use force to safeguard his or her own benefit.

Not surprisingly, economists seem to have become intrigued by a kind of Hobbesian intuition when writing about the emergence of law and order, statehood, or in trying to explain why some societies have failed to produce a Leviathan type of state that upholds the monopoly of violence. Economists began using the image of the warlord, who comes and loots a desperate population and then moves on to other areas, as a useful figure to model contemporary "new wars" (Kaldor, 1999; Münkler, 2002; critically on this: Kalyvas, 2001). These new wars are mostly intra-state, where the state's monopoly on violence has been transformed into an oligopoly that is shared with competing warlords. These "new" civil wars seem to be a form of private looting without popular support, where roving and stationary bandits (i.e. warlords) compete over who can best tax and expropriate resources from a desperate population. Violence becomes a means for conducting economic enterprise, exercised by undisciplined militias, private armies and independent warlords, and the state's monopoly on violence and thus social order has been lost to an oligopoly of violence shared by a number of bandits – a situation similar to Hobbes' state of nature.

A very influential contribution to this line of thinking has come from Mancur Olson (2000), who follows a Hobbesian reading in explaining the emergence of the modern nation state. While Olson did not intend to explain contemporary civil warfare, he used a warlord model to explain when and for what reasons a Leviathan kind of state was likely to develop – or not. Olson's empirical terrain was post-socialist transition and the difficulties faced of building strong, democratic states in many post-socialist countries. Olson's model is nevertheless useful at this point, as it explains the Hobbesian imagination in the language of collective action theory and rational choice.

Olson proposes a "bandit" model, arguing that politicians are like bandits and assuming that, when politicians are relatively unconstrained, they will rationally tend to grab as much as they can through holding office (or, in our case, by holding their guns). He distinguishes two types of bandit regime: the roving and the stationary. Olson notes that there is little production in anarchy and so little to steal. The more warlords can establish a territorial monopoly of violence and power, the more they may transform into stationary bandits: "If the leader of a roving bandit gang who finds slim pickings is strong enough to get hold of a given territory and to keep other bandits out, he can monopolize crime in that area – he becomes a stationary bandit" (Olson, 2000, p. 7).

Olson's distinction between stationary and roving bandits is particularly useful for application to civil wars (see, also, Tilly, 1985; Herbst, 1990; Tiemann, 2007; on war-making and state making in Europe and Africa). A stationary bandit has a greater interest in the territory he conquers to flourish economically, as this will increase his tax base. Thus, a stationary bandit has an interest to limit predation (and anarchic violence), because the social and economic losses resulting from predation will harm him economically, undermining the tax base. For this reason,

Olson concludes that the stationary bandit "becomes a benefactor to those he robs" (Olson, 2000, p. 9). Note that Olson's stationary bandit is not a Hobbesian Leviathan. His power does not emerge from the fear of free individuals, who hand over their freedom to the king to overcome anarchy, as Hobbes had suggested. Olson's bandit-turned-ruler is not legitimized by the people's own will, but through a clever economic strategy of resource appropriation; his "Leviathan" is the result of the business tactics of a warlord who provides protection cum taxation for the people of his territory.

Several economists have adopted, explicitly and implicitly, Olson's notion of a bandit model in their studies of violent conflict. But, in their models, the bandits are "real-life" warlords or clan leaders. Azam and Hoeffler (2002) analyze a warlord's trade-off between looting and fighting during ongoing warfare. Not surprisingly, they find that looting is economically more viable. Mehlum, Moene, and Torvik (2002) suggest a cost-benefit model of plunder and protection: roving warlords plunder versus stationary bandits providing "protection" for the people they tax or loot. In the latter case, the warlords must protect their own turf against competing warlords. Azam (2002) writes that more looting by one side entails more looting by the other and vice versa. He finds that looting during war is inefficient, as it would be possible to increase the joint utility of both sides by effectively banning looting. But a looting ban is often not Pareto-efficient and would require compensatory payments.

Skaperdas (2002, 2005) probes further into these warlord markets, where stationary bandits extract rents from the civilians of their territory and provide protection against roving or neighboring stationary bandits. Greater competition among rival groups increases the costs of providing protection and of defending one's share of rents. Much of the potential rent value is, however, eliminated by decreasing production. According to Skaperdas, this explains the gradual economic disintegration that occurs in civil wars. Bates, Greif, and Singh (2002) have provided a similar model regarding protection and production in stateless societies, where actors maximize or allocate specific periods for work, military preparation and leisure. They find that, in societies in which coercion is privately deployed for the raiding and protection of property (i.e. where there is no functioning state), the behavior in equilibrium "is likely to entail wasteful investments in military preparation and raiding" (Bates et al., 2002, p. 605). They call this equilibrium "anarchy equilibrium" and conclude that stateless societies trade off between production and protection. In societies with a functioning state, however, they claim that *both* production *and* protection are attainable and people can, therefore, live at a higher level of welfare.

The bandit or warlord models have focused on the economic incentives of warlords, rebels, soldiers, farmers, politicians and bandits in *ongoing* civil wars, indicating how a kind of looting equilibrium between different roving bandits is likely to emerge. A puzzle remains with the application of Olson-style models to the analysis of so-called new wars: Why don't we find the transition from roving to stationary bandits and, further, towards nation-state building in many contemporary civil wars? According to Olson's model, sooner or later the roving bandit changes his strategy toward stationary banditry, as it allows him to nurture the resources (and people that produce them) that he appropriates. It seems that in many contemporary wars this transition does not happen, or only as a result of outside interventions.

Paul Collier, an influential economist writing on violent conflict, has approached the problematic from a slightly different perspective. He has investigated the collective action dilemma pertinent in violent rebellion, that is, what causes civil wars to break out in the first place (Collier, 2000, Collier & Hoeffler, 2004). Rebellion is a risky enterprise with a free-rider dilemma, a problem not specifically addressed by Olson, but discussed in Kuran (1995): Why should someone be willing to take the risk of violent rebellion? Any rebellion may be suppressed and its proponents killed. It is less risky to free-ride and let others take up the job of rebellion, as the outcome – a better society – is a public good and will benefit those who undertook the rebellion as much as those who did not. If everybody thinks this way, however, no rebellion will ever occur. Collier solved this dilemma by arguing that, in those cases where there was opportunity to loot resources, potential rebels would calculate the potential benefits from future resource rents against the costs (risks) of rebellion. Rebellion would only be rational where sufficient resources are available for looting. Collier labels rebellion (against an incumbent regime) as a "quasi-criminal activity" (2000) and thereby implicitly accepts the Hobbesian conception.

Central to Collier's "greed" theory is the *opportunity to loot* (Collier, 2000; Cramer, 2002; Ginty, 2004), which depends on availability of resources and the technologies of resource appropriation and exploitation (Le Billon, 2001). He suggests that violent rebellion against an incumbent regime occurs when there is something to loot, when economic rents from exploiting natural resources can be captured and monopolized through rebellious activity. The kind of resources that rebels seek to loot can be manifold (Le Billon, 2001), but in the most protracted civil wars in Africa, these were often high value resources, such as oil, diamonds, or gold (Ross, 2004). Several authors have confirmed the link between the resource wealth of a society and its vulnerability to violent conflict (Auty, 2001; de Soysa, 2002; Le Billon, 2001; Ross, 2004). States endowed with minerals and oil are more likely to be autocratic, and less likely to be democratic, than are others. As these authoritarian states have access to economic rents independent of their citizens' tax payments, political elites in such states need not bargain with their citizens for support. However, Collier's analysis shows that, for competing groups in society, this rent is also an opportunity to loot and makes the risks of rebellion economically more attractive. Gates (2002) further refines Collier's analysis by showing how distance and geographical spread of rebel forces with regard to government strongholds affects rebel recruitment and allegiance.

Collier's analysis thereby points to the political economy of resource appropriation, which depends on what Konrad Hagedorn has called "the properties of transactions" (2003, p. 52). Philippe Le Billon has provided a further categorization of how the properties of a resource, its location and the required technologies of exploitation may impact upon the dynamics of rebellion and warfare (2001). In fact, Le Billon's analysis indicates that the physical properties of a resource and the material transformations that a resource has to undergo to become a high-value commodity are important determinants of its attractiveness for looting. However, he remains, albeit implicitly, within the overall paradigm of reading the agents in civil war through the lens of rational choice.

While Olson's bandit model, the warlord models, and Collier's greed model employ rational choice reasoning, the focus of each of them is slightly different: Olson and most warlord models look at the incentives for politicians, warlords or rulers when they are already occupying these roles, while Collier tries to explain how one *becomes* a warlord, although in more recent work, he has extended his analysis to the duration of conflict and the logic of ongoing war economies (Collier et al., 2004). Economic bandit models aggregate individual actors together in the form of "state", "warlord" or bandits. Bates et al. (2002), for example, acknowledge that they "ignore all issues relating to the internal organization of the actors, including collective action problems, decision-making processes and free riding. We simplify assuming two players" (p. 603). Collier, on the other hand, places the collective action dilemma center-stage and looks at an individual (potential) rebel's motivating forces. These models can, of course, only be as successful as their assumptions. And the assumptions made in rational choice models can be potentially problematic, as they abstract from the social embeddedness of violent actors.

3.3 The Anthropology of Violence

Anthropologists have long tended to read civil wars through a culturalist lens, explaining them as forms of "ethnic conflict" (Horowitz, 2001). Against this tradition, in the mid-1990s, a group of anthropological scholars started to deploy rationalist models to explain the political economy of civil wars. Two authors have been particularly prominent in this regard: David Keen and Georg Elwert. Both attempt to explain the internal social logic of warlordism and, thereby, though not using formal rational choice models, re-inscribe some of the arguments used by economists. At the same time, their analysis also differs from the economists' views, as they tend to emphasize the social embeddedness of warlords.

With his analysis of the "Economic Functions of Violence", Keen (1997, 1998) became one of the first anthropologists to reject culturalist claims that civil wars exhibited signs of mindless violence and "a coming anarchy" (Kaplan, 1994), coming from subconscious primitive instincts inherent in human nature. Based on his research in Sierra Leone and Sudan, Keen (1997) argues that the rational interests of rebel leaders and their economic interests contributed to a prolongation of fighting, destruction and human misery: a "rational kind of madness", he concluded.

Keen suggests that the political economy of war-fostering incentive structures made it rational for war entrepreneurs to continue fighting, since that was their source of ensuring resource rents. Georg Elwert (1997) uses the term "markets of violence" to describe the phenomenon of long-term violent interaction in modern civil wars, where the state's monopoly of violence has vanished, arguing that the decision whether to rob or to trade certain goods is contingent, not a priori given (p. 89). A warlord calculates costs and benefits in a triangle of violence, trade and space-time.

Elwert argues that markets of violence are pure, deregulated markets where the profit making motive is dominant, not emotional, primitive instincts or political grievances centering around ethnicity and identity, as has often been suggested (1997, p. 92). Elwert describes how spatially mobile predatory traders (*Räuber-Händler*) – who seem to be similar to Olson's roving bandits – appropriate high-value goods, such as diamonds, gold, drugs and weapons that are easy to transport and can be hidden away. Places where markets of violence emerge, often further attract such kinds of "illegal" trading and smuggling, and are provided protection by stationary bandits (territorially established warlords). As an externally provided opportunity to loot, food aid provided via international humanitarian machinery has also become a prime source of income for warlords (Anderson, 1999, Keen, 1994, Macrae, 2001). In addition to financing his personal expenditures, a warlord's entrepreneurial activities must provide sufficient revenue to pay for weapons and soldiers in order to reproduce himself as a warlord (Jean & Rufin, 1999).

The economic rationale of the war entrepreneur is embedded within an entrepreneurial symbolic politics of identity and fear. In order to recruit "volunteers", warlords play into political grievances and social demand for prestige, for example in societies where livestock raiding or violent rituals serve young males to demonstrate their maleness. Political "projects", such as struggles for justice, are useful tools to rally fighters. Mobilizing fighters can also build on a politics of fear. The fear of revenge after "mindless" acts of violence against others binds fighters more strongly to the warlord and stabilizes the collective system of a warlord's economic enterprise. Elwert suggests that modern communication devices have enabled warlords to effectively convey their propaganda, whereby the enemy is identified and defined, while also nurturing fear of the enemy (Elwert, 1997). Such propaganda, which creates friends and foes, frames conflict situations as ideological endeavors in the forms of, for example, a "freedom fight" or defense of "our honor" and "beliefs" (Schlee, 2004), for which diaspora communities often provide further financial or other assistance.

Keen's and Elwert's argument that violence in civil wars is economically rational resembles the reasoning of economists and their bandit models. But it also differs. Olson, Collier and game theoretical models work within the confines of methodological individualism and rational choice. Elwert argues that violent conflict follows culturally encoded patterns, has institutionalized forms and is controlled and directed in its appearance. It is, in short, socially embedded (Elwert, Feuchtwang, & Neubert, 1999): "Embedding is the ensemble of moral values, proper norms and institutional arrangements which create limits to a specific type of action and make simultaneously the outcome o these actions calculable" (Elwert, 2003, p. 2). Conflict has both, controlled, ordered and foreseeable aspects and an element of surprise, with Elwert calling this "partial embedding" (ibid.).

Elwert differentiates between normative conflict and actor conflict. In normative conflict, a person or a group of persons clashes with a norm and violates other people's rights. In actor conflict, actors (individual or group) clash in a field of action which has normatively defined boundaries, but neither side can claim norms protecting its goals (Elwert, 2003). The social practice of warring, such as with civil war or feuds, includes violent acts and physical harm, but is still confined by some rules whereby the types of victims, weapons as well as time and place of combat may be regulated. Elwert distinguishes such warring from destruction (e.g. genocide), where the goal is the total annihilation of the enemy or the other. In the latter case, there are no binding agreements, but there may still be rules, for example culturally encoded patterns of killing defining "proper" from "inhuman" killing.

Elwert's elaboration of the "markets of violence" shares with economic warlord models the need for abstraction from the messy ground realities in civil wars in order to produce a model with universal – or at least mid-range – applicability. Although Elwert refers to ethnographic field work, he does so ad hoc and in a way that suits his argument, not systematically. Through this, warlords appear, similarly to economic models, as existing outside of time and space: abstract agents acting in the model world of the economist or the anthropologist. What needs to be done, then, is to confront this model world with the ground realities of civil wars as we find them in the "real" world.

3.4 Ethnographies of Violence and Order

The rationalist explanations of civil war, both by economists and anthropologists, concentrate on one single category of agents in the political economy of war: the warlord or rebel. The category of "ordinary" people, however, is mostly missing. This is potentially problematic, as "what may be the most powerful aspect in studying war is not merely the violence that attends to it but the creativity the people on the front lines employ to reconstruct their shattered worlds" (Nordstrom, 1995, p. 131). If people are capable of manipulating norms, they will also find means to manipulate the norms of warlordism, the politics of fear and the political economy of war. It may be time to shift emphasis from the perpetrators of warlordism to the everyday forms of struggle, resistance and obedience within the political economy of violence and appropriation – a theme that was central to peasant studies in 1972 and the 1980s, though in a different empirical context.

In his seminal work *Weapons of the Weak*, James C. Scott describes the everyday forms of resistance through which poor peasants in Malaysia fought back against the experience of indignities, control, submission, humiliation, forced deference, and punishment, which shaped agrarian relations of exploitation and domination. These "small arms fire in the class wars" (Scott, 1985, p. 1) entail subtle peasant actions, from avoiding paying taxes to the state to jousting verbally with landlords, "slagging off" the rich behind their back or stealing crops by night from vulnerable neighbors. Scott's ethnographic case study is concerned with a relatively stable and hierarchically ordered polity, wherein class struggles dominate (Moore, 1986, p. 825). However, the question is equally valid concerning what the weapons of the weak may be in markets of violence and the political economy of violence and appropriation. In a sense, we might need to look at both, the weapons of the weak and the strong, at "two kinds of power, the power everybody has and the power only some people have, and whose intricate combination results in what we might refer to as the local arena" (Olivier de Sardan, 2005, p. 186).

More importantly, we can consider the political economy of violence and appropriation to be of particular heuristic value for the study of the intricate relations of violence, order and rule making. Conflict and violence are not alien to "society" or "order", but intrinsic to it. "Violence is never a totally isolated act" (Schröder & Schmidt, 2001, p. 3), but is rather tied to competitive social *relationships* and is the product of a historical process. Violence is never completely meaningless, to the actor or the victim. Violence is never totally idiosyncratic, and violent acts rarely target anybody at random, although an individual victim may be targeted at random as representative of a larger social category (ibid.).

It is an inherent character of social norms that they are "underlived" (Goffman, 1961). Norms are never adhered to one hundred percent, but they are sometimes followed, at times violated and occasionally bent and remade, as Norman Long (2001) suggests. Actors are capable of manipulating social norms, and they can mobilize different institutional logics to serve specific purposes. Through social practices, rules, orders and their logics may become internalized, "accepted" and shared, and can result in conformity, for example out of fear. But rules are not fixed, they are constantly remade through social practices, on different scales. While social practices are shaped consciously and unconsciously by the order(s) of rules, there are avenues for new forms of agency: limited certainly, but still agency. The volatility of military control and changing, multiply overlapping orders following shifting military dynamics create uncertainty, which can diminish or widen agency. Christian Lund (2006) argues that, in the context of institutional competition for public authority, "twilight" institutions emerge at the interface between authorities and the more or less mundane practices of "ordinary" people.

Sri Lanka's civil war offers illuminating material to study the "small arms fire" – the weapons of the weak, the mundane practices of everyday resistance and subordination – within the larger battles of the "ethnic" war that is being fought between the Liberation Tigers of Tamil Eelam (LTTE) and the Sinhalese-dominated Sri Lankan state. These mundane practices of everyday resistance and subordination illustrate the multiple linkages between struggle for survival and the political economy of violence and appropriation. Through these kinds of practices "markets of violence" emerge, enacted and produced by rebels, soldiers, bureaucrats, peasants and fishermen alike. Multiple orders and systems of rules evolve in the twilight of markets of violence that are both constraining and enabling, often at the same time (Korf, 2004).

The military and territorial dynamics of the Sri Lankan civil war and its political economy can tentatively be grasped using Olson's bandit model. In the initial stage of violent uprising in the early to mid 1980s, the LTTE was one among a number of Tamil militant groups that fought against the state. Guerrilla tactics and violent extraction of rents by these groups followed the logic of roving bandits. Increasingly, though, the LTTE outplayed other Tamil militant groups and became the strongest among them. When the Indian troops who had tried to pacify Sri Lanka's northeastern regions left the country in 1990, the LTTE was able to keep control over a sizable territory in the north and some smaller territorial pockets in the east. An oligopoly of territorial control by two stationary bandits – the LTTE and the Sri Lankan security forces – emerged. This duopoly of violence, authority and domination beyond the Sri Lankan state apparatus remained relatively stable in the east.

But the analysis of such cases needs to go beyond Olson's bandit model. Rather than simply studying the economic incentives for the two "bandits", the LTTE and the army, I want to demonstrate the complexity of the political economy of violence and appropriation and its multiple co-existing orders and systems of rules. The following ethnographies on the everyday practices of peasants and fishermen at the east coast of Sri Lanka describe the dialectics of violence and order and the intricate relationship between the weapons of the weak and the strong in the time period briefly before and after the ceasefire agreement in 2002. Note, that the ground situation has changed since then with the army conquering back most of the eastern territories in a large-scale military offensive in 2006 and 2007. Core questions asked in the ethnographic research have been: What kinds of rules prescribe the behavior of peasants and fishermen in the war zone? How do these rules affect their everyday livelihoods in terms of, for example, cultivating their fields, going out to sea for fishing, selling their products, going to the market town? What are their everyday struggles and forms of resistance in the political economy of violence and appropriation? In posing these questions, these ethnographies seek to illustrate how survival economies can be intricately linked with the political economy of violence imposed by combatant actors, in this case the Sri Lankan security forces and the LTTE.[1]

Bargaining and fighting between combatants over their relative realms of power, both territorially and ideologically, define the order of rules for peasants and fishermen in a given territorial space. As first approximation, we may broadly distinguish different "orders" imposed by the powerful agents involved in this particular case: the LTTE rule over particular territories, the attempt to keep order of

[1] Fore more details on the methods and empirical results of this research, please consult Korf (2004), Korf and Fünfgeld (2006), Korf (2006, 2007).

the Sri Lankan security forces, the authority of the state apparatus and the customary norms of caste, religion and class. But this overlap of orders is not a permanent and static equilibrium. The power differentials between the combatant groups change across time and space; subsequently, the order of rules changes with the shifting power differentials. These variations occurred on different time scales: heavy fighting, for example, could shift the borderline or frontier between the territory under government control and the territory under LTTE control (in the Sri Lankan context, the former were called "cleared", the latter "uncleared" or not yet cleared, areas). But these frontiers were not fixed, impermeable lines. Rather, the LTTE moved across the frontiers at night time, when the rebels controlled most of the territory and the Sri Lankan security forces withdrew to their camps.

For a peasant or fishermen, this implies that the rules may not only change with the shifting military battle lines, but the order of rules and the rulers are different during the day, when the security forces are in charge, than at the night, when the LTTE rules. However, this situation is not of the sort that would allow the peasant to simply switch to two different modes of living and two distinct orders of rule: the day and the night. Rather, throughout the day and the night, the institutional logic persists, in varying guises, and the rules do not just vanish. When performing an action during daytime, a peasant will also consider what the implications are for his life at night, or the other way round. For example, if the peasant pays taxes to the LTTE during the night, this will be a reasonable thing to do under the order of LTTE rule, but it may be a dangerous thing under the order of the military's rule during the day. When peasants move to specific places, the order of rules may change as well; when peasants living in an uncleared area under LTTE control, for example, want to sell their agricultural products, they need to go to market towns that are located in cleared areas. They pass the frontier line between LTTE rule and military rule, but both rulers will interrogate the peasants with suspicion. On top of these two orders, the state still maintained a considerable presence in the government-controlled areas where the formal, legal rules co-exist with the emergency rules imposed by the security forces.

Several implications arise from these observations that seem to contradict some commonly cherished assumptions in institutional economics (Korf, 2007). First, rules about what is appropriate behavior may change within short time periods. The ambiguity of the rule system creates cognitive dissonance as the reference system of order changes and multiple orders co-exist that need to be balanced. Political violence undermines commonly accepted norms. Moral hazards and opportunistic behavior become more common in such situations, with rules influencing strategic (conscious) and unconscious behavior: peasants can seek strategic cooperation with combatants in order to be able to move to specific places or just in order to be able to bring products to the market. This is the balancing act, the conscious "play" with the ambiguity of the (momentarily) existing rules. But, parallel to those strategies, the complexity of rules also affects the mental models of those who are subjected to such changes and upheaval. What people consider as normatively desirable behavior changes: opportunism gains more ground. Ideology often becomes an important anchor tool, such as the ideology that defines friend and foe along ethnic dividing lines.

Second, recognition and acceptance of rules is not voluntary, but coercively imposed by stationary and roving bandits. Rules are not followed because they are broadly conceived as being "fair", but rather out of fear. For example, peasants will not go to specific places that are considered "no-go"; they do this out of fear, whether they think it just or not. Families comply with an LTTE rule that forces each family to give one child to them, not because they want their child to become a rebel, but out of fear. Fishermen pay taxes to army commanders or the LTTE, not because they consider this to give them a specific advantage, but again out of fear. But by constantly performing such practices, they and the coercive rules that originate them become more and more "accepted" as rules, though not voluntarily. These orders of rules thus emerge as a result of an imposed mutual acceptance. In such a situation, rules reflect (coercively) routinized behavior, rather than reflecting normatively endorsed rules.

Third, fear results in acceptance of rules, even if there is no direct local threat. People follow rules even though the acts that have created a climate of fear have been conducted in a remote place, with other people having been victims of them. But the legacy of these violent acts has traveled to other places and occupies the consciousness of those who have not directly experienced them, but have heard witnesses' accounts or just rumors about these acts. Communication – including the mouth to mouth flow of information can trigger a remote response, spatializing the governance of intimidation beyond the place of violent acts or suppression. Even without being there, "they" (meaning the perpetrators of these acts) are around, "their" presence is felt.

While combatants enforce their rules largely coercively, they need be careful not to overstretch their coercive force and practices. The "strongest is never strong enough to be master all the time, unless he transforms force into right", says Jacques Derrida (2005, p. 93). Rulers need to find stories to legitimize their use of force and violence to their constituencies. If the LTTE is too harsh in imposing taxes from Tamil people, this may diminish the support base of the rebels among Tamil civilians: they may attract less recruits, find fewer places to hide in government-controlled areas and there may be more reports about their movements to the security forces. If the security forces are too strict and brutal in imposing their regime on Tamil civilians, they may increase the recruitment drives among Tamil youth, thereby strengthening the rebel basis. Therefore, forcefulness needs to be balanced out by something that combatants can offer to their constituencies, for example an ideology of shared belonging (the Tamil homeland) and economic benefits. Combatants plunder and protect at the same time that they make war and law (and order), indicating the existence of an important maneuvering space where combatants attempt to set the core rules of survival in the political economy of war and appropriation.

But there is also space for the "weapons of the weak": in this case, farmers or fishermen, who also have some (limited) leverage and negotiating power to pursue practices of everyday resistance and opportunism. Three simple examples taken from the time period 2000–2002 may be used to illustrate this point. First, Muslim traders in Sri Lanka have been able to navigate between the lines of combat. As they are neither Tamil nor Sinhalese, they could deal with both the LTTE and Sinhalese army officers. In many places at the Sri Lankan east coast, Muslim traders have managed to establish a kind of "ethnic" trade oligopoly, buying produce from Tamil farmers and fishermen and transporting it through a large number of military checkpoints to markets outside of the war zone. Tamil traders have been handicapped in this trade, as they could easily get in trouble at a checkpoint under suspicion of being an LTTE spy. But Tamil farmers can also pay back any Muslim traders for shady practices or unfair market exchanges by informing the LTTE, which then "visits" traders by night, taxing or intimidating them.

Second, the fear of one's neighbor offers opportunities for appropriating land parcels from the ethnic other. In the irrigated cultivation areas of the east coast, Muslim and Tamil paddy fields are located adjacent to each other in a jigsaw puzzle of property lines. With the shifting dynamics of territorial control and military dynamics, land markets have often developed patterns of forced sales and unequal exchange. Sometimes, Muslims have sold land at marginal prices to Tamil neighbors, when they do not feel safe going to their fields for cultivation. In other cases, Tamils have sold their land to Muslims. When Tamil–Muslim conflicts have emerged, Tamil farmers have harvested the crops of their Muslim neighbors who were afraid to go to their fields and vice versa. Third, Sinhalese farmers have used the protection of the military to block the flow of water to Tamil and Muslim fields at night, so that they could cultivate more of their own land. Tamil engineers from the irrigation department have been reluctant to stop these practices, as the Sinhalese farmers could outplay their political connections, knowing politicians who could order the transfer of engineers to even worse work stations or informing military personnel who could threaten them directly.

These mundane practices of everyday survival and entrepreneurial activities rely on small opportunisms, the pursuit of self-interest and struggle over resources in which "ordinary" people and combatants have each played their role. The hybridity and ambiguity of orders and rules in this region has created uncertainty and fear, while at the same time opening up spaces for resistance to subordination, oppression, forced deference and humiliation. But often the resistance to the political economy of violence has, in turn, produced new violence and opportunisms, mostly against the ethnic other. Contrary to Scott's peasant resistance against the ("bad") rich people, where "good" and "bad" are normatively defined through the analytical lens of class struggle, the weapons of the weak in Sri Lanka's civil war seem to be muddier and more opaque in the twilight of the political economy of violence and appropriation.

3.5 Conclusion

Garfinkel and Skaperdas (2000) have argued that rationality, defined as the pursuit of self-interest, includes actors with "grabbing" hands who conduct appropriation, predation, deception and enforced redistribution. Collier (2000) applied this argument to rebellion, making it a "quasi-criminal activity" of greedy agents. Elwert (1997) wrote that markets of violence are "pure" markets, governed solely by supply-demand pressures. But these pressures arise from a multiplicity of actions that are social, economic and political. Markets are socially embedded, as Granovetter (1985) suggested, and this holds true for markets of violence as well. Contrary to the "rationalist" reading of civil war, in this essay it has been argued that the political economy of violence and appropriation in civil wars entails a politics of domination, coercion and control as well as struggles of resistance and the everyday opportunisms of various actors.

The anthropologists Thomas Bierschenk and Jean-Pierre Olivier de Sardan (1997, p. 240, my emphasis) propose that, "conflicts are one of the best "virtual leads" for "penetrating" a society and revealing *its norms or codes* as well as its structures". I tend to agree with their view. Violence is not the opposite of order, it creates new order(s) and rules. In fact, my reading of the political economy of the Sri Lankan civil war suggests that some commonly proposed assumptions of institutional economics are difficult to uphold in the context of civil war. First, rules about what constitutes appropriate behavior (mental models) change within short time periods. Second, recognition and acceptance of rules is not voluntary, but coercively imposed. Third, fear results in acceptance of rules, even if there is no direct threat or coercion. And, at the same time, while these rules constrain people's choices and imaginations, there is room for emergence of the weapons of the weak: the small everyday resistance and opportunism played out, not by the powerful, the combatants, but by ordinary people.

"Make law, not war" was the Hobbesian logic: monopolize power in the hands of the monarch to avoid social anomy. According to the Hobbesian view, violence is the opposite of order and civilization. But "make law *and* war" seems to be what combatants, warlords, rebels, militants, army soldiers and police officers are doing in civil wars. This "make law and war" logic results neither in deadly stability nor pure anarchy. In the twilight of military contestation, multiple and competing orders of rules emerge, forming a political economy of violence and appropriation. These orders, as this essay has argued, are ambivalent, since there are multiple rulers and territorial control is contested. Power shifts in space and time. In the institutional competition for order and authority, rules are not shared norms, but are rather imposed, either violently or through the remote response of fear. Ordinary people are not only victims, but partly culprits, as they negotiate their mundane social practices of everyday life and, thereby, re-make some of the multiple rules that the different order(s) impose on them.

Acknowledgments

The following people have critically commented on earlier drafts of this chapter: Norman Backhaus, Michelle Engeler, Matthias Juninger, Urs Geiser, Tobias Hagmann, Urs Müller, Lilith Schärer and the editors.

References

Anderson, M. (1999). Do no harm: How aid can support peace – or war. Boulder CO: Lynne Rienner.

Auty, R. (2001). *Resource abundance and economic growth*. Oxford: Oxford University Press.

Azam, J. -P. (2002). Looting and conflict between ethnoregional groups. *Journal of Conflict Resolution, 46*, 131–153.

Azam, J. -P., & Hoeffler, A. (2002). Violence against civilians in civil wars: Looting or terror? *Journal of Peace Research, 38*, 429–444.

Bates, R. H. (2001). *Prosperity and violence: The political economy of development*. New York: W.W. Norton.

Bates, R., Greif, A., & Singh, S. (2002). Organizing violence. *Journal of Conflict Resolution, 46*, 599–628.

Bierschenk, T., & Olivier de Sardan, J. -P. (1997). ECRIS: Rapid collective inquiry for the identification of conflicts and strategic groups. *Human Organization, 56*, 238–244.

Blok, A. (1988). Book review of "The Anthropology of Violence" by David Riches. *Man, 23*, 785–786.

Collier, P. (2000). Rebellion as a quasi-criminal activity. *Journal of Conflict Resolution, 44*, 839–853.

Collier, P., & Hoeffler, A. (2004). Greed and grievance in civil war. *Oxford Economic Papers, 56*, 563–595.

Collier, P., Hoeffler, A., & Söderbom, M. (2004). On the duration of civil war. *Journal of Peace Research, 41*, 253–273.

Coutin, S. (1995). Ethnographies of violence: Law, dissidence, and the state. *Law and Society Review, 29*, 517–539.

Cramer, C. (2002). Homo economicus goes to war: Methodological individualism, rational choice and the political economy of war. *World Development, 30*, 1845–1864.

De Soysa, I. (2002). Paradise is a bazaar? Greed, creed and governance in civil war, 1989–1999. *Journal of Peace Research, 39*, 395–416.

Derrida, J. (2005). *Rogues*. Stanford: Stanford University Press.

Elwert, G. (1997). Gewaltmärkte. In T. von Trotha (Ed.), *Soziologie der Gewalt: Sonderheft No. 37 der Kölner Zeitschrift für Soziologie und Sozialpsychologie* (pp. 86–101). Opladen: Westdeutscher Verlag.

Elwert, G. (2003). *Conflict and institution*. (Impulse paper presented at the conference on "Conflict, violence and procedures", Hanse Institute for Advanced Study, Delmenhorst).

Elwert, G., Feuchtwang, S., & Neubert, D. (1999). *Dynamics of violence: Processes of escalation and de-escalation in violent group conflicts*. Berlin: Duncker & Humblot.

Garfinkel, M. R., & Skaperdas, S. (2000). Contract or war? On the consequences of a broader view of self-interest in economics. *The American Economist, 44*, 5–16.

Gates, S. (2002). Recruitment and allegiance: The microfoundations of rebellion. *Journal of Conflict Resolution, 46*, 111–130.

Ginty, R.M. (2004). Looting in the context of violent conflict: a conceptualisation and typology. *Third World Quarterly, 25*, 857–870.

Goffman, E. (1961). *Encounters: Two studies in the sociology of interaction. Fun in games & role distance.* Indianapolis: Bobbs-Merrill.

Granovetter, M. (1985). Economic action and social structure: The problem of embeddedness. *American Journal of Sociology, 91*, 481–510.

Hagedorn, K. (1996). *Das Institutionenproblem in der agrarökonomischen Politikforschung.* Tübingen: J.C.B. Mohr (Siebeck).

Hagedorn, K. (2003). Rethinking the theory of agricultural change in an institutions of sustainability perspective. In G. van Huylenbroeck, W. Verbeke, L. Lauwers, I. Vanslembrouck, & M. D'Haese (Eds.), *Importance of policies and institutions for agriculture* (pp. 33–56). Ghent: Academia Press.

Hagedorn, K. (2004). Property rights reform on agricultural land in Central and Eastern Europe. *Quarterly Journal of International Agriculture, 43*, 409–438.

Hanisch, M. (2003). *Property rights and social conflict: Vol. 15. Institutional change in agriculture and natural resources.* Aachen: Shaker.

Herbst, J. (1990). War and the state in Africa. *International Security, 14*, 117–139.

Hirshleifer, J. (1994). The dark side of the force. *Economic Inquiry, 32*, 1–10.

Horowitz, D. (2001). *The deadly ethnic riot.* Berkeley: University of California Press.

Jean, F., & Rufin, J. -C. (1999). *Ökonomie der Bürgerkriege.* Hamburg: Hamburger Edition.

Kaldor, M. (1999). *New and old wars: Organized violence in a global era.* Stanford: Stanford University Press.

Kalyvas, S. (2001). "New" and "old" civil wars: A valid distinction? *World Politics 54*, 99–108.

Kaplan, R. (1994). The coming anarchy. *Atlantic Monthly, 273*, 44–54.

Keen, D. (1994). *The benefits of famine: A political economy of famine and relief in Southwestern Sudan, 1983–1989.* Princeton: Princeton University Press.

Keen, D. (1997). A rational kind of madness. *Oxford Development Studies, 25*, 67–75.

Keen, D. (1998). The economic functions of violence in civil war. Adelphi Paper 320, International Institute of Strategic Studies.

Knight, J. (1992). *Institutions and social conflict.* Cambridge: Cambridge University Press.

Korf, B. (2004). *Conflict, space and institutions: Property rights and the political economy of war in Sri Lanka: Vol. 19. Institutional change in agriculture and natural resources.* Aachen: Shaker.

Korf, B. (2006). Functions of violence revisited: Greed, pride and grievance in Sri Lanka's civil war. *Progress in Development Studies, 6*, 109–122.

Korf, B. (2007). Contract or war? On the rules of the game in civil wars. *Journal of International Development, 19*, 685–694.

Korf, B., & Fünfgeld, H. (2006). War and the commons: Assessing the changing politics of violence, access and entitlements in Sri Lanka. *Geoforum, 37*, 391–403.

Kuran, T. (1995). The inevitability of future revolutionary surprises. *American Journal of Sociology, 100*, 1528–1551.

Le Billon, P. (2001). The political ecology of war: Natural resources and armed conflict. *Political Geography, 10*, 561–584.

Long, N. (2001). *Development sociology.* London: Routledge.

Lund, C. (2006). Twilight institutions: Public authority and local politics in Africa. *Development and Change, 37*, 685–705.

Macrae J. (2001). *Aiding recovery? The crises of aid in chronic political emergencies.* London: Zed Books.

Mehlum, H., Moene, K. O., & Torvik, R. (2002). Plunder and protection Inc. *Journal of Peace Research, 39*, 447–459.

Moore, M. (1986). Review of: Scott, J. C. (1985). Weapons of the weak: Everyday forms of peasant resistance. New Haven: Yale University Press. *Modern Asian Studies*, 21, 824–827.

Münkler, H. (2002). *Die neuen Kriege*. München: Beck.

Niemann, M. (2007). War making and state making in Central Africa. *Africa Today, 53*, 21–39.

Nordstrom, C. (1995). War on the front lines. In A. Robben & C. Nordstrom (Eds.), *Fieldwork under fire. Contemporary studies of violence and survival* (pp. 129–153). Berkeley: University of California Press.

Olivier de Sardan, J. -P. (2005). *Anthropology and development*. London: Zed Books.

Olson, M. (2000). *Power and prosperity: Outgrowing communist and capitalist dictatorship*. New York: Basic Books.

Ross, M. (2004). What do we know about natural resources and civil war? *Journal of Peace Research, 41*, 337–356.

Schlee, G. (2004). Taking sides and constructing identities: Reflections on conflict theory. *Journal of the Royal Anthropological Institute (N.S.), 10*, 135–156.

Schröder, I. W., & Schmidt, B. E. (2001). Introduction: Violent imaginaries and violent practices. In B. E. Schmidt & I. W. Schröder (Eds.), *Anthropology of violence and conflict* (pp. 1–24). London: Routledge.

Scott, J. C. (1985). *Weapons of the weak: Everyday forms of peasant resistance*. New Haven: Yale University Press.

Skaperdas, S. (2002). Warlord competition. *Journal of Peace Research, 39*, 435–46.

Skaperdas, S. (2005). An economic approach to analyzing civil wars. Department of Economics, University of California at Irvine. (unpublished paper)

Tilly, C. (1985). War making and state making as organized crime. In P. Evans, D. Rueschemeyer, & T. Skocpol (Eds.), *Bringing the state back in* (pp. 169–191). Cambridge: Cambridge University Press.

4 A Marathon Rather than a Sprint: The Reform of the Farmers' Pension System in Germany and its Impacts

Peter Mehl

Johann Heinrich von Thünen-Institut, Federal Research Institute for Rural Areas, Forestry and Fisheries (vTI), Institute of Rural Studies, Bundesallee 50, 38116 Braunschweig, Germany, E-mail: peter.mehl@vti.bund.de

Abstract. In 1994, the farmers' pension system in Germany was fundamentally reformed: the product of a long discussion process in which Konrad Hagedorn's analyses and recommendations played an important part. This paper analyses both the long road to the reform and its results and impacts. We first take a look back at the discussion about reform of the farmers' pension system during the 1980s and early 1990s and the reason why even small steps toward reform were not seen to be politically feasible at that time. Then we analyse the goals and main components of the reform in terms of its central features and their interplay. On this basis, the extent to which the targets intended by the reform were reached – or, rather, what intentional and non-intentional impacts emerged – is then analysed. With the reform, extensive improvements were achieved concerning social security for farmers' spouses, the stabilisation of the system, the dismantling of intersectoral advantages for the insured farmers and the compatibility of the farmers' pension system with other pension systems. The continuing discussion of the reform of the pay-as-you-go pension systems in Germany, however, clearly indicates that the farmers' pension system, despite the successful reform of 1994, will continue to be a topic of debate.

Keywords: Agricultural reform, Germany, Pension system, Political economy, Social security

4.1 Introduction

Social security for farmers is organised differently in the member states of the European Union. For example, in Germany, Austria, Poland and Italy, the farmers are insured through a special agricultural social insurance system. In contrast, in states like the Netherlands, the United Kingdom, or the Czech Republic, farmers belong to the common national social security system (Mehl, 1998). In the states with special agricultural systems, these organisations not only deliver farmers social security, they also fulfil policy tasks related to income and farm structure. The consequences of the sectoral systems are two-fold. On the one hand, they provide room for agricultural negotiation at the national level, a feature which has gained increasing significance in the course of developing a common agricultural policy for the European Union. On the other hand, the specially arranged agricultural social systems are facing significant pressure to adjust to the national social security systems due to structural changes taking place in agriculture and, increasingly, also due to changing societal expectations about agricultural economics and policy (Mehl, 2005a).

In Germany, the important role of the agricultural social security system (Landwirtschaftliche Sozialversicherung – LSV) can be seen in the fact that 3.7 billion Euros, or 72% of the national agricultural budget, was allotted to it in 2007. Of that, pension funds comprise the largest portion, with 2.37 billion Euros. At the same time, increasing pressure to reform this system has arisen because of its dominant role in the state budget.

When the farmers' pension system (Landwirtschaftliche Altershilfe – LAH) was founded in 1957, such a development could not have been anticipated. The pensions for farmers were originally conceived as modest cash supplements to the rights they retained on their farms in retirement and had to be financed solely by their own contributions. But, over the years, the extent and level of benefit payments have continually increased, mostly financed by national subsidies. Development of the Agricultural Accident Insurance (Landwirtschaftliche Unfallversicherung – LUV) and the Agricultural Health Insurance programmes (Landwirtschaftliche Krankenversicherung – LKV) was also marked by increasing national subsidies, and expenses for the agricultural social security system began to dominate the budget of the German Ministry of Nutrition, Agriculture and Forestry (Bundesministerium für Ernährung, Landwirtschaft und Forsten – BML). Efforts toward budgetary savings and structural reforms, which were started in the middle of the 1980s, had only limited impact on these trends. The extremely dynamic cost increases of the early 1990s, which coincided with the necessity to transfer the LSV to the new federal states following German reunification, provided the impetus for undertaking a basic reform of the agricultural social security system, which led to the Law to Reform Agricultural Social Security (Gesetz zur Reform des agrarsozialen Sicherungssystems – ASRG, 1994).

This paper analyses both the process of, and the long period of resistance to, the reform, and then explains the reform of 1994 itself, its results and impacts. For this purpose, Section 4.2 first takes a look back at the long discussion regarding amendments to the LSV during the 1980s and early 1990s. In Section 4.3, the main goals and components of the ASRG 1994 are analysed in terms of its central features and their interplay. On this basis, Section 4.4 shows the accomplishments and other more or less intended results of the reform. Finally, new questions currently arising from the farmers' pension system are discussed in Section 4.5.

4.2 Reform in the 1980s: Proposals and Resistance

Starting in the mid-1970s, calls for a reform of the LSV led to a whole range of reform proposals and attempted policy changes (Mehl, 1997, pp. 155–350). However, despite two large-scale reform attempts since the mid 1970s, a sustainable
adjustment of the LSV was only first achieved in 1994. Previously, the LAH
proved to be highly resistant to all reform attempts. It was not only that the basic
reform proposals were not able to be implemented: even small corrections were either blocked or changed through subsequent amendments which served to increase
the incomes of the insured farmers. The decision-making processes concerning the
LSV in the 1980s are marked by a distinct pattern composed of two phases. The
first phase is characterised by attempts targeting a basic re-creation of the LSV.
Accordingly, political developments wherein central actors urged reform can be
found in the years 1977/1978, 1981–1984, and 1987–1989. They all have in common that the proposals made could not be implemented. A second phase adjoining
the first contains amendments, focused primarily on an expansion of the intersectoral transfer function of the LSV.

4.2.1 The first attempt at reform

The development of the LSV was marked by dynamic expansion of costs until the
middle of the 1970s. From that time, the first demands for a basic reform, both
endogenous and exogenous to the system, were placed on the political agenda
(Hagedorn, 1986a; Scheele, 1990; Mehl, 1997). Pressure for reform came about,
on the one hand, through the interaction of endogenous expense dynamics of the
LAH, tied to sinking numbers of paying insured farmers (Hagedom, 1986b). At the
same time, a phase of "social policy for lean years" began in the 1970s (Schmidt,
1998, p. 98), marked by a range of laws reducing social benefits. Both aspects,
endogenous dynamics of the LAH as well as changing conditions of the political
framework, contributed largely to increasingly critical judgement of the LSV.

   An expression of the growing reform discussion about the LSV, and at the
same time an important input for this discussion, was a report from the Scientific
Council to the BML in 1979 (Wissenschaftlicher Beirat, 1979, p. 1) – mostly
based on research results from Konrad Hagedorn and developed under the chair-
manship of Prof. Günter Schmitt at the University of Göttingen (Hagedorn,
1982) – which came to the conclusion that the LSV was in need of basic reform
and included extensive and detailed recommendations for a reshaping of the system. The core concept of the experts' report was to limit the LSV to social policy
goals and to liberate it from tasks related to agricultural structure and income policy. For this purpose, according to the report the LSV system should to a large extent be reshaped on the basis of the statutory pension insurance, the national old age

pension system for employees (gesetzliche Rentenversicherung – GRV). Concretely, this meant that the contributions of the LAH should be determined on the basis of the contribution/benefit relations of the GRV. But benefits are set one third lower than the average benefit in the GRV in order to account for the payments from the farm successor to the retiree. The Scientific Council's report worked as the catalyser for the reform discussion, with the concrete proposals for change being at first of little political relevance, because they were simply too far from what the government administration and agricultural policy makers considered to be politically feasible at that time.

Temporarily, a second expert report, compiled a working group of the BML (Pfleiderer, Tenwinkel, Michels, & Schlagheck, 1981), became more significant. It was not only a critical response to the proposals of the Scientific Council's report, but also contained its own proposals for the "Further Development of Agricultural Social Security." An analysis of these proposals by Hagedorn (1982) contended that the recommendations of the BML Working Group should primarily serve to actually legitimise the independent system of agricultural pensions. The proposals were a response to the consolidation requirements seen to be urgent within the German Federal Budget at the beginning of the 1980s. They became a part of the political agenda much more quickly than planned, but ultimately failed due to resistance from the CDU (Christian Democratic Union) – and CSU (Christian Social Union) – dominated *Bundesrat*[1]. Only a short time after this first reform attempt had failed, the CDU and CSU took over the government together with the FDP (Free Democratic Party).

4.2.2 Redefinition of the reform problem (1984–1987)

The agricultural social policy of the newly elected Christian-liberal federal government in 1982 was at first marked by continuity. Two years after the change in government, however, a new phase in agricultural social policy began from an agricultural policy perspective. In 1982 and 1983, the focus was particularly on the dismantling of intersectoral benefits and, at the same time, on redistributing part of the federal subsidies to the LAH: to the benefit of owners of small and midsized farms and at the cost of farms with greater income potential. The emphasis shifted partially due to the impressions left by the reform of the Common Agricultural Policy (CAP) in 1983, especially the introduction of production quota in the milk sector and subsequent debates, but the social-cost burden of more weakly contributing farms continued to be seen as being in need of a political solution. However, the emphasis of the discussed approaches no longer rested on an intrasectoral

---

[1] The *Bundesrat* is one of the five constitutional bodies in Germany. The *Länder* (federal states) participate through the *Bundesrat* in the legislation and administration of the Federation.

redistribution of subsidies. Now, a reduction of the social costs should rather be financed without a reduction in the intersectoral transfer volume. Hence, the reshaping of the LAH was redefined as a necessary agricultural policy measure, compensating decisions of the CAP of the EU.

This negation of the reform requirements and the simultaneous agricultural policy instrumentation for the LSV was favoured largely through exceptional but temporary demographic conditions in 1981–1984 (Hagedorn, 1982, p. 165; Hagedorn, 1987, p. 251). Subsequently, the cost dynamic of the LSV increased significantly, because the endogenous system dynamics, the increasing costs per beneficiary, and the drop in contributors due to structural changes and applications for exemption grew through demographic influences. High rates of increase for the contributions of farmers and rapid growth in federal subsidies to LAH after 1987 were a consequence, so that a reform of the LAH again appeared quickly on the political agenda.

4.2.3 The second attempt at reform (1987–1990)

The second attempt to reform the LSV exhibits parallels to the first attempt in terms of course and results. As already at the beginning of the 1980s, in 1987 the administration of the DML was the driving force behind efforts to realise or prepare for the implementation of a basic reform of the LSV. As in the first attempt, a scientific report played a role in defining the problem which, however, in contrast to the first reform efforts at the beginning of the 1980s, found stronger acceptance by the government in its first draft. Nevertheless, the various proposals, which were constantly reduced in terms of their reform content, never reached the policy formulation stage, but rather failed again due to political resistance.

A concept created by the administration of BML in the first half of 1988 was unsuccessful due to resistance from parliament members close to agriculture and a feared "spill-over effect" of the proposed reform of the LAH onto the preparations for the reform of the GRV. The plan was to avoid making the proposed LAH pension for farm spouses a focus of concern for the GRV, where difficult compromises could be endangered (for a more comprehensive account see Mehl, 1997, pp. 319–321). Since the introduction of an independent pension for farm spouses within the LAH required a reshaping of central features of the LSV system, the forgoing of a solution to this question was, at the same time, a forgoing of a comprehensive general reform along the same lines. In the government, a coalition agreement was reached that the reform could be carried out in several steps. But the discussion and reference draft for a fourth Agricultural Social Extension Law (Viertes Agrarsoziales Ergänzungsgesetz – 4. ASEG; printed in Agra-Europe (1989)), to serve as the first step toward total reform of the agricultural social insurance, was not on the agenda of the Bundestag. Intervention, especially by parliamentary members of the FDP and CSU coalition fractions close to agriculture, made sure that this draft failed before an official discussion by the German Cabinet could be undertaken. Instead, just shortly before the end of the voting term, a minimal solution was approved securing ownership rights (Mehl, 1990).

4.3 The Agricultural Social Security Reform Law (ASRG)

The previously sketched reform discussions extended over two decades and ultimately came to a head in 1994 with the Agricultural Social Security Reform Law (ASRG), through which farm pension rights were thoroughly reformed: specifically, the LAH was replaced by the law for farm pensions (Alterssicherung der Landwirte – AdL).

4.3.1 The decision-making process and its rationale

The decision-making process for this reform and its ultimate shape were influenced by a number of factors, including (1) the change in position of the farm-interest representatives on the question about the need for reform, (2) the circumstance that funds for this reform were made available from other expiring measures, (3) the requirement that the LSV should be applied to the new German federal states, (4) the organisation of the reform preparations within the framework of a coalition working group and, ultimately, (5) the dynamic course of the political decision-making process. Each of these points is explained below:

1. Already in 1991, the leadership of the Farmers' Union advocated that the "long-planned agricultural social reform be carried out within this legislature period" (Agra-Europe, 1991a) and presented its own ideas in a discussion paper. The self dynamism of the LSV system, and its expected development without political correction, was decisive to the change in position of farm-interest representatives: from a strict defence of the status quo to becoming proponents of reform.
2. The reform of the Common Agricultural Policy of 1992 led to an increase in agricultural funding of 1.745 billion German Marks within the national budget for 1993. The compensation measures, together with the EC agricultural reform, were to be financed with these funds (Agra-Europe, 1992a). The LSV presented a possibility with regard to the ongoing reform discussion and, for this reason, seemed to be suitable because use of these funds in conformity with EC law appeared to be secure over the long term.
3. With the German reunification, a fully new situation developed for the LSV, with the political decision-makers now facing a dilemma:
   - if the transfer of the LAH to farmers in the new federal states ceased, then those farmers would not have access to extensive income transfers in the form of contribution reductions in the LAH.

- if the decision were to be made for a transfer, then a solution was hardly imaginable which could avoid disadvantaging farms operating in the form of corporations as compared to family farms (Hagedorn & Mehl, 1993a; 1994).
4. One working group of the coalition fraction was assigned the task of drafting a proposal in order to eliminate the kind of parliamentary blockades that had met previous reform proposals by the government administration. This approach can be understood as a result of learning from the earlier, failed reform efforts.
5. In the design of the first reference draft of September 1992, the position of large-scale financial scope was clearly expressed, which, however, due to differences in farm structures in the former and new federal states, led to a very uneven distribution of LSV funds. This circumstance then caused the agricultural ministers of the new federal states to object and demand that the farms in these states not be excluded from the income transfers of the AdL. The delays caused by consultation on these issues led to further discussion in the context of an initial discussion on necessary consolidation of the federal budget in 1993, which prompted further change of the proposal in some extremely generously designed areas; thus the changed drafts first did not receive approval from the German Cabinet until July of 1993 (Mehl & Hagedorn, 1994). Ultimately, the central point was that the government proposal required the approval of the Bundesrat, in which the SPD-lead federal states held the majority. Several negotiating rounds between the coalition and the SPD opposition ultimately led to a consensus and to approval of a reform law which resembled the original cabinet proposal only in terms of its basic goals, but was in some areas much more restrictive in design. With these modifications, objections against the design of the government's proposal, expressed during expert hearings at the German Parliament in 1993, were for the most part incorporated (Mehl & Hagedorn, 1993b). Konrad Hagedorn was among these experts. Some of the main results of his doctoral thesis of 1982 were only finally implemented in 1994 – it was a marathon, not a sprint.

4.3.2 Goals and main features of the reform law

The ASRG is characterised by the attempt to stabilise expenses and to orientate the AdL along the features of the GRV. The original features of the farmers' pension system, which were motivated by farm policy goals, are maintained only in a very much weakened form. The income-related elements of the ASRG were almost completely limited to the area of contribution subsidies, which were scaled according to the income of the contributor. Although the obligatory transfer of a farm to the successor in order to obtain pension payments (farm transfer clause) was maintained, it was eased significantly (Möller, 1994).

Discussion of the reform of the farmers' pension system was dominated by the question of linking the necessity to financially stabilise the system with the plan to establish a separate social security arrangement for farmers' spouses. In addition, the transfer of farm pensions to the new federal states (Mehl & Hagedorn, 1993b) and strong consideration of individual farm income in contribution subsidy laws were further significant goals of the reform. The main problem of the ASRG was to harmonise the first two goals and reduce the existing resistance against reform by the affected persons.

Separate insurance for farmers' spouses

A mandatory pension insurance for farmers' spouses was introduced. With this independent pension and disability insurance, the central role of spouses on farms was recognised (Stüwe & Zindel, 1991). All farm spouses not yet 65 at the time the reform was enacted were insured like farmers in the AdL, while farm spouses who were already 50 could choose between insurance or no insurance. All newly insured after 1995 needed to have mandatory coverage, although members of this group could also apply for an exemption under certain circumstances. With amendments to the Farm Social Reform Law of 1995, the exemption possibilities for the spouses of a special group of part-time farmers were extended for a limited period of time (Wirth, 1996).

The main point of independent insurance for the farmers' spouses and a simultaneous central incentive to participate in the AdL insurance was the form that pension entitlement would take. This was particularly relevant to older farmers' spouses, who, due to their advanced age, could only contribute for a limited time. For them, a pension entitlement was to be created through a splitting of the entitlement with farmers insured under the LAH according to years of marriage. The contributions by the farmer during his married period were thus calculated as entitlement years for the farm spouses drawn into the AdL, without a retroactive payment of contributions.

Financial stabilisation of the system

This new element in the ASRG increased the cost of the system, which was counteracted by a new form of pension calculation. Cost reducing and stabilising measures in benefits led to (a) a linearization of the pension calculation, meaning that the same result is arrived at for each contribution year, and (b) the dismantling of the marriage-supplement, which became obsolete due to the introduction of spouse insurance. Both regulations were to reach significant reductions in benefit expenditures for new members of the AdL. A comparison of contributions and benefits under the old and new laws shows the differences (Fig. 4.1).

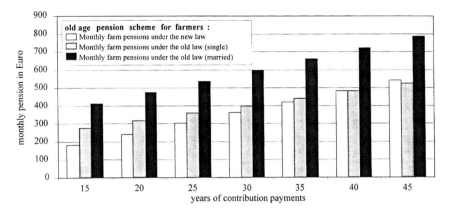

Fig. 4.1: Changes in farm pension benefits due to the ASRG
Note: Values for the first half of 2006 (former federal states); a continuation of the old law is assumed.

Figure 4.1 shows that particularly married beneficiaries with a short period of contributions will suffer severe repercussions. The pension benefits of a married farmer with 15 years of contributions would have been 413 Euros under those of the old laws. The higher valuation of the first fifteen years was explained in part because, under the old laws before the reform, there were no non-contributory supplementary periods calculated in case of disability. As an accompanying measure toward linearizing the pensions in the AdL, the non-contributory supplementary periods were analogised to the regulation of disability in the GRV. The linearization of the pension calculations on the basis of 40 years of contributions and the elimination of married pension benefits has led to a situation where farmers have markedly lower pension entitlements under the new law. But the financial losses in pensions will first become completely effective on July 1, 2009, because a grandfather clause is in effect from 1995 to 2009, with a melting rate of 1/15 per year, which means that the change from the old to new laws is gradual. Furthermore, the elimination of the supplement for married farmers can be compensated with the inclusion of the farmers' spouses in the AdL, as long as these persons were not exempted from the system.

Farm spouses insurance and system stability

The new form of pension calculation and the targeted use of part of the savings from benefit payments to build an independent pension system for farm spouses was the key to this reform, linking both of its central goals. In the years from 1995 to 1998, increasing expenses for the AdL could first be balanced with an increase of contributions by the insured as a consequence of the mandatory pension contributions of farmers' spouses. Here it was clear that the consequent expansion of the insurance obligations led in any case to a short term "health improvement" for the system, since demographic and agricultural structural influences were time delayed but effective. Here, the savings presented above in the benefit areas shall start and be introduced stepwise by 2009.

The retroactive calculation of the farmer' years of contribution served as the basis for the pension rights of their spouses, because each farmer received entitlement for the pension contributions he had made during the marriage until the end of 1994. The sum of these pension entitlements were limited by a capping regulation, so that these could, at the highest, reach the level of the spouse's supplement under the old law. Without this regulation, the incentive structure of the government proposal, together with the broad option and exemption possibilities, would have made only a short term stabilisation of the system possible (Hagedorn & Mehl, 1993b, 1994; Stüwe, 1996, p. 64). The significantly more restrictive splitting rules of the ASRG and the changed, very limited, option and exemption possibilities were to ensure that the goal of a mid-term to long-term stabilisation of the expenses not be counteracted through the introduction of the farm spouses' pension system.

Supplemental contribution reduction system

The introduction of mandatory pension insurance for farmers' spouses also faced the difficulty that the need for double contributions had to be explained to the farm couples. The new contribution formula was based on the GRV, but generated a 20% gap compared to the contribution-benefit relation of this system. This difference was explained in 1994 as the result of the reduced benefit spectrum of the AdL in comparison to the GRV (Rombach, 1995, p. 208). The gradually implemented reduction by 50% of this gap is explained by subsequent benefit reductions in the general pension system. As a consequence, the supplemental contribution reduction system became the AdL's only income policy instrument. That is why the new design of the supplemental contribution reduction system should be considered an important part of the reform.

Farmers with an income of up to 40,000 DM/ year (with their spouses up to 80,000) are eligible for further contribution reductions; the highest graduated contribution reductions are paid to farmers with an income of up to 16,000 DM/year (with their spouses up to 32,000/year). The incomes of both spouses were added together and each partner was assigned 50% of the total income. The supplement limit for married partners was thus (at first) 80,000 DM (40,903.35 Euros). In 1999 64.5% of all insured farmers were entitled for graduated contribution reductions and only 35.5% have to pay the standard contribution of 340,– DM. Farmers who are eligible for the highest graduated contribution reductions only had to pay a monthly contribution of 68, – DM, which is only 16% of the contribution, an employee in the statutory pension insurance is charged with. Hence, only about one third of the insured farmers have to pay the standard contribution in 1999 due to these graduated contribution reductions.

4.4 Effects of the Reform

Reforms often display significant differences between the postulated impacts (policy output) of a law actually passed and its true effects (policy impact). With the ASRG, the assumption that the goals of the reform – independent social security for farm spouses, financial stabilisation of the system and better consideration of individual income – cannot be realised to the same extent without conflict arising between them. Therefore, the effects of the law with regard to social security, financial consequences and distribution policy implications will now be analysed.

4.4.1 Effect on social security

The social security of farm families during old age and possible disability could be improved by a range of ASRG measures (a) easier access to drawing a pension, (b) improved mobility between the farm and statutory pension systems, (c) improved coverage in case of disability through a strong move in the direction of the statutory pension system. Evaluation of the reform's effects on social security functions needs to take into consideration the new design of the pension calculation (see above linearization) as well as the form and methods of the farm spouses' insurance programme.

Pension level

As described above, the linearization of pension calculation entails a reduction of the benefit level of a normal pension for an unmarried pension recipient if the average number of years of contributions is less than 40. With more than 40 years of contributions, the pension is somewhat above that of the old laws for married pension recipients. The comparison also depends on whether the spouse enters the AdL or is exempted from the system.

According to the annual report of the Farmers' pension system, the average number of contribution years for farmers receiving a pension in 2006 was 28.7; the comparable period for 65 year old retirees was 30.5 years. Of the 12,818 new retirees in 2006, only 678 (5.3%) had contributed for 40 years or more. The overwhelming majority of unmarried retirees is now entitled to less pension benefits (8% on average) than they would have been before the reform. These losses were slightly softened by the grandfather clause, which provided pensioners with one third of the difference between the old and new laws in the first half of 2005.

Married pension recipients could prevent this reduction in their pensions by opening a farm spouse's pension. For this purpose, the pension entitlement for the total years of marriage needs to be split from the contribution periods of the farmer. As a consequence, spouses of retirees showed an average of 29.6 eligible years in 2006. As the mandatory insurance for farmers' spouses has only been in place since 1995, a maximum of 11 years can be based on their own contributions. Thus, the losses resulting from the reform of the benefit law can be completely offset by this splitting of contribution times if the spouse joins the AdL. This will not, however, hold true for the future. Since the splitting of times for farm spouses is based on the years that the farmer had been insured prior to 1995, the portion of the split period of eligibility for younger spouses will successively drop overall. The pensions of spouses who have become insured by the AdL for the first time after 1995 rely solely on own contributions, as do unmarried farmers.

Claiming benefits from the farm spouses' insurance system

Whether and to what extent the ASRG improves social security for farmers' spouses not only depends on the benefit level obtained, but also on the numbers of newly insured spouses.

Since 1995, more and more farmers and their spouses have been trying to avoid paying contributions into the AdL and have applied for a corresponding exemption (Deutscher Bundestag, 1997, 2001, 2006) (Fig. 4.2).

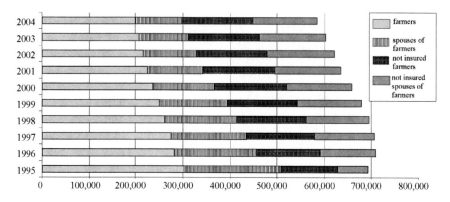

Fig. 4.2: Insured and exempted farmers and spouses in the AdL 1995–2004
Source: Own calculations, based on Geschäfts- und Rechnungsergebnisse der landwirtschaftlichen Altersklassen; Agrarbericht der Bundesregierung, verschiedene Jahrgänge

The number of farmers covered under the AdL is now about the same as the level of those with farm health insurance (LKV), implying that the possibility for exemption from the AdL is largely being used by all farmers who are eligible for it. In the case of spouses the existing exemption possibilities are even more intensively used: about 58% of farmers' spouses, who either have no insurance or were exempted from it, do not participate in the AdL.

As a consequence of the high exemption rate, the question emerges regarding how often married partners are both members of the AdL. Figure 4.3 shows the development in this area.

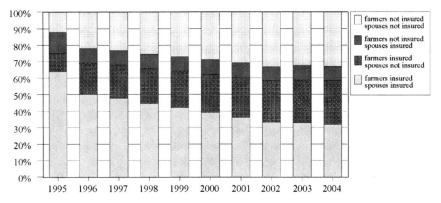

Fig. 4.3: Insurance for married couples in the AdL 1995–2004, in percent
Source: Own calculations, based on Geschäfts- und Rechnungsergebnisse der landwirtschaftlichen Altersklassen; Agrarbericht der Bundesregierung, verschiedene Jahrgänge

The number of farms in which both partners are insured by the AdL sank from about two thirds in 1995 to a scant third in 2004. In contrast, the number of married farm couples in which only the farmer is a member of the AdL rose significantly. Together with the group of farms in which only the spouse and not the farmer is a member of the AdL, the number of those households in which one partner was a member in 2004 was a generous third. The greatest increase since 1995 can be seen in the group in which neither partner is a member of the AdL, comprising one third of all farming couples.

Over the mid- and long-term, that is without the "grandfather clause" and the splitting of years of marriage, only farming couples now paying double contributions may in the future obtain the same or higher pensions as compared to the old laws. The strongly rising number of exemptions from mandatory insurance participation has led to a situation where the original purpose of the ASRG, to improve social security for the farmers' spouses, can only be achieved to a limited extent. And it seems as though AdL insurance coverage is increasingly being limited to that group of persons without exemption possibilities. On farms in which the farmer or his/her spouse is a member of the AdL, the pension to be expected from it is significantly below the pension level according to the old laws. Here, however, it must be taken into consideration that an exemption from the mandatory insurance obligations for farmer and spouse can only be granted if they are otherwise insured, usually through the GRV (Mehl, 2005b). From the perspective of the responsible federal ministry, the high portion of exemptions shows the flexibility of the system in meeting "the individual insurance needs and personal employment biography of farm families" (Schmidt, 2005, p. 17).

4.4.2 Stabilisation effects on costs and contributions

The above-outlined changes in the benefit and financing laws should induce a re-action to increased pension costs, which are themselves due to a shrinking community of contributors and multiple burdens on the government. Whether and to what extent the intended system stabilisation can be achieved through the ASRG can be shown via analysis of the burdens which have to be borne by the government and the effects of contributors following the reform rules in contrast to the old laws. Here a question emerges whether the cost of adjustment, especially its distribution between the group of contributors and the government, was simply shifted by the reform, rather than reduced. For this purpose, the fictitious effects of the old laws prior to reform are compared with the impacts of the reform. To achieve that, we contrast the forecasts of 1994 with the observed developments and the latest prognoses up to 2010. The presentation of the "actual development" until 2010 is based on the status report of the German government on the Farmers' pension system of 2001, which seems the most appropriate source from the perspective of 2005. The impact of the reform on the total costs of providing pensions has been a reduced rate of increase of these costs. Here, both the government and the contributors have benefited (Fig. 4.4).

The federal expenses are much lower than they would have been with a continuation of the old laws, and slightly lower than expected in the reform prognosis. During the passage of the reform, in 1995 a short-term savings of about 40 million Euros was expected, and then slightly increased costs for the government until 2000. From 2001 on, growing savings were predicted in comparison to the continuation of the old system, culminating in 168 million Euros saved for 2010.

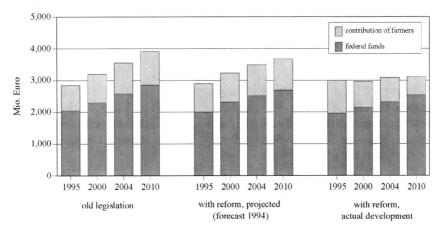

Fig. 4.4: Development of AdL, with and without reform, 1995 to 2010 (Mil. Euros)
Source: Own calculations, based on Geschäfts- und Rechnungsergebnisse der landwirtschaftlichen Altersklassen; Agrarbericht der Bundesregierung, verschiedene Jahrgänge

In fact, since 1995 the expenses of the government have always been less than
predicted. This is mainly due to the increased number of contributors, which ex-
ceeded expectations. One explanation here is that expectations about remaining
expenses for supplementary contributions reductions were particularly high, with
actual relief having come about due to reductions in the framework of the Balanced Budget Law of 1999. In 2004, the federal expenditures were 255 million
Euros less than under the old laws, and 176 million Euros less than under the
prognosis.

Looking at the distribution between contributors and the federal government in
terms of the financing of total pension expenditures, it can be seen that the growth
in new contributors to the AdL in the course of establishing the farmers' spouses
insurance plan relieved the budget of the federal government: the contribution of
which was 72.5% in 1993, but sank to 67.9% in 1995. Due to the unexpectedly
large number of contributors, the portion of federal funding was both absolutely
and relatively lower than the predicted figures. In the further course of the reform
implementation, this trend became reversed, in part due to a reduction in contributors: a consequence of the exemptions from mandatory insurance participation.
Consequently, federal share of total expenditures rose from 72.7% (2000) to 76%
(2004) and is anticipated to reach 82% in 2010. Thus, the relative portion of federal participation is much higher than under the old laws, where the federal share
would have been relatively consistent at about 73%. At the same time, the absolute level of federal participation is much less than the sum would have been under
a continuation of the old laws. The cause for this is the reduction of total beneficiaries, which can also be traced back to the development of exemptions. These exemptions had a double effect: They reduced the input from contributors, but also
limited the expenditure for pensions because those exempted cannot be beneficiaries.

Through the new financing system, contributors have much higher planning security concerning future contribution levels than before the reform. This is due to
the coupling of the contributions with developments in the general pension system
and the taking over of payments not covered by the contributions by the federal
government.

The differences in the actual development of contribution levels from those
calculated via the prognoses 1994 are relatively minimal (Fig. 4.5). However, the
cause for this is not the ASRG itself, but rather the different measures taken to
stabilise the level of contributions in the GRV in the area of benefits, as well as
the increase in federal subsidies in this area.

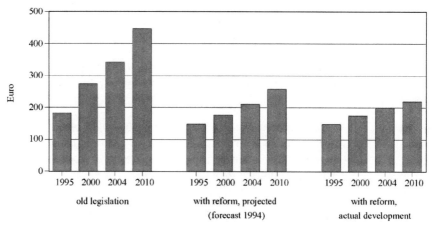

Fig. 4.5: Development of AdL contributions, with and without reform, 1995–2010 [Euros per
month]
Source: Own calculations, based on Geschäfts- und Rechnungsergebnisse der landwirtschaftlichen Altersklassen; Agrarbericht der Bundesregierung, verschiedene Jahrgänge

The consolidation measures to secure the level of contributions to the GRV had a
stabilising effect as a consequence of the coupling with the contributions to the
AdL. Despite the stepwise reductions of differences between the AdL and the
GRV from an original 20–10% through the Balanced Budget Act of 1999, the contribution for AdL members in 2004 was 10 Euros less than the reform prognosis in
1994 and 141 Euros under the contribution that would have been required had
there been no reform and had the former law continued. Here, however, it must be
taken into consideration that, according to the reform, in some cases two contributions must be paid, one each for farmer and spouse. The enormous expense dynamics of the old system are revealed when compared to the situation after reform; in 2010, individual contribution under the old law would be 446 Euros per
month higher than for the AdL, as predicted by the 2001 status report. Overall, it
can be said that the financial stability of the system was attained to a greater extent
than predicted, with the cost of reform-related adjustments having to be borne by
all participating groups: contributors, beneficiaries and federal government.

4.4.3 Distribution effects

The adjustment of contributions into the AdL to mirror the contribution-benefit relation of the GRV brought about a situation in which the previous significant advantage of the farmers' pension system now extended only to the graduated contribution reductions following the reform (Hagedorn, 1982; Mehl, 1997; Hagedorn & Mehl, 2001). However, the contribution-benefit relationship for the AdL is in part still much less costly for the beneficiaries eligible to graduated contribution reductions than that of the general pension system (Fig. 4.6, upper part).

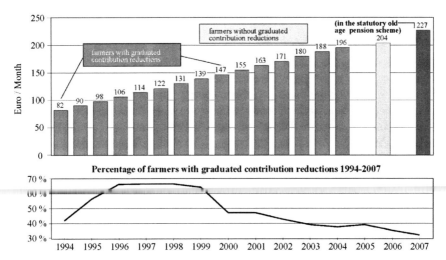

Fig. 4.6: Contributions per month to AdL and GRV for the same level of benefits (2005)
Source: Own calculations, based on Agrarberichte der Bundesregierung (1994–2007)

The bottom part of Fig. 4.6 charts the development of the subsidy entitlement since 1994. Through the ASRG, from 1995 to 1999, the group of persons entitled to subsidies was initially significantly expanded in comparison to the old laws, with the rationale being to make the new regulation regarding double contribution as a consequence of the new spouse insurance more attractive by granting contribution subsidies. Among the insured members in the AdL during 1996–1999, about two thirds received a contribution subsidy at the beginning of each year; among the group of insured farm spouses, almost three quarters received a subsidy. According to the old laws, in 1994 only 41.9% of the contributors would have received a subsidy. The large drop in the number of those entitled to subsidies after 2000 can largely be traced back to the fact that subsidy limitations were put into place within the framework of the Balanced Budget Act of 1999. On the one hand, the upper limit of yearly contribution subsidies was reduced from 40,000 to 30,000 DM (today 15,500 Euros) for single persons and from 80,000 to 60,000 DM (today 31,000 Euros) for married households. Furthermore, the highest contribution subsidy was reduced from the original 80 to 60% of the standard contribution. Thus, the group of people entitled to subsidies was limited and the relative preferability of the AdL as opposed to the general pension system was decreased. Income increases for the insured farmers with static subsidy limits led to a continuing drop of persons with entitlement to subsidies. In 2007, only about 32% of all insured persons were entitled to a subsidy. Without dynamisation of the limits for subsidy entitlement, the previously significant income policy component of the AdL will gradually be phased out (Möller, 2007, p. 125).

4.5 Reform Evaluation and Perspectives

With the arrival of the ASRG in 1995, new regulations for the farm pension fund were put in place, which can doubtlessly serve as a fundamental and long-term reform, with the following benefits: extensive improvements for the social security for farmers' spouses, stabilisation of the pension system itself through dismantling of intersectoral advantages for the AdL-insured farmers, and improved compatibility of the AdL with other pension systems. The main difficulties encountered regarding the reform of the farmers' pension system were the stabilisation of costs for the farmers' pension system (AdL); establishment of an independent social security plan for farm spouses, mostly women; and acceptance of the reform by the insured persons.

These difficulties were for the most part successfully overcome with the ASRG: first, with the linearization of the pension calculation (meaning that for each year of contributions the same yield is calculated) and then with the dismantling of the marriage supplement (which became obsolete due to the introduction of pension insurance for spouses). The latter led to major reductions in benefits, unless both farmer and spouse were insured. The contribution to the AdL is coupled with the contributions to the general pension system and tied to its development. Expenditures for benefits that are not covered by contributions will in the future be covered by the federal government (deficit coverage). Ultimately, an independent, mandatory insurance for spouses was put in place. That must be considered as an important step in terms of social security for this group, irrespective the numerous exemptions. Here the retroactive eligibility to count the husbands' years of contribution served as the basis for pension rights, particularly for older farmers' spouses. However, the pension eligibility rights which were split in this manner were limited by a capping regulation. The highest level of these rights is receipt of the spousal supplement according to the old laws, but in many cases the entitlements are much lower. They show a significant evening out of the increase in pension-related expenses, from which the government and contributors profit, at the expense of the beneficiaries in the future. A transitional plan for the years 1995–2009, with a melting factor of 1/15 per year, allowed the change from the old to the new laws to take place gradually and, with the takeover of deficit coverage by the federal government and the temporary expansion of the eligibility group until 2000, in part hard losses for affected farmers were softened. Overall, the ASRG can be called a justly carried out reform. A decisive factor in this new reform orientation was the harmonisation of the AdL with the general pension system through the ASRG, which led to broad-reaching legal parallels (Wirth, 2007, p. 99): since 1994, all significant reform measures in the area of the GRV have been transferred, with the same level of effectiveness, to the AdL (e.g., reform of the disability pension or increase of the pension age to 67).

While the system still faces criticism from insured farmers, it is difficult to decide whether this is a problem of acceptance of the special system, or an expression of general displeasure with state pension systems (Möller, 2005). The further shrinking of actively insured, the growing share of federal subsidies in the financing of the AdL, as well as continuing discussion about reform of the pay-as-you-go financed pension systems in Germany signal that the special system of farm pensions, despite the successful reform of 1995, will continue to be a topic of discussion. However, the AdL is in no way badly positioned when one considers the reform discussions regarding the GRV. There, topics like the necessity for supplementary private insurance, better insurance for women or a minimum insurance are vital points of discussion. The AdL presents a partial insurance concept that requires private supplementation. At the same time, it contains an independent mandatory insurance for spouses, mostly women. Furthermore, the AdL has significant elements of a minimum pension through its contribution subsidy concept. Currently, modifications of special aspects of the AdL, such as changes of the "farm transfer clause" (Zindel, 2005) or the dynamisation of the upper limits for contribution subsidies, are being discussed. Both measures should improve acceptance of the system by the insured persons and will not conflict with the essential nature of the reform course adopted since 1994.

References

Agrarbericht der Bundesregierung. Verschiedene Jahrgänge. Bonn, Berlin.

Deutscher Bundestag. (1997). *Unterrichtung durch die Bundesregierung: Lagebericht der Bundesregierung über die Alterssicherung der Landwirte 1997.* Bundestags-Drucksache 13/ 8919 vom 03.11.1997.

Deutscher Bundestag. (2001). *Unterrichtung durch die Bundesregierung: Lagebericht der Bundesregierung über die Alterssicherung der Landwirte 2001.* Bundestags-Drucksache 14/ 8072 vom 04.12.2001.

Deutscher Bundestag. (2006). *Unterrichtung durch die Bundesregierung: Lagebericht der Bundesregierung über die Alterssicherung der Landwirte 2005.* Bundestags-Drucksache 16/ 907 vom 09.03.2006.

Geschäfts- und Rechnungsergebnisse der landwirtschaftlichen Alterskassen. Verschiedene Jahrgänge. Kassel.

Gesetz zur Reform der agrarsozialen Sicherung – Agrarsozialreformgesetz 1994 (ASRG 1995) – vom 29. Juli 1994 (BGBl. I p. 1890).

Gesetz zur Änderung des ASRG 1995 (ASRGÄndG) – vom 15. Dezember 1995 (BGBl. I p. 1814).

Hagedorn, K. (1981). Probleme der Alterssicherung mitarbeitender Familienangehöriger. *Agra-Europe*, 22, 1–11.

Hagedorn, K. (1982a). Der Plan der Bundesregierung zur Weiterentwicklung der agrarsozialen Sicherung. *Agrarwirtschaft, 31*, 65–77.

Hagedorn, K. (1982b). *Agrarsozialpolitik in der Bundesrepublik Deutschland: Kritik und Alternativmodelle zur Alterssicherung in der Landwirtschaft*. Berlin: Erich Schmidt.

Hagedorn, K. (1984). Drittes Agrarsoziales Ergänzungsgesetz: Soziale Umverteilung oder "soziale Optik"? *Sozialer Fortschritt, 33*, 212–214.

Hagedorn, K. (1986a). Reformversuche in der Geschichte der Agrarsozialpolitik. *Zeitschrift für Agrargeschichte und Agrarsoziologie, 34*, 176–215.

Hagedorn, K. (1986b). Ökonomische und politische Auswirkungen der rückläufigen Bevölkerungsentwicklung auf die Finanzierung der agrarsozialen Sicherung. In P. von Blanckenburg & H. de Haen (Eds.), *Bevölkerungsentwicklung, Agrarstruktur und Ländlicher Raum* (pp. 259–272). Münster-Hiltrup: Landwirtschaftsverlag.

Hagedorn, K. (1987). Alternative Modelle zur Finanzierung der landwirtschaftlichen Alterssicherung. *Landbauforschung Völkenrode, 36*, 249–267.

Hagedorn, K., & Mehl, P. (1993a). Die agrarsoziale Sicherung im Prozess der Vereinigung Deutschlands: Probleme des Übergangs zu einem sektoral gegliederten Sozialversicherungssystem. *Deutsche Rentenversicherung, 3*, 120–147.

Hagedorn, K., & Mehl, P. (1993b). Eigenständige soziale Sicherung der Bäuerin und finanzielle Stabilisierung des agrarsozialen Sicherungssystemp: Überlegungen zum Gesetzentwurf der Bundesregierung zur Reform der agrarsozialen Sicherung (ASRG 1995). *Agra-Europe, 34*, Sonderbeilage 1–9.

Hagedorn, K., & Mehl, P. (1994). Die Übertragung des landwirtschaftlichen Alterssicherungssystems auf die Neuen Bundesländer im Gesetzentwurf der Bundesregierung zur Reform des agrarsozialen Sicherungssystemp. *Landbauforschung Völkenrode, 44*, 77–90.

Hagedorn, K., & Mehl, P. (2001). Social policy reforms for German agriculture: Challenges and recommendations. *International Social Security Review, 54*, 85–100.

Mehl, P. (1990). Soziale Sicherung. Zuschüsse neu verteilt. *DLG-Mitteilungen, 105*, 226–228.

Mehl, P. (1997). *Reformansätze und Reformwiderstände in der Agrarsozialpolitik der Bundesrepublik Deutschland: Politikinhalte und ihre Bestimmungsgründe von 1976 bis 1990*. Berlin: Duncker & Humblot.

Mehl, P. (1998). Transformation of the social security system in agriculture in East Germany: Lessons for Central and Eastern European countries? In K. Frohberg & P. Weingarten (Eds.). *The significance of politics and institutions for the design and formation of agricultural policies* (pp. 139–156). Kiel: Vauk.

Mehl, P. (2005a). Soziale Sicherung der Landwirte in Österreich: Modell für eine Reform des agrarsozialen Sicherungssystems in Deutschland? *Soziale Sicherheit in der Landwirtschaft, 3*, 235–258.

Mehl, P. (2005b). Zehn Jahre Bäuerinnenrente: Die Bäuerinnenrente als zentraler Bestandteil der Reform der landwirtschaftlichen Alterssicherung. *Ländlicher Raum, 56*, 13–16.

Möller, B. (1994). *Die neue Alterssicherung für die landwirtschaftliche Familie*. Bonn: Deutscher Agrar-Verlag.

Möller, B. (2005). Zehn Jahre Bäuerinnenrente: Bäuerinnensicherung aus der Sicht des Deutschen Bauernverbandes. *Ländlicher Raum, 56*, 18–19.

Möller, B. (2007). Ist die LSV für die Zukunft gerüstet? *Soziale Sicherheit in der Landwirtschaft, 2*, 235–258.

Pfleiderer, K., Tenwinkel, E., Michels, R., & Schlagheck, H. (1981). *Weiterentwicklung der agrarsozialen Sicherung*. Münster-Hiltrup: Landwirtschaftsverlag.

Rombach, W. (1995). *Alterssicherung der Landwirte: Das neue Recht nach dem Gesetz zur Reform der Agrarsozialen Sicherung.* Freiburg: Haufe.

Scheele, M. (1990). *Die politische Ökonomie landwirtschaftlicher Einkommenspolitik im Rahmen der Agrarsozialpolitik in der Bundesrepublik Deutschland.* Kiel: Vauk.

Schmidt, B. (2005). Zehn Jahre Bäuerinnenrente aus Sicht des Bundesministeriums für Gesundheit und Soziale Sicherung und des Bundesministeriums für Verbraucherschutz, Ernährung und Landwirtschaft. *Ländlicher Raum, 56,* 16–17.

Schmidt, M. G. (1998). *Sozialpolitik: Historische Entwicklung und internationaler Vergleich.* Opladen: Leske + Budrich.

Stüwe, E. (1996). Ein Jahr Agrarsozialreformgesetz. *Soziale Sicherheit in der Landwirtschaft, 1,* 59–76.

Stüwe, E., & Zindel, G. (1991). Die Agrarsoziale Sicherung der Bäuerin: Bestandsaufnahme und Verbesserungsmöglichkeit. *Soziale Sicherheit in der Landwirtschaft, 1,* 129–156.

Wirth, C. (1996). Änderung des Agrarsozialreformgesetzes. *Soziale Sicherheit in der Landwirtschaft, 1,* 36–58.

Wirth, C (2007). 50 Jahre Alterssicherung der Landwirte. *Soziale Sicherheit in der Landwirtschaft, 2,* 96–102.

Wissenschaftlicher Beirat beim Bundesminister für Ernährung, Landwirtschaft und Forsten. (1979). *Agrarsozialpolitik: Situation und Reformvorschläge.* Münster-Hiltrup: Landwirtschaftsverlag.

Zindel, G. (2005). Zehn Jahre Bäuerinnenrente: Die Bäuerinnensicherung aus der Sicht der landwirtschaftlichen Sozialversicherung. *Ländlicher Raum, 56,* 10–13.

5 Complex Policy Choices Regarding Agricultural Externalities: Efficiency, Equity and Acceptability

Clem Tisdell

School of Economics, The University of Queensland, St Lucia, Queensland, 4072, Australia,
E-mail: c.tisdell@economics.uq.edu.au

Abstract. A feature of the research contribution of Konrad Hagedorn is his proposals for the integration of economic, social and political dimensions of agricultural policy. His holistic approach involves, in part, an extension of new institutionalism to public policy. This article identifies a number of difficulties that arise in choosing public policies for regulating externalities generated by agricultural activity. Firstly, it is noted that finding an economically efficient agricultural policy can be difficult because the functions involved can be irregular and may involve features associated with the mathematics of catastrophe. This adds to the complexity of public decision-making and increases the bounds on rational choice. Secondly, in light of the research results of behavioural economists and other considerations, it is shown that efficient economic solutions to resource allocation are not independent of the distribution of property rights, inevitably requiring consideration of whether the distribution of these rights is equitable. Thirdly, the importance of institutional structures for the transaction costs (or more generally administrative costs) of implementing agricultural policy are stressed and illustrated. Fourthly, the political acceptability or feasibility of implementing policies is demonstrated to be a relevant consideration in choosing agricultural policies, and it is noted that these are influenced by existing social structures and cultural factors. Some of these issues are briefly illustrated by public policies (such as those implied by the International Convention on Biological Diversity) designed or intended to extend property rights in genetic materials.

Keywords: Agricultural externalities, Agricultural policy, Environmental policy, Institutional economics, Politics

5.1 Introduction

As originally pointed out by Arthur Pigou (1932) and as is now well known, economic externalities (whether favourable or unfavourable) can be an important source of market failure. However, the mere presence of externalities does not mean that they are Pareto relevant. When unfavourable externalities are infra-marginal, they are often irrelevant. However, if alternative production techniques or consumption methods are available with different sets of externalities, market failure can still occur (Tisdell, 1993, Chs. 2 and 3). Even if no significant externalities are observed from an economic activity, for example when a particular type of farming is adopted, an alternative type of activity or set of farming practices may generate large positive externalities and be socially superior. In such cases, market failure can also occur, even though no actual externalities are observed. This implies that, in order to assess whether externalities could be Pareto relevant, one has to consider not only the marginal external effects of economic activities, but also their total effects (Tisdell, 2005, Ch.3). Evaluation of externalities is much more complex than has been traditionally realised and cannot be done accurately by adopting only a marginalist point of view.

Note that failure to take adequate account of externalities is not peculiar to market systems, but also occurs in non-market systems, including state decision-making about resource-use. Failure to take proper account of externalities in state decision-making might also be more widespread in societies where democracy and freedom of speech and communication are limited, such as appeared to be the case in many centralised communist countries. There is considerable evidence that inadequate attention was given to the effects of adverse environmental externalities in former communist countries. One of the many examples includes the decision by the Soviet Union to extensively use waters feeding the Aral Sea for irrigating cotton, with subsequent seriously adverse effects on the Aral Sea itself. Not only does state decision-making often fail to take sufficient account of environmental spillovers, but inadequate attention is sometimes given to sustainability issues as well. A recent example is Indonesia's transmigration programme from Java to Kalimantan. The Indonesian government has sponsored resettlement projects intended to grow rice on peat lands in Kalimantan, although soil quality is such that agricultural production is not sustainable on these lands. In addition, these land areas are often a source of fires that cause air pollution in Southeast Asia and add to greenhouse gas emissions (Singleton et al., 2004, p.70).

As pointed out by Galbraith (1952, 1967), the presence of democracy and freedom of speech do not ensure that governments take adequate account of externalities in their decision-making. Political lobbying and associated mechanisms can also result in economic failure of a Paretian type.

In this article, the patterns and nature of agricultural externalities and their relationship to agricultural sustainability are discussed first. These can give rise to complicated mathematical relationships and add to the difficulties of rationally choosing agricultural policies. The nature of such externalities has normative implications affecting the range of choices for public policies intended to regulate agricultural spillovers, as outlined below. While the main emphasis in this article is on environmental externalities from and within agriculture, attention is also given to agricultural externalities arising from adverse selection. This aspect, together with the regulation of agriculture's environmental externalities, is being addressed under the EU's new Common Agricultural Policy. The implications of agricultural environmental policy choice are explored with regard to features often associated with the new institutional economics, such as transaction costs; aspects of uncertainty in policy formation and implementation are also considered. Subsequently, attention is given to political and social acceptability as influences on agricultural policy decisions. Then, agriculture's role in biodiversity conservation is considered as a particular case in order to illustrate the theories outlined in this chapter. In line with the polycentric approach of Konrad Hagedorn, topics in this analysis are considered from multiple points of view, and institutional structures are shown to be important in relation to economic efficiency and political acceptability.

5.2 Types of Agricultural Externalities

Externalities involving agriculture can be classified in varied ways. The public's attitude about how externalities involving agriculture should be regulated are likely to be influenced by their nature. The following types of relevant spillovers involving agriculture can be a source of market failure:

1. *Spillovers from non-agricultural sectors of the economy affecting agriculture.* Agriculture can experience adverse environmental externalities from airborne pollution caused by emissions of particulate matter, metallic dust, acidic vapour and particles as well as water pollution due to wastes from factories and mining. For instance, horse breeders from the Scone area in the Hunter Valley of New South Wales, Australia, complain that coal dust from open-cut coal mines causes their naturally alkaline soils to turn acidic. It is claimed that this has adverse consequences for the development of the bones of their thoroughbred horses and makes them less fit for racing.
2. *Spillovers from agricultural to non-agricultural sectors of the economy.* Agriculture may, for example, create and sustain landscapes favoured by the public, such as heathlands, or in some cases, ones that are disliked by the public, such as weedy areas, for example areas of gorse in New Zealand. Similarly, while some types of agriculture conserve wild species desired by the public, they also result in the loss of others. Water run-off from agricultural land containing chemicals leached from fertilisers and livestock manure as well as soil particles results in nutrient-enrichment of water bodies and this stimulates growth of

aquatic algae and weeds, accelerating eutrophication of some water masses. Run-off from agricultural lands (particularly land for growing sugar cane in northern coastal Queensland) is claimed to have an adverse impact on the corals in parts of the Great Barrier Reef, which do not survive in dirty, nutrient-rich water.

3. *Spillovers confined to agriculture itself.* Unfavourable ones include dryland salting (if the effect extends beyond a farm where land clearing occurs), salination of watercourses as a result of land clearing, herbicide or pesticide drift, adverse externalities from water use and possible cross-fertilisation of GM (genetically modified) and non-GM crops. Favourable externalities within agriculture can result from pest control by farmers having pests on their property.

Externalities may also be classified according to the mathematical nature of the spillover benefits or costs that they generate. Institutional neoclassical economic analysis usually supposes that these functions are continuous and differentiable. This, however, is a special case. In some cases, including in agriculture, marginal external economic impacts may only arise once the level of an activity exceeds some thresholds. In other cases, marginal external economic impacts of an economic activity may fall to zero once the level of the activity reaches a particular threshold. Or both aspects may occur. In many cases, the relationships involved are best modelled using the mathematics of catastrophe (Zeeman, 1976; Poston & Stewart, 1978; Arnold, 1992; Anonymous, 2008), given the knowledge that this mathematics is not only relevant to the modelling of catastrophes, but can also be applied to a whole host of irregular functional relationships. When such thresholds occur and different techniques of production generate varied spillover impacts, policy choices for regulating economic activities in order to attain economic efficiency can become very complicated. Often, one can no longer rely on marginal effects to determine Paretian efficient policies but must estimate total effects. Furthermore, views about what is equitable can alter, for example, whether or not farmers should be subsidised for creating favourable externalities that are inframarginal. The next section demonstrates the significance of these complications.

Before, however, considering this section, it might be noted that its models relate to thresholds that involve cusp points in the rate of change of net social benefit functions. They imply that the second derivatives of the net social function are discontinuous at these points. The total net social benefit functions themselves may also have cusp points or be discontinuous at particular points. At these points, their corresponding marginal curves are discontinuous. In these cases, similar complexities occur to those considered in the next section. Discontinuities and lack of differentiability of relevant functions should not be ignored in assessing environmental externalities.

5.3 Complications Arising from Thresholds in the Economic Effects of Externalities

The purpose of this section is to show how the presence of thresholds in the external economic effects generated by externalities can complicate policy choices for their regulation. Traditional neoclassical analysis does not take such complications into account. Several possibilities are considered here. In the first case, the spillover depends on the type of technique used for production, but in this case the Paretian efficient technique is not adopted in a free market. In the illustrated case (Fig. 5.1), all production should be accomplished through using the technique with a favourable externality. In the second case (illustrated by Fig. 5.2), economic efficiency requires a portion of supply to be provided by a technique generating a favourable externality and the remainder to be supplied by a technique involving no externalities. It is then pointed out that many externalities can be Paretian irrelevant and that thresholds can create further complications for evaluating externalities, for example, in cases where adverse externalities from the use of a method of production only emerge once the extent of its use exceeds some threshold. Often such complications imply that, to achieve economic efficiency, an 'ideal' mixture of techniques should be used in production. Evaluating the economic consequences of the different available techniques in order to determine this ideal could be a Herculean task, especially if some of the available techniques have not been used or empirically tested on a large scale.

   Note that in the theory outlined in the remainder of this section, the assumptions of neoclassical economics are adopted. However, thresholds are allowed for in this analysis, whereas in neoclassical analysis they are not. There are reasons to believe that thresholds could be significant in relation to externalities generated by agriculture. For example, external demand for the supply of particular agricultural landscapes may drop to zero once their supply exceeds a particular threshold. Or the external demand for particular landscapes might be zero, until their transformation by agricultural production reaches a particular threshold. To give another example, the external benefits of conserving traditional breeds and crop varieties may be zero, until the level of agricultural production using 'improved' breeds and crop varieties reaches a particular threshold. This type of analysis has implications for the efficiency (and equity) of subsidising agriculture production methods in the European Union that have favourable externalities (Van Huylenbroeck & Durand, 2003; Vanslembrouck & Van Huylenbroeck, 2005). With this background in mind, let us consider some specific theoretical possibilities which allow for thresholds.

5.3.1 A Paretian relevant externality

For simplicity, assume that only two methods of producing an agricultural product are available. Method I has no external costs or benefits and involves the lowest private cost of production. Represent the market demand for this agricultural product by line DD in Fig. 5.1 and let S_1S_1 represent its market supply curve when technique I is adopted. Using this method of production, the market would come into equilibrium at E_1. Suppose that a second method (Method II) is available, but involves higher private costs of production. Consequently, the supply curve S_2S_2 applies in this case. This alternative method generates a favourable externality, for instance by creating desirable landscapes, and the marginal external value obtained is assumed to be equal to the difference between curve ABCF and line DD. However, production using method II generates no marginal externality once its level exceeds X_4.

Taking into account the favourable externality, economic welfare benefits from agriculture production are maximised when only method II is used and X_3 of the agricultural product is supplied. This could be achieved by only allowing the use of method II and paying a subsidy of CE_3 on each unit of product X supplied. However, the externality could be infra-marginal in some cases.

5.3.2 An infra-marginal externality which is Paretian relevant for policy and which complicates social decisions

A more complicated case is illustrated in Fig. 5.2. As in the previous case, demand for greater quantities of the favoured landscape eventually falls to zero, but in this case, satiation with the supply of the landscape occurs before market equilibrium is reached. Satiation with the landscape *incidentally* supplied as a result of agricultural activity occurs when X_1 of product X is produced using technique II. Otherwise, the same assumptions as in the previous case are made. In the absence of intervention, X_3 of product X will be supplied using only technique I. However, because of landscape externalities, it is socially optimal that X_0 of the product be supplied using technique II with $X_3 - X_0$ being supplied by technique I. At X_0, the marginal value of the externality, BG, is just equal to the difference in the marginal cost of production using the alternative technique.

In the case represented by Fig. 5.2, economic optimality can be achieved by paying a minimum subsidy on each unit of X produced equal to the excess marginal cost of its production using technique II rather than I, up to an aggregate level of production of X_0. No subsidy is paid for production exceeding X_0. The per-unit subsidy is lower in this case than in the previous case.

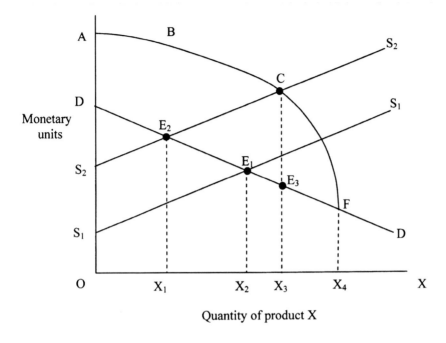

Quantity of product X

Fig. 5.1: A case where a favourable externality can be generated by agricultural production if a technique of production is adopted by farmers that does not minimise their private costs of production. For simplicity, only two alternative techniques, I and II, are assumed to be available. The use of technique I generates no externalities and results in an industry supply curve indicated by line S_1S_1. The market demand for the agricultural product X is shown by the line DD. If technique I is adopted, market equilibrium will be established at E_1, with X_2 of the product being supplied. The private marginal cost of using technique II is higher than for technique I, and the industry supply curve, if it is adopted, is as shown by line S_2S_2. This would result in a market equilibrium corresponding to E_2. In a free market, technique I rather than II will be adopted by farmers. However, use of technique II generates a positive externality, the marginal value of which is equal to the difference between the curve marked ABCF and the line DD. If the potential Paretian improvement criterion of economic efficiency is adopted, it is desirable that technique II should be adopted rather than technique I. However, merely banning the use of technique I will not give rise to an efficient economic outcome, because it will only result in production of X_1 of the agricultural product arising from technique II. The wealth-maximising ideal level of production corresponds to point C (the point where the social marginal benefit from extra supplies of X using technique II equals the marginal private cost of its supply) and implies that agricultural production should be X_3. Economic incentives, such as a production subsidy, are needed to bring about the most efficient economic result

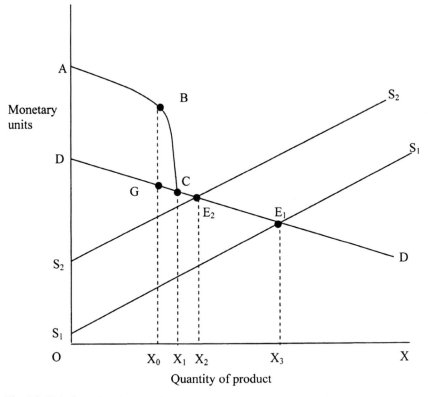

Fig. 5.2: This figure has the same interpretation as Fig. 5.1 and is based on the same theoretical assumptions. However, whereas the favourable externality was extra-marginal in Fig. 5.1, here it is infra-marginal compared to the market equilibrium, E_2. Here there is no marginal external benefit from producing more than X_1 of the agricultural product using technique II, but in the case illustrated in Fig. 5.1, that does not happen until more than X_4 of X is produced using technique II. This complicates the efficient economic allocation, because it requires some of the agricultural production to be supplied using technique II and some to be supplied using technique I. The combination required for economic efficiency is easily identified in Fig. 5.3

The optimality condition given the situation in Fig. 5.2 can be clarified by reference to Fig. 5.3, where curve KLM represents the marginal value of the externality when technique II is used, which falls to zero for a level of production of X_1 or more. The marginal opportunity cost of using technique II rather than I to produce X is represented by OH, indicating the difference between S_2S_2 and S_1S_1 in Fig. 5.2, the difference in the per unit production cost between the techniques. The optimal outcome corresponds to point L, where the marginal external value obtained by using technique II just equals the marginal opportunity cost of using it.

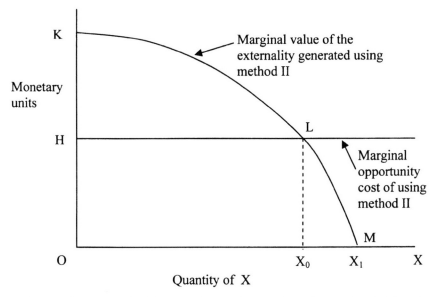

Fig. 5.3: An illustration of the 'efficient' solution to the situation depicted in Fig. 5.2. The difference between the social marginal value of using technique II rather than technique I to produce X is shown by curve KLM. This falls to zero when X_1 or some of X is produced using technique II. The line HL indicates the difference between the private marginal cost of using technique II rather than I to produce X. It is equivalent to the distance between lines S_2S_2 and S_1S_1 in Fig. 5.2. The efficient economic solution is for only X_0 of X to be produced using technique II and for the remainder of demand $(X_2 - X_0)$, as shown in Fig. 5.2 to be met using technique I. This complicates agricultural policy-making. Note that use of technique II is still generating positive marginal externalities when it is efficient to switch to technique I to provide required extra supplies of the agricultural product

In the situation illustrated in Fig. 5.2, a regulating authority requires more information than in the case shown in Fig. 5.1 to regulate externalities so as to achieve a Paretian optimum. In most cases of this type, a regulatory authority is unlikely to have sufficient information to regulate economic activity optimally. However, it may be able to obtain an idea of when beneficiaries are likely to be satiated by a favourable environmental feature. It will never be optimal to proceed beyond the satiation point, and, if opportunity costs are involved, it will usually be socially optimal to supply less of the environmental amenity than results in satiation with it.

5.3.3 Some externalities are Paretian irrelevant

The economic evaluation of externalities is complicated further by the fact that some externalities are Paretian irrelevant (Tisdell, 1970, 1993 Chs. 3–4; Walsh & Tisdell, 1973). For example, an infra-marginal externality can be Paretian irrelevant in relation to the equilibrium of a market. This is because it does not affect the market equilibrium. If the externality is favourable, there is no economic efficiency argument for providing a subsidy to its suppliers, assuming that the socially optimal technique has already been adopted by suppliers. If, on the other hand, the infra-marginal externality is an unfavourable one, its total effect needs to be assessed. This is because the total social cost of supplying the commodity may exceed its economic value. In that case, it is economically efficient to ban production of the commodity (Tisdell, 2005).

5.3.4 Further complications

Some externalities do not occur until the level of production or economic activity exceeds a threshold. The presence of such externalities further complicates the choice of policies to maximise economic efficiency. For example, the loss of traditional breeds of livestock or plant varieties may not involve external costs until production using 'improved' breeds or modern crop varieties exceeds some threshold level. Significant social economic costs from the displacement of traditional breeds and crop varieties only emerge after this threshold is reached. Only after this point is it likely to become efficient to subsidise the conservation of traditional breeds and plant varieties, at which time social decisions will need to be made about how much traditional agricultural genetic material should be conserved: taking into account the potential (or actual) externality and public good attributes of this material.

The above discussion indicates that, when agricultural externalities occur, a mixture of techniques or methods to produce the aggregate level of supply of a commodity is often efficient from an economics point of view. Neoclassical economics has not given enough attention to factors influencing the optimal *mixture* of methods or techniques for production that takes into account externalities

5.4 Adverse Selection as an Unfavourable Externality and Possible Threshold Effects

The phenomenon of adverse selection of products involves unfavourable externalities. It arises when there is asymmetric information about a product and occurs when buyers are unable to easily ascertain the quality of a product by inspection, even though its quality is known to suppliers. The problem then arises when products of inferior quality cost less to produce than those of superior quality, that the inferior ones may be traded as being of top or acceptable quality. This can cause the whole market for the products to collapse or result in only the inferior ones being traded (Akerloff, 1970; Varian, 1987, pp. 630–635). This happens even though buyers have an effective demand for the superior products.

The conditions under which agricultural products are produced are often difficult to determine by inspecting the final product. Therefore, there is a high risk of adverse selection occurring for agricultural products. It is often not clear, for instance, from inspection whether food products are produced under hygienic conditions, are organic produce or not, or are derived from free-range animals or not. Furthermore, it is usually not clear from inspection whether agriculturally based products are derived from GMOs or not, whether their production involved a lack of consideration of animal welfare, whether production techniques were used that pose a potential health risk to humans, (for example, mad cow disease), or whether they actually do originate from the regions or areas from which they are claimed to come from.

Processes of adverse selection can also be subject to thresholds and sharp variations (spikes). For example, when the proportion of defective or inferior products traded in a market (or sub-market) reaches a particular proportion, the market may collapse altogether or the rate of decline in the demand for the product may suddenly alter: from falling at a declining rate to falling at an increasing rate. The latter involves a cusp (a spike) in the relationship. Furthermore, once a market collapses, it may be very difficult to re-establish trust in the products involved and re-create the market. This means that hysteresis is present. It is a type of path-dependence. This phenomenon is not taken into account in neoclassical economic theory, but is one of the focal interests of the mathematics of catastrophe.

Governments can help to overcome some of these problems by requiring the correct labelling of products and by imposing penalties for non-compliance. Also laws may be passed specifying that minimum hygiene conditions are to be complied with in producing and trading in commodities that could pose a health risk. Governments may be active in enforcing these laws, and non-compliance with them is likely to make sellers subject to claims for damages from injured buyers. Standards may also be attested to by trusted non-government organisations and other bodies.

Other institutional arrangements can also evolve to address the phenomenon of adverse selection. For example, some large retailers, such as supermarkets, attest to the quality of the products that they sell and offer money-back guarantees. They check the products supplied to them and are able to enforce quality and other conditions on their suppliers. Similarly, the sellers of some branded products are able to establish trust in their brands. These institutional arrangements can, however, create significant barriers to entry of new suppliers of quality products.

Adverse selection can result in lack of sustainability of agricultural production of superior products, can reduce regional production of specialities and, in some cases, could lead to the complete collapse of individual agricultural markets. Elimination of adverse selection benefits both buyers as well as sellers of superior or sought after products. Some institutional arrangements are more prone to the occurrence of adverse selection than others. For example, depending on the type of products being traded, free market institutional arrangements often need to be supplemented by additional institutional structures to prevent major losses in economic efficiency and in order to sustain the operation of socially desirable markets. In many cases, hybrid governance or institutional structures evolve (or may only evolve) to address such problems, supporting the sustainability of markets (Van Huylenbroeck et al. this volume). These institutional structures may evolve on their own accord and, in other cases, they may be able to evolve with government assistance. The social and economic attributes of the hybrid systems that evolve need to be examined carefully to decide on how beneficial they are and whether superior systems are possible.

5.5 Environmental Externalities and Sustainability

Lack of sustainability of agricultural production and of incomes often, but not always, arises from adverse environmental externalities affecting agriculture (Tisdell, 1999, Ch. 4). Examples include depletion of shared water bodies, such as aquifers, as a result of open-access or poorly regulated access to the water, spillovers from salting such as reduced water quality, or environmental pollution caused by other industries that adversely impact on agricultural production. It is also possible that loss of genetic diversity could eventually have adverse consequences for the sustainability of agricultural production.

However, lack of sustainability of the productivity of agriculture cannot always be attributed to environmental externalities. Taking into account the discount rates which landholders apply, it may pay them to mine their land. The higher their discount rate, the more likely landholders are to do this. A higher discount rate results in stronger preferences for farm income now rather than in the future. Rising relative returns from investing off-farm rather than on-farm and easier access to off-farm investment opportunities can also have a similar effect. In both cases, lack of agricultural sustainability is a consequence of private decisions by farmers rather than a consequence of externalities.

Sometimes, particular institutional arrangements for the use of shared resources (subject to adverse externalities) can increase the economic efficiency of their use and promote the sustainability of agricultural production. For example, co-operative arrangements between persons for the management of a shared natural resource may benefit all (Swallow and Meinzen-Dick this volume). Nevertheless, co-operative agreements may only evolve if the number of effective parties is relatively small or if legal obligations provide a stimulus for their formation, as in the case of the New York City water supply, where the water authority was legally required to supply water which met a minimum standard of quality. The water authority decided that rather than incur extra costs to treat this water, the most economical solution would be for farmers in its water catchment to plant trees to improve water quality and was able to reach a co-operative agreement with these farmers to achieve this, as reported in Swallow and Meinzen-Dick in this volume.

In other cases, institutional reform which results, for example, in the introduction of tradable permit systems may result in the more efficient use of shared resources. However, such systems will only result in sustainability if production of the aggregate allowable use of the shared natural resource does not lead to its overexploitation. Furthermore, systems of tradable resource rights are more complex than is commonly realised and can involve a high level of transaction costs, as pointed out by Tisdell (2009, Ch.6). These systems involve hybrid economic governance structures (Van Huylenbroeck et al. this volume) in the sense that they combine government regulation with the use of market forces to manage the shared use of natural resources.

5.6 Equity, Efficiency and Agricultural Externalities

The presence of externalities is often believed to provide a case for public intervention in an economy in order to bring about a Paretian improvement, particularly if the transaction costs involved in intervention are low or zero. Nevertheless, externalities can be Paretian irrelevant (see Section 5.3), in which case there are no economic efficiency grounds for intervention.

Whether there are equity grounds for public intervention when externalities are Paretian irrelevant is less clear. If an externality is favourable and Paretian irrelevant, should those who benefit from it have to pay those who generate it? The case for this seems to be weak, because those who engage in the activity already gain from it in any case, and it is coincidental that the external beneficiaries also gain. Compared to its absence, there is a Paretian improvement as a result of the activity occurring. But what if an adverse externality is involved? Those creating the adverse externality gain from it, but those who suffer from it lose compared to the original situation. Even if the adverse externality is Paretian irrelevant, there could be a case in such circumstances to compensate the victims on distributional grounds.

The above indicates that the case for transferring income to agriculturalists on the basis that they create favourable externalities is sometimes weak on economic grounds. The externalities may be infra-marginal and Paretian irrelevant. However, compensation to farmers seems justifiable when it is required that they alter their activities at a cost to themselves in order to change the nature or extent of the favourable externalities they create. The minimum necessary compensation in such cases would be the extra cost the agriculturalists incur to comply with the policy. To the extent that farm income supports under the Common Agricultural Policy (CAP) focus on this aspect, they could be regarded as being equitable and as promoting economic efficiency. In practice, however, it is debatable whether environmental policies can be so finely tuned. It may be that some agricultural subsidies are being paid for the generation of Paretian irrelevant externalities or that a greater amount is being paid than the costs to farmers of generating additions to favourable externalities. The presence of infra-marginal and extra-marginal externalities complicates the formulation of environmental policies.

A further set of economic efficiency versus equity issues are raised by the Coase theorem (Coase, 1960), which Coase illustrated by an agricultural example. This theorem was welcomed by strong advocates of private property rights and seemed to provide solid support for those, such as Posner (1981), favouring aggregate wealth maximisation as the desirable goal for the organisation of society. Nevertheless, a serious shortcoming of Coase's theorem is that it ignores equity issues and only concentrates on economic efficiency, asserting that in the absence of transaction costs, a Paretian optimum can be achieved if either polluters have the legal right to pollute or if others have the right to a pollution-free environment. However, the distribution of income is entirely different, depending on whether those generating the adverse externality are given the right to pollute or those affected by it are given the right to a pollution-free environment. A choice between the alternatives must be made on the grounds of justice. It is less well known that Coase's efficient solution to the externality problem is sensitive to the distribution of property rights.

This second limitation of Coase's theorem means that the Paretian efficient use of shared natural resources varies with the distribution of property rights in these, that is with the distribution of resource entitlements. Consequently, the efficient economic solution to Coase's resource-use problem cannot be divorced from the distribution of those rights. There are at least two reasons why this is so. As is well known in neoclassical welfare economics, changes in resource allocation which are able to bring about a Paretian improvement depend upon the initial endowments of those involved in economic activity: they restrict, for example, points on the contract curve which can result in a Paretian improvement compared to the original position (Tisdell & Hartley, 2008). However, a very important effect can also be the status quo or endowment effect.

Research by behavioural economists finds that the willingness of individuals to pay (WTP) for an environmental good is generally less than their willingness to accept compensation (WAC) for its loss. This has been described as the endowment or status quo effect (Kahneman, Knetsch, & Thaler, 1991; Knetsch, 1989, 1990). This effect results in different bargained outcomes, when Coase's analysis is applied, depending upon whether those creating an adverse externality have the right to create it or whether those adversely affected by it have the right to disallow it. Hence, the efficient economic solution is sensitive to the distribution of rights. This can be illustrated by a simple example.

Suppose an area of land in a relatively natural state is privately owned and suitable for agriculture. The owners are basically agriculturalists and would like to transform the land so its agricultural productivity can be raised. They need to clear the land of trees (of forest), but this creates an adverse externality for others whom we shall call conservationists.

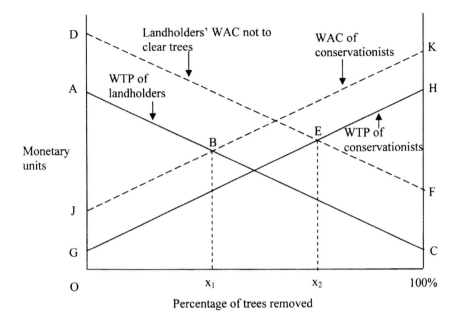

Fig. 5.4: Coase (1960) argued that in many cases the clear specification of property rights in environments would facilitate an efficient economic response to the occurrence of externalities.
However, because willingness to accept compensation for loss of these rights usually exceeds
willingness to pay for them, an efficient economic outcome is sensitive to the legal distribution
of property rights in the environment. This means that economic efficiency and equity are not independent. In the case illustrated, it is assumed that landholders obtain an economic benefit from
clearing trees on their land, whereas conservationists suffer an economic loss. If landholders
have the legal right to all trees on their land, they will find it profitable to remove them all in the
absence of compensation to refrain from this. In the case shown, the marginal willingness of
conservationists to pay landholders to refrain from removal of trees is indicated by line GEH,
and the willingness of landholders to accept compensation is indicated by the broken line DEF.
In the absence of transaction costs, a bargained solution (an efficient solution) corresponding to
point E should emerge. This will result in x_2% of trees being removed. On the other hand, if the
property rights in the trees are reversed, the bargained outcome would correspond to point B.
This efficient economic solution would result in only x_1% of trees being removed. Thus, even in
the absence of transaction costs, the Paretian efficient solution depends on the distribution of
property rights

If agriculturalists do not have the right to clear the land of trees, their marginal
willingness to pay conservationists to allow this might be as indicated by line
ABC in Fig. 5.4. On the other hand, if agriculturalists have the right to land clearing, their marginal willingness to accept compensation to forgo land clearing
might be as indicated by line DEF. Similarly, the marginal willingness to pay
curve (to avoid deforestation) for conservationists might be as indicated by line
GEH, while their marginal willingness to accept payment for deforestation might

be as shown by line JBK. It follows, if landowners (agriculturalists) have the right to clear their land, that E is the Coasian bargained solution. If, on the other hand, conservationists have the right to tree-cover of the land, B is the Coasian bargained solution. In the former case, a larger percentage of the land is cleared, x_2, than in the latter case, which involves x_1 of the land being cleared. The efficient economic result therefore varies with the distribution of property rights.

The reasons why the endowment or status quo effect exists and can be quite large has not yet been fully explained in the available economic literature. It may, however, be reinforced by the income effect.

In reality, the presence of transaction costs can be expected to hinder or block the realisation of an efficient Coasian bargained outcome to the control of environmental externalities. In some cases, transaction costs will be least if the government intervenes to address the externality problem directly. Direct government intervention to regulate environmental externalities is sometimes (but not always) the most economical policy option. Determining the most efficient institutional structures for regulating externalities is a challenging task, because it requires account to be taken of transaction costs and the possible presence of asymmetric information. These aspects are ignored in neoclassical economic analysis and, therefore, some new institutional economists have branded it Nirvana economics. Let us consider transactions costs and asymmetric information in relation to the regulation of externalities. Coase (1960) failed to take account of these despite his being a pioneer of transaction cost economics (Coase, 1937).

5.7 Transaction Costs Involved in Public Regulation of Externalities

While public regulation of externalities can bring Paretian gains, this is by no means assured. Agency costs (transaction costs) are involved in the public regulation of externalities. This can be so high as to prevent a Paretian gain which would otherwise occur. Information deficiencies on the part of regulators are also a problem, and improved knowledge can only be obtained at a cost which in some cases can prove to be excessive.

Furthermore, principal-agent problems (which partly occur because of asymmetry of information) can arise if public servants look mainly towards their own self interest. They may try to maximise their income, and that of their agency, from their regulatory activities. They may fail to regulate environmental spillovers in a least-cost manner and could absorb all the revenue obtained from environmental charges (or more if funded from general public revenue) in their administrative expenditures.

The problem can be illustrated by Fig. 5.5. For simplicity, suppose the point emission of a water pollutant that adversely affects agriculturalists and other water users. Suppose that the marginal externality costs imposed by the emission of the pollutant are as indicated by line OBD in Fig. 5.5 and that line ABC represents the marginal benefit to polluters of being able to pollute. In the absence of regulation, polluters will emit x_2 of the water-borne pollutant per unit of time. This results in a social economic deadweight loss equivalent to the area of triangle BCD. A potential Paretian improvement is possible by reducing the level of these emissions from x_2 to x_1.

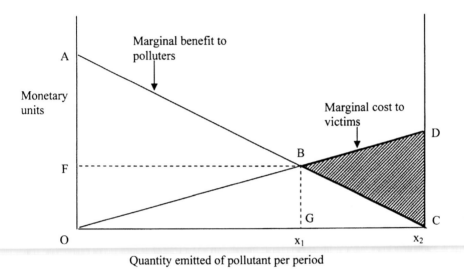

Quantity emitted of pollutant per period

Fig. 5.5: When transaction and related costs are taken into account, the cost of public regulation of externalities can exceed the social economic benefits otherwise obtained. In the case illustrated here, in the absence of regulation polluters will emit x_2 units of the pollutant per period of time. A potential Paretian gain can be achieved by reducing the level of emissions to x_1. This results in a potential net economic benefit equal to the area of triangle BCD. However, if the government's administrative expenditure to bring this about exceeds the area of the triangle, this regulation results in a net Kaldor-Hicks economic loss

This could be achieved by the government imposing a charge of OF on each unit of the pollutant emitted. This would yield the equivalent of the area OFBG in public revenue. However, a Kaldor-Hicks loss will occur if the cost of administering the scheme exceeds the area of triangle BCD. This means that the economic gainers from the intervention (victims of pollution and the government) would not be in a position to potentially compensate losers (polluters) for the intervention. Observe that the final welfare impact of such a scheme would depend on how the public revenue obtained from it is used. This type of analysis leaves such an issue unresolved. Furthermore, the equity question would remain of whether the victims of the water pollution should be fully compensated for their losses. In this case, even if emissions are reduced to x_2, victims of the pollution still suffer an economic loss equivalent to the area of triangle OBG, and so the reduction in emissions from x_2 to x_1 does not fully satisfy them.

The economic efficiency of different institutional mechanisms for the management of natural resource use varies in their economic efficiency when account is taken of transaction costs. In addition, they often vary in their equity consequences and their political acceptability. For example, a system of tradable pollution rights may involve lower administration costs than a system of government charges on pollution emissions. However, both will involve administration costs. Furthermore, tradable permit systems can vary significantly in their nature (Tisdell, 2009, Ch.5) and, therefore, in their effects on economic efficiency and equity. For instance, if tradable pollution rights are auctioned, this will result in a transfer of income to the government, but if they are allocated free of charge to existing polluters (a process known as grandfathering), polluters may end up with a windfall economic gain. In the latter case, they have a valuable asset which they may sell. Grandfathering can politically facilitate the introduction of government regulation of externalities.

5.8 The Political Acceptability of Economic Policies

Economic policies cannot usually be implemented unless they are politically acceptable. This means that the policies likely to yield the greatest economic benefits cannot always be implemented. What factors influence the political acceptability of policies?

Social values and ethics play a role in policy formulation. These change or evolve with the passage of time and are subject to influence by propaganda and other means. Secondly, institutional constraints may also impact on what is politically acceptable. Given these constraints, constituents will be limited in the ways in which they can object to political decisions, and the costs that they must incur to try to change these decisions will also be affected. Such costs can result in passive acceptance of political decisions that may be unpopular. Therefore, those policies that are politically acceptable will vary with the historical background and institutional structures of nations.

While economists are often only concerned about the ultimate economic consequences of policies, political approaches tend to put much more emphasis on the procedures used for social decision-making. Some of these politically acceptable procedures (such as majority voting systems) can actually add to economic costs, but constituents seem to be prepared on occasions to accept these in return for greater political or social involvement.

The type of conflict that can arise between preferences for political procedures and social economic benefits can be illustrated by Fig. 5.6. There, on the X-axis a set of political procedures are in theory valued from the least acceptable, which are closest to its origin, to the more acceptable, which are further from the origin. For simplicity, these procedures are assumed to be continuous, but need not be. The Y-axis indicates the social economic benefits from these alternative political procedures, only one of which may be chosen. These social economic benefits may for example be for alternative possible policies relating to the regulation of environ-mental externalities in agriculture. Curve ABCD represents the frontier of possibili-ties, and W_1W_1 and W_2W_2 are social indifference curves of the Bergson type.

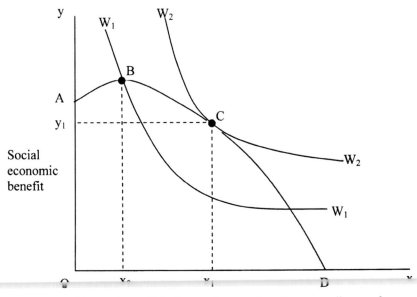

Alternative political procedures ordered by ascending preference

Fig. 5.6: Policies that are economically efficient or create the greatest social economic benefit are not always politically acceptable. In this figure, curve ABCD shows the relationship between political procedures adopted and social economic benefits obtained. Political procedures corre-sponding to x_0 yield the greatest economic benefit, but this combination of political procedures and their economic outcome is not socially ideal, because preferences exist about the political procedures adopted in society for decision-making. Given the preferences represented by the so-cial indifference curves W_1W_1 and W_2W_2, the ideal political procedure corresponds to x_1, even though it does not maximise social economic benefit

Given the possibilities illustrated in Fig. 5.6, the combination corresponding to point C is socially ideal. However, it does not result in the best 'attainable' eco-nomic outcome, nor does it correspond to the most desired political procedure. Note that the ideal solution in Fig. 5.6 corresponding to point C can change if the social indifference curves vary or if the ordering of possible political procedures alters, other things being constant.

Although the presentation in Fig. 5.6 is more illustrative than definitive, it helps to support the view expressed by Hagedorn (1993) that agricultural economists should take account of the political acceptability of economic policies when they propose them. At the same time, it can be important (from a social point of view) for economists to point out economic benefits forgone by adopting politically ac-ceptable procedures and policies that yield inferior economic results.

5.9 Property Rights in Agricultural Genetic Material and Externalities

It is often difficult to sustain property rights in agricultural genetic material, and in the past, genetic material was frequently taken from those originally possessing it without any payment being made for its use. This is still possible today, but this possibility has now become more limited due to laws granting intellectual property rights to those who develop new plant varieties and patents or similar protection for those who create new genetically modified organisms (GMOs).

The introduction of new organisms usually results in incompletely or unknown environmental risks. The more demanding the screening required to determine these risks is, the less profitable it is likely to be for enterprises to engage in such development. Furthermore, the greater the environmental restrictions on the use of new organisms by the customers of their developers, the lower is the demand for these and the less incentive there is to develop them. For example, the more restrictions there are on the use of GM soya beans resistant to the herbicide glyphosate, the lower is the profitability of this innovation for Monsanto. Thus to some extent, a company such as Monsanto will profit from fewer environmental restrictions on the use of its GM seed. On the other hand, very loose regulations could result in serious environmental problems and, in turn, this could generate a political backlash for developers of GM seed. It may be that the co-existence rules for the growing of transgenic crops and non-GMO crops provide an appropriate compromise between political acceptability and environmental risk (see Beckmann, Soregaroli, & Wesseler, 2006). Nevertheless, politically speaking, the appropriate level of environmental risk to take with new GMOs is uncertain.

On the other hand, public regulations ostensibly intended to protect the public against environmental risk often protect the party or parties that are the source of this risk. This is sometimes true of regulations that prescribe particular tests be carried out by those proposing to market a product for, say, use in agriculture. Provided the tests are conducted and show no problem, the seller may be free of further legal liability if a subsequent environmental problem emerges. The legal liability of the seller may be curtailed even further if a public body exists which authorises the use of the product (Tisdell, 1993, Ch.5).

While intellectual property rights in new plant varieties and GMOs could be justified on the basis that they provide economic incentives and rewards for research and innovation, the argument for property rights in existing natural genetic material (or that developed as a result of communities pursuing their own self-interest) appears to be more tenuous. Such rights might only be defensible on income distributional grounds or if the payment would result in conservation of a genetic material which otherwise would not be saved. If the conservation of the material would have occurred in any case, payment for it would not be compensation for supplying a service. In such cases, the conservation of the genetic material is Paretian irrelevant. Apart from the huge transaction costs that would be involved if users of natural genetic agricultural material were required to pay the 'original' possessors of this material for its use, this might have little effect on the conservation of natural genetic materials utilised in agriculture. Therefore, payment in such cases is essentially a rental payment. Consequently, it is surprising that the International Convention on Biological Diversity puts so much store on property rights in genetic material as a way of conserving biodiversity: a result that is widely believed to be environmentally desirable and to be favourable to sustaining economic development.

The granting of property rights to entities developing new genetic material, such as new plant varieties and genetically modified organisms, has become of growing importance in recent decades. In agriculture, a major concern has been that this new genetic material might give rise to unknown or unanticipated negative externalities. There is considerable debate about how one can best balance the potential economic benefits from such genetic developments against the environmental risks and uncertainties they entail and about the institutional structures that might be best to address these problems. Different countries have developed different structures presumably influenced by their varying political backgrounds and evolutionary aspects of governance (Beckmann et al., 2006; Beckmann & Wesseler, 2007). Although an economic case exists for granting property rights to entities that develop new genetic agricultural material, there is a need to be more cautious about granting such rights to all extant natural genetic material to the region where that material has originated from. The economic argument for such property rights appears to be weak, except in cases where these rights would result in the conservation of wanted genetic material that otherwise would not be conserved. The International Convention on Biological Diversity assumes that by the granting of such property rights in genetic materials originating locally to indigenous people, traditional farmers and similar entities, this will be effective for ensuring biodiversity conservation (thereby supporting sustainable development) and will also result in an equitable outcome. However, the transaction costs involved in implementing such a policy could be huge and could more than outweigh any economic benefit. While there could be some circumstances in which this property rights policy generates the desired results, success may be restricted to special cases. Furthermore, it was found from a sample survey in Australia that there was little public support for the sustainable use of wildlife as a strategy to conserve biodiversity and, therefore, this policy has limited political acceptability in Australia (Tisdell, Swarna Nantha, & Wilson, 2007). The commercial (and subsistence) use of species was most strongly opposed in cases where their existence was endangered or they were believed to be vulnerable to extinction, presumably because proponents thought this would be an ineffective conservation policy.

Although the transaction costs involved in implementing public policy pose a formidable barrier to the practical application of the International Convention on Biological Diversity, these barriers can be reduced by institutional changes, such as the formation of farmers' and tribal co-operatives to secure payment from other users for genetic material conserved or developed in their area. The cost of the political momentum for implementing policy varies with institutional structures. As Hagedorn (1993, 2003, 2005); Hagedorn, Arzt, and Peters (2002) has emphasised, social organisational structures are highly significant in determining the economics, political prospects and practicability of implementing public policies to manage the supply of public goods. Hagedorn's approach, therefore, has extended the contribution of Williamson (1975), which has concentrated on the economics of business management, to the wider sphere of public policy. This has resulted in new insights into processes involved in political economy.

5.10 Concluding Comments

Herbert Simon (1957, 1961) stressed the importance of bounded rationality as an element in administrative decision-making. This theme was extended and developed by Williamson (1975), who placed a high degree of emphasis on the importance of transaction costs in influencing the evolution and optimality of organisational structures. In Williamson's theories, the assumption of rational behaviour is of central importance, as it is in neoclassical economics, whereas Simon (1957, 1961) was critical of this assumption. Hagedorn (1993, 2003, 2005); Hagedorn et al. (2002) has extended the new institutionalist framework of Williamson to the analysis of public policy-making in relation to agriculture and the management of natural resources.

This paper has demonstrated that, even ignoring transaction costs and equity considerations as well as other limitations, finding the most efficient economic solution to the regulation of agricultural externalities can be much more complex than is commonly realised. This is because the mathematical functions that underlie such relationships are often not smooth and continuous everywhere, contrary to the assumptions of neoclassical economics. This complexity suggests that policymakers are likely to be faced by the types of bounded rationality problems raised by Simon (1957, 1961). These 'irregular' functional relationships also raise new questions about the economic efficiency consequences of subsidising favourable agricultural externalities as well as the equity of such policies. A further difficulty for the rational design of agricultural policy arises because the economic efficiency of resource use is not independent of the distribution of property rights in resources, as results from behavioural economics were used here to demonstrate. This means that one has to consider what is the just distribution of rights in assessing agricultural policies in order to select the appropriate efficient economic policy.

However, the transaction costs involved in implementing agricultural policy cannot be ignored from an economic efficiency point of view. These costs vary with the institutional arrangements for policy implementation. In some cases, hybrid institutional systems may minimise transaction costs, but not in all cases. Systems of tradable resource use and the issue of permits provide an example of such hybrid systems.

The political economy challenges involved in designing agricultural policy for regulating externalities and the supply of public goods are increased by the fact that such policies need to be politically acceptable if they are to have a reasonable chance of being adopted. As pointed out by Hagedorn (1993), it is possible to identify particular institutional structures that can facilitate the acceptability of proposed public policies. Political acceptability or practicality, therefore, is a constraint on the implementation of agricultural policies. It means that the most efficient policy from an economic point of view may not be able to be implemented because of political considerations. Similar constraints may also occur in relation to the implementation of agricultural policies that are considered to be equitable. Property rights in agricultural genetic material were discussed briefly in order to illustrate some of these issues.

Acknowledgements

I wish to thank Volker Beckmann and Martina Padmanabhan for their constructive comments on the first draft of this paper. This paper has also benefited from comments received, especially those of Dr. Eduardo Pol, when it was presented at a seminar of the School of Economics, Wollongong University, Australia in June, 2008. The usual caveat applies.

References

Akerloff, G. (1970). The market for lemons: quality, uncertainty and the market mechanism. *Quarterly Journal of Economics, 84*, 488–500.
Anonymous. (2008). Catastrophe theory, from *Wikipedia.* http://en.wikipedia.org/wiki/Catastrophe_theory.
Arnold, V. I. (1992). *Catastrophe theory*. Berlin and New York: Springer.
Beckmann, V., Soregaroli, C., & Wesseler, J. (2006). Coexistence rules and regulations in the European Union. *American Journal of Agricultural Economics, 88*, 1193–1199.
Beckmann, V., & Wesseler, J. (2007). Spatial dimension of externalities and the Coase theorem: Implications for coexistence of transgenic crops. In W. Heijman (Ed.), *Regional externalities* (pp. 223–242). Berlin and Heidelberg: Springer.
Coase, R. H. (1937). The nature of the firm. *Economica, 4*, 386–405.
Coase, R. H. (1960). The problem of social cost. *Journal of Law and Economics, 3*, 1–44.
Galbraith, J. K. (1952). *American capitalism: The concept of countervailing power*. Boston: Houghton Mifflin.
Galbraith, J. K. (1967). *The new industrial state*. London: Hamish Hamilton.
Hagedorn, K. (1993). Institutions and agricultural economics. *Journal of Economic Issues, 27*, 849–886.
Hagedorn, K. (2003). Rethinking the theory of agricultural change in an institution of sustainability perspective. In G. Van Huylenbroeck, W. Verbeke, L. Lauwers, I. Vanslembrouck, & M. Dhose (Eds.), *Importance of policies and institutions for agriculture* (pp. 33–56). Gent: Academic Press.

Hagedorn, K. (2005). *The dichotomy of segregative and integrative institutions and its particular importance for sustainable resource use and rural development.* Paper presented at the workshop in political theory and policy analysis colloquium, Mini Series, Bloomington.

Hagedorn, K., Arzt, A., & Peters, U. (2002). Institutional arrangements for environmental co-operatives: A conceptual framework. In K. Hagedorn (Ed.), *Environmental co-operation and institutional change: Theories and policies for European agriculture* (pp. 3–25). Cheltenham and Northampton: Edward Elgar.

Kahneman, D., Knetsch, J. L., & Thaler, R. H. (1991). The endowment effect, loss aversion and status quo bias. *Journal of Economic Perspectives, 5,* 193–206.

Knetsch, J. L. (1989). The endowment effect and evidence of non-reversible indifference curves. *American Economic Review, 79,* 1277–1284.

Knetsch, J. L. (1990). Environmental policy implications of disparities between willingness to pay and compensation demanded. *Journal of Environmental Economics and Management, 18,* 227–237.

Pigou, A. C. (1932). *The economics of welfare.* London: Macmillan.

Posner, R. A. (1981). *The economics of justice.* Cambridge and London: Harvard University Press.

Poston, T., & Stewart, I. (1978). *Catastrophe theory and its applications.* London and San Fransisco: Pitman.

Simon, H. (1957). *Models of man.* New York: John Wiley.

Simon, H. (1961). *Administrative behavior.* New York: The Macmillan Company.

Singleton, I., Wich, S., Stephens, S., Admoko, S., Leighton, M., Rosen, N., et al.. (Eds.). (2004). *Orangutan population and habitat viability assessment: Final report.* Apple Valley: IUCN/SSC Conservation Building Specialist Group.

Tisdell, C. A. (1970). On the theory of externalities: As relevant and as not. *The Economic Record, 46,* 14–25.

Tisdell, C. A. (1993). *Environmental economics.* Aldershot and Brookfield: Edward Elgar.

Tisdell, C. A. (1999). Economics, aspects of ecology and sustainable agricultural production. In A. K. Dragun & C. Tisdell (Eds.), *Sustainable agriculture and the environment* (pp. 37–56). Cheltenham and Northampton: Edward Elgar.

Tisdell, C. A. (2005). *Economics of environmental conservation.* Cheltenham and Northampton: Edward Elgar.

Tisdell, C. A. (2009). *Resource and environmental economics: A modern approach.* Singapore, River Edge, New Jersey and London: World Scientific.

Tisdell, C. A., & Hartley, K. (2008). *Microeconomic policy: A new approach.* Cheltenham and Northampton: Edward Elgar.

Tisdell, C., Swarna Nantha, H., & Wilson C. (2007). Biodiversity conservation and public support for wildlife harvesting: A case study. *The International Journal of Biodiversity Science and Management 3,* 129–144.

Van Huylenbroeck, G., & Durand, G. (2003). *Multifunctional agriculture: A new paradigm for European agriculture and rural development.* Aldershot: Ashgate.

Vanslembrouck, I., & Van Huylenbroeck, G. (2005). *Landscape amenities: Economic assessment of agricultural landscapes.* Dordrecht: Springer.

Varian, H. (1987). *Intermediate microeconomics: A modern approach.* New York and London: W.W. Norton and Company.

Walsh, C., & Tisdell, C. (1973). Non-marginal externalities as relevant and as not. *The Economic Record, 49,* 447–455.

Williamson, E. O. (1975). *Markets and hierarchies: Analysis and anti-trust implications.* New York: Free Press.

Zeeman, E. C. (1976). Catastrophe theory. *Scientific American, 234,* 373–388.

Part II
Institutions, Governance and Sustainability

6 Multi-level Governance and Natural Resource Management: The Challenges of Complexity, Diversity, and Uncertainty

William Blomquist

Department of Political Science, Indiana University Purdue University Indianapolis (IUPUI), Indianapolis, IN 46202, USA, E-mail: blomquis@iupui.edu

Abstract. Most human-environment interactions with regard to any natural resource occur on multiple scales. Furthermore, the "human" aspect of human-environment interactions always involves multiple communities of interest and identity, and the "environment" aspect always involves multiple dimensions, uses, and values of any natural resource. These facts pose a significant challenge in the design of institutions to aid in the sustainable management of those human-environment interactions. Literature addressing that challenge spreads across several disciplines, including resource economics, ecology, law, and political science. Any quest for the "right" scale of resource management institutions may end up being unsuccessful, but this does not mean there is no difference among institutional alternatives. Some arrangements offer more favorable conditions than others for information collection, deliberation, learning, and adaptation. This chapter provides arguments in support of the conclusion that polycentric arrangements operating (albeit imperfectly) in a number of settings improve human beings' prospects for handling the challenges of complexity, diversity, and uncertainty and, therefore, enhance the possibilities for human societies to organize and maintain more nearly sustainable management of natural resources.

Keywords: Complexity, Decision making, Institutions, Multi-level governance, Resources

6.1 Introduction

Most human-environment interactions with regard to any natural resource occur on multiple scales. Furthermore, the "human" aspect of human-environment interactions always involves multiple communities of interest and identity, and the "environment" aspect always involves multiple dimensions, uses, and values of any natural resource. These facts pose a significant challenge in the design of

V. Beckmann, M. Padmanabhan (eds.), *Institutions and Sustainability*,
DOI 10.1007/978-1-4020-9690-7_6, © Springer Science+Business Media B.V. 2009

institutions to aid in the sustainable management of those human-environment interactions.

Any quest for the "right" scale of resource management institutions may be unsuccessful, but this does not mean there are no differences among institutional alternatives. Some arrangements may offer more favorable conditions than others for information collection, deliberation, learning, and adaptation. This chapter discusses a theoretical rationale, and provides some empirical support, for the proposition that multiple and polycentric arrangements operating (imperfectly) in a number of settings may offer prospects for more nearly sustainable management of natural resources.

The chapter opens with a review of current conceptions that have influenced thinking about the sustainable management of natural resources. The next section focuses upon the elements of complexity and uncertainty that have strongly influenced the changed conceptions of natural resource management. Then the implications of complexity and uncertainty for natural resource management, as well as for the design of institutions, are explored and discussed in the following two sections of the chapter. A subsequent section presents some alternative institutional arrangements as they relate to the governance and management of human activities with regard to natural resources. The concluding section summarizes the argument for polycentric institutions as keys to sustainability in natural resource management, in light of the challenges posed by complexity, diversity, and uncertainty.

6.2 Current Conceptions of Natural Resource Systems

In the past half century, at least three significant changes in the conception of natural resources have emerged: the view of natural resources in terms of ecosystems, beginning approximately forty years ago; the closely related conception of "complex adaptive systems", which came into prominence approximately twenty years ago; and the more recent examination, within the past decade, of the interactions between humans and the biophysical world in terms of linked "social-ecological systems". Although these changing conceptions of natural resources have developed in response to the felt need of scientists to develop better analytical tools, these changed ideas also bear substantial implications for the management of natural resources and, thus, for the questions of institutional design. Therefore, in order to get to the topic of institutional design for natural resource management, it is worthwhile to at least briefly consider the factors that have contributed to these changed conceptions about natural resources.

Ecosystem concepts have become a more common element of natural resource management. Closely associated with the idea of the ecosystem is that of the complex adaptive system, which was captured elegantly by Low, Ostrom, Simon, and Wilson (2003, p. 103): "complex adaptive systems are composed of a large number of active elements whose rich pattern of interactions produce emergent properties which are not easy to predict by analyzing the separate system components." Ecosystems similarly consist of multiple interacting elements, the conditions and behavior of which change over time in ways that can yield unpredictable shifts and outcomes. These two ideas (ecosystems and complex adaptive systems) have generated a significant literature, contributed to by scholars from many disciplines.

Resource economist James Wilson (2002) has contrasted the Newtonian world of controllable non-adaptive systems with the ecosystem world of complex adaptive systems. A problem with the latter is the pervasiveness of nonlinear relationships, making it difficult to trace movement or changes in one object in the system and predict the reactions of other objects. Past approaches to natural resource management, even as the ecosystem concept emerged, typically assumed that this tracing was possible. Earlier experiences with those past approaches suggest that this Newtonian view does not apply readily to complex adaptive systems, and perhaps not at all. The incorporation of ecosystem concepts necessitates some replacement of modern, often engineering-based management with broader, less precise, and less controlled approaches, such as adaptive management (Holling, 1978).

The presence of human societies and their interaction with natural resources adds further complexity and creates additional potentials for unexpected dynamic responses. Carl Walters (1986, p. 2), another early advocate of adaptive management, pointed out that focusing resource management on the physical landscape alone overlooks "the socioeconomic dynamics that are never completely controlled by management activities" either. The need for analytical tools capable of incorporating the social as well as ecological dimensions of sustainable natural resource management has motivated the work of Konrad Hagedorn on the Institutions of Sustainability (IoS) framework and the work of Elinor Ostrom – first, on the application of the Institutional Analysis and Development (IAD) framework to common-pool resources and, more recently, on a multi-tier framework for analyzing social-ecological systems (SESs).

Close attention to the interactions between human beings and the biophysical world is the focus of the emerging literature on SESs. Contributors to Berkes and Folke (1998) addressed "linked social-ecological systems," and the term was also used the following year in Wilson, Low, Costanza, and Ostrom (1999). The literature on SESs, which has developed rapidly since the late 1990s, emphasizes the challenges of institutional design, resource management, and conservation in light of the complex, multi-dimensional characteristics of such systems (see Berkes, Colding, & Folke, 2003; Ostrom, 2007).

6.3 Complexity and Uncertainty in Adaptive Systems

Although they are distinct from one another, these newer conceptions of natural resource systems exhibit common elements. One is a recognition of, and a focus upon, complexity (see especially Janssen, 2002). Another is a recognition of, and a focus upon, uncertainty, particularly in the work on complex adaptive systems and on social-ecological systems. The complexity of systems, and the uncertainty associated with them, have important ramifications for management prospects and institutional design and, thus, deserve closer attention here.

"Uncertainty" is used in several contexts. Often it signifies insufficient data or a lack of complete information. Sometimes it means the presence of "noise" or error due to the randomly varying nature of some process. Such views of uncertainty share an "assumption that we know or believe we know the basic cause-and-effect relationships – the system structure – in [...] whatever we are studying" (Wilson, 2002, p. 333). Although we understand a system's structure, we lack enough data to be more precise and accurate, or our predictions contain errors because of known or random variability in the system.

But there is another, and one might say deeper, type of uncertainty which involves more than a lack of reliable data or the presence of random variation. This deeper uncertainty involves a lack of knowledge or absence of agreement about the nature of the resource system itself and of its dynamic behavior. This uncertainty includes lack of agreement about what elements of the system are the best indicators of its overall condition as well as lack of agreement about what changes in those indicators mean (Jordan & Miller, 1996). More or better data, by themselves, would not necessarily diminish or eliminate this kind of uncertainty.

Because the latter type of uncertainty has been discussed by some authors in the literature on complex adaptive systems, it is possible to confuse this sort of uncertainty with complexity. The difference between the two, however, was usefully articulated by Roe (2001, p. 111): "Issues are uncertain when causal processes are unclear or not easily understood. Issues are complex when they are more numerous, varied, and interrelated than before."

There are at least three reasons why this deep uncertainty is characteristic of complex adaptive systems: differing rates of change among system components, scale differences, and disturbance processes.

6.3.1 Differing rates of change

The factors that make up an ecosystem, complex adaptive system, or social-ecological system typically change at different rates. Species populations, ambient environmental conditions (e.g., air, water, and soil composition, temperatures), and anthropogenic impacts (e.g., harvesting behavior or technologies) all change at different rates. By themselves, differential rates of change would present a complexity problem rather than an uncertainty problem; the latter arises rather from the fact that elements in the system respond to changes in other elements. Therefore, the effects of differential rates of change are contingent, and may yield alterations that are not merely linear extensions of trends. "State shifts" may occur, even as a result of a small change in a single system element, depending upon the configuration of the conditions of all other system elements at that moment. Conversely, with a different configuration of the conditions of all other system elements, that same small change in the remaining element may yield little or no observable perturbation at all.

6.3.2 Scale differences and near decomposability

Interactions and effects also occur across space and time scales, a phenomenon that has gained a great deal of attention lately, especially in the work of Young (1994, 1995, 2002) and colleagues. Because these complex systems are heterogeneous, the effects of a condition change in one portion or local area of the system may be relatively insulated from the rest, while the same change occurring in a different portion or local area of the system generates system-level transformations. For this and other reasons (e.g., Wilson et al., 1999), a change of condition in one portion of the system cannot be automatically "scaled up" to predict system level effects. Discontinuities in the relationships between system elements and system effects make it "very difficult to extrapolate results from one scale – frequently the plot scale – to higher spatial scales" (Swallow, Johnson, & Meinzen-Dick, 2001, p. 451; see also Gunderson, Holling, & Light, 1995, p. 531). "Scaling down" is difficult as well: it is unclear how changes occurring at a systemwide scale will manifest themselves in effects at particular locations within the system.

6.3.3 Disturbance processes

System processes and behaviors may be interrupted by disturbances. In social-ecological systems, these include effects of infestation and disease, natural disasters, and shifts in the ambient environment. Added to the natural variability of the resource systems themselves, this kind of uncertainty allows for "unknowable responses, or true surprises [due to] the self-organizing, ever-changing character of ecosystems and their response to perturbations that are unprecedented (at least to the current ecosystems)" (Carpenter, 1996, p. 120). Rapid changes may occur for reasons that are not only poorly understood but even unforeseen. Disturbance processes introduce an element of deep uncertainty – not merely complexity – into the challenge of resource management.

6.4 Implications for the Approach to Management

Without agreement on which elements of a system best indicate its overall condition, scientists and resource managers are likely to also lack agreement on what a
change in one or more of those indicators at any particular time signifies. It is difficult to know, even after the fact, which changes in system conditions represent
trends and which do not. The selection of policy "targets" becomes especially unclear, and so does our understanding of how alternative policy actions relate to
those targets. Furthermore, if resource managers focus their attention on a few selected policy targets, undesired and undesirable results may occur as other elements of the system shift in unanticipated ways (Carpenter, 1996, p. 147).

In the protection and management of complex adaptive systems, both the scientific problem and the management problem are qualitatively different from what
they would be if we understood the fundamental dynamics of the system and simply needed more data. Uncertainty boosts the chances for decision making to result in misguided or maladaptive policies. Management systems are prone to error.

Failure to recognize and acknowledge uncertainty can magnify that error-
proneness. Unfortunately, decision makers tend to overestimate their understanding of problems and underestimate the uncertainty involved in them (Low et al.,
2003). Failure to acknowledge uncertainty reduces the likelihood that policy makers will develop and implement management practices that have learning elements
designed into them, a practice recommended by Korten (1980) years before. Failure to incorporate learning processes into institutional designs may expose us to
more "catastrophic" errors that can result from an incomplete understanding of the
resource system (Wilson, 2002, p. 332). This makes error correction even more
important. Error correction depends upon error detection, and this raises questions
about what sorts of institutional designs could enhance the prospects for error
detection.

In the management of complex resource systems, the predictions underlying
policy actions must be closely and continually compared with observations of the
resource system. Furthermore, this close monitoring will need to incorporate multiple indicators and take place at multiple scales. Arrangements are therefore needed that will enhance the collection of information, the detection of errors, and the
opportunities for adaptation.

6.5 Implications for the Design of Institutional Arrangements

As the preceding sections have suggested, the changed conceptions of natural resource systems have substantial and far-reaching implications for decision making
as well as for the institutional structures human beings devise and employ. Dis-
agreement continues among researchers and practitioners over, for instance, the

relative merits of comprehensive regulation through integrated agencies versus multi-centered or polycentric institutional arrangements. The desire for comprehensive decision making still holds significant attraction in the literatures on integrated resource management and is implicitly associated with the notion of some integrated decision-making apparatus. Other authors, however, are skeptical of using an integrated decision making organization for the management of complex adaptive systems. Their rationale for multi-centered or polycentric institutional arrangements appears to be composed of a number of common themes:

1. the recognition of scale diversity,
2. the desire to reduce error-proneness and promote learning,
3. the recognition of limitations on human information processing capabilities,
4. the presence of multiple goals for resource management, and
5. the recognition of the diversity of human interests and values associated with most complex natural resource systems.

6.5.1 Recognition of scale diversity

In light of the observations about scale differences in complex resource systems, institutional analysts have incorporated scale diversity – and its implication, organizational multiplicity – into considerations of institutional design. According to this view, the management and protection of complex resource systems may require the involvement of multiple organizations at a variety of scales (Berkes, 2006, 2007). Gunderson, Pritchard, Holling, Folke, and Peterson (2002, p. 262) observed that "resource systems that have been sustained over long time periods increase resilience by managing processes at multiple scales." Both the IoS and IAD frameworks incorporate the presence of multiple scales as well as interactions between them.

Such thinking is predicated substantially upon the concept of "near decomposability," which Simon (1996, 2000) developed in connection with the analysis of organizations, but which others have applied to the analysis of biophysical systems as well.[1] Ostrom (2007), for example, writes that "SESs are partially decomposable systems" (2007, p. 15182). The concept of near decomposability opens the possibility that, even for a system composed of interacting elements, it may be possible to organize management around those elements as well as at the level of the system as a whole. Indeed, Simon sees it as more of a necessity than merely a possibility: "If we design complex systems to operate efficiently, we must incorporate near-decomposability in the design" (Simon, 2000, p. 753).

---

[1] Such an extension does no harm to the original concept, however, as Simon himself has recognized that its scope extends beyond human organizations: "Most of the complex systems seen in the world are nearly decomposable systems." (Simon, 2000, p. 753).

Such a multiorganizational arrangement would include smaller local organizations attending to particular subsystems, as these subsystem levels are more nearly amenable to close monitoring and to the development of improved understanding of patterns of activity. Smaller organizations would be combined with overlapping organizations at larger scales. These can serve as forums for sharing of information across subsystems, and as a check on local structures that behave in ways detrimental to other subsystems (Low et al., 2003, p. 106; also Berkes, 2007). One finds examples of such arrangements in irrigation systems that have small-scale, farmer-managed units that are served by intermediate-scale, community-managed distribution canals, which are fed by large-scale, sometimes publicly-managed, headworks diverting water from a river or other water body (see Tang, 1994; Ostrom, 1992; Lam, 2006).

6.5.2 Reducing error proneness and promoting learning

A second theme is the importance of reducing error proneness and promoting learning, an effort that may be aided by some degree of duplication and redundancy of organizational structures. Learning is essential to the kind of adaptive management that has been advocated for complex resource systems (Walters, 1986, Lee, 1993). Learning is likely to be maximized and accelerated in a diversified institutional setting where multiple interventions are being undertaken and compared within the same system simultaneously, with opportunities to exchange results and observe the experiences of others (Wilson, 2002, p. 345–347, see also Holling, 1986; Ostrom, 2005).

In addition to promoting learning, such experimentation may reduce the prospects of large-scale errors. In Ostrom's view, taking advantage of the partial decomposability of resource systems means that "policies can be explored in one part of a system without imposing uniform formulas on the larger system that might lead to a large-scale collapse" (Ostrom, 2007, p. 15182). From this perspective, it may be important to avoid reliance upon a single management organization in situations where deep uncertainty, information loss, and information distortion can cascade into dramatically erroneous decisions and actions.

The point made earlier about the importance of error detection comes into play at this point. Limited attention to a few selected indicators of system conditions is dangerous, but this is what individuals trying to operate a single organization charged with monitoring and managing a complex system will be inclined to do. A century of research on organizational behavior suggests that more nearly centralized organizations are susceptible internally to distortions of information and communications that can allow poor policies and practices to persist for undesirably long periods (see Rozelle and Swinnen in this volume).

6.5.3 Recognizing the capabilities and limitations of human beings

Paraphrasing Jones (2001), institutional design for complex resource management is more likely to be successful if it accounts for the limits and potentialities of human nature. Human decision making has limitations, which have been identified, characterized, and studied empirically for decades, usually under the rubric of bounded rationality, which is attributed to Herbert Simon (1957, 1996).

A boundedly rational individual possesses both limited cognitive processing capabilities and limited information. People are goal-oriented and purposive, but limited in their cognitive competence (Simon, 1957). Boundedly rational individuals can learn and adapt to their immediate environment, and over time, learn and adapt to changing environments. Such learning and adaptation will be episodic and disjointed, however, because of the structure and operation of their cognitive architecture (Jones & Baumgartner, 2005). Boundedly rational individuals are also influenced by norms and by their interactions with other individuals, an important finding that opens up possibilities for cooperative behavior, as emphasized by Arild Vatn in this volume.

The above analysis suggests that comprehensive, integrated decision making will rapidly overwhelm people's cognitive capabilities. Because of the complexity and uncertainty associated with resource systems, "no one individual or group could hope to adequately address the learning problem" (Wilson, 2002, p. 341; see also White, 1998, p. 25; Walther, 1987).[2] Furthermore, these problems of limits of understanding and cognition may not be solved merely by the often-prescribed organizational fix of "scale matching," that is, creating organizations to correspond with the outer boundaries of a complex resource system (Gunderson et al., 1995, p. 531; for analysis of a specific case demonstrating this, see Wilson et al., 1999).

In addition to having imperfect information-processing abilities, boundedly rational people operate in a costly world. They must expend resources developing, implementing, monitoring, enforcing, and revising institutional arrangements. Those transaction costs shape and constrain the types of institutional arrangements that people devise (Williamson, 1985). People are not free to design any type of institution or policy they desire. People thus confront both cognitive and cost limitations in developing and selecting policies, limitations that tend to direct them away from comprehensive, integrated approaches.

---

[2] In a recent comparison of two cases, Slaughter and Wiener (2007) found that the concentration of decision making in a single agency operated less effectively at detecting and solving complex problems in a watershed than polycentric arrangements in another one.

6.5.4 Multiple management goal

Although limited in their capabilities, people are not similarly limited in their wants. A vital reality of complex resource system management is that people want it to achieve multiple goals. Two dimensions of the multiple-goal issue are important to consider. First, the multiple goals people desire may conflict in some respects and under some conditions. This is not fatal, since tradeoffs are often feasible, but it is an important fact to be kept in view. Second, different goals are more pertinent to some scales or subsystems within a resource system than they are to others; for example, recreational opportunities and demands might be more relevant within one portion of the overall resource system, while subsistence needs are more critical in another. An implication of the fact that resource management involves the simultaneous pursuit of multiple goals at multiple scales is that people trying to achieve a variety of goals within a resource system could sensibly opt to organize several overlapping institutional arrangements.

6.5.5 Recognizing diversity of human communities and interests

Managing and protecting complex adaptive resource systems would be challenging enough even if human uses, interests, and values were not at stake. The entrance of human beings into the problem brings an additional set of multiple scales (Lebel, Garden, & Imamura, 2005; Berkes, 2006). Just as the physical dimensions of a resource system appear at different scales, so do the multiple human uses and behaviors that occur and interact with that system, complicating further the tasks of decision making, monitoring, and enforcement (Adger, Brown, & Tompkins, 2006). Handling such diversity is difficult within a single governance structure. People often choose instead to create a variety of different types of government and organization.

It is especially important not to approach the problem of institutional design with the assumption that management decisions will be made by like-minded resource users or like-minded policy makers. If we recognize instead that communities of users within a complex resource system are likely to hold different values, norms, and preferences, our expectations regarding the design and performance of decision making processes will be affected substantially. As we contemplate individuals and communities interacting with natural resources, the "how" questions about decision making arrangements are compounded by "for whom" questions (Hooghe & Marks, 2003, p. 241).

Overlaid upon the differences in people's physical situations within a complex resources system (upstream versus downstream, adjacent to valuable resources versus farther away, etc.) are the many social, economic, and cultural distinctions among people. Distinctions of wealth, ethnicity, religion, occupation, social status and the like will also exist among and between individuals and the groups or communities with which they identify (Lebel et al., 2005). Under these circumstances, the questions of who gets to decide and how are as important as, often more important than, the questions of what shall be done.

As the "for whom" questions join the "how" questions of resource management, it is essential to pay attention to boundary issues concerning who belongs "in" the decision making processes and who does not. Defining boundaries is a matter of determining (whether we acknowledge it explicitly or not) who is in and who is out; who "counts", and how much; and who doesn't count at all. Deborah Stone (1988) has observed that, although "who gets what" is as important as how they get it, defining the "who" and the "how" are not simple. There are multiple available definitions for each, and each definition invokes different values and different notions of equity. The distinctions made will therefore be contested: either by people who want to get in and be counted or those who wish to escape and avoid being included in a decision process that is likely to involve burdens as well as benefits.

To adopt the attractive-sounding rhetoric that "all affected interests" should be included simply raises more questions, such as what it means for someone or some group to have an "interest" in the resource system? Does it mean to live within the physical boundaries of the system? To use its resources? To care about the resource system even though one never expects to live or visit there? Can one "have an interest" in a resource system by merely "taking an interest" in it?

Ultimately, debates over who should be included within decision making processes are debates over which values should be given the greatest weight. Political theorist E.E. Schattschneider (1960) called such strategies "managing the scope of conflict": one set of interests is likely to advocate defining the situation in ways that keep the scope limited, while another set of interests may try to define the situation in ways that draw in more participants, each anticipating the effects that the narrower or broader scope will have on the likelihood of their preferences prevailing. In complex resource systems, it is unlikely that there is a single boundary, or set of boundaries, that will be clear to all participants or upon which all potential participants will be willing to agree.

As countless authors have observed, human communities have rarely been organized to coincide with ecosystem boundaries. Neither form of organization is likely to displace the other, and reconciling them adds further complexity to the task of institutional design (Barham, 2001). Neither a single decision making principle nor a single organization at a single scale is therefore likely to suffice. As a result, institutional arrangements suited to decision making about complex adaptive systems may themselves need to exhibit some features of complexity and adaptability (Berkes, 2006). The challenge was described well by Blatter and Ingram (2000, p. 464) with regard to water resource systems:

> Common goods such as water are multidimensional (drinking, shipping, power generation, irrigation, recreation, ecological functions, economic development, et al.). For this reason, [a single principle] does not work very well as an instrument to define the one

best size of a geographical area for governing water. Instead of applying economic criteria or markets to the task of creating boundaries, a political process of trading values off against one another must take place. It is necessary to determine the most important function(s), create the government structure(s) corresponding to these functions, and find some mechanisms to deal with the interdependencies and spillovers between these functions.

Finally, conflicts and policy choices concerning complex resource systems are not fixed in time. Changes in population concentrations or economic activities will bring different values to the fore. Neither defining communities of interest broadly, nor giving pride of place to geographically local communities, guarantees that a particular set of values will be pursued consistently over time as the resource setting and its context changes.

6.6 A Closer Look at Institutional Options

Establishing the rationale for multi-organizational structures is one matter, articulating how they look and work is another. For that, it is useful to turn to contributions to the literature on governance structures for a closer look at some options for multi-organizational arrangements.

6.6.1 Type I and Type II organizations

Usefully distilling decades of theoretical development about the organization of governing jurisdictions, Hooghe and Marks (2003) distinguished between "Type I" and "Type II" governance structures. Type I structures are *constituency-defined multi-service or multi-function organizations*: general-purpose governments, such as a city or province, encompassing a defined group of residents and providing an array of services. Type I structures are usually nested vertically – cities and counties encompassed by states or provinces, provinces or states within a nation, and meso and supra levels, such as regional and international organizations – and do not overlap horizontally (e.g., the territory and population of one a Type I jurisdiction do not carry over into a neighboring one).

Type II governmental structures are *functionally* defined, and their boundaries vary from one service or function to another. Type II structures are established at whatever geographical scale may be suited to funding and delivering a particular service, such as an irrigation district serving a collection of farmers and the like. Type II governments can and often do overlap horizontally, and many may operate with different functional responsibilities in the same geographic area (Hooghe & Marks, 2003, p. 236–240).

Type II governments have the advantages of functional specialization and geographical flexibility. On the other hand, because of their specialization they are usually not engaged in making decisions regarding trade-offs or bargaining among service priorities – for example, whether to devote more resources this year to policing or to street maintenance – which are usually facilitated by Type I governmental structures. Nonetheless, although these governance forms differ, Hooghe and Marks also underscore their compatibility and complementarity. In most (perhaps all) complex resource systems, combinations of Type I and Type II governance structures will exist, additional ones may be created and existing ones modified, and the relationships among them adjusted from time to time.

6.6.2 Public economies

The theory of public economies provides another way to make sense of complicated and multi-layered governing arrangements. It was developed to explain complex polycentric systems, such as the governance of metropolitan areas in the absence of a metropolitan government (Ostrom, Tiebout, & Warren, 1961; Bish & Ostrom, 1973; U.S. ACIR, 1987; Oakerson, 1999). The application is particularly apt, since so many contemporary debates about how best to govern resource systems echo earlier debates among scholars and practitioners concerning metropolitan government. The most important components of public economies theory are the provision-production distinction, organizational specialization, economies and diseconomies of scale, and coordination versus hierarchy.

In all social settings, decisions may be made concerning the provision of desired resources, goods, and services without actually engaging in their production. Members of a household, for instance, decide how (and how much) they will obtain of the necessities and conveniences of life – housing, food, schooling, entertainment – but do not necessarily produce these items or services themselves. Similarly, a community of individuals may organize a town, a water district, or a Web page and decide what services they want to receive, what forms and amounts of revenue they will contribute, what content they want to disseminate, and so forth. These are provision decisions. They do not imply that the individuals in the community will actually police the streets, construct wells or pipes, or make the Web page. They may choose to procure any or all of those services from other individuals or organizations that offer them (Oakerson, 1999), who may then be engaged by provider units through a variety of arrangements (partnerships, contracts, and so on).

In addition to this distinction between provision and production arrangements, the theory of public economies incorporates the concept of functional specialization. As implied in the discussion of Type I and Type organizations above, there often are advantages in organizing activities by taking advantage of specialization. Whether to add a responsibility to an existing organization or create a specialist organization for that function is an important institutional choice, but one for which there is no a priori correct answer. The choice about whether to add another organization or increase the responsibilities of an existing one will depend upon matters such as the skills required for the function, the resources available within existing organizations, the costs of coordination if a new organization is created, and the political issues of governance and control.

Another concept that follows closely with those of specialization and the distinction between provision and production is that of scale. Some activities can be less costly and more efficiently accomplished if organized on a large scale. Others exhibit diseconomies of scale, becoming inefficient or cumbersome when too many people or too diverse a set of interests is involved.

Of course, advantages of specialization and scale could be overwhelmed by the costs of coordination among multiple organizations in such a public economy. Why not just organize a single authority encompassing all these activities? Interorganizational coordination is costly, of course, but the alternatives are not costless either. As suggested above, organizational integration also has costs – of internal coordination and communication, information distortion, control of losses, and the like – as described in the political economy literature on bureaucratic pathologies (see e.g., Simon, 1955; V. Ostrom, 1989; Knott & Miller, 1987; Chisholm, 1989; Miller, 1992). On balance, whether organizational integration or inter-organizational coordination is more costly is an empirical question, and the answer will vary from one situation to another.

6.6.3 Integrative and segregative institutions

The work of Konrad Hagedorn has provided an additional way to think about the alternative institutional arrangements that may be combined in a multi-organizational or polycentric structure associated with a complex resource system (Hagedorn, 2005; Hagedorn, Arzt, & Peters, 2002). Recognizing that there is a large menu of governance structures that could contribute to sustainable resource use – markets, hierarchies, cooperatives and other hybrid organizations, co-production, federal and other multi-level systems, and so on – Hagedorn has recommended instead that analysts focus on the effects that organizational structures would have upon people and their decision-making processes.

Integrative institutions have the effect of promoting decision making that addresses

1. the interactions among elements of the physical systems and
2. the interdependencies and externalities of individuals' decisions and actions. Such institutions promote, for instance, liability of individuals for adverse effects their actions have on resources or other resource users, or rewards to individuals whose actions generate benefits for other resource users or the physical

system itself. Integrative institutions are important components of sustainable resource governance, but they do come with costs. Decision making processes that must take interactions and interdependencies into account will tend to be more laborious, with substantial transaction costs, as well as some inhibiting effects on individuals' ability to act quickly and engage in innovative behavior.

Segregative institutions allow individuals to isolate aspects of a particular resource system and to isolate (or at least parcel) the positive and negative effects of their decisions and actions. Such institutions take advantage of the near decomposability of complex resource systems and of the social structures within which human beings live and interact. As the discussion earlier in this chapter indicates, such institutions can also be important components of sustainable resource governance, but they too come with costs. When decisions and actions are governed by segregative institutions, it is possible for harmful social or ecological consequences to persist unacknowledged or unaddressed and pose dangers to long-term and large-scale conditions.

6.7 Concluding Remarks: Institutional Diversity and Methodological Diversity

The foregoing discussion indicates that there can be value in having multiple sizes, types, and responsibilities of organizations for managing complex resource systems. Success under such conditions is by no means guaranteed, but prospects for success may be enhanced. In the view of many scholars, institutional richness may be valuable in the complex and uncertain world of social-ecological systems. Multi-scale institutional arrangements, including small and local organizations linked horizontally with each other and vertically with larger scale organizations, may be able to achieve

1. close monitoring of local (subsystem) conditions;
2. representation of diverse interests associated with different physical components of the system as a whole;
3. error correction when management practices undertaken with respect to one element of the system create unanticipated negative effects elsewhere in the system; and
4. opportunities to communicate and exchange information across subsystem elements and to discuss subsystem interactions and system-wide conditions, without necessarily trying to manage all parts of the system with a comprehensive organization.

The case for institutional diversity in the management of complex resource systems has already been made well, by Hagedorn (2005), Ostrom (2005), and others. Nevertheless, it bears reiterating here. The theme that underlies all of the preceding discussion in this chapter is the observation that there is no single management approach, governance structure, or other institutional design that will fit the enormous diversity of social-ecological systems in the world or accomplish the multiple goals and satisfy the diverse values of human beings. The wiser course of action, for practitioners as well as for researchers, is to keep a diversity of options available and pursue processes that incorporate opportunities and capacities for learning and adaptation.

By a similar logic, a good deal of methodological diversity is worthwhile as well. There is great value in having multiple researchers from many disciplines, applying a diversity of methods, studying the management of complex resource systems (Ostrom, 2007, p. 15185). As researchers from diverse traditions encounter one another's work, their prospects for learning are multiplied as well. This is among the contributions of this volume and of Professor Hagedorn's work which has inspired it.

Acknowledgments

The argument presented in this paper was developed and applied to the case of watershed management in Schlager and Blomquist (2008).

References

Adger, W. N., Brown, K., & Tompkins, E. L. (2006). The political economy of cross-scale networks in resource co-management. *Ecology and Society, 10*, article 9, from: http://www.ecologyandsociety.org/vol10/art9/.

Barham, E. (2001). Ecological boundaries as community boundaries: The politics of watersheds. *Society and Natural Resources, 14*, 181–191.

Berkes, F. (2006). From community-based resource management to complex systems: The scale issue and marine commons. *Ecology and Society, 11*, article 45, from: http://www.ecologyandsociety.org/vol11/iss1/art45.

Berkes, F. (2007). Community-based conservation in a globalized world. *Proceedings of the National Academy of Sciences, 104*, 15188–15193.

Berkes, F., Colding, J., & Folke, C. (Eds.) (2003). *Navigating social-ecological systems: Building resilience for complexity and change.* Cambridge: Cambridge University Press.

Berkes, F., & Folke, C. (Eds.). (1998). *Linking social and ecological systems: Management practices and social mechanisms for building resilience.* Cambridge: Cambridge University Press.

Bish, R., & Ostrom, V. (1973). *Understanding urban government.* Washington, DC: American Enterprise Institute.

Blatter, J., & Ingram, H. M. (2000). States, markets and beyond: Governance of transboundary water resources. *Natural Resources Journal, 40*, 439–474.

Carpenter, R. A. (1996). Uncertainty in managing ecosystems sustainably. In J. Lemons (Ed.), *Scientific uncertainty and environmental problem solving* (pp. 118–159). London: Blackwell Science.

Chisholm, D. (1989). *Coordination without hierarchy: Informal structures in multiorganizational systems.* Berkeley: University of California Press.

Gunderson, L. H., Holling, C. S., & Light, St. S. (1995). Barriers broken and bridges built: A synthesis. In L. H. Gunderson, C. S. Holling, & St. S. Light (Eds.), *Barriers and bridges to the renewal of ecosystems and institutions* (pp. 489–532). New York: Columbia University Press.

Gunderson, L. H., Pritchard, Jr. L., Holling, C. S., Folke, C., &. Peterson, G. D. (2002). A summary and synthesis of resilience in large-scale systems. In L. H. Gunderson & L. Pritchard, Jr. (Eds.), *Resilience and the behavior of large-scale systems* (pp. 249–266). Washington, DC: Island Press.

Hagedorn, K. (2005, June). *Integrative and segregative institutions.* (Paper presented at the TransCoop workshop "Problems of polycentric governance in the growing EU", Berlin).

Hagedorn, K., Arzt, K., & Peters, U. (2002). Institutional arrangements for environmental co-operatives: A conceptual framework. In K. Hagedorn (Ed.), *Environmental cooperation and institutional change: Theories and policies for European agriculture* (pp. 3–25). Cheltenham and Northampton: Edward Elgar.

Holling, C. S. (1978). *Adaptive environmental assessment and management.* New York: John Wiley & Sons.

Holling, C. S. (1986). Resilience of ecosystems, local surprise and global change. In W. Clark & R. E. Munn (Eds.), *Sustainable development of the biosphere* (pp. 297–317). Cambridge: Cambridge University Press.

Hooghe, L., & Marks, G. (2003). Unraveling the central state, but how? Types of multi-level governance. *American Political Science Review, 97,* 233–243.

Janssen, M. A. (2002). *Complexity and ecosystem management.* Cheltenham and Northampton: Edward Elgar.

Jones, B. D. (2001). *Politics and the architecture of choice.* Chicago: University of Chicago Press.

Jones, B. D., & Baumgartner, F. R. (2005). *The politics of attention: How government prioritizes problems.* Chicago: University of Chicago Press.

Jordan, C. F., & Miller, C. (1996). Scientific uncertainty as a constraint to environmental problem solving: Large-scale ecosystems. In J. Lemons (Ed.), *Scientific uncertainty and environmental problem solving* (pp. 91–117). London: Blackwell Science.

Knott, J., & Miller, G. (1987). *Reforming bureaucracy: The politics of institutional choice.* Englewood Cliffs: Prentice-Hall, Inc.

Korten, D. C. (1980). Community organization and rural development: A learning process approach. *Public Administration Review, 40,* 480–511.

Lam, W. F. (2006). Foundations of a robust social-ecological system: Irrigation institutions in Taiwan. *Journal of Institutional Economics, 2,* 203–226

Lebel, L., Garden, P., & Imamura, M. (2005). The politics of scale, position, and place in the governance of water resources in the Mekong region. *Ecology and Society, 10,* article 18, from: http://www.ecologyandsociety.org/vol10/iss2/art18.

Lee, K. N. (1993). *Compass and gyroscope: Integrating science and politics for the environment.* Washington, DC: Island Press.

Low, B., Ostrom, E., Simon, & Wilson, J. (2003). Redundancy and diversity: Do they influence optimal management? In F. Berkes, J. Colding, & C. Folke (Eds.), *Navigating social-ecological systems: Building resilience for complexity and change* (pp. 83–114). New York: Cambridge University Press.

Miller, G. (1992). *Managerial dilemmas.* New York: Cambridge University Press.

Oakerson, R. (1999). *Understanding local public economies.* San Francisco: ICS Press.

Ostrom, E. (1992). *Crafting self-governing institutions for irrigation systems.* San Francisco: ICS Press

Ostrom, E. (2005). *Understanding institutional diversity.* Princeton: Princeton University Press.

Ostrom, E. (2007). A diagnostic approach for going beyond panaceas. *Proceedings of the National Academy of Sciences, 104,* 15181–15187.

Ostrom, V. (1989). *The intellectual crisis in American public administration.* Tuscaloosa: University of Alabama Press.

Ostrom, V., Tiebout, C. M., & Warren, R. (1961). The organization of government in metropolitan areas: A theoretical inquiry. *American Political Science Review, 55,* 831–842.

Roe, E. (2001). Varieties of issue incompleteness and coordination: An example from ecosystem management. *Policy Sciences, 34,* 111–133.

Schattschneider, E. E. (1960*). The semisovereign people: A realist's view of democracy in America.* New York: Holt, Rinehart, and Winston.

Schlager, E., & Blomquist, W. (2008). *Embracing watershed politics.* Boulder: University Press of Colorado.

Simon, H. (1955). A behavioral model of rational choice. *Quarterly Journal of Economics, 69,* 99–118.

Simon, H. (1957). *Models of man.* New York: Wiley.

Simon, H. (1996). *The sciences of the artificial.* Cambridge: MIT Press.

Simon, H. (2000). Public administration in today's world of organizations and markets. *PS: Political Science and Politics, 33,* 749–756.

Slaughter, R. A., & Wiener, J. D. (2007). Water, adaptation, and property rights on the Snake and Klamath Rivers. *Journal of the American Water Resources Association, 43,* 308–321.

Stone, D. (1988). *Policy paradox and political reason.* New York: Harper Collins.

Swallow, B. M., Johnson, N. L., & Meinzen-Dick, R. S. (2001). Working with people for watershed management. *Water Policy, 3,* 449–455.

Tang, S. -Y. (1994). *Institutions and collective action: Self-governance in irrigation.* San Francisco: ICS Press.

United States Advisory Commission on Intergovernmental Relations (U.S. ACIR). (1987). *The organization of local public economies (Report A-109).* Washington, DC: U.S. Advisory Commission on Intergovernmental Relations.

Walters, C. (1986). *Adaptive management of renewable resources.* New York: Macmillan.

Walther, P. (1987). Against idealistic beliefs in the problem-solving capacities of integrated resource management. *Environmental Management, 11,* 439–446.

White, G. F. (1998). Reflections on the 50-year international search for integrated water management. *Water Policy, 1,* 21–27.

Williamson, O. (1985). *The economic institutions of capitalism.* New York: The Free Press.

Wilson, J. (2002). Scientific uncertainty, complex systems and the design of common pool institutions. In E. Ostrom, T. Dietz, N. E. Dolsak, P. Stern, S. Stonich, & E. U. Weber (Eds.), *Drama of the commons* (pp. 327–359). Washington, DC: National Academy Press.

Wilson, J., Low, B., Costanza, R., & Ostrom, E. (1999). Scale misperceptions and the spatial dynamics of a social-ecological system. *Ecological Economics, 31,* 243–257.

Young, O. R. (1994). The problem of scale in human environment relationships. *Journal of Theoretical Politics, 6,* 429–447.

Young, O. R. (1995). The problem of scale in human environment relationships. In R. O. Keohane & E. Ostrom (Eds.), *Local commons and global interdependence: Heterogeneity and cooperation in two domains* (pp. 27–45). London: Sage Publications.

Young, O. R. (2002). *The institutional dimensions of environmental change: Fit, interplay, and scale.* Cambridge: MIT Press.

7 Constraints on Rural Governance in the European Union: A Role for Co-operative Associations?

Markus Hanisch

Division of Cooperative Studies, Humboldt-Universität zu Berlin, Luisenstr. 53, 10099 Berlin, Germany, E-mail: ifg-berlin@rz.hu-berlin.de

Abstract. In this contribution I argue that the concept of polycentricity that has evolved from the body of literature on governance problems in metropolitan areas (Tiebout, 1956, Ostrom, Tiebout, & Warren, 1961, Marks & Hooghe, 2003, Frey & Eichenberger, 1999) may not be easily adapted to address current governance problems in the rural areas of the EU-27. The chapter explores some of the likely limits of the concept in the context of rural development in the European Union. I first explore the foundations of the concept of polycentricity, along with its assumptions and theoretical conclusions. I then characterize typical contemporary problems in the rural areas of the EU after the enlargement from EU-15 to EU-27. I then show that phenomena like rural poverty, local budget crises, and scale economies in service provision in areas like health-care, infrastructure and education lead to situations where the assumptions of multi-level governance are not met. Finally, I draw a few theoretical and practical conclusions, which are in line with the basic tenets of the concept of polycentricity, about the potential of co-operatives for solving governance problems in the rural areas of the European Union.

Keywords: Consumer democracy, Local government, Multi-level governance, Public goods dilemma, Theory of the co-operative firm

7.1 Introduction

Along with the recent EU-enlargement, a discussion has emerged about how to delegate authority and how to adequately divide tasks and labor among various decision making units spread across different regions in the European Union. In this discussion there seems to be agreement among scholars that the emerging architecture of the system of European governance substantially differs from some larger form of unitary government. It is claimed that the internal heterogeneity of a growing European Union affords a complex, multi-tier system of sometimes competing decision-making units which allows citizens to actively choose between service alternatives, to self-organize and, therewith, to adjust decision-making units to the growing scope and diversity of problems (Marks & Hooghe, 2003).

One immediate outcome of this discussion is the view that a traditional division of labor and resultant model of governance that allocates the responsibility for the production of different types of goods to different types of sectors is way too simplistic to cover the diverse modes of the division of labor between the various groups and jurisdictions within the EU. As a consequence both, the role of government and its locus have to be redefined. Concepts like Polycentricity (Ostrom, 1972), Multi-level governance[1] (Marks & Hooghe, 2003, pp. 223–249) or Frey, Luechinger and Stutzer (2004) FOCJ (Functionally Overlapping Competitive Jurisdictions) represent attempts at answering the question of how non-private goods can be produced in the absence of a central coordinator. Common to these approaches is the hope that a multi-level architecture would improve the overall performance of non-private service provision. However, with the stepwise or full dissolution of unitary government, the question arises of what other principles might direct and justify the production of non-private goods. Tiebout (1956), Ostrom et al. (1961) as well as Ostrom (1972) have hypothesized that – compared to monocentric systems – the introduction of elements of competition and participation of civil society in the process of the production of public services would increase the efficiency of decentralized public service provision.

In this chapter I argue that multi-level concepts of governance, which have mainly evolved from a body of literature on governance problems in *metropolitan areas*, may not be easily adapted to addressing emerging governance problems in the *rural areas* of the EU-27. My aim is to explore some of the likely theoretical constraints to the applicability of such approaches to rural areas. After this has been achieved, in light of the theory of multi-level governance, I will clarify both the function and the historical and the potential future roles of a particular type of self-help organization: the rural co-operative.

The reminder of this chapter is structured as follows: I first introduce the basic concepts of multi-level governance and present the main theoretical arguments for them. I then sketch important structural problems of rural development following the enlargement from the EU-15 to the EU-27 and give examples of how the notions of polycentricity and multi-level governance have entered both the EU policy dialogue and the EU's current rural development paradigm. After that, I briefly analyze the theoretical implications of such problems for the applicability of multi-level governance concepts in rural areas. Discussion of a stylized model of rural development at the end of the 19th century reveals that, prior to the formation of modern public service industries, various types of self-help organizations

---

[1] In this chapter I will use the latter term, "multi-level governance", to represent the main ideas of these concepts.

have formed the backbone of collective service provision in rural areas. I conclude with a few theoretical and practical theses about the roles and potential of old and new forms of associative membership organizations for solving governance problems in ways that are in line with multi-level governance concepts.

7.2 The Multi-Level Governance Concept

Concepts of multi-level governance begin from the assumption that centralized government is not well-suited to accommodating diversity. Marks and Hooghe (2003) describe the emerging architecture of multi-level governance in the EU-27 as a system consisting of mainly two types of nested decision-making units (governance types), among which members and functions are divided (see Table 7.1). Federalistic elements of general purpose jurisdiction with non-intersecting memberships and only a few well-separated jurisdictional levels share a universal system-wide architecture (Type I). More variable elements of special purpose jurisdictions (Type II), with intersecting memberships across infinite numbers of jurisdictional levels but with non-intersecting tasks, complement this structure. Type II jurisdictions are nested in a more distinct Type I governance system. The combination of both types allows actors with different governance problems to flexibly adapt governance structures to problem particularities.

Table 7.1: Attributes and types of a multi-level governance system

	Governance types	
	Type I	Type II
Attributes	General purpose jurisdictions	Task-specific jurisdictions
	Non-intersecting membership	Intersecting memberships
	Limited number of governance levels	Unlimited number of decision making levels
	System-wide architecture	Flexible designs

Source: Marks and Hooghe (2003, p. 236), adapted

Confronted with a particular problem of non-private goods production, actors may decide to move away to another community in order to cope with an existing set of general services (general purpose jurisdictions) or to self-organize or demand additional service provision in the form of "special purpose jurisdictions". This concept is in line with Vincent Ostrom's polycentricity thesis, "[c]ompetitive public economies can emerge in highly federalized systems of government where substantial fragmentation and overlap exists among diverse government units" (Ostrom, 1994, p. 231), and with Hirschman's concepts of "exit, voice or loyalty"

(Hirschman, 1970)[2]. Polycentric governance may be analyzed as the outcome of multiple decision-making processes: "rational choices" among individual or collective actors. In multi-level governance structures, decision-making represents the trade-off between the costs of participating in the creation, and maintenance of an additional governance unit, and the cost of moving to a community in which a preferred combination of public services already exists (Williams, 1971, p. 29)[3]. In a fully polycentric system, the hope is that elements of representational self-organization (e.g., special districts) together with overlapping and co-operating or competing jurisdictions (Frey & Eichenberger, 1999) would improve the overall performance of the production of public services to an extent approximating the process of private goods production in a perfect-market environment. Normative statements about multi-level governance (if made) would have to be judged against this claim. Theoretical concepts of multi-level governance are applied to study governance problems in metropolitan areas where multiple jurisdictions often interact formally and informally with each other (Ostrom et al., 1961; Young, 1971; Orbell & Uno, 1972). Necessary background conditions for the application of a multi-level governance perspective are pretty demanding: local jurisdictions must have the authority to tax and residents should elect public managers by direct vote (Frey et al., 2004); spatially distributed choice alternatives among various communities and types of public goods and services should exist; households should be mobile (Tiebout, 1956); and an active civil society with rich capacities to self-organize should inhabit these communities (Ostrom, 1994, pp. 223–249). Where this is the case, decision making on the production or provision of some service (local expenditures) is relatively trivial. Regarding cases of insufficient service provision, for example, citizens may reveal their preferences to public managers by adopting communities which offer preferred services. Another solution is that citizens stay and, through various means of self-organization (voting, referendum, petition, association, special district), demand the production of preferred services. After successful self-organization, new service structures may become integrated in the overall public services system by being granted the right to self-tax their members (Frey & Eichenberger, 1999). Given a wide variety of competing self-organized service providers, together with a citizenry which is willing to either "make or move"[4], citizens may govern and governance in the absence of some unitary form of government (Peters & Pierre, 1998) may appear feasible.

---

[2] Theoretical concept derived from the work of Albert O. Hirschman (1980) which elaborates on two essential options in organizational decline, being exit and voice.

[3] Williams explains this idea thus: "There are essentially two options for those who wish to employ a location strategy to change their access within the urban complex. They can move or they can change the characteristics of the place they presently occupy."(1971, p. 29).

[4] I use the term "make or move" in analogy to Oliver Williamson's term "make or buy", which is often used by transaction cost theorists in order to characterize decisions about appropriate firm size (Williamson, 1990).

7.3 Theoretical Foundations

7.3.1 The Samuelsonian preference-shirking[5] dilemma

This view is in sharp contrast to Samuelson's influential paper "A Pure Theory of Public Expenditures" (Samuelson, 1954, p. 388), in which he laid the theoretical foundations for what is often called "the private-public sector dichotomy" (Sikor, 2008, pp. 89–106). According to Samuelson's theory, the main problem related to the production of non-private goods is for the public manager to assess residents' true willingness to pay for non-private services[6]. In the absence of a decentralized pricing mechanism, consumers of non-private goods have strong incentives to hide their true preferences for these goods in order to shift some of the production cost into the public domain. Thus, the production of non-private goods creates free-riding opportunities for rational players, with the result that efficient allocation of non-private resources appears to be difficult. Samuelson's prominent conclusion was often used to legitimize unitary government as some sort of a centralized mechanism to overcome the involved collective action dilemma and to bring public services not at optimal but at least to desired production levels. In Samuelson's own words: "No decentralized pricing system can serve to determine optimally these levels of collective consumption" (1954, p. 388).

7.3.2 Tiebout's spatial economy and the shopping tour metaphor

The theoretical foundations of all multi-level concepts of governance go back to Tiebout's (1956) reply to Samuelson, where he developed a theoretical solution to the problem Samuelson had raised, namely that public spending was necessarily inefficient. In his "A Pure Theory of Local Expenditures", the single most important mechanism through which consumers are "forced" to reveal their preferences for non-private goods is known as "the shopping tour metaphor". As Tiebout explained,

---

[5] I use the term "preference shirking" in analogy to the terms "output, input and quality shirking", as used in contract theory (Hayami & Otsuka, 1993).

[6] Samuelson (1954) explains his argument as follows: "One could imagine every person in the community being indoctrinated to behave like a 'parametric decentralized bureaucrat' who reveals his preferences by signaling in response to price parameters or Lagrangean multipliers, to questionnaires, or to other devices. But there is still this fundamental technical difference going to the heart of the whole problem of social economy: by departing from his indoctrinated rules, any one person can hope to snatch some selfish benefit in a way not possible under the self-policing competitive pricing of private goods; and the 'external economies' or 'jointness of demand' intrinsic to the very concept of collective goods."

just as the consumer may be visualized as walking to a private market place to buy his goods, the prices of which are set, we place him in the position of walking to a community where the prices (taxes) of community services are set. Both trips take the consumer to market. There is no way in which the consumer can avoid revealing his preferences in a spatial economy (1956, p. 422).

In the same way in which Samuelson's model points to a centralized authority, Tiebout's analogy allows him to promote a fully decentralized (spatial) architecture of metropolitan governance.

But the assumptions for Tiebout's model are by no means innocent. Here, the hands of local public managers are not bound by being at subordinated levels of a central authority. Local managers are authorized to levy taxes and invest; they are also free to develop entrepreneurial skills and compete with each other by offering alternative programs of public service production. They have all the incentives to do so, because they are directly elected by tax-paying community residents. In the respective metropolitan areas, a large variety of competing public-service offers exist, provoking residents to reveal their preferences while choosing at the "market for public services". In the words of Ostrom et al. (1961, p. 841): "If consumer-voters are fully mobile, the appropriate local governments, whose revenue-expenditure patterns are set, are adopted by the consumer-voters".

Tiebout (1956) was well aware of the rigid assumptions of his model of local government and restricted the analysis of his "spatial economy" to *metropolitan areas*. The same holds true for a later article of Ostrom et al. (1961). One of the reasons for this is that densely populated metropolitan areas may, under certain conditions, sufficiently approximate the shopping tour metaphor in which supply, not demand, drives the selection process. Interestingly, Tiebout claims that, the greater the number of communities in a region and the greater their variance, the closer the citizen will come to realizing allocative efficiency (Tiebout, 1956, p. 418).

7.3.3 Voice and loyalty as direct articulations of preferences

In Hirschman (1970), Orbell and Uno (1972), Ostrom (1972), and Ostrom and Ostrom (1994), the consumer-voter is offered more options to reveal preferences than in the Tiebout (1956) model. These authors highlight the role of self-organizing and co-productive capabilities of citizens as additional mechanisms by which preferences for non-private goods and services can be directly articulated. Not only moving away to another community (exit), but also active participation in the production process or in lobbying activities demanding particular services (voice) in a particular community, or the long-term acceptance of a tolerable level of production of non-private goods (loyalty) can be interpreted as mechanisms of preference articulation.

In Ostrom's theory of polycentric governance (Ostrom, 1972), voice is an expression of societies' self-organizing capacities. The better these capacities are developed, the more "governance without government" is realized and the better is the match between consumer-voter's preferences and a communities' given set of non-private goods and services (efficient allocation of non private goods). However, the social dilemma situation which led Samuelson to his seminal conclusion cannot be denied. The process of organizing collective action may be costly and may, therefore, be riddled by free-riding attempts and lack of incentives to participate. Hirschman (1980, p. 432) refers to this point as follows: "On the one hand, such participation is equivalent to expressing a demand for certain public policies, and since such public policies, once established, can be enjoyed or 'consumed' by everyone in the community, the demand for public policies has the earmarks of the demand for public goods". But Ostrom (1990) has convincingly demonstrated that many examples exist in which communities successfully overcome such social dilemma problems. Among other structural variables, a collective's ability to control and police individual contributions as well as to maintain clear boundaries of membership and eligibility are crucial for creating situations in which collectives can overcome such problems (Ostrom, 2005, pp. 199–201). Another equally important ingredient of successful collectives is the issue of voluntary entry and exit (Ostrom, 2005, p. 8). Starting from the assumption that exiting a particular situation is in general costless while voice is not, Hirschman (1980, p. 433) analyzes a situation in which voice is a preferred option over exit.

"If active concern with the public happiness can on occasion be felt as a benefit and as an important contribution to the private happiness rather than as a subtraction from it and as a cost, then voice will have an occasional edge over exit in those situations that clearly impinge on the public happiness. This means that voice can be expected to play a role in relation to those goods and in particular to those dimensions of goods and services that have a strong public interest component [...] the primary handicaps of voice in relation to exit will be reduced and, on occasion, eliminated".

Whether or not a particular good has "a strong public interest component" not only depends on the character of the good or service. Hagedorn and Hanisch (2005) have argued that the character of the involved actors and the character of the possible transactions between those actors will have consequences for the overall level of production of that good or service. The marginal contribution to the production of a non private good may be higher in close-knit communities in which reputation and mechanisms like ostracism and retaliation (Knight, 1992) may play their roles. Thus compared to metropolitan areas, the organization of "voice" may sometimes be comparatively cheaper in smaller, informally structured communities (Putnam, 1993, p. 165). In addition, spatial distance between settlements may serve as a natural boundary which enables exclusion of strangers and, thus, counteracts free-riding attempts of service consumers who do not live and contribute to collective goods production in the respective community.

7.3.4 Some preliminary conclusions

Concepts of multi-level governance deliver polycentric answers to the preference-articulation problem Samuelson has accurately described in his 1954 paper. Tiebout has hypothesized that the more communities per area exist, the better the competitive process between them should work. Other authors have claimed that – if citizens, be it for reasons of reduced household mobility or for other reasons – cannot be forced to reveal their preferences, other decentralized mechanisms of preference articulation may still work. Residents may show preferences through self-organization, lobbying or tolerating a given level of non-private goods production (loyalty).

7.4 Structural Problems of Rural Areas in the EU-27

As explained above, the theoretical preconditions for the applicability of these claims in densely populated metropolitan areas are pretty demanding. In this section, I highlight important features of rural areas in the EU-27, arguing that great disparities between living conditions in its metropolitan areas and those in its rural areas may put the applicability of multi-level governance concepts for rural areas into question. Consequently, multi-level governance may not be the expected governance mechanism resulting from ongoing rural-development processes. My list of structural problems below is neither meant to be complete nor very detailed. Following through on the arguments raised in the theory discussion above, the emphasis here is laid on relative terms and the comparison between rural areas and metropolitan areas (see Table 7.2), because most of the arguments in favor of multi-level governance concepts have been raised in a metropolitan context[7].

7.4.1 Population density

With the latest two rounds of enlargement in the years 2004 and 2006/7 (EU-15/ -27), 12 more countries joined the EU. While the overall size of rural areas in the EU almost doubled, the total amount of people living in rural areas increased by only 5% from 53 to 58 percent (EC, 2006, p. 30).

Rural areas in the European Union now comprise 93% of its territory and have a population density that is in general 40–60% below each national average (EC, 2005).

---

[7] This statement holds for Tiebout (1956) and the later papers of Ostrom, Tiebout and Warren (1961) and Ostrom (1972).

According to OECD standards, rural areas are classified into two categories "Predominantly Rural Areas (PRAs)" and "Significantly Rural Areas (SRAs)". The latter comprise 36% of the EU territory, the former 57% (EC, 2006, pp. 30–32). In SRAs, between 15 and 50% of the population lives in rural communities, whereas in PRAs over 50% of the population lives in rural communities. These categories and figures already indicate that more than half of the European population lives in some sort of rural community. Across the 27 diversely populated EU member countries, 57% of the territory is populated by, on average, only 39 inhabitants per square kilometer (EC, 2006). As a consequence, EU enlargement has led to a substantial increase in remote and loosely populated rural areas.

7.4.2 Unemployment and rural migration

Migration of the younger segments of the labor force away from rural areas is a widespread but not generalizable phenomenon (NIAE, 2004; EC, 2007, p. 2). Relatively high unemployment rates and, in comparison to urban areas, a higher proportion of elderly residents characterize most of the countryside of the new member states of the EU (NIAE, 2004; EU, 2007, p. 2). Thus, moving might not only express preferences towards particular packages of public services. Moving might as well represent a "nothing to lose" reality for young people who have not yet invested in housing or having their own family. In addition, consumer-voter mobility may not only reveal preferences for public goods and services. Preferences for private services might be equally involved in residents' decision making.

7.4.3 Weak service sectors and lower household income

In the majority of the EU-27 countries, the level and quality of public services is generally lower in rural areas than in urban ones. Service provision in rural areas is dominated by publicly managed industries, whereas in metropolitan areas private industries dominate (EC, 2006, p. 20; EU, 2007, p. 1). Many people who live in rural regions of the New Member States, and especially those in Predominantly Rural Areas, are poor as judged by the level of GDP per capita, relative to the standards of the EU-15. Some are living under conditions of extreme poverty, particularly in Latvia, Romania and Bulgaria (NIAE, 2004). There is generally a wide disparity between the incomes of those who live in cities and those who live in rural regions. The per capita income of PUA`s is almost double that of Predominantly Rural Areas (EC, 2007, p. 2). But also within the rural areas of the rest of Europe, the absolute distribution of income between rural dwellers is less equal than in metropolitan areas (NIAE, 2004). In the same way as low income may foster migration, low household income may constrain household mobility, because larger proportions of income are invested in rural real estate, the prices of which often vary with proximity to metropolitan areas.

7.4.4 Lower educational standards

The quality of rural education in the new member states is reported to be, in general, lower than in the larger towns and cities, due to difficulties in attracting teachers, worse school equipment, less access to information technology, few special schools and, finally, budget-crisis problems in the public sectors (NIAE, 2004). With only a few exceptions, the quality of other typically public services (hospitals, kindergartens, public transport, police) is also lower in rural areas as compared to urban ones. A large proportion of the labor force either commutes to urban areas or works in agriculture (EU, 2006). Lower educational standard may create additional constraints on household mobility in rural areas, because rural dwellers may become disadvantaged on the labor market.

7.4.5 Budget crises, ageing and low tax revenues

Public infrastructure is one of the key factors fostering rural development (NIAE, 2004). However, budget crises in rural communities have been a widespread phenomenon throughout the EU. In some areas, a vicious cycle is already in place whereby poor infrastructure induces migration which, in turn, further reduces the tax base and a community's future opportunities to attract money from outside. The Network of Independent Agricultural Experts (NIAE, 2004) refers to this point as follows:

"Stated by more than one country are the ageing of the population and migration, which may prove to be a vicious circle, the low absorption of structural funds because of problems in mobilizing own financial resources, the lack of required reforms, the further decline in traditional agriculture and industry and finally, the further marginalization of remote areas and growing disparities".

7.4.6 Lack of authority to levy taxes

Frey et al. (2004) observe that European public managers of service units often do not have the *power to tax* citizens for the functions they perform. As a consequence, local politicians have to engage in widespread rent-seeking activities with the central administration or in the application of project funds from external sources[8]. In many cases, they have to please political decision makers on a higher level to obtain funds. Once funds are granted, they have few incentives not to spend them completely and to thus waste them, as such funds have the character of a "free good" (Frey et al., 2004, p. 10). For rural areas, it can be assumed that public managers are even less powerful vis-à-vis central-level decision makers than their metropolitan colleagues. As rural politicians, they bargain on the basis of a comparatively smaller political support base (electorate). In service areas in which local decision makers have the authority to tax, the shape of the production function for non-private goods comes into play (Kollock, 1998, p. 190). In situations in which the number of taxpayers (consumer-voters) is relatively small, while increasing returns to scale characterize the production process; it is thus unlikely that rural public managers can offer public good at qualities and prices competitive to their colleagues in metropolitan areas. As a consequence, in a situation in which service providers have to realize economies of scale in order to be competitive, the market mechanism generates fewer service centers in rural areas than around larger agglomerations of tax payers. This becomes a self-enforcing mechanism of rural centralization (not decentralization) in which not only consumer-voters adopt service providing communities, but also one in which relevant service-industries adopt agglomerations of consumers. Given that the provision of services at a competitive level of taxation may often have to do with the prior realization of scale economies, once it has started to gain momentum, it may not be easy to turn a local downwards trend in public revenues and service provision around. A process of the continuous growth and concentration of public service industries, first in the form of regional service centers and later from rural to peri-urban and urban areas, may be the result (Frey et al., 2004, p. 12). Remaining rural residents are then confronted with the closing down of more and more services such as hospitals, schools, kindergartens and police, as the concentration of those services into just a few regional service-centers proceeds.

7.4.7 Disparities between metropolitan and rural areas

Table 7.2 summarizes most of the salient differences between rural and metropolitan communities in the EU-27. Where such differences characterize the rural/metropolitan divide, "exit" might not be a viable option for all, but rather the younger players only. In the same vein and in the presence of migration, it is questionable to simply assume that in such rural areas the self-organizing capacities of the players ("voice") may suffice to bring about needed services at desirable production costs and levels. Finally, it is not adequate to interpret for example elderly,

---

[8] For example, the LEADER initiative offered various opportunities for rural players to attract outside money.

less educated or poorer rural dwellers' "reluctance to move" as "loyalty", in a Hirschmanian sense.

Table 7.2: Main differences between rural and metropolitan areas in the EU-27

	Rural areas	Metropolitan areas
No. of consumers/km2	Small (e.g. 10–200/km2)	Large (e.g. 1000–4000/km^2)
Income/tax revenue	Lower	2x Higher
Service infrastructure like: Health, transport, sport	Weak	Good
Main income opportunities	Few (Agriculture, tourism)	Many
Education/information	Worse	Better
Labor market	Weak	Better
Cost of moving	Higher	Lower
Service quality	Worse	Better
Service alternatives	Few	Many

Source: Complied from EC (2006, pp. 30–32), EC (2007, pp. 1–3), NIAE-Group (2004)

Extending the Tiebout model to rural areas means, then, accepting the idea that the wish to live and work in rural areas represents a preferred lifestyle of a subset of actors in society. Thus, living in rural areas is to be treated as a matter of tastes and as one out of many other preferences for which, at least in part, the choice alternatives and service advantages of more densely populated areas are purposefully given up. Conflicting preferences, like a rural lifestyle combined with the wish to achieve higher income or receive better education or health services, may materialize in the form of commuting to work, living in suburbs, acceptance of having to travel longer distances before reaching medical care, or it may materialize as moving to the city while maintaining a weekend house at the countryside.

One theoretical conclusion of this premise would be that, by definition, rural areas can either be expected to be less price-competitive than metropolitan areas, which generates the scenario of a stepwise concentration process of service production around larger agglomerations of consumers. Or, another interpretation would be that rural inhabitants voluntarily forego the benefits of cheaper metropolitan services because they have different sets of preferences with regard to non private goods production. Both explanations may be valid, but will not cover all reasons for rural residency. The important aspect here is that it is changeable interpretations which decide on the right governance structures for non-private goods production in rural areas. Interestingly, if the spatial economy model works and economies of scale exist, competition between rural and metropolitan communities (not a central authority!) will concentrate resources around metropolitan agglomerations of consumers.

The problem with Tiebout´s spatial economy is that residents who move away can no longer express their preferences in the community they have left. Thus competition of preferences within the community or competition between different packages of services will have to take place on the level of local political agendas. Without having a choice within one particular community, for the individual the process of preference articulation will rely on political representation. After elections are held, a minority of unsatisfied consumer-voters would always have to move. A different mechanism (organization) through which the revelation of alternative tastes for non-private services within one and the same community, the discovery of true individual willingness to pay for these services and exit opportunities *within* the community are linked would be desirable.

7.5 Empowerment: Strengthening Self-Organizing Capacities of Rural Communities, but How?

Up to now, I have concentrated on the structural problems in European rural areas and on the likely impact these problems will have on the feasibility of applying the concept of multi-level rural governance there. Tiebout's model of a spatial economy and the shopping tour metaphor have been helpful for understanding the conditions under which multiple levels of decision making may improve local public service provision. But the problem with the multi-level governance model is that the production of non-private goods and services is often subject to scale economies and boundary problems. Where this is the case, rural communities as compared to metropolitan communities will offer less variety and lower quality of services, because the level of competition in a certain area as well the expectable total budget for local expenditures will depend on the number of residents and their tax payments, which is likely to be smaller in rural areas. This argument gains additional momentum in the presence of the structural problems which at the moment characterize rural areas in the new member states of the EU-27 (see Table 7.2). As I will explain below mechanisms of voice and self-organization seem to be better suited to addressing the current problems of rural governance in the EU than the mechanism of exit in a spatial mobility model. The question is than how to bring self-organizing capabilities about?

Contemporary decision-makers in the EU-27 are well aware of the above-described developments: the increasing influence of ideas of multi-level governance in the EU rural policy debate (EU White Paper on Governance, 2001, Frey et al., 2004); the widening urban-rural disparities; and the local budget crises and increasingly disintegrating public service infrastructure in many of the rural areas of the member states. Growing problem awareness has triggered a renewed emphasis on rural community development and "bottom-up" initiatives in the rural development debate (Goodwin, 2004). The "empowerment" of communities and active citizens has been promoted in the EU Cork Declaration[9] – which states that rural

---

[9] The European Conference on Rural Development met in Cork in 1996. The outcome was a ten-point program on European rural development, agreed upon by stakeholders and decision

policy must be "as decentralized as possible", based on rural partnerships and co-operation between public and private organizations (European Conference on Rural Development, EC, 2007, p. 11). Development schemes such as the LEADER I, II, and LEADER + prioritize partnerships and now demand participation of community representatives in order for a partnership to win, or even take part in, the bidding process for receiving project money. Policies reflect the appreciation of the idea that, in times of scarce resources, neither exit nor competition between communities can reduce migration and stabilize rural areas, but rather only through self-organization and the organization of "voice", which is to say achieving a better match between local preferences and provided services. The hope is that funds from the private sector will co-produce public efforts. A coalition between the public sector and local private organizations should improve the responsiveness of local service provision to local preferences. Missing funds are being partially covered by EU project funding and the initiative of local partnerships between private and public counterparts. Among other authors[10], Goodwin (2004, p. 17) criticizes the actual practice of forming these "initiated partnerships" and the often inadequate representation of community members in them, offering the following observation: "Often however, this [community representation] can amount to little more than the co-option of key individuals. In fact 'the community' representative is often chosen from a 'representative' organization – the local authority itself in some cases, local voluntary associations or even the chamber of commerce – rather than from the community itself. The substance of community involvement is variable [...]. As such, it could be argued that the much vaunted 'community engagement' is simply used by many partnerships as a 'resource' which must be enrolled and demonstrated in order to secure funding [...]. This in turn raises questions as to who is being 'empowered', and for what ends? [...] Moreover, the ways in which these practices are developing are raising interesting questions about how partnerships might be made more democratic and produce more effective participation."

In the meantime, a growing concern about an outsider-expert and elite bias in the emerging community partnerships has been raised because members of the communities are not always willing to participate. In other cases, outsiders and experts formulate development goals and community strategies. For example, of the one hundred and fifty-four rural partnerships analyzed by Edwards, Goodwin, Pemberton and Woods (2000), only two listed "the community" as one of their active partners. Goodwin (2004, p. 16) states that, because of a lack of time in preparing bids (project applications) it is not members of a particular community,

---

makers. In point number 10 it is stated that: "The administrative capacity and effectiveness of regional and local governments and community-based groups must be enhanced, where necessary, through the provision of technical assistance, training, better communications, partnership and the sharing of research, information and exchange of experience through networking between regions and between rural communities throughout Europe".

[10] Cavazzani and Moseley (2001) critically compare the results of 24 intensive case studies of rural partnerships in six European countries.

but rather representatives of "community organizations" who are often asked to take positions as "representatives of their local communities". Where this is so, policy-induced partnerships may have little to do with empowerment of local actors and the desired vitalization of self-organization capacities. To the contrary, such partnerships may even override existing grass-root initiatives of local self-help, and the money influx from outside may outcompete long-standing local activities, generating dependencies and unequal power relations (Post, 2002).

Another outcome of community partnership-oriented development strategies in the EU-27 is an emerging, uneven geographical patterns of partnership-rich versus partnership-poor structures (Goodwin, 2004, p. 20), where partnership-rich regions have advantages in applying for follow-up activities. Because competition takes place among members of the applying consortiums, neither a communal voting mechanism nor some other mechanism involving the revelation of preferences of community inhabitants regarding the financed measures is involved. In other words, more and more application-experienced groupings of private-sector managers, public sector managers, project consultants and planners are competing with one another for EU project funding, based on criteria open to interpretation and set by EU bureaucracies. Little can be said about the responsiveness of such measures to local preferences and their relative performance vis-à-vis possible alternatives that are not implemented.

The above discussion shows that political efforts to stimulate citizen participation and self-organization may reach non-sustainable or even counterproductive results. The reasons are manifold. Frey et al. (2004) argue that preconditions for the functioning of a multi-level system of European governance included that service providers possess the power to levy taxes, that residents pay directly for what they consume as well as elect public managers, and that fair competition between communities exists. Any political undertaking in favor of a multi-level governance approach will have to take these preconditions into account. European decision makers have inhaled the ideas of multi-level governance, active community participation and decentralized governance. However, the ways in which policies are applied seem to have little to do with these ideas.

7.6 Governance Without Government in Rural Areas

7.6.1 Foundations

Frey et al. (2004, p. 20) compare their vision of multi-level governance (FOCJ) with historical forerunners in the Holy Roman Empire or competing structures between nation states at the end of the 19th century. With regard to rural governance, it may be rewarding to look at the history of non-private goods production at the local level: how did rural residents historically deal with the Samuelsonian dilemma of preference articulation?

"Governance without government" has not really been a "new concept" for most of the rural communities in the EU-27. In the same sense in which one could claim that farmers have always been "organic farmers" prior to the invention of chemical fertilizers, at the end of the 19th century, prior to the emergence of specialized exchange economies[11], the history of non-private goods production in rural areas is one of self-organization. As such, one could argue that relying on self-organizing capabilities instead of relying on local government lies at the heart of any concept of rurality (Cloke et al. 1997). In fact, in rural areas of the EU-27 and the US there is a strong tradition of self-organization among rural dwellers (farmers and rural craftsmen)[12]. Apart from organizing market access to machinery, agricultural supplies and products, associations based on membership and democratic rule have often managed to collectively organize various types of services like telecommunication, insurance and health care, credit and microfinance. Thus, since the second half of the nineteenth century, free co-operative associations have pioneered the provision of most important rural services for their members, but also for the communities in which they operate. Today, most co-operatives are part of complex, multi-tiered member-owned network structures that combine a diverse set of functions and services, such as social services and elder care, rural finance, insurance, consumer services, processing, transportation, rural supplies, agricultural extension, recreation, water, forest and land management, hunting grounds, regional labeling and education.

Initiated by a "social movement" during the period between 1850 and 1930, co-operative networks emerged in countries like France, Germany, Italy, England, Austria, Switzerland, Denmark, Norway, Holland, Sweden and Finland. The decisive contribution these co-operative systems made to the development of rural economies across Europe and the USA is well documented (Fairbairn, 1994; Clark, 1943; Guinnane, 2001). Even compared to mass movements such as European unionism and the larger social democratic movements of that period, the co-operative movement is considered to be the largest social movement in Europe (Fairbairn, 1994, p. 4).

In order to better understand rural governance problems and organizational change in the rural areas of Europe, one has to understand the factors that constitute the leading role self-organizing capabilities once played for economic development during the co-operative movement era and those factors responsible for

---

[11] The term "specialized exchange economy" is borrowed from Ronald Coase's "The nature of the firm" (1937. p. 390). The concept denotes the division of labor between sectors, such as the public and the private, and the division of labor among branches and subsectors. Specialization affords exchange and generates the problem of social cost, which is a dominant subject of his later oeuvre (Coase, 1960).

[12] After the Second World War, in some of the New Member States from Central and Eastern Europe, these traditions were broken up by the transformation of market economies into soviet-type economies (Todev, Rönnebeck, & Brazda, 1994).

their reduced roles in a specialized exchange economy today. Once this has been understood, the potential role of policy-led initiatives for the multi-level governance of problems related to rural development in the EU-27 can be better assessed.

7.6.2 A stylized historical model: collective rural entrepreneurship

The key to understanding why co-operatives became so actively involved in the development of their communities lies in an understanding of the institutional context of their formation. Let us imagine a simplified model of a historical rural community in Europe in which, apart from a basic school and a church, no public services exist. Let us further assume that in the mid-eighteen hundreds in that community, between 80 and 90% of the population lived mainly from subsistence-oriented agriculture (Henkel, 2004). As a result, local tax revenue in our model community may be considered low. In the larger cities of that time, service provision is slightly better in that hospitals and some public transportation may exist. Rural household income varies with stochastic events such as droughts, pests, floods and the like. Some simplified assumptions about household mobility may add to that characterization: In the western world, the cost of mobility has continuously dropped over the last 100 years (Tullock, 1967, p. 77), so it is reasonable to assume that voting with one's feet had a relatively more substantial price some hundred years ago. Decisions, such as moving along with the household to some other area, take the form of "once in a lifetime" events.

Let us further assume that it is not only with regard to public services that the situation is unsatisfactory. At some "proto-capitalistic market-end" of private service provision, the situation is not much better. In the countryside, market failure results in either monopolistic or inferior quality private services: think, for example, of usurers as representative of the private financial services sector, quack-doctors in the area of private health services and tinkerers[13], instead of well educated engineers, as being widespread phenomena (Faust, 1965).

In Germany, for example, following the institutional liberalization of individual choice of profession and the freeing of the peasantry from relations of medieval servitude *(Gewerbefreiheit, Bauernbefreiung)*, exchange, investment and specialization in the rural economy became increasingly riskier than operating among guild-members, family members, neighbors, clan structures or religious groupings. As a consequence of the rather poor economy, village or community mayors were endowed with relatively few resources (tax revenue) for offering preferred communal services to the members of their community. In a nutshell: In this early version of a rural public economy, actors found themselves in a situation in which specialization was risky and access to outside markets costly, and most of what is today called "community services" were missing.

---

[13] Tinkerer here means a clumsy repairer or worker, a meddler.

Table 7.3: Governance by co-operative principles versus multi-level governance

Rules/purpose	Governance	
	Co-operative Principles	Multi-Level Rural Governance
Entry/Access	Voluntary, Open	Voluntary, Open
Fees, Contributions/ Tax basis	Membership	Membership self-taxing
Benefits	Exclusive	Exclusive
Representation	"One man one vote"	Direct democracy
Specialization	Specialized or Multi-Purpose	Specialized or Multi-Purpose
Organizational Levels	3 Tiers: local-regional-central	As many as needed
Competition	No	Yes, if not voted against
Scale Economies	Yes	Yes
Ownership	Collectively owned private entity	Publicly owned, public jurisdiction

Source: Principles in the version of 1844, Ostrom (1972), Marks and Hooghe (2003), Frey et al. (2004), Birchall (2005)

Returning to our model, village residents predominantly live from subsistence agriculture and may choose between staying in the village, moving to some other village or moving into a city. Given the financial and educational constraints at the countryside, joining some low-income industrial labor force (for example, mining in hilly regions) or emigrating is the likely alternative to staying in the village or town[14]. In this rather extreme model, the role of rural government is quite limited, because taxable income, if any, remains low. "Governance without government" is, in this situation, not a desired outcome, but rather a consequence of immature institutional and market development. This does not, however, mean that local government is inactive. Tight budget constraints on public management create incentives for the rural mayors to either leave or to actively promote the local self-organization of whatever service industry serves best to stabilize the incomes of rural residents (Hanisch, 2006, p. 12)[15]. Historically, these conditions gave rise to a new type of self-help association among rural dwellers: the modern co-operative. Looking at the organizational principles of rural co-operatives[16] reveals some

[14] Rural poverty in Europe at the end of the nineteenth century is well documented in Tagungsbericht Armut und ländliche Gesellschaft (2006), while poverty in contemporary Europe is discussed in Buchenrieder and Knüpfer. (2002, pp. 353–364).

[15] The initiators of the German co-operative movements are reported to have been mainly civil servants, such as small town mayors (Friedrich Wilhelm Raiffeisen), district judges, members of parliament (Hermann Schulze-Delitzsch), or police chiefs (Haas).

[16] The principles of the famous "equitable pioneers of Rochdale" or the principles of the first version of the German Co-operative Law of 1868 describe similar features regarding co-operative self-help associations, according to which a co-operative is an autonomous

similarities to the organizational principles suggested by contemporary proponents of the multi-level governance concept and by scholars of collective action theory (see Table 7.3).

In the subsistence-oriented economy of our example, farmers mainly produce what their families consume and, without further access to markets, forego gains from specialization and scale. Given some homogeneity of village residents' needs, agricultural services to improve household income may represent an almost perfect match between villagers' private and public interests (storage, processing, machinery, rural credit, rural supplies, transportation, communication or crop insurance) and afford collective investments. Farmers manage to vertically integrate production, investment for services and processing and market-price risks into one and the same type of membership organization, such as the rural supplies co-operative; in Germany an example would be the Raiffeisen Warehouse Co-operative[17]. Those village residents not willing to pay for such services had the option to simply refuse membership in the co-operative.

7.6.3 Democratic governance and membership as surrogates for competitive pricing

The organization of dairy co-operatives is a prominent example of how such coops work (Bonus, 1986). Farmers do not integrate farms by merging their entire businesses into one production unit, but prefer instead to choose a more federal governance type that combines the advantages of farming independently with the advantages of producing and consuming services collectively in one larger unit (scale economies). Because investments on both sides (on farm and in the dairy) are highly specific and, therefore, subject to hold-up problems (Williamson, 1975) member-user ownership solves a dilemma which would otherwise likely prevent necessary investments from being undertaken. Once input and extension services have accomplished a stabilization of member-household production, finding profitable ways for marketing excess production becomes the dominant task of the dairy management. Both issues, stabilizing production and linking members to new marketing channels, are interconnected.

Up to now, the model shares most of the features discussed by proponents of the club theory (Buchanan, 1965; Olson, 1965; Sandler & Tschirhart, 1980). Membership is open or closed. Depending on the type of co-operative, goods and

---

association of persons united voluntarily to meet their common economic, social, and cultural needs and aspirations through a jointly-owned and democratically-controlled enterprise (Birchall, 2005).

[17] Until today, co-operative warehouses, credit unions and rural supply associations dominate the agricultural input markets in countries like Germany, the US or Austria.

services are impure or pure public goods. The co-operative may, then, be inclusive or become exclusive over time.

In their decision to become co-operators, rural dwellers compare their situation without a co-operative with their situation as a member, assessing benefits versus marginal cost of membership before joining a coop. Note, given the previously described market imperfections, it is incorrect to speak of a competitive price for service provision because, in our simple model, the coop is a pioneer organization and competing services do not yet exist. Villagers articulate their preferences for non-private co-operative services by means of their membership decision and related individual contributions to service production. Adjustments to norms of exchange (prices) are made on the basis of general assemblies and institutionalized voting procedures.

Apart from "voting with one's feet", the principle of voluntary association offers an additional mechanism of preference revelation within a rural community: So long as additional members generate benefits for the incumbent membership, co-operative management is forced (by consumer-voter control) to offer services which follow the preferences of existing members and potential members (in order to attract them). Membership fees or any other contribution to service provision adequately represents the preferences of a variable membership. Democratic decision-making creates a direct link between preferences and fees, so that in this situation the co-operative serves as a self-taxing mechanism of internal pricing, a "surrogate" for a market for rural services.

Compared to other mechanisms, the co-operative club has advantages. The co-operative benefits from local knowledge about individual talents (screening), trustworthiness of its members (reputation), pooled investment risks and liabilities[18] and pre-tested self-organizing capabilities derived from existing modes of rural religious, cultural, or professional associations (Putnam, 1993, p. 163).

7.6.4 The rise and decline of co-operative associations

Where the co-operative is successful, members benefit, and rising household income may generate a future basis for the community to develop publicly organized services on the basis of taxes. Collective entrepreneurship, on the basis of an agreed-upon internal pricing mechanism for co-operative services, in a situation in

---

[18] For example because locals know best about the qualities of the people they live with, a self-organized micro-credit system is suitable for internalizing the credit risk that an outsider organization would otherwise have to bear. In the early credit associations of the Raiffeisen type in Germany, members were jointly responsible and indefinitely liable for each credit granted. This strategy eliminated a considerable amount of the cost of credit risk and, thereby, avoided dealing with the established system of middlemen and usurers (Guinnane, 2001).

which no other pricing mechanism exists generates valuable knowledge about the value of crucial resources for entrepreneurial activities.

Co-operatives are known to have generated the first functional (because democratically agreed upon) business plans for rural service industries. Successful co-operatives have served as blueprints for successor organizations and opened up new opportunities for the development of both competitors, in the form of privately organized services, and the public service industry. After members of the community have revealed their preferences via self-organizing service production, public managers from within the community or from outside may consider the creation of public service industries on a similar price-cost scheme[19]. Because open access to membership is an organizing principle of co-operative organization, the relevant information about price-cost ratios "spills over" and becomes a local public good. Co-operatives may therefore be understood as mechanisms for groups in a particular community to reveal their preferences, just in the same way as the shopping tour metaphor works in the Tiebout model. The difference is that co-operatives "take consumers to the co-operative" in a situation in which the costs of mobility or lobbying politicians may be considered very high. Internal pricing on the basis of democratic decision making (not competition) and "willingness to join" were the mechanism that created the substance of the co-operative movement and, therewith, community development in the rural areas of Europe and America at the end of the 19th century, in a situation in which both private-service market development and the development of public services are in their infancy.

Under certain conditions, then, the mechanism of co-operative association may be considered as a surrogate for a market: when "the cost of using the price mechanism"[20] outside the co-operative is too high, either because communities are dispersed and the cost of mobility is high – because population density does not allow for many competing service industries existing in parallel – or because information about the reliability of community members is costly to process for potential investors from outside.

This interpretation neatly tallies with the transaction cost theory of the firm (Coase, 1937), in which the comparative cost of using the price mechanism (the

---

[19] There are many examples of co-operatives which have developed into public service industries. In Germany, the organization of dams at the German coast provides a good example of such a development in which local co-operatives have, over time, developed into special purpose associations (Zweckverbände). The emergence of private dairies and rural supply firms may serve as an example of informational spillovers which fostered the organization of private services in rural areas.

[20] The cost of using the price mechanism is Coase´s main argument for the existence of firms: "The main reason why it is profitable to establish a firm would seem to be that there is a cost of using the price mechanism. The most obvious cost of 'organizing' production through the price mechanism is that of discovering what the relevant prices are. This cost may be reduced but it will not be eliminated by the emergence of specialists who will sell this information" (1937, p. 390).

market) is the reason why entrepreneurs choose to organize transactions in hierarchical structures (within the firm). However, looking at the formation of co-operatives from a multi-level governance perspective allows us to explain the importance of the co-operative association for rural development in Europe as well as for many other places in the world where neither markets nor public services exist in meaningful ways. At the same time, this perspective offers a dynamic explanation for the disappearance of co-operatives over time that goes hand in hand with the development of what Coase has called "specialized exchange economies" (1937, p. 390). Once members of a rural community have successfully established service industries on the basis of open and democratic member associations, information spillover effects occur, with the preferences of this group regarding services and prices being revealed and becoming local public information. Without other competitors, service provision takes the form of a regional monopoly, controlled by consumer-voters who are at the same time the owners of the enterprise. Note that, without competition in this model, free entrance and the revealed willingness to join the coop ensure that consumers do benefit from established cost price ratios (Tullock, 1967, p. 77)[21]. So long as there is no alternative mode of service provision, consumers will join the coop until the per-member cost of contributing to service provision exceeds the individual benefit from service availability. The logic here is "better some service than no service". The "size of the club" then depends on the form of the production function of the service produced (Kollock, 1998, p. 190). If economies of scale and stages in the production function are at stake, incentives for sizeable service industry formation may exist (Kollock, 1998, p. 190). Where this process has begun, benefits from collective action emerge and the community becomes wealthier. Political or private entrepreneurs may now use the co-operative price-cost scheme as an organizational blueprint for non-self-organized forms of service industries (public corporations, shareholder value-oriented firms). Thus, outside observers of the goings on of the co-operative model receive for free what would otherwise be costly: the most valuable information about available techniques, risk management, needed managerial skills, more or less talented employees, price-cost ratios and preferences of local residents. This spillover effect lowers risks for other models of organization that are not co-operative-based. The more alternatives emerge, the better the market price mechanism works. At the same time, the reason for organizing services in the particular form of a collective, risk-minimizing, democratically governed local service mo-

---

[21] In his geographical ice-cream truck model of monopolistic competition, Tullock (1967, p. 72) compares three optima: monopolistic competition, coop and competitive market. He concludes that, in the presence of competition, only the monopolistic competition optimum reaches a socially desirable allocation of ice-cream trucks along some road in a spatial economy of ice cream consumers who reside along this road. The reason is that, otherwise, either one truck for any ice consumer or an almost non-computable price system differentiating the utilities of various coop members which live at different distances from the co-operatively owned ice cream truck would be necessary to satisfy some criteria of Pareto-optimality within a co-operative.

nopoly becomes obsolete, because valuable information about how to organize, which services at what cost is generated as a spillover. Because, according to the theory of the firm, some sort of more or less functional market usually produces this type of information (Williamson, 1975), the co-operative appears to be an alternative mechanism of pricing – a market surrogate and pioneer enterprise.

7.7 Conclusions

In this paper, I have analyzed the structural problems of the rural areas in the EU-27. My aim has been to explore constraints on rural governance and the validity of the multi-level governance concept, especially the ways in which it is being applied to rural areas. Without the element of self-organization, the promise of multi-level governance for the rural areas of the EU-27 remains obscure. But the capacity to self-organize cannot simply be assumed as a given or be easily politically implemented in rural areas. At a time of budget crises in many communities of the EU-27, it is reasonable to assume that public and private service industries will have to stepwise pull out. Where this is the case, conditions similar to those in the rural areas of Europe some hundred years ago may apply, in which communities are dispersed over sizeable, loosely populated territory, the costs of mobility are high and educational, employment and income opportunities differ greatly from metropolitan areas. In such situations, the scope for promotion of civil society development or self-help by means of policy intervention is limited. Likewise, the validity of the concept of multi-level governance for rural areas in the presence of these structural problems in the EU-27 is limited.

Surely, the preferences of the rural dwellers of today will largely differ from those of their ancestors some 150 years ago. However, multi-level governance, rightly understood, means that residents should be enabled to self-determine the scale and level on which they intend to approach a particular problem (special purpose jurisdiction). In the face of budget crises, it is not the residents but rather important branches of public services (hospitals, police departments, elderly care) that might be the first to be relocated or consolidated in larger settlements. The remaining residents are often left with the decision to self-organize these services on a scale that best suits them or to move. One problem is that, in the face of shrinking or ageing communities, existing public service industries may prevail but may no longer provide services at tolerable fees. In many of the European countries, communal services are organized in the form of special purpose associations *(Zweckverbände)*. These are frequently protected by law and represent local monopolies.

One way to motivate self organization is, then, to "institutionally liberalize" alternative ways to produce rural services. This means opening up possibilities for rural dwellers to challenge the price worthiness of existing communal services by self-organizing important services. The historical example of nineteenth century

Germany has shown that giving people a choice may unleash hitherto unknown self-organizing capabilities. Recent examples of this phenomenon in the areas of land development, privatization of schools, local energy plants, wastewater management and the self-management of formerly communal recreational facilities show that the self-organization of typically communal services in the form of rural co-operative associations can pay off (Eisen, 2002). In such cases, co-operatives once again represent self-organized mechanisms of preference articulation and pricing in situations in which neither markets nor public service industries satisfy consumer-voters' needs. Contemporary constraints on rural governance in the EU-27 may well generate renewed interest in and re-examination of a prominent instance of self-organization which solved basic problems of rural governance in Europe some 150 years ago.

References

Birchall, J. (2005). Co-operative principles ten years on. *Review of International Co-operation, 98*, 45–63.

Bonus, H. (1986). The cooperative association as a business enterprise: A study in the economics of transactions. *Volkswirtschaftliche Diskussionsbeiträge, 81*, Münster: Institut für Genossenschaftswesen.

Buchanan, J. M. (1965). An economic theory of clubs. *Economica, New Series, 32*, 1–14.

Buchenrieder, G., & Knüpfer, J. (2002). Ländliche Armut in Transformationsökonomien: Wirtschaften ohne ausserlandwirtschaftliches Einkommen. In M. Brockmeier et al. (Eds), *Liberalisierung des Weltagrarhandels: Strategien und Konsequenzen* (pp. 353–364). Münster-Hiltrup: Landwirtschaftsverlag.

Cavazzani, A., & Moseley, M. (Eds.). (2001). *The practice of rural development partnerships in Europe: 24 case studies in six European countries*. Soveria Mannelli: Rubbettino.

Clark, L. (1943). Credit unions in the United States. *The Journal of Business of the University of Chicago, 16*, 235–246.

Cloke, P., Milbourne, P., & Thomas, C. (1997). Living lives in different ways? Deprivation, marginalization and changing lifestyles in rural England. Transactions of the Institute of British Geographers, New Series, 22, 210–230.

Coase, R. (1937). The nature of the firm. *Economica, 4*, 386–405.

Coase, R. (1960). The problem of social cost. *Journal of Law and Economics, 3*, 1–44.

Edwards, B., Goodwin, M., Pemberton, S., & Woods, M. (2000). *Partnership working in rural regeneration*. Bristol: Policy Press.

Eisen, A. (2002). Die Genossenschaft ist ein Zukunftsmodell: Neue Genossenschaften und neue Perspektiven für genossenschaftliche Lösungen. In M. Hanisch (Ed.), *Genossenschaftsmodelle zwischen Auftrag und Anpassung* (pp. 201–218). Berlin: Institut für Genossenschaftswesen.

European Commission. (2005). *Fact sheet: New perspectives for EU rural development*. Brussels: European Commission, from http://ec.europa.eu/agriculture/publi/fact/index_en.htm.

European Commission. (2006). Employment in rural areas: Closing the jobs gap. Communication from the Commission to the Council and the European Parliament. EC Reference: COM (2006) 857 final, Brussels, from: http://ec.europa.eu/agriculture/ publi/reports/ ruralemployment/com857_en.pdf.

European Commission. (2007). Territorial agenda of the European Union: Towards a more sustainable and competitive Europe of diverse regions, from: www.cor.europa.eu/ COR_cms/ui/ViewDocument.aspx?siteid=default&contentID=4c3c41dc-7d16-48fd-87f-a8317c0f3667

Fairbairn, B. (1994). History from the ecological perspective: Gaia theory and the problem of cooperatives in turn-of-the-century Germany. *The American Historical Review, 99,* 1203–1239.

Faust, H. (1965). *Geschichte der Genossenschaftsbewegung: Ursprung und Weg der Genossenschaften im deutschen Sprachraum.* Frankfurt am Main: Knapp.

Frey, B. S., & Eichenberger, R. (1999). *The new democratic federalism for Europe: Functional, overlapping and competing jurisdictions.* Cheltenham and Northampton: Edward Elgar.

Frey, B. S., Luechinger, S., & Stutzer, A. (2004). *Valuing public goods: The life satisfaction approach.* Working Paper No. 184, University of Zurich, Institute for Empirical Research in Economics.

Goodwin, M. (2004). *Rural governance: A review of relevant literature.* Paper prepared for ESRC, Countryside Agency and DEFRA. Institute of Geography and Earth Sciences.

Guinnane, T. W. (2001). Cooperatives as information machines: German rural credit cooperatives, 1883–1914. *The Journal of Economic History, 61,* 366–389.

Hagedorn, K., & Hanisch, M. (2005, August). *Institutions of sustainability and the concept of integrative and segregative institutions.* Paper presented at the 99th seminar of the EAAE – European Association of Agricultural Economists, Copenhagen.

Hanisch, M. (2006). Eine Theorie genossenschaftlichen Wandels. In H.-H. Münkner, G. Ringle (Eds.), *Zukunftsperspektiven für Genossenschaften: Bausteine für typengerechte Weiterentwicklung* (pp. 297–323). Bern: Haupt.

Hayami, Y., & Otsuka, K. (1993). *The economics of contract choice: An agrarian perspective.* Oxford: Clarendon Press.

Henkel, G. (2004). *Der Ländliche Raum: Gegenwart und Wandlungsprozesse seit dem 19. Jahrhundert in Deutschland.* Stuttgart: Borntraeger.

Hirschman, A. O. (1970). *Exit, voice, and loyalty: Response to decline in firms, organizations, and states.* Cambridge: Harvard University Press.

Hirschman, A. O. (1980). Exit, voice, and loyalty: Further reflections and a survey of recent contributions. *The Milbank Memorial Fund Quarterly. Health and Society, 58,* 430–453.

Knight, J. (1992). *Institutions and social conflict.* Cambridge: Cambridge University Press.

Kollock, P. (1998). Social dilemmas: The anatomy of cooperation. *Annual Review of Sociology, 24,* 183–214.

Marks, G., & Hooghe, L. (2003). Unravelling the central state, but how? Types of multilevel governance. *American Political Science Review, 97,* 233–243.

NIAE (2004). *The future of rural areas in the CEE new member states: Network of independent agricultural experts in the CEE candidate countries.* Halle: IAMO.

Olson, M. (1965). *The logic of collective action.* Cambridge: Harvard University Press.

Orbell, J. M., & Uno, T. (1972). A theory of neighborhood problem-solving: Political action versus residential mobility. *American Political Science Review, 66,* 471–489.

Ostrom, E. (1990). *Governing the commons: The evolution of institutions for collective action.* Cambridge: Cambridge University Press.

Ostrom, E. (2005, June). *The complexity of collective action theory.* Paper presented at the conference "Analyzing problems of polycentric governance in the growing EU", Berlin.

Ostrom, V. (2004). Polycentricity. In V. Ostrom (Ed.), The meaning of American federalism: Constituting a self-governing society (pp. 198–232). San Francisco: Institute for Contemporary Studies.

Ostrom, V. (1972, September). *Polycentricity*. Paper presented at 1972 Annual meeting of the American Political Science Association, Washington, DC.

Ostrom, V., & Ostrom, E. (1994). Public goods and public choices: The emergence of public economies and industry structures. In V. Ostrom (Ed.), *The meaning of American federalism: Constituting a self-governing society* (pp. 162–197). San Francisco: Institute for Contemporary Studies.

Ostrom, V., Tiebout, C. M., & Warren, R. (1961). The organization of government in metropolitan areas. *American Political Science Review, 55*, 831–842.

Peters B. G., & Pierre, J. (1998). Governance without government? Rethinking public administration. *Journal of Public Administration Research and Theory: J-PART, 8*, 223–243.

Post, D. (2002). Closing the deception gap: Accession to the European Union and environmental standards in East Central Europe dynamics of regulatory change: How globalization affects national regulatory policies. *UCIAS Edited Volume 1*, Year 2002, Article 5.

Putnam, R. (1993). *Making democracy work: Civic traditions in modern Italy*. Princeton: Princeton University Press.

Samuelson, P. A. (1954). The pure theory of public expenditure. *The Review of Economics and Statistics, 36*, 387–389.

Sandler, T., & Tschirhart, J. T. (1980). The economic theory of clubs: An evaluative survey. *Journal of Economic Literature, 18*, 1481–1521.

Sikor, T. (2008). (Ed.). *Public and private in natural resource governance: A false dichotomy?* London: Earthscan.

Tagungsbericht Armut und ländliche Gesellschaften (2006, October). *Zwischen Tradition und Moderne: Philanthropie und Selbsthilfe in Europa, 1850–1930*. Tagung, Trier, from: http://hsozkult.geschichte.hu-berlin.de/tagungsberichte/id=1400.

Tiebout, C. M. (1956). A pure theory of local expenditures. *Journal of Political Economy, 64*, 416–24.

Todev, T., Rönnebeck, G., & Brazda, J. (1994). *Perversion einer Idee*. Berlin: Duncker & Humblot.

Tullock, G. (1967). *Toward a mathematics of politics*. Ann Arbor: University of Michigan Press.

Williams, O. P. (1971). *Metropolitan political analysis*. New York: Free Press of Glencoe.

Williamson, O. E. (1975). *Markets and hierarchies: Analysis and antitrust implications*. New York: The Free Press.

Williamson, O. E. (1990). *Die ökonomischen Institutionen des Kapitalismus: Unternehmen, Märkte, Kooperationen*. Tübingen: Mohr Siebeck.

Young, D. R. (1971). Institutional change and the delivery of urban public services. *Policy Sciences 2*, 425–438.

8 Making Environmental Administration More Effective: A Contribution from New Institutional Economics

Regina Birner[1] and Heidi Wittmer[2]

[1] International Food Policy Research Institute (IFPRI), 2033 K Street, NW, Washington, DC 20006-1002, USA, E-mail: R.Birner@cgiar.org
[2] Helmholtz Centre for Environmental Research – UFZ, Permoserstr. 15, 04318 Leipzig, Germany, E-mail: heidi.wittmer@ufz.de

Abstract. During the past 40 years, many countries have adopted policies and laws aimed at protecting the environment and ensuring the sustainable management of natural resources. Yet implementing such policies and laws requires efficient public administration. This chapter presents a conceptual framework that identifies the factors influencing the performance of environmental ministries, departments and agencies (MDAs). Based on this framework, the chapter explores how New Institutional Economics, specifically transaction cost economics, can be applied to derive hypotheses regarding the institutional design of environmental MDAs. Four questions concerning institutional design are discussed: To which extent should environmental functions be integrated into sector ministries? What is the appropriate level of autonomy for different MDAs? What is the appropriate level of decentralization? And how should they interact with civil society and the private sector? The case of Uganda is used to illustrate the arguments derived from the transaction cost approach.

Keywords: Decentralization, Delegation, Institutions of environmental administration, Transaction costs economics, Uganda

8.1 Introduction

Since the second half of the 20th century, environmental concerns have entered the political agenda, both in industrialized and in developing countries. To varying degrees, most countries have developed policies and enacted laws aimed at protecting the environment. Implementing these laws and policies has required the development of institutions for environmental administration. To that effect, countries have set up specialized environmental ministries, and/or added environmental functions in the form of departments to existing ministries. They have also created

V. Beckmann, M. Padmanabhan (eds.), *Institutions and Sustainability*, DOI 10.1007/978-1-4020-9690-7_8, © Springer Science+Business Media B.V. 2009

independent environmental agencies. In line with a trend towards decentralization, on the one hand, and regional integration, on the other, some environmental functions have been transferred to supra-national administrative bodies, whereas others have been decentralized to local governments. In spite of their efforts to create environmental administration institutions, many countries still face an implementation gap. Environmental degradation continues worldwide, in spite of the laws and policies that have been set up to protect the environment. There are various reasons for this implementation gap, including problems of political economy. Ultimately, however, it is environmental administration institutions that fail to implement the provisions that legislators set up to protect the environment. Therefore, organizing environmental administration institutions more effectively can go a long way towards reducing the implementation gap in environmental policy. This paper uses concepts from New Institutional Economics to derive design principles for environmental administration which may help policy-makers to reform their country's own environmental administration institutions and increase their effectiveness. The paper is inspired by Konrad Hagedorn's work on the institutional dimension of environmental policy (see e.g. Hagedorn, 2002, 2004) and by the innovative ways in which he and his followers have used transaction cost economics to analyze institutional issues in agriculture and natural resource management (see e.g. Beckmann, 2000).

Our contribution is organized as follows: Section 8.2 provides a conceptual framework for the analysis of environmental administration institutions. On this basis, Section 8.3 identifies the goals and functions of environmental ministries, departments and agencies (MDAs). Section 8.4 specifies how transaction cost economics can be used to analyze essential questions regarding the institutional design of environmental MDAs, with Section 8.5 using the case of Uganda to illustrate the application of transaction cost economics for their analysis. Section 8.6 discusses the framework and draws some conclusions.

8.2 A Conceptual Framework for Analyzing MDAs

The conceptual framework for the analysis of environmental MDAs presented here draws on standard approaches in organizational assessment (e.g., Lusthaus, Adrien, Anderson, Carden, & Montalván, 2002) and on specific applications in the field of agriculture and natural resource management (e.g., Birner et al., 2006). Figure 8.1 illustrates the elements of this framework and their interrelationships, further explained below.

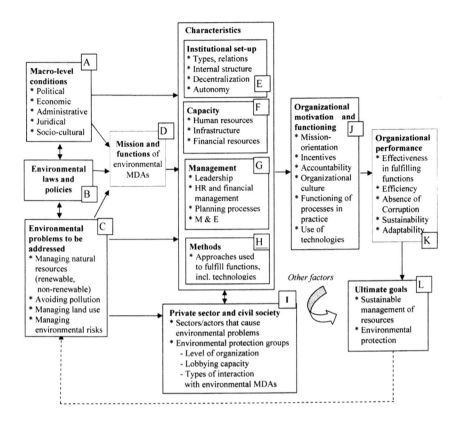

Fig. 8.1: Conceptual framework

8.2.1 Mission and functions

The starting point for assessing the design of environmental MDAs is to identify the functions that they should fulfill (Box D in Fig. 8.1). Their mission and functions should be derived from the environmental policies and laws of the country under consideration (Box B), which are influenced by macro-level factors (Box A). These include the country's political and administrative system, its level of economic development as well as socio-cultural conditions. The functioning of the juridical system is particularly important with regard to environmental management. Environmental policies and laws are also influenced by different types of environmental problems that need to be managed, as further specified in Table 8.1.

8.2.2 Characteristics of MDAs

The framework indicates that the mission and the functions that MDAs are supposed to fulfill, together with macro-economic factors and the type of environmental problems to be solved within the sector, determine how environmental MDAs should be designed and managed. Important aspects in this regard include the following:

Institutional set-up (Box E)

The institutional set-up of the MDAs, which can also be referred to as governance structures, includes the following aspects:

1. *Types of MDAs and relations between them*: The various environmental functions could be organized in one ministry, but in practice they are often distributed over several. In this case, the relations between the environmental MDAs are important for their overall functioning and performance.
2. *Internal structure*: Important aspects of the internal structure of a ministry include, for example, the number and types of departments it has and the levels of hierarchy that exist within it.
3. *Decentralization*: MDAs can be associated with different levels of government, depending on the overall structure of government in the country under consideration.
4. *Autonomy*: Departments and agencies can enjoy different degrees of autonomy from the ministry to which they belong. They may also be independent of any ministry.

Changes in the institutional set-up typically require legislative action, and, therefore, they are often part of general public sector reforms, such as decentralization. The institutional set-up typically also reflects a historical legacy, which in many developing countries still relates to the colonial system of public administration that they inherited, but it may also reflect the various trends of public sector reforms that have occurred since then.

Capacity (Box F)

The mission and the functions of MDAs influence the capacities that they require in terms of human resources, physical infrastructure and financial resources:

1. *Human resources*: This aspect refers to the numbers, qualifications and skills of staff in different units and at different levels within environmental MDAs;
2. *Physical infrastructure*: This refers to the buildings, vehicles, communication infrastructure, and equipment that MDAs have at their disposal;

3. *Financial resources*: The ability of MDAs to fulfill their functions depends on the amount of financial resources available for salaries, maintenance of infrastructure, investment, and operations, as well as on the predictability and reliability of resource flows. MDAs may also be able to generate their own revenues.

Management (Box G)

While institutional set-up and capacity can be considered to be the "hardware" of environmental MDAs, the ways in which resources available to MDAs are managed can be considered to be the "software." Important aspects of managing environmental MDAs include the following:

1. *Leadership* roles and styles that MDA managers have at different levels;
2. *Management of human resources*, including strategies that are applied to create incentives, using rewards and sanctions, as well as strategies to maintain and increase skill and qualification levels of staff members;
3. *Financial management*, understood in terms of transparency, timeliness, accountability and auditing;
4. *Planning processes* used at different levels, including coordination of planning processes between different levels; involvement of stakeholders in the planning process; aligning planning with budgets and implementation activities;
5. *Monitoring and evaluation* systems as well as use of information from M&E for management purposes; and
6. *Information flows and coordination mechanisms* within and among MDAs as well as between MDAs and other actors.

Methods and technologies (Box H)

MDAs can use different approaches, methods and technologies to fulfill their functions. The technologies that environmental MDAs use, for example, to detect and monitor environmental problems, have an important influence on the results they are able to achieve.

Relations with private sector and civil society (Box I)

The functioning and performance of environmental MDAs is not only influenced by their institutional set-up, capacity, organization and management, but also by the ways in which they interact with private sector and civil society, particularly with the actors that cause environmental problems, on the one hand, and the groups that advocate environmental protection, on the other. Environmental protection groups, for example, can exercise pressure on environmental MDAs and support their implementation activities. Enterprises that cause environmental problems may cooperate with environmental MDAs to solve problems, or they may use political channels to undermine implementation efforts.

Organizational motivation and functioning (Box J)

The foregoing characteristics of MDAs and their interaction with environmental actors influence what can be called the "organizational motivation" (Lusthaus et al., 2002), and the actual functioning of MDAs. It is important to acknowledge organizational motivation and functioning of MDAs as an "intermediate outcome" which influences their performance. It is often assumed that reforming MDAs by restructuring them, retraining their staff, and putting new technologies and processes in place will lead to increased performance. However, one first needs to ask questions such as the following: Do these reforms indeed increase the incentives, motivation and mission-orientation of MDA staff? How do the new processes actually work in practice? Are new technologies actually used? It is not unusual, for example, that computers introduced by development projects are, after a short while, not used any longer. Thus, to what extent changes in the institutional design, capacity, management and methods of MDAs will lead to better results *depends on the way in which the staff reacts* to these changes. Therefore, it is important to analyze the organizational motivation and functioning of MDAs, paying attention to the following aspects:

1. *Mission-orientation* and professional ethics of the staff members;
2. *Incentives* that staff members have to fulfill their tasks;
3. *Accountability* that is created within the MDAs, as well as with regard to politicians and stakeholders;
4. *Organizational culture* within MDAs;
5. *Actual functioning of processes*, such as planning and budgeting in practice; prevalence of informal processes that may support or undermine formal processes; and
6. *Actual use of technologies*, such as computers, software, etc.

Organizational performance (Box K)

The ultimate goal of public sector reform is improving the organizational performance of MDAs. The important dimensions of which include the following:

1. *Effectiveness* in fulfilling their functions;
2. *Efficiency*, which is influenced, among other factors, by the extent to which *corruption* can be controlled;

3. *Sustainability* of operations; and
4. *Adaptability* to new tasks and challenges.

More specific performance indicators can be developed for the different functions that environmental MDAs are in charge of.

Achievement of environmental goals (Box L)

The performance of MDAs influences achievement of the ultimate environmental goals for which they were created, such as sustainable resource use and environmental protection. To assess environmental MDAs, it is essential to collect indicators on these ultimate outcomes, while taking into account that these outcomes are also influenced by factors that may lie outside their control. For example, pollution of rivers may be caused by other countries that share them.

The feedback arrow leading from the sector goals to the characteristics and environmental problems (Box C) indicates that the framework has to be seen from a dynamic perspective. With economic development, the functions of environmental MDAs will change over time, which should induce appropriate changes in their institutional set-up, capacity, management and methods. For example, with industrial development, new types of environmental problems arise, and environmental MDAs have to be adjusted to meet these challenges.

In summary, the outlined framework identifies key factors that influence the performance of environmental MDAs and their contribution towards the achievement of environmental goals. What the framework does not capture is the *process* of organizational change, which is required to create and reform environmental MDAs. Reforming public sector institutions is a challenging task, since it is inherently a political process, which is influenced by organizational politics within MDAs and by external actors, including political decision-makers, private sector and civil society organizations, as well as donor agencies that may pursue or resist change. Analyzing the dynamics of institutional change is beyond the scope of this paper, but the final section does take the question into consideration.

8.3 Functions and Activities of Environmental MDAs

As shown in Fig. 8.1, the mission and the functions that environmental MDAs are supposed to fulfill (Box D) depend on the types of environmental problems that need to be solved (Box C). There are many different ways in which environmental problems can be classified. Gerelli and Patrizii (1996), for example, suggest a classification according to the sectors involved, the type of recipient medium, and the type of polluting agent. Table 8.1 provides a classification scheme that includes (a) the types of environmental problems, (b) the subjects of protection (or the medium to be protected), and (c) the sectors that cause environmental problems.

Table 8.1: Classification of environmental problems

Environmental problems to be managed	Subjects of environmental protection	Sectors that potentially cause environmental problems
• Pollution, e.g. waste, toxic substances, noise • Hazards • Disasters • Unsustainable use of natural resources • Climate change	• Human health • Air / atmosphere • Water • Soils • Biodiversity • Landscapes • Ecosystems	• Agriculture • Forestry • Fisheries • Mining • Energy • Industry • Transport • Households

The first column in Table 8.1 lists the types of problems. They include pollution, which may occur in the forms of waste, toxic substances, and noise; hazards, which may be caused by industrial or agricultural production; natural disasters, which may be promoted by human interventions in ecosystems; unsustainable use of natural resources; and climate change. The second column of Table 8.1 lists the subjects of environmental protection. These include human health, air and atmosphere, water resources, soils, biological diversity (including genetic resources), landscapes and ecosystems (including forests and rangelands). The sectors that potentially cause environmental problems are listed in the third column, including agriculture, forestry and fisheries, the mining sector, the energy sector, the industrial sector, transport, and households. Some types of industrial production, such as the chemical industry, are particularly contributory to environmental problems. Likewise, some agricultural technologies, such as pesticides and genetically modified crops, are more environmentally problematic than others.

To manage environmental problems, environmental MDAs have to fulfill a range of different functions, classified in Table 8.2. They include policy formulation; planning and the development of guidelines and regulations; conducting environmental risk assessments; monitoring of environmental problems; enforcement of environmental policies and regulations; coordination among public sector, private sector and civil society, and coordination across different levels of government; environmental education and advisory services; and research on environmental problems and solutions.

Table 8.2: Types of environmental functions

Type of functions	Examples
Policy formulation	Drafting environmental policies and laws
Planning Developing guidelines and regulations	Preparing environmental strategies and action plans Preparing land use plans Devising zoning regulations
Conducting environmental risk assessments	Environmental impact assessment Risk assessment for pesticides and genetically modified crops
Monitoring	Measuring pollution and resource use Identifying illegal resource use
Enforcement	Ensuring that violations of environmental laws and guidelines are prosecuted
Coordination	Coordinating between different environmental MDAs, between different levels of government; and between public sector, private sector and civil society organizations that are concerned with environmental problems
Educational and advisory functions	Advising producers on environmentally safe production; educating households on environmental issues
Research	Conducting scientific and socio-economic research on environmental problems and strategies to solve them

8.4 Designing Environmental MDAs: The Contribution of the New Institutional Economics

Various disciplines, such as organizational sociology and administrative science, can contribute towards identifying how environmental MDAs should be designed and managed to achieve high levels of performance. In the spirit of the work of Konrad Hagedorn, this chapter concentrates on the contribution that New Institutional Economics, especially transaction cost economics, can make in this regard. Concepts from New Institutional Economics can contribute most to the analysis of the institutional set-up of environmental MDAs. Therefore, in terms of Fig. 8.1, the analysis presented here concentrates on the factors listed in Box E, while still taking into account the other factors included in the framework.

The analysis here mainly follows the transaction cost concept as developed by Oliver Williamson (1985, 1991, 1999), an approach also applied by Guido Van Huylenbroeck et al. (this volume) to analyze hybrid governance structures. To assess the comparative advantage of different governance structures, Williamson (1991) developed the "discriminating alignment hypothesis", according to which transactions that differ in their attributes are to be aligned with governance structures that differ in their costs and competence, so as to effect an economizing result. Williamson uses a cost-effectiveness approach, which compares the costs involved in achieving a set of defined outcomes using different governance structures. In terms of the framework presented above, these outcomes could either be identified at the level of organizational performance (Box K) or ultimate goals (Box L). To apply the transaction cost approach to environmental administration institutions, one needs to (a) specify possible governance structures for environmental MDAs, (b) identify the transactions to be carried out, (c) identify the types of costs involved in carrying out the respective transactions, and (d) identify the attributes and context-specific factors that influence the comparative advantage of different governance structures for the transactions in question. These steps are further detailed below:

(a) The concept of "governance structures" can be applied to the institutional aspects of environmental MDAs that have been discussed above for Box E. For this article, we have limited our scope to concentrating on only four dimensions of environmental MDA governance structures: integration, autonomy, decentralization, and relations with civil society and the private sector.

(b) To identify the transactions carried out by environmental MDAs, one can use Table 8.2 above as a starting point. The functions listed therein are associated with different types of transactions. The challenges involved in carrying out the respective transactions may, however, differ considerably depending on the type of environmental problem and the sector concerned. For example, the activities required to enforce compliance with environmental regulations are easier to organize if they apply to a limited number of large-scale industrial plants as compared to a large number of small-scale farmers.

(c) With regard to public administration, the classification of costs into transaction, production or other costs is largely a matter of definition. For example, one may classify all expenditures associated with regulatory activities as transaction costs. For the purpose of the analysis presented here, it is important to consider the *total* costs associated with carrying out a certain transaction, since the cost-effectiveness approach aims at identifying the governance structure that involves the lowest total costs. Therefore, defining transaction costs and production costs in different ways will not change the considerations presented here.

(d) Regarding the attributes of transactions, Williamson's work focuses on asset specificity, uncertainty, and frequency. As further specified below, additional attributes need to be considered to address the specific features of environmental administration institutions. Section 8.5 will also identify the types of literature that can help to identify attributes as well as context-specific factors.

8.5 Analyzing the Governance Structures of Environmental MDAs

This section uses the transaction cost approach to derive hypotheses regarding the comparative cost-effectiveness of different governance structures for environmental MDAs, focusing on the case of Uganda, where data were collected during a field visit in 2007 involving expert interviews, interviews with representatives of different environmental MDAs, and a review of policy documents. The case of Uganda is used here primarily to show how environmental MDAs are structured in a concrete case.

8.5.1 Level of integration

Since environmental problems are caused by different sectors (Table 8.1), the question arises as to what extent administrative environmental functions should be incorporated into the respective sector ministries – such as, the ministries in charge of agriculture, energy or transport – and to what extent they should be integrated in one separate ministry or agency in charge of the environment. This is related to the question of whether integrative or segregative institutions are better suited for environmental management, which has been analyzed by Hagedorn (2005) and is further discussed by William Blomquist in this volume. In the case of Uganda, environmental functions are to a considerable extent incorporated into different sectoral ministries, implying a segregation of environmental functions.

1. *The Ministry of Agriculture, Animal Industry and Fisheries*, hereafter referred to as the Ministry of Agriculture, is in charge of promoting sustainable management activities related to agriculture, rangelands, pastures and fisheries. The Farm Development Department of the Ministry of Agriculture also deals with watershed management, including soil and water conservation and irrigation and drainage. The ministry has overall responsibility for the National Agricultural Advisory Services, established in 2001 as a semi-autonomous agency under the Ministry of Agriculture, which hires agricultural extension agents on a contract basis. The advisory services have a strategy that aims at incorporating natural resource management issues into extension work plans and into the contracts with service providers.

2. *The Ministry of Tourism, Trade and Industry* oversees the Uganda Wildlife Authority, which is in charge of managing the country's protected areas. To protect wildlife resources, the Wildlife Authority also works with communities outside protected areas.
3. *The Ministry of Energy and Mineral Development* is in charge of the management of minerals and energy. Its mandate includes the promotion of renewable energies.
4. *The Ministry of Lands, Housing and Urban Development* has the responsibility for ensuring "security of land tenure and productive use of land resources." This ministry is in charge of land administration, which includes land registration and the development of a Land Information System.
5. Uganda also has a ministry that is responsible for the overall coordination of environmental protection. This is the *Ministry of Water and Environment,* which oversees the *National Environment Management Authority.* This agency has the mandate to monitor, plan and coordinate environmental matters in all sectors. The implementation, however, remains the responsibility of the relevant sectoral ministries. The Ministry of Water and Environment is also responsible for the management of water resources, forests and woodlands. The National Forest Authority, which is in charge of managing the country's Central Forest Reserves, falls under the jurisdiction of this ministry as well.

The question arises as to whether the far-reaching incorporation of environmental functions into different sectoral ministries, as opposed to their integration into a single environmental ministry, is an appropriate governance structure. One important trade-off to be considered in this regard is the following: On the one hand, the incorporation of administrative environmental functions into the respective sectoral ministries can reduce the costs of fulfilling these functions, because incorporation makes it possible to use existing staff, infrastructure and knowledge. For example, to reach important environmental goals in the agricultural sector, it is necessary to influence the farming practices of hundreds of thousands, if not millions, of farmers. Therefore, it is advantageous to incorporate educational and advisory services for environmental protection in the agricultural sector with the agricultural extension system, as is the case in Uganda. This will be more cost-effective than setting up a separate service to advise farmers on environmental issues. Similarly, it is advantageous to incorporate research on sustainable natural resource management into the agendas of existing agricultural research organizations (Crosson & Anderson, 1993).

However, incorporating environmental functions into existing sectoral ministries presents its own challenges. Importantly, it is often politically difficult to pursue environmental goals in sectoral ministries, since their main goals are often in conflict with environmental ones, at least in the short run. Therefore, the staff in such ministries often lacks sufficient incentives to promote environmental protection. Moreover, sectoral ministries, such as agriculture, energy and transport, are typically subject to intensive lobbying by producer groups that consider environmental protection to be a burden and lobby against it. Hence, there is a trade-off between the reduction in costs due to incorporation and the failure to achieve a desired level of environmental protection. Incorporation involves another trade-off. If environmental functions are part of different sectoral ministries, the costs that arise for coordination across different sectors will increase. As pointed out by Blomquist in Chapter 5 of the present volume, it is an empirical question whether organizational integration or inter-organizational coordination is more costly, and the answer will depend on context-specific factors.

The interviews with stakeholders and experts conducted in Uganda indicate that the trade-offs discussed here are in fact relevant. There are concerns that the National Agricultural Advisory Service is not particularly effective in promoting sustainable resource management, because this is not a priority for the agricultural administration. Likewise, there are concerns about limited coordination between different ministries. For example, wildlife conservation requires coordination with forest and rangeland management, but each of these three resource systems is assigned to a different ministry. This is perceived to be a problem because – as the respondents pointed out – existing rules and communication procedures in Uganda's public administration do not facilitate inter-ministerial coordination.

These considerations suggest that four attributes of transactions influence the comparative advantages of incorporation: (1) specificity; (2) transaction-intensity; (3) scope for interest capture; and (4) need for coordination. Taking these attributes into account, one can formulate the following hypotheses: If environmental functions are closely interlinked with sector-specific activities, it will, all else being equal, be more cost-effective to incorporate these functions into the respective sectoral ministry. This is especially the case for environmental functions that are "transaction-intensive", a term indicating that the required transactions are frequent and at the same time widely distributed in space as in the case of advising farmers (Pritchett & Woolcock, 2004). However, if environmental functions are subject to lobbying by special interest groups, the cost-effectiveness of incorporating these functions into sector ministries will be reduced. The same applies if there is a need to coordinate environmental activities in one sector with environmental activities in other sectors.

8.5.2 Level of autonomy

The above description shows that environmental MDAs in Uganda differ in their degree of autonomy. The National Environment Management Authority, the National Forest Authority and the National Wildlife Authority enjoy a considerable degree of autonomy from the ministries to which they belong. The National Agricultural Advisory Services unit does not have the same level of autonomy, but it is still more independent from the Ministry of Agriculture than a typical ministerial

department. The question arises: Which factors need to be considered when deciding on the appropriate level of autonomy of an environmental unit?

The transaction cost framework can also be applied to answer this. The literature on political transaction costs and delegation (Dixit, 1996; Calvert,
McCubbins, & Weingast, 1989) provides important insights on the attributes that
matter in this regard, suggesting that delegation of authority to an independent
agency can reduce problems of "political interest capture," which arise, for example, if there is a strong trade-off between short-term and long-term interests. The
creation of independent central banks is a well-known example.

Figure 8.2 illustrates how the transaction cost approach can be used to derive
hypotheses on the appropriate level of autonomy.

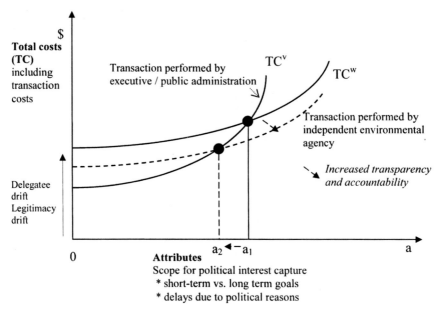

Fig. 8.2: Comparative efficiency of different governance structures: Degree of autonomy

The diagram displays hypothetical cost curves for the respective transactions under a more autonomous governance structure, w, and a less autonomous governance structure, v. The vertical axis indicates the total costs arising for the respective transaction. The horizontal axis displays the attribute "scope for political
interest capture", which increases the comparative advantage for autonomy, as
explained above. As shown in Fig. 8.2, from point a_1 onwards, an independent
agency can perform the respective transaction at a lower cost than the public administration, because in this cost-effectiveness consideration, the benefits of reduced political interest capture translate into a lower slope for the respective hypothetical cost curve. For $a < a_1$, however, an independent agency does not have a
comparative advantage, because delegation also involves costs. These costs have

been attributed to "legitimacy drift" and "delegatee drift" (Voigt & Salzberger, 2002). Legitimacy drift occurs if the public does not attribute the same legitimacy to the independent agency that they would attribute to a governance structure with less delegation. Delegatee drift occurs if the independent agency pursues goals other than those that the policy-makers had in mind when they created the agency. Delegation may also lead to increased coordination costs and reduced possibilities for monitoring.

With regard to delegatee drift, it is necessary to consider whether an independent agency or the executive/public administration is likely to be subject to interest group capture, either by the industry or by environmental groups. In Fig. 8.2, it is assumed that the independent environmental agency can take steps to increase transparency and accountability that a department – being part of a ministry and bound by its rules – cannot undertake. One can hypothesize that such measures will make it easier to achieve the required outcome, which is indicated by a downward shift of the respective cost-curve. The level from which an independent agency has a comparative advantage over an integrated department moves, then, from a_1 to a_2.

The expert interviews conducted in Uganda suggest that the independent environmental agencies (National Environment Management Agency, Uganda Wildlife Agency, National Forest Authority), in fact enjoy high reputations. They are considered to be more effective than typical government departments and to show stronger commitment to environmental goals. The National Forest Authority, for example, resisted a plan for the conversion of the Mabira Forest Reserve into a sugar cane plantation, which was based on a deal between political leaders and a sugar corporation and was widely perceived as a case of interest capture. This resistance of the National Forest Authority against the plan can be seen as an indication for the merits of its autonomy. However, the government reacted by sacking the entire board of the agency, and it was only massive public protest organized by environmental interest groups that eventually prevented the conversion of the forest (Howden, 2007).

8.5.3 Level of centralization/decentralization

Next to the levels of integration and autonomy, the level of decentralization is a third important dimension of environmental MDA governance structures. Since Uganda has undergone a far-reaching process of decentralization, local governments are also in charge of environmental functions. Uganda's local government system has five tiers: District, County, Sub-county, Parish and Village. The following two levels are most important for environmental MDAs:

1. *District level*: Under the District Administration, the District Forestry Services are in charge of managing the forest resources in the district (except

those managed by the National Forest Authority and the Uganda Wildlife Authority). The Department of Land Management is in charge of the environment and wetlands. The Directorate for Production, Marketing and Agricultural Extension Services is responsible for agricultural activities and also oversees the district coordinator of National Agricultural Advisory Services.

2. *Sub-county level*: The sub-counties develop and execute their own budgets. Similar to the district level, they have administrative staff, a Sub-county Executive as political head, and a Sub-county Council of elected members. However, there is no officer from the environmental administration posted at this level. The National Agricultural Advisory Services have staff members, since contracts to service providers are awarded at the sub-county level.

Which factors should be considered when deciding on the appropriate levels of decentralization for different environmental functions? As Blomquist (this volume) points out, this question is particularly important in natural resource management, since ecosystems differ in scale. The transaction cost approach can be used to identify the factors that influence appropriate levels of decentralization. Figure 8.3 shows hypothetical cost curves for environmental transactions under a more centralized governance structure, x, and a more decentralized governance structure, y. The vertical axis indicates the total costs arising for each respective transaction. The horizontal axis displays the attributes which increase the comparative advantage for a decentralized organization of the respective transaction.

The environmental federalism literature provides important clues on the attributes that matter in this respect. As can be derived from the work of Oates (2004), the nature of a particular environmental problem plays an important role. If environmental MDAs are supposed to produce local public goods, a more decentralized governance structure has advantages. In cases of local public goods with spill-over effects, coordination between decentralized environmental MDAs is typically more appropriate than centralized decision making, especially if preferences are heterogeneous. Economies of scale in performing the respective activity are an important attribute favoring more centralized approaches. These may differ, however, between types of environmental transactions. The economies of scale in the activities to be carried out by environmental MDAs are linked to their "transaction intensity." As indicated above, this attribute reflects the frequency and spatial dispersion of transactions. If local knowledge, for example knowledge of local environmental conditions, rather than expert knowledge is required to perform the transaction well, a decentralized organization has advantages, too.

In Fig. 8.3, the horizontal axis displays attributes that increase the comparative advantage of a decentralized governance structure (i.e. local public goods, increasing transaction-intensity, need for local knowledge). The more these attributes matter, the greater is the increase in the hypothetical costs for performing the respective transaction under the centralized governance structure, x.

In the case of the decentralized governance structure y, the total costs increase at a slower pace, which is indicated by a smaller slope of the respective hypothetical cost curve. If the respective attributes are not relevant (moving towards the left-hand side along the horizontal axis), a centralized governance structure has a comparative advantage over a decentralized one. In this case, one can save the costs of establishing a decentralized system, which may require considerable investments for building capacity at the local level. From point a_1 onwards, a decentralized governance structure has a comparative advantage over a centralized one for performing the respective transaction.

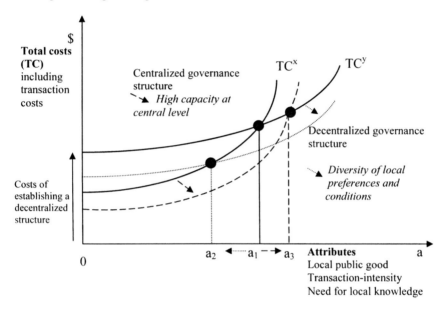

Fig. 8.3: Comparative efficiency of different governance structures: Level of decentralization

Figure 8.3 also displays the effects of context-specific factors, for example, the role of heterogeneous local conditions and preferences. This factor increases the comparative advantage of a decentralized agency, resulting in a downward shift of the cost curve that indicates decentralized administration. Accordingly, the point from which decentralized management becomes more efficient moves to a_2. In contrast, if the capacity of a national environmental agency is increased, the cost curve of the centralized agency is shifted downwards. This may occur, for example, if the central agency is able to hire better qualified and more motivated staff than local governments are able to. Accordingly, the point at which a centralized organization of the respective transaction begins to have a comparative advantage over a decentralized organization moves from a_1 to a_3.

The interviews conducted in Uganda suggest that the trade-offs discussed here are, in fact, relevant. Uganda is rather heterogeneous with regard to agro-ecology and ethnicity, and many environmental activities are transaction-intensive. These factors support a decentralized organization of environmental MDAs. At the same time, the challenge to build sufficient capacity for environmental administration institutions at the local level remains an important challenge for the decentralized approach.

8.5.4 Interaction with private sector and civil society

The transaction cost economics approach can also be applied to other dimensions of institutional design besides integration, autonomy and decentralization. One important question is related to interaction with the private sector and civil society (Box I in Fig. 8.1). As can be derived from the previous sections, there is a wide spectrum of forms that this interaction may take. For example, commercial enterprises may seek political alliances to undermine environmental MDAs. Environmental groups may put pressure on the public administration to pursue their goals more effectively. In general, civil society can play this role most effectively if citizens have the right to environmental information and if public interest associations have the right to contest environmental cases in court.

An important approach for involving civil society and the private sector in environmental MDAs in a constructive way is the formation of boards or other governing bodies in which these groups are represented. In the case of Uganda, this approach is applied in the case of the autonomous or semi-autonomous agencies, such as the National Forest Authority, the Uganda Wildlife Authority and the National Agricultural Advisory Services. Such organizations can be considered to be hybrid governance structures, which, as pointed out in Chapter 9 of this volume, have a considerable potential for promoting sustainable resource management.

Transaction cost economics can also be used to assess trade-offs that may arise with regard to the establishment of such hybrid governance structures. An important trade-off is the following: On the one hand, participation by the private sector and civil society can reduce the costs of environmental administration, especially by creating legitimacy. On the other hand, participation may increase transaction costs, because multi-stakeholder decision-making processes involve time and resources. An important attribute with regard to this trade-off is "contest-intensity." In areas where environmental conflicts are prevalent, participation can play an important role, not only as a goal in its own right, but also as a tool to reduce the costs of implementation.[1]

---

[1] See Birner and Wittmer (2004) for a more detailed analysis of this question.

8.6. Discussion and Conclusions

This chapter has proposed a conceptual framework for analyzing the performance of environmental ministries, departments and agencies (MDAs). On this basis, theoretical concepts of the New Institutional Economics, specifically transaction cost economics, were used to derive hypotheses on the institutional design of environmental MDAs. The framework and the transaction cost approach developed in this chapter can be used to guide future empirical research on environmental MDAs. Note that in most of the empirical applications of transaction cost economics found in the literature, neither attributes nor transaction costs are empirically measured. The approach displayed in Figs. 8.2 and 8.3 has rather been used to derive hypotheses regarding the comparative advantages of different governance structures. Empirical studies have then been used to test whether the observed choice of governance structures can be explained by the key attributes of the transactions in the way predicted by transaction cost economics.[2]

This approach is best suited to studying profit-oriented organizations, where competition forces enterprises to select governance structures according to cost-economizing criteria. However, one cannot assume that, in practice, the empirically observed design of environmental MDAs follows cost-effectiveness criteria. Therefore, to apply this framework quantitatively, it is necessary to empirically measure the transaction costs arising for the performance of environment-related functions. The costs incurred by environmental MDAs can be estimated on the basis of information acquired from them. As these costs are typically part of an agency's budget, measuring them is easier than measuring the transaction costs incurred by other actors, such as business enterprises who incur costs, for example, due to delays in regulatory decisions. Various studies have shown, however, that it is possible to empirically measure transaction costs arising with regard to environmental management (Mburu & Birner, 2002; Kuperan et al., 1998) and public administration (Mann, 2000).

The framework proposed here can also be used for policy dialogue, in particular to inform efforts at reforming environmental MDAs. The framework can help to structure discussions on controversial topics of institutional design by identifying the factors and trade-offs to be considered when making choices on issues such as decentralization and autonomy of environmental MDAs. Obviously, the reform of environmental MDAs is a political process, in which both interest-group politics and bureaucratic politics play an important role. For reasons of scope, the political economy of organizational reform has not been covered in this paper, but its importance should not be underestimated, as the work by Konrad Hagedorn has made clear (see e.g. Hagedorn, 1996).

In applying the framework proposed here, one needs to take into account that the transaction cost approach focuses on the role that institutional design (Box E

---

[2] See Shelanski and Klein (1995) for a review of the empirical transaction cost economics literature.

in Fig. 8.1) can play for the performance of MDAs. The framework makes it clear, however, that institutional design covers only one set of relevant factors. Equally important are capacity (Box F), management (Box G) and methods (Box H). Obviously, the best institutional design will not be effective if environmental MDAs face a lack of qualified personnel and financial resources. In developing countries, this is often a major challenge. Likewise, the best institutional set-up will have little effect if management practices, administrative procedures and techniques are inadequate. In this respect, institutional design can be considered as the "hardware" of MDAs, while management and methods constitute their "software." Public sector management is a field of its own, and there is a large literature on the "software" dimension of MDAs which could not be covered here for reasons of scope. However, the framework provided in Fig. 8.1 clearly implies that an interdisciplinary approach is best suited towards analyzing and supporting reforms of environmental MDAs. By drawing attention to the role of macro-level conditions (Box A), the framework also reminds us that the analysis of governance structures has to be seen in a broader political and socio-economic context, a point that is given great consideration in the work of Konrad Hagedorn.

References

Beckmann, V. (2000). *Transaktionskosten und institutionelle Wahl in der Landwirtschaft: Zwischen Markt, Hierarchie und Kooperation*. Berlin: Edition Sigma.

Birner, R., Davis, K., Pender, J., Nkonya, E., Anandajayasekeram, P., Ekboir, J., et al. (2006). *From best practice to best fit: A framework for analyzing agricultural advisory services worldwide*. Washington, DC: DSGD Discussion Paper No. 39, Development Strategy and Governance Division, International Food Policy Research Institute.

Birner, R., & Wittmer, H. (2004). On the efficient boundaries of the state: The contribution of transaction costs economics to the analysis of decentralisation and devolution in natural resource management. *Environment and Planning C: Government and Policy, 22*, 667–685.

Calvert, R., McCubbins, M. D., & Weingast, B. R. (1989). A theory of political control and agency discretion. *American Journal of Political Science, 33*, 588–611.

Crosson, P., & Anderson, J. R. (1993). *Concerns for sustainability: Integration of natural resource and environmental issues in the research agendas of NARS* (The Hague: ISNAR Research Report No. 4). International Service for National Agricultural Research.

Dixit, A. K. (1996). *The making of economic policy: A transaction-cost politics perspective*. Cambridge: MIT Press.

Gerelli, E., & Patrizii, V. (1996). Information bases for environmental policies. In I. Musu & D. Siniscalco (Eds.), *National accounts and the environment* (pp. 107–132). New York: Springer.

Hagedorn, K. (1996). *Das Institutionenproblem in der agrarökonomischen Politikforschung*. Tübingen: J.C.B. Mohr (Paul Siebeck).

Hagedorn, K. (Ed.). (2002). *Environmental co-operation and institutional change: Theories and policies for European agriculture*. Cheltenham and Northampton: Edward Elgar.

Hagedorn, K. (2004). Institutionen der Nachhaltigkeit: Eine Theorie der Umweltkoordination. In S. Dabbert, W. Grosskopf, F. Heidhues, & J. Zeddies (Eds.), *Perspektiven in der Landnutzung: Regionen, Landschaften, Betriebe. Entscheidungsträger und Instrumente* (pp. 65–73). Münster-Hiltrup: Landwirtschaftsverlag.

Hagedorn, K. (2005, June). *Integrative and segregative institutions*. Paper presented at the TransCoop workshop "Problems of polycentric governance in the growing EU", Berlin.

Howden, D. (2007). African forest under threat from sugar cane plantation. *The Independent*, 10 July, 2007.

Kuperan, K., Mustapha, N., Abdullah, R., Pomeroy, R. S., Genio, E., & Salamanca, A. (1998, June). *Measuring transaction costs of fisheries co-management*. Vancouver, http://www.indiana.edu/~iascp/Drafts/kuperan.pdf, (Paper presented at the 7th Biennial Conference of the International Association for the Study of Common Property).

Lusthaus, C., Adrien, M. -H., Anderson, G., Carden, F., & Montalván, G. P. (2002). *Organizational assessment: A framework for improving performance*. Ottawa, http://www.idrc.ca/en/ev-23987-201-1-DO_TOPIC.html: The International Development Research Center (IDRC).

Mann, S. (2000). Transaktionskosten landwirtschaftlicher Investitionsförderung: Ein komparativer Ansatz [Transaction costs of agricultural investment promotion: A comparative analysis]. *Agrarwirtschaft*, 94, 259–269.

Mburu, J., & Birner, R. (2002). Analyzing the efficiency of collaborative wildlife management: The case of two community wildlife sanctuaries in Kenya. *Journal of Organizational Theory and Behaviour, 5*, 359–394.

Oates, W. E. (2004). *Environmental policy and fiscal federalism: Selected essays of Wallace E. Oates*. Cheltenham and Northampton: Edward Elgar.

Pritchett, L., & Woolcock, M. (2004). Solutions when the solution is the problem: Arraying the disarray in development. *World Development, 32*, 191–212.

Shelanski, H. A., & Klein, P. G. (1995). Empirical research in transaction cost economics: A review and assessment. *Journal of Law, Economics and Organization, 11*, 335–361.

Voigt, S., & Salzberger, E. (2002). Choosing not to choose: When politicians choose to delegate power. *Kyklos, 55*, 289–310.

Williamson, O. E. (1985). *The economic institutions of capitalism: Firms, markets, relational contracting*. New York: The Free Press.

Williamson, O. E. (1991). Comparative economic organization: The analysis of discrete structural alternatives. *Administrative Science Quarterly, 36*, 269–296.

Williamson, O. E. (1999). Public and private bureaucracies: A transaction cost economics perspective. *Journal of Law, Economics and Organization, 15*, 306–341.

9 Public Good Markets: The Possible Role of Hybrid Governance Structures in Institutions for Sustainability

Guido Van Huylenbroeck, Anne Vuylsteke and Wim Verbeke

Department of Agricultural Economics, Ghent University, Coupure Links 653, 9000 Gent, Belgium, E-mail: Guido.VanHuylenbroeck@ugent.be, Anne.Vuylsteke@UGent.be, Wim.Verbeke@UGent.be

Abstract. Based on a review of the concept of markets, a more comprehensive definition of markets is developed. Within this concept it is argued that hybrid governance structures, which are defined as structures in which actors with autonomous property rights transfer part of these rights to a transaction partner without losing all property rights, play an important role. Based on the theory of hybrid governance structures for private goods, the concept of hybrid organisations in public good markets is conceptualised. We are convinced this may contribute to the further elaboration of the "institutions of sustainability" concept developed by Konrad Hagedorn.

Keywords: Action arena, Hybrid governance, Institutions, Public good markets, Transaction costs

9.1 Introduction

In a major part of his work, Konrad Hagedorn focuses on institutions of sustainability (see among others Hagedorn, Arzt, & Peters, 2002; Hagedorn, 2003, 2005). A basic hypothesis in his line of thinking is that there is a need of finding rules and regulations that integrate all dimensions of sustainability. Public good market creation is conceived as one of the possible ways to arrive at more sustainability in agriculture and natural resource management. Examples here include water markets in irrigation schemes or agri-environmental payment schemes in the field of agri-environmental management. Market instruments are also being used in resource management. An example are, tradable permits or quotas markets, not only used for issues like CO_2 emission rights (see Swallow and Meinzen-Dick this volume), but also in fish resource management (tradable fish quota) or in manure policies (tradable manure production rights). Without exception, these examples

V. Beckmann, M. Padmanabhan (eds.), *Institutions and Sustainability*,
DOI 10.1007/978-1-4020-9690-7_9, © Springer Science+Business Media B.V. 2009

are concerned with issues of contemporary debate that figure high on global, European, national and regional political agendas.

In this contribution, we build further on the ideas already put forward in Van Huylenbroeck (2003), where we argued that hybrid governance structures, defined as cooperative arrangements between different actors (private as well as public stakeholders), may facilitate the functioning not only of private but also of public good markets. Our hypothesis is, therefore, that hybrid governance structures should receive more attention when creating sustainable institutions for public goods. Our contribution is organised as follows: first we revisit briefly the market concept from a neo-institutional point of view and propose an extended market concept, integrating the action arena theory as set forth by Ostrom (1998) with the four layers theory of Williamson (2000). Next, we focus on the importance of institutional arrangements in the functioning of markets and on the role hybrid governance structures may play in this respect, drawing heavily on the work of Menard (1995, 2004, 2007) on hybrid governance structures in private markets. Following that, we extend the theory of hybrid governance to public markets, concluding that an extension of the hybrid governance concept to public markets deserves more attention in future research and can indeed contribute to the further development of Hagedorn's "institutions of sustainability" concept.

9.2 The Market Concept Revisited

Despite the fact that "markets are at the centre of economic activity, and many of the most interesting questions and issues in economics concern how markets work" (Pindyck & Rubinfeld, 1998), attempts to grasp what exactly a market is are surprisingly rare and rather recent in economic thought. Moreover, understanding of the functioning of the market hinges on one's conceptualisation of the market and the attributes of the society in which it operates. In economic literature, the issue of defining the market is rarely explicitly addressed, as Nobel prize winner George Stigler makes clear: "Economic theory is concerned with markets much more than with factories or kitchens. It is, therefore, a source of embarrassment that so little attention has been paid to the theory of markets" (1967: 291).

Menard (1995) suggests that variations in conceptualising the market are in general not formal but rather a reflection of diverging analyses. For example, a market can be understood as a public place where goods are being offered for sale, or as a public gathering held for buying and selling of goods (as in Arndt, 1979; Barnhill & Lawson 1980; Callon, 1998), or as a group or organisation of buyers interested in buying goods, or a sub-division of the population considered as prospective buyers, that is, a group of people sharing similar needs and wants, who are willing and able to engage in the exchange of goods or services that can satisfy them (as in Kotler, 1997). Lindblom (2001) defines the market as the "interaction between suppliers and demanders, where the interaction is voluntary and where access to the market is open to everyone". Conversely, some economists conceptualise markets as specific organisational forms (Arrow, 1974), or as one large organisation (Arrow, 1964; Hurwicz, 1987), while others consider markets to be institutions where consensus over prices and qualities is established (McMillan, 2002; Hodgson, 1999), or a specific "institutional arrangement" or "governance structure" where a large number of voluntary transfers of property rights take place (Williamson, 1991; Menard, 1995). Clearly, the definition of the market is still confusing. Indeed, Menard (1995) considers it "paradoxical how variously and vaguely defined the concept of the market is".

Some of the perspectives mentioned above partly capture the thinking about markets under the neoclassic economics paradigm, in which the market is pictured as an interaction of supply and demand but free of any institutional structures. Simply reduced to a price-making mechanism, the market serves more as a theoretical construct than as a characterisation (or concretisation) of the actual exchange process. New Social theorists (Granovetter, 1985; Swedberg, 1994; Fukuyama, 2002) have challenged this notion of the market, arguing that they consist of more than an act of exchange. They see the market as a specific type of social structure which offers a continuous and extended range of social interaction. This means that economic action is embedded in non-economic networks, institutions and relations and that market transactions occur only within an already institutionalised setting. This model assumes that the market is composed of a network of buyers and sellers engaged in competition as well as exchange. Therefore, exchange assumes a wider context in terms of prices, competition and market culture, which are socially constructed, and can involve different elements depending on the applicable social norms, habitual routines and established institutions.

New Institutional Economics and, in particular, the discipline of transaction costs have brought the understanding of markets closer to reality by taking up this idea and pointing out that exchange between economic actors in markets is costly and institutions are required to lower this cost. From this perspective, institutional constraints are added to the neo-classical market model. To work as they should, markets require new or modified institutions to resolve institutional constraints.

From the new institutional perspective, markets are therefore regarded as institutions that shape the behaviour of actors. Both formal rules, including laws, policies, constitutions, contracts and treaties, as well as informal rules, resulting from established customs and conventions concerning norms of behaviour and trust, facilitate coordination or govern relationships between individuals or groups (World Bank, 2003). By providing for more certainty in human interaction, institutions have an influence on the behaviour of actors and therefore on outcomes such as economic performance, efficiency, economic growth and development (North, 1990). From Menard's (1995) viewpoint, institutions establish and delineate the conditions under which goods are produced and exchanged. Hurwicz (1987), on the other hand, provides a more restrictive definition of institutions by defining it as an information mechanism that coordinates the actions of different agents. Hurwicz's definition underscores the critical point of departure between neoclassic economic theory, for which only price coordinates the behaviour of actors, and neo-institutional economics, according to which the behaviour of actors is coordinated by institutions.

Davis and North (1971) have successfully distinguished between "institutional environment" and "institutional arrangements", a distinction later extended by North (1991, 1994). According to these authors, the institutional environment refers to the set of fundamental political, social, and legal grounds that establish the basis of production and distribution. In other words, the institutional environment is the broader set of institutions in which transactions occur. The institutional arrangements are, on the other hand, the "arrangements between economic units that govern the ways in which these units can cooperate and/or compete" (Williamson, 2000). They are in other words the contracts or arrangements set up for particular transactions, also referred to as "governance structures". They can be regarded as a means by which to infuse order into a relationship where potential conflict threatens to undo or upset opportunities to realise mutual gains (Williamson, 2000).

Ostrom (1998) sees the market as a place where different actors (buyers and sellers) encounter each other to perform transactions. Basically, this point of view is close to the idea of markets as a public gathering space for buying and selling, as previously indicated. However, Ostrom (1998) also incorporates the idea of social interaction into her conceptualisation of markets, specifically through introducing the market as an "action arena", defined as the social space(s) within which individuals interact, exchange goods and services, solve problems, dominate one another, fight or compete. Action arenas include both an action situation as the actors within it (Ostrom, 1999a). The structure of an action situation is identified according to various situation variables, such as the types of participants, their positions, possible actions, information, and outcomes. Preferences, resources, information-processing capabilities and selection criteria characterise actors, understood as being goal-oriented but also fallible learners with limited resources and cognitive capacities, functioning in uncertain environments (Ostrom, 1999b). Action situations and actors then form the action arena, which is framed and constrained by contextual variables, such as the physical and material world within which the actors interact, the attributes of the community, and the formal rules and informal norms that define the "rules-in-use". These exogenous constraints jointly affect the types of action that individuals can take, the benefits and costs of these actions, and the (likely) outcomes resulting from them (Ostrom, 1999b).

Trying to bring together all the above perspectives, Kyeyamwa (2007) proposes in his work on livestock markets in Uganda to conceptualise markets as depicted in Fig. 9.1. In the centre is placed Ostrom, Gardener, and Walker (1994) actors' arena, embedded in the wider institutional environment that influences which institutional arrangements are possible. These, in turn, direct the incentives confronting actors and their subsequent behaviours. Hence, the market is nested in a structure of rules within rules, guiding the interactions and decisions of actors. Given a set of exogenous constraints, actors within an action arena consider the

costs and benefits of various behaviours and act according to their personal preferences, expected benefits and perceived incentives. The aggregate patterns of interaction lead to outcomes with which market institutions can then be evaluated according to relevant criteria (e.g., efficiency and effectiveness). Outcomes dyna-
mically feed back to both the action arena and to higher institutional levels,
potentially causing pressure that will ultimately change the rules in use or the contextual variables, hence feeding back to change perceived incentives within the action arena. In essence, self-enforcing institutional change is a continuous process
of adjustment across these nested levels of contextual variables, always trying to
find the most optimal outcome. Institutions provide the micro-foundations of behaviour while, at the same time, players shape institutions through their strategic
interactions (Mittenzwei & Bullock, 2004). From this perspective, the market is
circumscribed by a nested set of institutions that are in equilibrium at any given
time as a consequence of "repeatedly played games" between the stakeholders
who are active in the action arena.

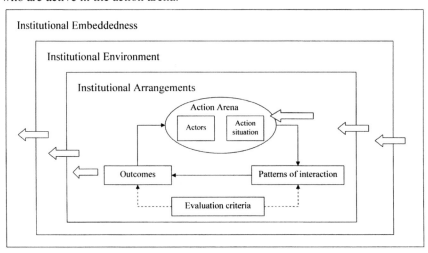

Fig. 9.1: A conceptual nested market model (based on Kyeyamwa, 2007)

In summary, the market model described assumes markets to be a social construct
in which transactions are coordinated by mechanisms beyond the neoclassical
price mechanism. In the action arena, model actors receive incentives for cooperation, more specifically through the reduction of transaction costs. Mechanisms
used for coordination are the result of social interaction. This market model also
acknowledges that ongoing networks of social relations between people discour-
age fraud. People guide their choices based on past interactions (experiences
stored in memory) with other actors and continue to deal with those they trust.
Eventually, positive experiences and mutual trust may even yield preferred supply-demand relationships, which may allow even further reduction of transaction
costs. In this way, economic exchange needs to be looked at as a social exchange

process. Levels of trust have effectively been shown to have an important influence on transaction costs in economic relationships (Platteau, 2000).

Within the nested market framework, actors make choices based on their own preferences, the costs and benefits that they assign to alternative actions and outcomes, and strategic considerations (i.e., expectations concerning the behaviours of others). One of the possible choices can be to become part of a given market arrangements or to establish new arrangements. Actors respond both individually and as members of groups, according to the ways in which different strategies impact on them collectively and individually. The patterns of interaction represent the collective choices and decisions made by individuals in response to physical attributes and institutions (Alavalapati & Mercer, 2004).

9.3 Hybrid Governance Structures

Transaction Cost Economics (TCE) posits that, within the above-explained nested market system, a governance structure will be chosen in order to economise on transaction costs. Governance structures, such as information centres, contracts, networks, bureaucracy, cooperation or markets, are organisational solutions for making institutions effective; they are necessary for guaranteeing the rights and duties of actors involved and their use in transactions, which themselves differ in their attributes and are systematically aligned with different governance structures. Transactions differ in the degree to which relationship-specific assets are involved, the amount of uncertainty about the future and about other parties involved, the complexity of trading arrangements and the frequency with which such transactions occur (Williamson, 1985, 2004). According to these arguments, governance structures are developed to improve the functioning of transaction markets and can be presented along a continuum. At the one end of the spectrum, we find pure, anonymous spot markets, in which market prices provide all relevant information and competition is the main safeguard. Adaptation to changing market conditions is guided individually and incentives to maximise profits are high. At the other end of the spectrum lies the fully integrated arrangement or hierarchy. Hierarchies mitigate risk, but provide only weak incentives to maximise profits, while also incurring additional bureaucratic costs (Boger, 2001). In between the market and the hierarchy are hybrid governance structures. This continuum of governance structures introduces two important issues. First, when transaction costs increase (or decrease), a different governance structure may be optimal for carrying out the transaction. Second, such a shift in governance structure has attendant costs. These factors are important, because they represent the conditions under which institutional choice and institutional change may occur.

Menard (2004) argues that in real market situations hybrids are more the rule than the exception (spot markets and firms are the extreme cases). Hybrid governance structures are characterised by actors with autonomous property rights, but who have transferred part of these rights to the transaction partner. Property autonomy elicits strong incentives, but at the same time the agreed coordination between partners, implying the transfer of property rights such as exploitation or allocation rights, attenuates incentive intensity. Menard (2004) identifies three common characteristics for all hybrids:

1. The partners in a hybrid governance structure pool (part of) their resources and their strategic decision rights, but at the same time keep the majority of their property rights and their associated decision rights distinct;
2. The relationships between partners are regulated by contracts, but these are in general incomplete and not tailored to suit the particular purpose; and
3. Competition persists between the partners in a hybrid as well as between hybrids and alternative organisational forms.

The mechanisms that can be deployed for coordination and safeguarding are – in increasing order of authority – information systems, contracts, external regulation and, finally, formal organisation. According to Menard (2007), hybrid organisations will develop if the benefits of coordination outweigh the costs or, in other words, if there are cooperation rents to capture. However, usually the higher the advantages of coordination, the higher the costs for organising it will be (e.g. because of the need for higher safeguard mechanisms to avoid free riding by actors who are attracted by the appealing benefits without accounting for a share of the costs), and so the more centralised the coordination mechanisms used will be, implying higher governance costs. A consequence of this is that different hybrid structures co-exist in practice, depending on the benefits of coordination.

Menard (2007) identifies four key mechanisms of coordination, each exercising different degrees of authority:

1. Information devices
   These are used in cases of asymmetric information between partners. Information devices are usually bi-directional: amongst partners and as an interface with the external environment (e.g. labels).
2. Contracts
   Contracts have always had a significant role in cooperation and collective organisations, but their role has been overstated, overlooking the problem of incompleteness and the need for adaptability in a changing world. Neo-classical contracts are typical for hybrid organisations; these are conceived as self-enforcing mechanisms that can be formal or informal and as facilitators for organising the relationship between partners.
3. Exogenous regulator or monitor
   Incomplete contracts and/or an exogenous impulse to cooperate are motives for the establishment of exogenous monitoring. A distinction can be made here between monitoring initiated and carried out by public authorities, private monitoring initiatives and a combination of public and private monitoring (e.g. a

private certification body that is recognised by the government to perform certain controls).

4. A governing body of its own

   The final coordination mechanism is the establishment of a formal framework within which contracts are initiated, negotiated, monitored, enforced and terminated. This entails the building of a formal authority, can take different forms and involves a significant degree of centralisation, formalisation and control over property rights.

One form of hybrid organisation consists of relations of trust, meaning that decisions are decentralised and coordination relies on mutual "influence" and reciprocity, mainly based on information exchange and peer review, such as in the case of farmers selling at weekly farm markets obeying certain loosely defined rules of conduct. Van Huylenbroeck (2003), based on the work of Verhaegen and Van Huylenbroeck (2002), describes this as a framework or open group form of governance. At the other end of the spectrum, we find hybrids close to integration, with tight coordination through quasi-autonomous governing bodies or "bureaus", sharing many attributes of a hierarchy. Menard (2004) calls this formal government, such as in the case of a new formal organisation owning a brand name. In between these polar cases, we find mild forms of "authority" based on relational networks or on leadership. Relational networks mainly rely on tighter coordination than trust, with formal rules and conventions based on long-term relationships, complementary competences, and/or social "connivance" (Powell, 1990), such as relationships seen in cooperatives. Van Huylenbroeck (2003) calls this coordinating governance. By contrast, hybrids known as leader governance (Menard, 2004) or captain-of-channel strategies leave little room for autonomy, such as with franchising or contracts imposed by retailers.

9.4 Extension to Public Good Markets

So far the theory on hybrid governance structures has mainly been developed for private good markets. However, in the context of the proposed market model illustrated by Fig. 9.1, we can easily extend this theory to public good markets in which the market is seen as an action arena occupied by a public body demanding services and private agents able to provide them. In this case also, hybrid structures may be a tool to improve the functioning of the "public" market. Two main differences between private and public markets are important, however (Rangan, Samii, & Van Wassenhove, 2006). The first is that there are benefits (positive externalities) generated for third parties not directly involved in the transaction (e.g. citizens in agri-environmental schemes). In such cases, it is well known that, because of individual rationality (oriented toward maximum private benefits at minimum private costs) and the nontrivial governance costs of collective action (i.e., fair allocation of costs among all potential beneficiaries and enforcement of sanctions against free riders), public "goods" tend to be underprovided. This calls for public actors to step into the market. The second difference is the position of public actors, which are different from private actors in the sense that they have more legal authority, which can be used to change the institutional environment as a tool for shaping and regulating the behaviour of other actors.

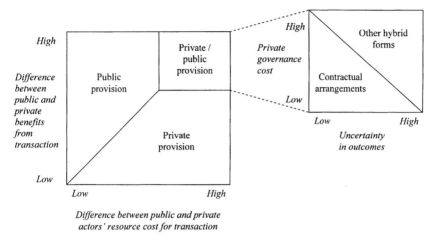

Fig. 9.2: Conceptualisation of the choice between public, private or public-private action (adapted from Rangan et al., 2006)

According to Rangan et al. (2006), it is important when bringing public actors and public benefits into the analysis not to contrast private-resource costs against governance costs, as is done in traditional transaction cost economic analysis, but to trade-off the difference (wedge) between public and private benefits, on the one hand, against the difference in public and private resource costs for making the transaction possible, on the other. They show, based on the model represented by Fig. 9.2, that when public benefits are relatively high and public resource costs relatively low, public action is the most economical strategy (e.g. pure nature conservation, such as in cases with low operational costs to maintain a reserve). In case of the opposite result, private market creation will be most appropriate. In the latter case, the role of public authorities can be reduced to providing the required legislative rules, changing the institutional environment. Illustrative cases here are tradable permits to regulate CO_2 or manure production or common pool resources, such as access to fisheries. In these cases, the public transaction and coordination costs of public governance would be far too high compared to the public benefits to be gained. By providing a legislative constraint on the amount of resources available or the amount of externalities that may be produced, and by providing an initial division of resource rights, a market institution can be created.

However, when there are both high positive externalities involved as well as high public resource costs relative to private-actor resource costs (e.g. in nature conservation practices implying highly specific agricultural methods or in irrigation schemes), partnerships between public and private actors will be optimal. Public actors want to get involved because of positive externalities and the great potential public benefits, but they will be hesitant to get involved alone, because the effectiveness and efficiency implications indicate otherwise. Private actors, on the other hand, will be reluctant to invest in such transactions by themselves because, while they might have resource (i.e., cost) advantages, they do not have the governance advantages required to close the public-private wedge and to adequately reap positive net benefits.

It is in the latter case that we can expect to see constructive partnerships, that is, active alliances between private and public actors. These public-private governance relationships can take different forms. As long as there is low uncertainty and private governance or transaction costs are perceived to be not too high, contracts will be the most adequate governance structure. Illustrative for this situation are agri-environmental contracts for rather simple conservation practices, such as maintaining hedgerows or other landscape elements. In such cases the governance cost and uncertainty can be kept low: payment for a direct service that is easily observable. However, in cases where private governance costs are high and there is also high uncertainty about private benefits – because, for example, there is a need for specific technology or knowledge or complex interactions with other providers – there is scope for other governance structures.

For such cases, we may think about more advanced hybrid governance structures such as trusts, user associations, cooperatives, private or public agencies and other intermediate structures to lower transaction and governance costs. In particular for transactions that require highly specific knowledge, technology and/or investments, such elaborated hybrid structures for public-private coordination will be more efficient than working on an individual contractual basis. Examples of such institutional arrangements include water user associations for the management of irrigation schemes (Herrera, 2005), environmental cooperatives for agri-environmental conservation (Slangen & Polman, 2002) and private-public organisations for the protection of property rights of genetic resources and biodiversity (Van Huylenbroeck & Espinel 2007).

Following the work of Williamson, Bougherara, Grolleau, and Mzoughi (2007) provide us with a first attempt to systemise public governance structures, seeking to classify regulatory instruments for environmental policy: based on measurement problems, on the one hand, and required safeguards on the other. They argue that, with raising measurement problems and desire for safeguards, more regulatory instruments will be used, while in cases where measurement costs and risks are low, contractual approaches will be preferred. However, although their analysis is a good first attempt, it is flawed because (1) they focus only on the role of the state to mitigate negative externalities and (2) in our opinion they neglect the possibility of hybrid forms in which private stakeholders organise themselves to contract with the government as well as the possibility of public-private investment agencies or collaborations.

Another indication that we need more systematic research on alternative public-private governance structures is given by Ducros (2007). In her analysis of agri-environmental schemes, based on contract and principal-agent theory, she proves that in cases where the principal (public authorities) is in a situation of high asymmetric information and uncertainty (leading to high public coordination costs) and farmers face high specific investments, individual agri-environmental contracts are not very successful. This is demonstrated by comparing the low uptake of this kind of contract with the greater uptake levels of rather simple measures, such as buffer strips and field margins, which involve low uncertainty in terms of outcomes and low specific investments, unlike individual contract measures requiring more specific knowledge (e.g. botanical management), highly specific investments (e.g. mechanical weeding) or complex interactions (e.g. late mowing). In such cases, governance structures based on cooperation among farmers (e.g. a contracting cooperative that makes specific investments and is paid from the individual payments farmers receive) would facilitate market development.

Hybrid governance structures will be advantageous in particular in cases where either (1) different stakeholders possess specific assets which need to be pooled in order to make the transaction possible or (2) when the public service requires highly specific investments which are impossible for individual stakeholders and where only a pooling of available resources makes the investment, and thus the transaction of the public good or service, possible. An example of the first category is the maintenance of a typical regional landscape for which it does not make sense to make individual contracts with farmers, as the value of the measure lies in the combination of different farm types, crops or practices. In such cases an intermediate structure is needed in which the rules (in Ostrom's sense) are negotiated and fixed. An example of the second category is investment in irrigation installations or machines for maintenance of hedges which are too costly for individual farmers and where water user associations or environmental cooperatives may be the ideal intermediary, and thus hybrid, structure.

The systematic analysis of hybrid governance types for public good markets is certainly still an underdeveloped field of research. That is why this chapter has not been able to undertake a full characterisation or classification of these types, but only provide some examples. A way forward for research would be to formulate a systematic categorisation of these structures, the involved stakeholders (private actors and/or public agencies), the legal entities formed, their motivations and so on. We propose to use a conceptual framework similar to that developed by Menard (2007) for classifying and evaluating hybrid governance structures in private good governance. This framework proposes distinguishing between two types of elements. On the one hand, it considers (see Fig. 9.3) the drivers for the development of hybrid governance structures, including the mutual dependency of stakeholders, (measurement) uncertainty about outcomes, expected social gains from transactions and so on. On the other hand, it looks at elements influencing the kinds of partnership and governance structures that can be formed, such as the existing institutional environment, path dependency (existing governance structures), asset specificity for necessary investments, expected rents and necessary safeguards for their protection or division among actors, consequential uncertainty and so on.

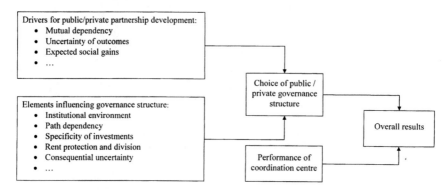

Fig. 9.3: Conceptual framework for the analysis of public-private hybrid governance structures (based on Menard, 2007)

Based on the theory of hybrid governance and the specificities of public goods, we may regroup hybrid institutions for public goods according to the same four categories outlined in Section 9.3, with the following specifications:

1. Information devices: hereby the coordination centre only provides information for coordination of the actions of individual actors, with the objective of achieving higher overall performance than would be the case with uncoordinated actions. Although the public authority may give some regulatory power and support to the coordination centre in order to stimulate coordination efforts, there is no, or only a very slight, shift in property rights to the coordination centre itself. Examples here include regional landscape centres for landscape maintenance and protection, natural parks, water protection areas.

2. Contractual arrangements: hereby the coordination centre remains a state body that makes individual contracts with private actors who can render a service to society. Classic examples include agri-environmental contracts, but also the attribution of tradable or non-tradable quotas, such as for fishing, can be considered in this category. All property rights not regulated by the contract remain in the hands of the individual actors

3. Exogenous regulator or monitor: hereby the state uses an external (private, or public-private) body as an intermediate body for coordinating the actions of individual actors. This intermediate body can take the form of cooperatives (agri-environmental cooperatives), associations (water user associations), or a private or state body regulating the trade in CO_2 or fishing quotas or any other legal form. This body receives from the state authority the regulatory and incentive power and instruments (mostly on a contractual basis) to regulate, coordinate and monitor the actions of its members or those actors that fall under its power.

In most cases, membership or entrance in a coordination system remains voluntary, but, once entered, individual actors are highly bound by the rules of the exogenous regulator. However, the individual actors keep a great part of their property rights.

4. A governing body: in extreme cases the governing authority can decide to pass all legal power to a new public, private or public-private body, which receives juridical and other power. Different from the previous coordination instruments, adherence to rules is more mandatory and there is a great shift in property rights to the governing body. Examples include natural parks (or similar devices), where a state-installed authority receives the power to manage the park and most of the relevant property rights (e.g. on the land), or a polder council that receives authority over dams in lowland areas near the seaside to regulate water levels in order to avoid floods and so on.

When evaluating the outcomes of different governance structures for public goods it is of course important to also take into account the performance of the "coordination centre". Indeed the final result of a certain governance structure will also depend on how well the coordination centre formed out of hybrid governance arrangements performs its tasks. As already explained, a coordination centre can take different organisational and legal forms, depending on the tasks allocated to it and the legal environment in which it operates (see the examples above). Therefore, as also indicated by Rangan et al. (2006), the valid calculus for the choice on a governance structure will depend on the presence, breadth, and quality of the ambient institutions of governance – including norms and laws regarding private property, courts, enforcement units and, last but not least, markets – as perceived by the private actors contemplating the focal transaction. In a place or time where ambient institutions of governance are not well developed, private willingness to engage will be perceived as low and the public-private wedge as large.

Finally, as also described by Hanisch (this volume), all these hybrid structures can co-exist within a so-called polycentric governance system consisting of different public and private actors and hybrid networks used to coordinate the transaction. In such cases it is important to analyse the mutual relations, competition, influence, and conflicts among the different structures to understand the spectrum of outcomes of the overall governance structure.

Another aspect to take into account here is the degree of centralisation or decentralisation, both at state level as well as within hybrid governance structures, because this may influence overall transaction costs, as explained by Birner and Wittmer (this volume). Here a trade-off will exist between the capacity of the central level to economise on regulatory costs (because of economies of scale) and the more precise regulation possibilities of decentralised structures, which gain in importance the higher the diversity of the transactions at stake.

9.5 Conclusion

Understanding the functioning of private and public markets requires a comprehensive conceptualisation of markets themselves. The framework presented here views the market as an action arena, nested in a set of institutional structures that directly constrain and guide the behaviour of actors.

The comprehensive model makes it possible to understand why hybrid governance structures may contribute to the proper functioning of markets, both private and public. It helps indeed to understand that coordination among stakeholders may help to lower the transaction costs in an action situation where individual actors do not have all specific assets to make the transaction possible, do not have sufficient resources to make the required investments in specific assets, or face too much uncertainty about the outcomes. Depending on the amount of pooled assets or resources, uncertainty about the outcomes and required safeguards to protect individual interests, different types of hybrid governance structures will emerge. In cases where the required amount of pooled specific assets and uncertainty and safeguards are low, only very loose coordination centres will be necessary (such as an information centre), while in cases where the amount and role of specific assets increases and uncertainty and required safeguards gain importance, more coordination will be required and, thus, also stronger forms of relationship. We are convinced that using an enlarged concept of markets and an extension of the hybrid governance concept to public markets can contribute to the further development of Hagedorn's "institutions of sustainability" concept and the better understanding of governance structures for public good markets. We have argued that markets should not be conceptualised as places of pure exchange, but rather as social structures in which exchanges or influences on actors' property rights take place. Within these social constructions, hybrid governance arrangements help to foster better allocation of public goods and their development. We therefore recommend a more systematic theoretical and empirical analysis of the role of hybrid governance structures in public markets in future research.

References

Alavalapati, J. R. R., & Mercer, D. E. (Eds.). (2004). *Valuing agro-forestry systems.* Dordrecht: Kluwer Academic Publishers.

Arndt, J. (1979). Toward a concept of domesticated markets. *Journal of Marketing, 43,* 69–75.

Arrow, K. J. (1964). Control in large organizations. *Management Science, 10,* 397–408.

Arrow, K. J. (1974). *The limits of organizations.* New York: Norton.

Barnhill, J. A., & Lawson, W. M. (1980). Toward a theory of modern markets. *European Journal of Marketing, 4,* 50–60.

Boger, S. (2001). *Agriculture markets in transition: An empirical study of contracts and transaction costs in the Polish hog sector: Vol. 4. Institutional change in agriculture and natural resources*. Aachen: Shaker.

Bougherara D., Grolleau, G., & Mzoughi, N. (2007). How can transaction costs economics help regulators choose between environmental policy options. *Research in Law and Economics* (forthcoming)

Callon, M. (1998). *The laws of the markets*. London: Blackwell Publishers.

Davis, L. E., & North, D. C. (1971). *Institutional change and American economic growth*. Cambridge: Cambridge University Press.

Ducros, G. (2007) Efficacité et coûts de transaction des contrats agro-environnementaux. PhD thesis, University of Rennes.

Fukuyama, F. (2002). Social capital and development: The coming agenda. *SAIS Review, 22*, 23–37.

Granovetter, M. (1985). Economic action and social structure: The problem of embeddedness. *American Journal of Sociology, 91*, 481–510.

Hagedorn, K. (2003). Rethinking the theory of agricultural change in an institution of sustainability perspective. In G. Van Huylenbroeck, W. Verbeke, L. Lauwers, I. Vanslembrouck, & M. Dhaese (Eds.). *Importance of policies and institutions for agriculture* (pp. 33–56). Gent: Academic Press.

Hagedorn, K. (2005, October). *The dichotomy of segregative and integrative institutions and its particular importance for sustainable resource use and rural development*. Paper presented at the workshop in political theory and policy analysis colloquium Mini Series, Bloomington.

Hagedorn, K., Arzt, A., & Peters, U. (2002). Institutional arrangements for environmental co-operatives: A conceptual framework. In K. Hagedorn (Ed.). *Environmental co-operation and institutional change. Theories and policies for European agriculture* (pp. 3–25). Cheltenham and Northampton: Edward Elgar.

Herrera, P. A. (2005) Institutional economic assessment of the governance of irrigated agriculture: The case of the Peninsula of Santa Elena, Ecuador. PhD thesis, Faculty of Bioscience Engineering, Gent: Ghent University.

Hodgson, G. M. (1999). *Economics and utopia*. London and New York: Routledge.

Hurwicz, L. (1987). Inventing new institutions: The design perspective. *American Journal of Agricultural Economics, 69*, 395–402.

Kotler, P. (1997). *Marketing management: Analysis, planning, implementation, and control*. New Jersey: Pentice Hall.

Kyeyamwa, H. (2007). Integration of smallholder cattle farmers in the livestock market of Uganda. PhD thesis, Faculty of Bioscience Engineering. Gent: Ghent University.

Lindblom, C.E. (2001). *The market system*. New Haven: Yale University Press.

McMillan, J. (2002). *Reinventing the bazaar*. New York: Norton

Menard, C. (1995). Markets as institutions versus organizations as markets? Disentangling some fundamental concepts. *Journal of Economic Behavior & Organisation, 28*, 161–182.

Menard, C. (2004). The economics of hybrid organizations. *Journal of Institutional and Theoretical Economics, 160*, 345–376.

Menard, C. (2007, June). *The governance of hybrid organizations*. Paper presented at the Emnet conference on economics and management of networks, Rotterdam.

Mittenzwei, K., & Bullock, D. (2004). Rules and equilibria: a formal conceptualization of institutions with an application to Nowegian agricultural policy making. In G. van Huylenbroeck, W. Verbeke & L. Lauwers (Eds.), *The role of institutions in rural policies and agricultural markets* (pp. 109–121). Amsterdam: Elsevier Press.

North, D. C. (1990). *Institutions, institutional change and economic performance*. New York: Cambridge University Press.

North, D. C. (1991). Institutions. *Journal of Economic Perspective, 5*, 97–112.

North, D. C. (1994). Economic performance through time. *American Economic Review, 84*, 359–368.

Ostrom, E. (1998). The institutional analysis and development approach. In E. Tusak-Loehman & D. Kulgur (Eds.), *Designing institutions for environmental and resource management* (pp. 68–90). Cheltenham: Edward Elgar.

Ostrom, E. (1999a). Coping with the tragedies of the commons. *Annual Review of Political Science, 2*, 493–535.

Ostrom, E. (1999b). Institutional rational choice: an assessment of the IAD framework. In P. Sabatier (Ed.), *Theories of the policy process* (pp. 35–72). Boulder, Colorado: Westview Press.

Ostrom, E., Gardener, R., & Walker, J. (1994). *Rules, games & common pool resources.* Ann Arbor: University of Michigan Press.

Pindyck, R. S., & Rubinfeld, D. L. (1998). *Microeconomics.* Upper Saddle River: Printice-Hall Inc.

Platteau, J. P. (2000). *Institutions, social norms, and economic development.* Amsteldijk: Harwood Academic Publishers.

Powell, W. W. (1990). Neither markets nor hierarchies. Network forms of organisations. In B. M. Staw & L. L. Cunnings (Eds.), *Research in organisational behaviour.* Greenwich, Connecticut: Jai Press Inc.

Rangan, S., Samii, R., & Van Wassenhove, L. (2006). Constructive partnerships: when alliances between private firms and public actors can enable creative strategies. *Academy of Management Review, 31*, 738–751.

Slangen, L. H. G., & Polman, N. B. P. (2002). Environmental co-operatives: a new institutional arrangement of farmers. In K. Hagedorn. (Ed.), *Environmental co-operation and institutional change. Theories and policies for European agriculture* (pp. 69–90). Cheltenham and Northampton: Edward Elgar.

Stigler, G. (1967). Imperfection in the capital market. *Journal of Political Economy, 75*, 287–292.

Swedberg, R. (1994). Markets as social structures. In R. Swedberg & N. J. Smelser. (Eds.), *The handbook of economic sociology* (pp. 255–282). Princeton: Princeton University Press.

Van Huylenbroeck, G. (2003). Hybrid governance structures to respond to new consumer and citizens' concerns about food. In G. Van Huylenbroeck, W. Verbeke, L. Lauwers, I. Vanslembrouck, & M. Dhaese (Eds.), *Importance of policies and institutions for agriculture* (pp. 191–206). Gent: Academic Press.

Van Huylenbroeck, G., & Espinel, R. L. (2007). Importance of institutions and governance structures for market access and protection of property rights of small farmers in developing countries. In E. Bulte & R. Ruben (Eds.), *Development economics between markets and institutions: Incentives for growth, food security and sustainable use of the environment* (pp. 327–344). Wageningen: Academic Publishers.

Verhaegen, I., & Van Huylenbroeck, G. (2002). *Hybrid governance structures for quality farm products. A transaction cost perspective: Vol. 6. Institutional change in agriculture and natural resources.* Aachen: Shaker.

Williamson, O. E. (1985). *The economic institutions of capitalism.* New York, NY: Free Press.

Williamson, O. E. (1991). Comparative economic organization: The analysis of discrete structural alternatives. *Administrative Science Quarterly, 36*, 269–296.

Williamson, O. E. (2000). The new institutional economics: Taking stock, looking ahead. *Journal of Economic Literature, 38*, 595–613.

Williamson, O. E. (2004). Transaction cost economics and agriculture: An excursion. In G. van Huylenbroeck, W. Verbeke & L. Lauwers (Eds.), *The role of institutions in rural policies and agricultural markets* (pp. 19–39). Amsterdam: Elsevier Press.

World Bank. (2003). *World development report 2003: Building institutions for markets.* New York: Oxford University Press for the World Bank.

Part III

Property Rights, Collective Action and Natural Resources

10 A Century of Institutions and Ecology in East Africa's Rangelands: Linking Institutional Robustness with the Ecological Resilience of Kenya's Maasailand

Esther Mwangi[1] and Elinor Ostrom[2]

[1] Kennedy School of Government and the University Center for Environment, Harvard University, 503A Rubenstein Building, 79 JFK Street, Cambridge, MA 02138, USA, E-mail: esther_mwangi@ksg.harvard.edu
[2] Workshop in Political Theory and Policy Analysis, Indiana University, 513 N Park Ave., Bloomington, IN 47408, USA, and Center for the Study of Institutional Diversity, Arizona State University, PO Box 872402, Tempe, AZ 85287, USA, E-mail: ostrom@indiana.edu

Abstract. In analyzing the interactions between institutions and ecology, it is useful to evaluate the robustness of the designed governance system and the resilience of the ecological system that together comprise a Social-Ecological System (SES). In this chapter, we will examine the patterns of interaction between ever-changing governance institutions related to the highly variable ecology of Eastern Africa extending in time from prior to the British colonial rule until early in this century. That will enable us to examine three questions: (1) Which of the institutions that have existed during this time are more robust and why? (2) How does institutional robustness influence ecosystem resilience? and (3) What assumptions can be made about human behavior and incentives in light of this sweep of human history? We find that the indigenous institutions of the Maasai people were the most robust of the set of institutions studied over time since pre-colonial days until contemporary times. And, these robust institutions were associated with a more resilient ecology.

Keywords: Ecological resilience, Institutional robustness, Kenya, Maasai, Pastoral systems, Social-ecological systems

10.1 Introduction

Working with Konrad Hagedorn on various projects involved in understanding how institutional arrangements facilitate or deter investments by resource users in maintaining complex ecosystems of high value has been a wonderful experience. A central purpose of this chapter is to examine questions related to the linkage between institutions and ecology, which we hope will be of interest to Konrad as well as a contribution to a further understanding of these complex connections. We will explore the dynamic interactions between institutions and ecology by trying to draw out characteristic features of institutions that are more likely to enhance the robustness of social systems and the resilience of ecological systems when these are brought together as Social-Ecological Systems (SESs). We share a deep concern with Vatn (this volume) concerning the sustainability of resource systems given contemporary uses. The term "social-ecological system" underscores the integrated concept of humans-in-nature and that any boundaries between social and natural systems are artificial (Berkes & Folke, 1998).

Since the publication of "The Tragedy of the Commons" by Garrett Hardin in 1968, many scholars have presumed that those who rely heavily on ecological systems to support their livelihoods, such as pastoralists, are trapped in social dilemma situations and cannot engage in self-governance. Social dilemmas characterize an extremely large number of settings in which individuals make independent choices that affect themselves and others. If each individual in such situations selects actions based strictly on individual, short-term maximization of individual returns, together they generate worse outcomes for the group as a whole. Hardin predicted that each pastoralist would place as many animals as they could on a shared pasture, leading to substantial overharvesting. Further, he presumed that the pastoralists themselves could not establish their own rules and norms to extract themselves from the tragedy of overuse. In other words, they could not govern themselves.

Governance is a process of devising rules for a variety of operational or day-to-day situations, such as where to pasture animals for today, the next week, and then the week thereafter, and so on. Governance processes are undertaken by governments (which are one type of organization) as well as by organizations of all types and at all scales (for further elaboration of this, see Blomquist, this volume). Contrary to the presumption made by Hardin, and many others following his general theory, many groups of harvesters from ecological systems do engage in self-governance (McCay & Acheson, 1987; NRC, 1986, 2002; Dietz, Ostrom, & Stern, 2003). A self-governed ecological system is one where actors, who in this case are major harvesters of the resource, are involved over time in making and adapting rules within collective-choice arenas regarding such matters as the inclusion or exclusion of participants, what are agreed-upon harvesting strategies, the obligations of participants, how rules will be monitored and sanctioned, and how conflicts will be resolved.

Some isolated ecological systems are governed entirely by harvesters and are not governed at all by external authorities. In most modern political economies, however, it is rare to find any resource systems, including the treasuries of private for-profit corporations, that are governed *entirely* by participants without rules made by local, regional, national, and international authorities also affecting key decisions (V. Ostrom, 1997, 2008). Thus, in a self-governed system, participants make many, but usually not all, of the rules that affect the sustainability of the resource system and its use.

When we speak of the governance of ecological systems, basically we mean the regimes that regulate one or more of the following:

- who is allowed to harvest resource units (trees, grasses, animals);
- the timing, quantity, location, and technology of harvesting;
- who is obligated to contribute resources to provide or maintain the ecological system itself;
- how harvesting and obligation activities are to be monitored and enforced;
- how conflicts over appropriation and obligation activities are to be resolved; and
- how the rules affecting the above will be changed over time along with changes in the performance of the resource system and the strategies of participants.

Diverse forms of self-governance are found in most societies, some of which are amazingly robust even though others are fragile and still others fail (E. Ostrom, 1990). Robustness is a concept developed in engineering to characterize designed systems that are able to continue to perform their core functions when subjected to external, unpredictable perturbations or disturbances (Carlson & Doyle, 2002). A robust bridge, for example, is one that continues to provide safe passage across a chasm when challenged by earthquakes or traffic jams. In ecology, a somewhat similar term – resilience – is used to evaluate the amount of a disturbance that will transform the maintenance of an ecological system from one group of mutually reinforcing structures and processes to a different set (Holling, 1973). A resilient ecosystem is one that has the capacity to withstand perturbations, such as fires, floods, or migration of new species, and to rebuild or renew itself afterwards. In analyzing the interactions between institutions and ecology in any particular region, it is useful to evaluate the robustness of the designed governance system and the resilience of the ecological system that together comprise an SES (see Anderies, Janssen, & Ostrom, 2004; Janssen, Anderies, & Ostrom, 2007).

In this chapter, we examine the patterns of interaction between ever-changing governance institutions related to the highly variable ecology of Eastern Africa, extending in time from prior to British colonial rule until early in the present century. That will enable us to examine three questions: (1) Which of the institutions that have existed during this time have been the most robust and why? (2) How does institutional robustness influence ecosystem resilience? and (3) What assumptions can be made about human behavior and incentives in light of this sweep of human history? In order to answer these questions, we use archival records, literature reviews, including published material that draws heavily from empirical work conducted by the authors.

Since we are analyzing human decisions as they impact on ecological systems, let us lay out our basic assumptions immediately, so that we can later assess whether they are reasonable in light of evidence. We assume that:

1. Human decisions occur within tiers of decision-making units that extend from an individual to higher tiers.
2. Within all tiers of decision making, fallible individuals make decisions that are intended to increase net benefits to themselves and, potentially, to others.
3. Individuals learn from their experiences and from culturally transmitted experiences.
4. Human decisions at all tiers are affected by the cultural values of the individuals involved, the resources they possess, the information they obtain, the incentives and disincentives they face, the internal learning and choice processes used, and the time horizon invoked.
5. Decisions at any one tier affect the conditions, information, incentives, and time horizon (and, perhaps the cultural values, resources, internal choice processes) of others at that tier, at present and future time periods, and sometimes at other tiers.
6. Thus, human choice is interdependent within tiers, at times between tiers, and across time and space. Impacts may be horizontal, upward, and downward.
7. Physical and biological processes also affect the information, incentives, and time horizon that are used in human choice as well as being affected by human choice.

In the conclusion, we will briefly assess whether we need to change any of these assumptions in light of the evidence we review in this chapter.

Following a brief description of the ecological dimension of an SES, the second section of this chapter provides the backdrop for later sections, outlining the precolonial environmental and institutional conditions among pastoral Maasai. This as well as the third and fourth sections consider the interplay between institutions and environment during colonial rule (1890–1963) and after 1963. The final (fifth and sixth) sections discuss the factors that influence institutional robustness and ecological resilience, connecting back to the assumptions that were posed in the introduction. Overall, this chapter presents a series of institutional changes over time and attempts to tie these together with their implications for the ecological system.

10.2 The Ecological Side of an SES

Dryland ecosystems are interchangeably referred to as savannahs, rangelands, bushlands, and the like. They cover about 40 percent of Africa's landmass (Scholes & Walker, 1993) and support close to 50 percent of its population (Thomas, Twyman, & Harris, 2002; Anderson et al., 2004). At a global level, pastoral areas represent some 25 percent of the global land area (FAO, 2001) and are home to about 103 million rural poor (IFAD, 2000). Many dryland environments are confronted with persistent drought shocks. Pastoralists, the dominant groups that inhabit these areas, are among the poorest peoples in the world (Lybbert, Barrett, Desta, & Coppock, 2004). In Kenya, for example, the highest incidence of poverty is found in the arid and semi-arid lands, where more than 65 percent live below the poverty line (GoK/ILRI, 2003).

Rainfall over much of Maasailand, which forms the context of this analysis, is low and variable (see Fig. 10.1), distributed in a bimodal pattern, with short rains from October to December and long rains from March to May. Annual rainfall in Kajiado District, for example, is strongly influenced by altitude. Loitokitok, on the foothills of Mount Kilimanjaro in the south, has the highest average rainfall of about 1,250 mm (49 inches). Lakes Magadi and Amboseli, the lowest points in the district, have the lowest average rainfall of less than 500 mm (20 inches) per annum. Heavy rains also occur around Ngong Hills, Chyulu Hills, the Nguruman escarpment, and the slopes of Mount Kilimanjaro. Apart from being low, the rainfall is highly variable from year to year.

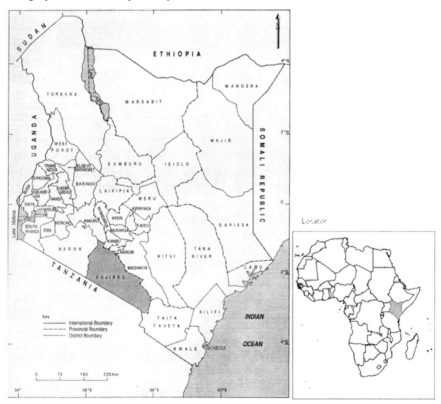

Fig. 10.1: Location of Kajiado District in Kenya
Source: Kenya Republic, 1990

Temperatures in the district also vary with altitude and season. The highest temperatures of about 34°C (93°F) are recorded around Lake Magadi, while the lowest minimum of about 10°C (50°F) is experienced at Loitokitok, on the eastern slopes of Mount Kilimanjaro. The mean maximum of Loitokitok is about 22°C (71°F). The coolest period is between July and August and the hottest is from November to April.

Based on these rainfall and temperature regimes, the Kajiado district has been divided into five agro-climatic zones with varying ecological potentials. Most (55 percent) of the district falls under agro-climatic zone V and 37 percent under agro-climatic zone VI: classified as semi-arid and arid, largely suited to livestock ranching. Rain-fed agriculture is possible only in a very small part (8 percent) of the district, mainly on the slopes of major hills and mountains and on the flood-plains of the Ewaso Ng'iro River, one of the three major rivers in the area.

In general, the Maasai live in a highly constrained and risky ecological setting, where livelihood options are limited and access to patchy resources are ever more critical. They are pastoralists, and livestock are central to their livelihoods and social relations. While some Maasai may periodically fall out of pastoralism because of drought or disease, or become cultivators or hunter-gatherers, they have been known to switch back to the pastoral mode as soon as they have rebuilt their herds (Waller, 1993).

The trajectory of change within SESs in Kenya's Maasailand is instructive for other parts of Africa and the developing world more broadly. Institutional reforms that address property rights are at the center of development policy in Kenya, with a push away from exclusive state claims towards decentralization and marketization. This push has tended to support one form of property structure, that is, individual ownership, regardless of the social and ecological setting. An analysis of the links between institutional robustness and ecological resilience over a defined time period shaped by major, externally-driven changes in property rights, in a defined ecological and cultural setting, can provide insights into how local institutions function to mitigate and/or absorb these changes and the effects of these functions on ecology. Such knowledge will help to generate a deeper understanding of how SESs are linked in order to improve governance and policy at a time when humans and nature are faced with many uncertainties and challenges.

10.3 Governance of the SES Prior to 1890: A Probable Balance

The Maasai in Kenya are comprised of twelve sections that occupy a specified territory, broadly governed by an autonomous political structure based on an age-grade system.[1] During the period prior to colonial rule, the boundaries of each

---

[1] The territorial organization of the Maasai has been extensively documented by prior scholars, from whose descriptions the following account is drawn: Spencer (1997), Mol

section were well recognized, and defended against unauthorized intrusion by a warrior age-set. Ecologically, most sections represented a mosaic of different eco-system types and could include high-potential forest, low-potential semi-arid scrubland, and wetlands. Access and use were coordinated, and highland pastures often reserved for dry-season grazing, while areas closest to settlements were set aside for young, old, and sick stock. Elders' councils and the warrior groups enforced access and use rights. In times of environmental stress, herds were moved within the section and across sectional boundaries, depending on pasture availability (Galaty, 1994a, 1994b). Sectional alliances allowed access outside the territory of each section. Under extreme environmental stress, intersectional conflict over resources would often escalate into war.

Each section was further divided into localities and localities into neighborhoods. Each locality had a council of elders for coordinating resource access and management, settling disputes, and enforcing customary law. The locality was the basis of the Maasai transhumant herding system and involved herd and family movements between dry- and wet-season pastures. Local organization through the elders ensured that Maasai stock had access to both types of pasture and that various traditional management techniques were employed, such as the regular burning of portions of grassland to help regenerate new grass growth and the judicious grazing of goats to prevent destruction of grass roots. Rights to resources were secured by families through continued residence in the locality and by participation in rites and rituals.

Each locality was divided further into common residential areas, or settlements, that comprised several households. Different neighborhoods would grant grazing access to herders who were temporarily passing through the area. There were also neighborhood controls on grazing. Each neighborhood had, for example, two types of dry-season grazing areas, one to be used in the early to middle of the dry season, and the other in the late dry season. Elders enforced these rules and also forbade the construction of permanent settlements in these areas. Despite cooperation at the settlement level, where households pooled labor for herding and security as well as for enforcement of use and management rights, herd ownership was individualized. Each household was autonomous and regulated its own affairs independently.

Maasai pastoralism allowed for a variety of accommodations with cultivating communities living in the region, such as the Kikuyu. Through marital exchange, the Maasai solidified friendship bonds that facilitated complementarities. The Maasai could seek agricultural produce in exchange for livestock, obtaining for instance superior steers from Borana pastoralists of northern Kenya and southern Ethiopia. Maasai dependence on trade increased during times of crisis, such as drought or epidemics.

(1996), Galaty (1989), Ingule (1980), Berntsen (1979), Baxter and Almagor (1978), Jacobs (1965), and Bernardi (1952).

Knowledge on the ecological status of Maasailand in the precolonial era is based on anecdotal information from early travelers and colonial administrators. Maasailand comprised a diversity of landscape and vegetation conditions (Thomson, 1885). The southern part of Maasailand comprised what Thomson called the "Nyika dry savannah," which was sparsely vegetated with grass. Here, water was scarce and rainfall so little that there was "hardly a blade of grass to be seen." These areas included the regions surrounding the Maparasha Hills, Oldonyo Orok, and the Amboseli plains. To the north of this area, in the Kaputiei plains (i.e., present-day northeastern Kajiado District), Thomson found a grand expanse of undulating country, the hollows of which were "knee-deep in rich and succulent pasture ... and ridges covered in trees of moderate size" (1885, p. 170).

Similar observations were made by Governor Charles Eliot a decade later when commenting on the pasturage potential of the East African Protectorate. According to Eliot (1905, p. 170), Maasailand would "afford excellent grass to cattle owned by both natives and Europeans." He further suggested that the quality of the pasturage may have been due to long periods of continuous grazing by native cattle, which involved regular burning to improve the quality of grass, to clear pests, and to remove woody vegetation. On the other hand, Talbot (1972) suggested that, ranging over broad territories, the Maasai may never actually have achieved a balance with their environment. Their emphasis on large herds, close herding in tight groups, and use of few watering points by large concentrations of livestock resulted in overgrazing, which was typical of Maasai pastoralism, as it comprised an adaptation to a difficult environment. Movement to new pastures allowed the recovery of overgrazed and/or degraded areas. Jacobs (1980) points out that past traditional localities seemed to have been stable, with adequate quantities of both wet- and dry-season pastures and considerable mobility between the two. Nevertheless, the absence of surface water, periodic droughts, and livestock disease limited livestock production and maintained the balance of the SES.

The influence of traditional pastoralism on the historical development of ecological regimes in Maasailand is inconclusive, yet these early accounts suggest that Maasai pastoralism may have been attuned to resource productivity. Under traditional herd management practices and other self-regulatory mechanisms, exhaustion of pasture was temporary and probably not serious, since the pastoralists had sufficient opportunities to move their herds elsewhere. Herd mobility may well have enabled the achievement of a dynamic balance between pasture resources and livestock holdings.

The preceding account reveals two major features of an interactive SES that may permit, and possibly enhance, the resilience of the ecological system against periodic disturbances such as drought and disease: (1) a multilevel governance structure at multiple and nested spatial scales and (2) rules (and norms) for resource access and conflict resolution that were legitimate and broadly accepted. During this era, households were nested within neighborhoods and settlements, nested within localities, nested within sections. Each level corresponded to a spatial scale and was interlinked. Yet, failures at any one level did not necessarily devastate decisions at another level, because each level had a fair amount of autonomy to make and enforce rules for resource appropriation and provision that were recognized and accepted at other levels.

These features of polycentric and multiple governance (concepts that are also developed by Blomquist, this volume) provided pastoralists with the flexibility to adapt and respond to disturbances, including drought. Mobility was a key component of resource use, management, and sustainability. Rules and norms served to coordinate access, to prevent or manage conflicts among multiple users, and to provide degraded areas with sufficient time to recover. Importantly, if one level did not function well for whatever reason, the whole system was not necessarily compromised, as other levels would continue to function.

10.4 Governance of the SES During the Colonial Era: Institutions and Ecology in Jeopardy

British interests in East Africa in the late nineteenth century encouraged the settlement of European farmers in Maasailand. The agricultural and commercial activities of the incoming settlers were expected to contribute towards making the New British Protectorate self-financing and less reliant on budgetary support from the London office. The Maasai, whose use of land was seasonal, were relocated from the northern, better-watered areas of their territory to land further south, where most of them resided at the time. Close to two million hectares of land used by the Maasai was converted to private, individually owned farms and commercial ranches.

The land areas where the Maasai were relocated were either too small or too arid to support transhumant pastoralism. The most valuable water supplies were included in the land allocated to the Europeans (James, 1939). Land in the south was also tick-infested and already populated by other Maasai sections (Tignor, 1976; Sandford, 1919). Of the 10 million acres of the Maasai reserve, 2 million acres were arid or semi-arid; 800,000 infested with tsetse fly; and 300,000 subject to East Coast fever (Lewis, 1934, cited in Kipury, 1989).

More land was later taken for the creation of protected areas. Between 1946 and 1965, a total of 25,792 km^2 of present-day Kajiado District was converted into national parks, reserves, or conservation areas (Kituyi, 1990). Most of this land constituted dry season highlands or swamplands and salt licks – strategic resources for the Maasai.

The Maasai were eventually confined to the southern reserve (Halderman, 1989; Kipuri, 1989; Sandford, 1919), their herds restricted from regular, traditional movement to prevent mixing with new breeds from England. This restriction also blocked traditional trade and exchange between the Maasai and the northern Borana pastoralists.

Lack of market offtake and the introduction of veterinary services within the Maasai reserve led to herd proliferation. Herd growth was also aided by "authorized" raiding against non-Maasai communities, as British officers employed the Maasai as mercenaries who were paid with captured cattle (Bridges, 1991; Halderman, 1989). By 1932, colonial administrators were expressing concern about the large herds, which they presumed were responsible for soil erosion and land degradation. In 1904, cattle were estimated at only 50,000 and shoats at 600,000.[2] By 1914, Maasai cattle were 600,000 and shoats over 1 million. In later years, even after the droughts of 1933 and 1934, cattle had increased to 700,000 and sheep and goats to 800,000.

Administrators attributed soil degradation in the Maasai reserve to Maasai "irrationality."[3] The Maasai's "cattle complex," a psychological attachment to the beast, led to an emphasis on quantity over quality, resulting in overgrazing and environmental degradation (Herskovits, 1926). This destruction was viewed as a threat to the large herds of wildlife in the Maasai reserves. Maasai perceptions of the origins of the problem were, however, different (Campbell, 1993). For them, degradation was a consequence of constrained grazing following large-scale appropriations for European settlement. It was also a consequence of losing the remaining good-quality grazing to cultivation.

The official solutions to the problem of degradation undertaken by the British involved appointing a series of commissions to divine ways of controlling stock levels in tune with carrying capacities and to explore land tenure options. The first was the Kenya Land Commission (Carter Commission) of 1932, which recognized customary tenure in the Maasai reserve, but recommended gradual privatization and eventual individualization of land. The commissioners were opposed to returning appropriated land back to the Maasai, since they thought the Maasai were tying up prime land and not exploiting it efficiently. The commission suggested that the Maasai be forced to lease out land, particularly to cultivating communities.

The Carter Commission ended the theoretical security over land rights that the Treaty of 1911 had given to the Maasai. It also introduced a new structure for land and livestock management: the grazing schemes, which turned on the reduction of livestock numbers, the provision of water supplies, disease control and the creation of livestock markets through British financing. Each scheme was administered by a livestock officer, with the assistance of a grazing committee comprising twelve elders, who were responsible for the enforcement of regulations. Livestock officers acted under special ordinances and bylaws that conferred broad powers upon them. They determined who could graze livestock in the scheme, the number of animals each could graze, and where they could graze, while also enforcing

---

[2] This unnamed and undated citation, titled "Section VII: The Masai Extra Provincial District," was retrieved from Box File A in the library of the Catholic Church in Kajiado town.

[3] The notion of Maasai irrationality has since been forcefully refuted (Livingstone, 1977, 1986; Helland, 1980).

fines on violators. The bylaws did not provide for appeal against a livestock officer's decisions.

Grazing schemes were introduced at the level of the Maasai section. But first,
in 1946, a model ranch unit was set up in Konza in order "to demonstrate to the
Maasai how a permanent water supply can be most beneficially used and the advantages of control grazing, that is relating the number of cattle to the carrying capacity of the land."[4] The Konza scheme was also aimed at demonstrating the improved stock breeding practices and at conducting experiments in pasture
improvement. The first Maasai families to participate in this scheme, chosen by
elders, took up residence in January 1949. Each agreed to weekly livestock dipping, giving prophylactic injections, following rotational grazing plans, and restricting livestock to prescribed numbers. A manager was resident from the start of
the ranch until 1958.

One commentator characterized the scheme as a drastic failure (Fallon, 1962).
Many things went wrong: fencing fell into disrepair and did not keep out game
animals; residents did not restrict livestock numbers; and the drought of 1959
forced residents out. Cattle population increased substantially. By 1954, the number had grown from 1,400 to 2,300, and by 1958 it had grown to 2,441, far exceeding the stated maximum of 1,700. In 1958, a new limit of 2,000 was set. Then
came the drought; by mid-1961, the ground was bare and all residents had left. By
this time, most of Kajiado District was severely overgrazed and range resources
badly degraded. Watering points, grazing schemes, and demonstration ranches
were the sites of severe degradation. The destruction was so severe that, where the
"model range" was located, a jagged, bare, red-earth scar in the savanna landscape
was now visible from a high-flying airliner through the blowing dust. Residents of
the Konza scheme failed to honor their commitment to reduce livestock. All other
grazing schemes (in the Ilkisonko and Loodokilani sections) were eventually
abandoned.

Overall, grazing schemes did not function during droughts, and water development contributed to significant resource depletion (Fallon, 1962). Destocking
proved difficult (Jahnke, 1978): many Maasai were already living at submarginal
levels. Stock reduction further reduced the supply of meat and milk for the household; culling programs did not fit into the traditional social patterns that were built
on an intricate system of human bonds established by lending, renting, exchang-
ing, and sharing livestock for different reasons in different situations.

A second commission, the East Africa Royal Commission (also known as the
Dow Commission) of 1952, was initiated to provide solutions for land tenure. This
commission viewed Maasai communal ownership of land combined with individual livestock ownership as the root cause of land degradation. The commissioners
recommended that land be individualized and customary rights eliminated as they
were inefficient. However, the commission also recommended that collective
rights in pastoral areas be maintained, but only as an intermediate stage towards

---

[4] See footnote 1.

individual ranching. It proposed ranches, access to markets, better breeding practices, and commercialization of stock farming as solutions to the "pastoral problem."

The Swynnerton Plan of 1954, crafted during a time of great political crisis, superseded but drew heavily from both the Carter and Dow Commissions. It proposed a sweeping registration and individualization of land tenure in Kenya. Since the outcome of individualized tenure in the Kikuyu areas of central province had been landlessness and political unrest, however, the Swynnerton Plan promoted grazing schemes and group ranches. These were to be managed according to "scientific principles," such as grazing rotation. Water and veterinary facilities were to be provided and small-scale irrigation encouraged. Soil conservation, afforestation, and rehabilitation were to be taken up to restore denuded areas. To ensure that these innovations were strictly followed, the government was to impose strict measures such as "grazing guards," fines, and imprisonment for pastoralists who broke the rules. Livestock marketing, controlled grazing, water supply, and tsetse and livestock disease eradication were additional interventions. The objective was to exploit the potential of Maasai stock to contribute to the national economy.

What do we make of these changes in the SES during the colonial era (1890–1963)? How can institutional robustness be linked to ecological resilience? Clearly, the entry of officials from the British administration introduced a new set of powerful actors and institutions at the national and local levels. These new sets of institutions did not solve the long-standing problem of drought and land/soil degradation, but rather intensified it. The key features of the SES during the colonial era that are important to robustness and resilience include:

1. A new and powerful actor, the government and government officials, with clear objectives regarding land management, but with insufficient understanding of ecosystem processes. These objectives, which included limiting livestock numbers, and new rules and structures for land and livestock management, were at odds with the Maasai production system and institutions that supported it.
2. A decline in spatial scale for the operation of Maasai resource management institutions and production system. Mobility was constrained within grazing schemes and the Maasai Reserve. Elders were, in turn, required to enforce rules made by government officials (e.g., those for constraining livestock numbers), while their authority was undermined.
3. Removal or reduction of the risk of disease, water distribution, and a declining scale of the system (or a concentration of livestock with reduced mobility) reversed these supposed gains in risk reduction and increased the severity of disturbances.
4. New government institutions at nested administrative levels, competing with and/or replacing Maasai institutions. This competition and replacement also included the content of the institutions, which was not only at variance with Maasai institutions, but also poorly matched with the ecological situation.

In sum, a general decline occurred in the diversity of institutions, the autonomy of Maasai institutions, the spatial scale of livestock production, and the institutional levels of indigenous institutions. This resulted in the reduction of both the robustness of institutions as well as the resilience of the ecosystem, whose vulnerability to disturbances was amplified. In order to cope with the severity of the disturbances, the Maasai abandoned the new/imposed institutional structures and, instead, resorted to prior arrangements of mutual reciprocity, which allowed for mobility.

10.5 Governing the SES in the Post-Colonial Period: The Introduction of Group and Individual Ranches

The Dow Commission and the Swynnerton Plan resulted in the establishment of individual ranches[5] and group ranches in Maasailand. Instead of attempting to directly control herders and their livestock management techniques, the government instead sought to formalize land rights. Land in the former reserves was demarcated, surveyed, and registered, with the expectation that the Maasai would adjust their herd management strategies, destock, and conserve the resource base.

Individual ranches were intended to serve as a model for the rest of the Maasai to emulate (Jahnke, Ruthenberg, & Thimm, 1972). Low-interest credit for purchasing superior breeds and for farm infrastructure, such as boreholes and water pans, was made available through the Agricultural Finance Corporation as part of World Bank financing to Kenya's livestock sector under the Kenya Livestock Development Program (KLDP). The individual ranchers also had support from livestock extension officers from the Ministry of Agriculture and Livestock Development.

The first individual ranch was established as early as 1954 (Campbell, 1993), but most of the approximately fifty-two ranches were established between 1963 and 1965 (Hedlund, 1971; Rutten, 1992). Individual ranches were first created in better-watered areas of Kajiado District. The first owners of individual ranches were all Maasai, most of whom, once having acquired their large ranches, sold off portions to Kikuyu cultivators (Simpson, 1973).

The progressive development of individual ranches, each averaging between 300–800 hectares (Grandin, 1987), raised concerns among administrators and ordinary Maasai alike, who feared a landgrab by influential Maasai and insecurity as land was easily transferred to non-Maasai. These concerns were captured in the Lawrance Report of 1965–1966 (Kenya Republic, 1966), which recommended the establishment of group ranches, which were seen as an alternative way of realizing the same goals of accelerating pastoral development, but with the added advantage

---

[5] An individual ranch is a production enterprise in which an individual member of a "tribal" society may, with community consent and the authorization of the local country council, legally register communal land as private property.

of safeguarding against alienation to non-Maasai. They were expected to provide tenure security, creating incentives for the Maasai to invest in range improvement and, ultimately, to reduce overaccumulation of livestock.

A "group" meant a tribe, clan, section, family, or other group of persons whose land under recognized customary law belonged communally to its members. The exact grouping was determined by a committee that comprised officials of the Lands Department and elders from each section of the Maasai. Under this law, a Registrar of Group Ranches, whose job it was to oversee their functioning, was also created by the Lands Ministry. He or she would convene a meeting of the members of the group, encouraging them to adopt a constitution and elect representatives. Every registered member of the group ranch is a joint owner of group land and holds equal shares. Each member is entitled to reside on group land with family and dependents.

The group representatives are expected to ensure that the rights of any person under recognized customary law are safeguarded. In consultation with other group members, they are authorized to hold property on behalf of the group, acting on its behalf and for its collective benefit. Each group can craft its own rules regarding the running of its own affairs, but is required by law to hold a general meeting of its members every year. Decisions made at these meetings are binding if at least 60 percent of group members are present and a similar proportion of those present vote for them. In addition, members elect a management committee by open ballot, comprised of a chair, vice-chair, secretary, treasurer, and three other members elected from the group representatives. The committee encourages members to manage the land or graze their stock in accordance with sound principles of land use, range management, animal husbandry, and commercial practice. It can raise credit and is involved in development planning. Every member is required to accept and comply with decisions of the committee and, if aggrieved by a committee decision, has the formal right to appeal to the group representatives, the registrar of group representatives, or to a subordinate court having jurisdiction in the area. Group ranch dissolution can occur only after a written application signed by a majority of the group representatives is followed by a resolution passed by a 60 percent majority in a meeting specially convened for that purpose.

The Kenyan government, newly independent in 1963, received loans and grants from the World Bank, USAID, the Swedish Aid agency, Canadian Development Agency, and the United Kingdom. Loans were granted under the KLDP and implemented jointly by the Ministry of Lands and Settlement, the Range Management division of the Ministry of Agriculture, the Ministry of Water Development, and the Agricultural Finance Corporation. A total of fifty-two group ranches were created under two phases of the KLDP between 1968 and 1979.

Although the Maasai did not agree with, or even understand, some features of the group ranch, such as grazing quotas, boundary maintenance, and the management committee, they accepted the idea of group ranches primarily because it afforded them protection against further land appropriation from the government, against the incursion of non-Maasai, and from a landgrab by the elite Maasai

(Fratkin & Smith, 1994; Campbell, 1991; Goldschmidt, 1980; Hopcraft, 1980; Halderman, 1972; Hedlund, 1971). Group ranch development also promised water development in the form of dams and boreholes, and improved livestock husbandry through introduction of dipping facilities and regular vaccination against prevalent animal diseases (Davis, 1970). An evaluation conducted in the fourth year of the program found that the Maasai viewed the program as a means of increasing herds and assuring a larger and steadier supply of milk and blood to feed their families (Axinn, Birkhead, & Sudholt, 1979).

Group ranches are now generally thought to have failed to meet their intended objectives. An indicator of this failure is increasing demands for their dissolution and subsequent division into individual, titled units for distribution among their registered members. Disintegration began in the mid-1970s for the Kaputiei ranches. By 1985, twenty-two group ranches in different parts of Kajiado had resolved to subdivide; seven went ahead and subdivided (Munei, 1987). By 1996, all of these twenty-two group ranches had actually subdivided and individual land titles had begun to be issued (Kimani & Pickard, 1998). Eleven other group ranches were in various stages of subdivision. By 2000, thirty-one group ranches had subdivided and been issued titles (Mwangi, 2007a). Fourteen others resolved to subdivide and were being surveyed and demarcated. Only twelve had resisted subdivision. According to official records in 2006, out of a total of fifty-two group ranches, thirty-two are subdivided, and fifteen are in progress, seven of which are disputed and under court injunction, five have not subdivided (Mwangi, 2007b).

A variety of reasons have been offered to account for the failure of group ranches. Some scholars note that group ranches were undermined by a lack of ecological viability (Kipuri, 1989; Halderman, 1985, 1989; Hopcraft, 1980; Njoka, 1979). Ranches were not sufficiently extensive to allow pastoralists to exploit the discontinuity and heterogeneity of resources within their environment adequately. Group ranch boundaries were not respected in times of drought and Maasai continued to rely on movement across group ranches under traditional norms of reciprocity via kinship and friendship ties. Thus, the incentive to invest in pasture management and stinting is weakened, as those who did not invest effort would still benefit from the investments of others (Hopcraft, 1980). Munei (1987) argues that, while the enclosure of group ranches served to intensify droughts and increase movement, this would have been less severe if appropriate infrastructure had been developed within the ranch. Because the committee was not vested with sufficient authority to control livestock numbers (livestock are owned individually) and grazing patterns, group ranches experienced an overgrazing problem (Evangelou, 1984; Hopcraft, 1980).

Misappropriation of funds, difficulties in enforcing loan repayment, and low/delayed returns were additional problems that locked out group ranches from their principal source of development funds (Galaty, 1994b; Kipuri, 1989; Munei, 1987; Doherty, 1987; Migot-Adholla & Little, 1980). The above suite of reasons was provided by observers in the very early stages of group ranch disintegration. Later studies echo these problems. They also provide additional insights about the increasing uncertainty regarding individual shares in group land, population increases, and governance failures, especially difficulties in enforcing livestock quotas and subsequent distributional problems (Mwangi, 2007a, 2007c; Davis, 2000; Simel, 1999; Galaty, 1992, 1994b).

What have been the effects of these institutional changes that have taken place during the post-colonial era (after 1963) on ranch ecology? A series of unrelated studies and evaluations using different methodologies and based on different group ranches provide insights on the implications of group ranches on local ecologies. One evaluation of group ranches observed that, four years after launching the program, committees had not yet implemented grazing quotas, save for a general rule that restricted grazing from a two-mile perimeter around water facilities (Jahnke et al., 1972). The same evaluation also noted that the notion of committee decision making on behalf of others was a new one for the Maasai, who traditionally rely on group consensus. In addition, livestock is owned by individuals, and the idea of the livestock quota tends to favor either an egalitarian distribution of herds or a freezing of a given distribution pattern, both of which were not valid for the Maasai production system, which has been fluid and motivated by risk reduction and cultural obligations. Talbot (1972) views group ranches and grazing schemes as "resource degrading development activities," in which overgrazing and drought losses are proportional to the amount of development suffered. The projections of the early evaluations were confirmed by empirical studies in later years.

Ecological studies comparing a broad range of ecological indicators before the creation of group ranches in 1967 and during their operation in 1977 observed a deterioration in range condition, with an increase in the incidence and cover of undesired/less palatable species relative to desired/palatable ones (Njoka, 1979). Range management seemed to be a more important factor influencing the decline, including a roughly two-fold increase in cattle and water facilities, even as vaccination and other treatments decreased mortality. Despite ecological decline in group ranches, they seemed to fare better than their closely associated individual ranches (Rutten, 1992). Other studies using community perceptions – backed by aerial photography and topographical maps – revealed similar trends over a thirty-year period, comparing conditions before and after group ranches were subdivided (Macharia & Ekaya, 2005). Communities indicated that areas of bare ground were more prevalent and more extensive than they were before, while sustained overgrazing reduced cover, quality, and productivity; changed plant composition from perennial to annual species; and encouraged bush encroachment.

Group ranch subdivision and privatization is associated with a steady decline in the capacity of the land to support livestock populations (Thornton et al., 2007; Boone, Burnsilver, Thornton, Worden, & Galvin, 2005) and with a precipitous (72 percent) decline in wildlife populations in the subdivided areas adjacent to protected areas, due to habitat fragmentation (Reid et al., 2007). In spite of the subdivisions, herders are now adopting new institutional arrangements that increase opportunities for herd mobility and access to forage (Burnsilver & Mwangi, 2006;

Mwangi, 2007b; Rutten, 1992) and are also reconsolidating subdivided parcels and pursuing joint management, while continuing with large-scale movement during severe droughts and reciprocal arrangements of herd redistribution. These arrangements at local and broader scales are based on pre-existing social relationships, networks and norms among age-sets, clan members, friends, and stock associates. An evaluation of the ecological implications of these arrangements is instructive (Mwangi, 2007a, Chapter 7): Valuable perennial grass species show consistently higher cover values where groups reconsolidate parcels and jointly manage pastures, while weedy shrubs colonize unconsolidated parcels, where individuals enforce their boundaries and livestock concentrated over smaller areas.

Features of the SES after 1963 include:

1. The national government is an established actor that uses formal law to embed its objectives, which are intended to create incentives for better range management.
2. Government objectives do not change across time.
3. Creation of group and individual ranches side-by-side, both replace the council of elders as the organization that governs resource allocation and management. Individual owners now make decisions for individual ranches, while a new bureaucratic structure with new decision-making rules – the management committee – is the locus of decision making on land matters for the group ranch. The accountability of the management committee was primarily to the organization that had oversight over group ranch functions – the registrar of group ranches, a government official – rather than to the group members.
4. The evolution of an elaborate and ineffective system of financing and operation that involved multiple donors, with multiple expectations and mechanisms of financing group and individual ranches. This system did not work.
5. The spatial scale of pastoralism is further circumscribed with the creation of hard boundaries between group ranches.
6. The condition of the range declines further, and the group ranches eventually subdivide into individually titled parcels, the viability of which is questionable, even as herders adopt new arrangements.

10.6 Discussion

We began this chapter by asking three questions: which institutions are more likely to be robust over time, how robustness (or lack thereof) may influence ecological conditions, and what kinds of assumptions those exploring linked social-ecological systems can make in their inquiries.

Robust institutions are those that can weather repeated disturbance and reconstitute themselves to perform their functions. Our cross-time analysis demonstrates that, at prior to colonial rule Maasai institutions regulated resource use and access within and among different subgroups of the Maasai. These councils of elders were organized locally, but they were also nested and replicated at higher spatial scales and governance levels. Thus, the neighborhood was nested within a settlement, the settlement was nested within a locality, and the locality was nested within a section.

At lower levels, the rules established by these governance arrangements regulated access and relationships between households and neighborhoods, at higher levels between Maasai sections or sub-tribes, and between them and non-Maasai (see Marshall, 2008 for development of the concept of nesting). These access relationships included seasonal herd movements between wet and dry season pastures, daily livestock movements in localities, and pasture management techniques such as burning. Mobility between different resource patches was possible. The effects of overgrazing and degradation, which were posited by colonial officials as typifying Maasai pastoralism, were tempered by the capacity to move to new pastures. The different spatial scales for resource appropriation were well matched with the multilevel structure of institutions, allowing sufficient control and flexibility over use, thus checking sustained damage/degradation of the ecological conditions. Institutions were well adapted to a risky ecological setting.

The colonial rule (ca. 1890–1963) represents the beginning of radical changes in the linked SES. The introduction of external, formal, governmental institutions and personnel was grafted onto preexisting traditional institutions and systems. Formal institutions competed with and/or replaced the functions of traditional institutions, reducing their autonomy and restricting their reach to very small spatial scales. Soil erosion, land degradation, and increased severity of droughts were the result. The new institutional rules, such as those requiring the reduction of stocking levels, were ineffective simply because they overlooked cultural, ecological, and nutritional imperatives that necessitated an accumulation of livestock among herders. Despite heavy capital and financial investments, these new institutions and organizations were unable to adapt to ecological exigencies. At best, the introduction of water points and veterinary services served to reduce risks faced by herders. At worst, these interventions were incomplete, and only served to increase the severity of environmental disturbance, such as drought, when it occurred.

The Maasai tended to abandon the imposed grazing schemes and their rigid rules. Instead, they resorted to prior and well-tested mobility to exploit heterogeneously distributed resources, while using familiar norms of reciprocity among kin and friends to facilitate movement. The elders councils – the primary governance arrangement controlling resource access and distribution – were undermined by the introduction of formal government rules and organization. They subsequently lost control. This was then reflected in declining ecological resilience. However, other traditional institutions, such as norms of reciprocity, were remarkably robust and allowed herders to adapt to the declining conditions and still be able to move their herds to some degree, despite their confinement in smaller spaces.

During the post-colonial era, after 1963, radical changes from the colonial rule (ca. 1890–1963) were further adopted and entrenched under an independent

Kenyan government. Full-scale privatization of the range was pursued with the creation of individual and group ranches. Again, the official objective was to stabilize a degrading environment and to change Maasai herds from being a subsistence asset to a marketable commodity. The strategy was different in that it involved a formal change in the rules of resource access for the Maasai by creating and formalizing boundaries between Maasai subgroups by way of formal land ownership. In the group ranches in particular, a management committee was constituted that served to replace the council of elders in land and resource allocation. Committees were, by law, granted additional powers, including the regulation of livestock numbers in the group ranches by enforcing livestock quotas. Finally, group consensus in decision making was replaced by a majority voting rule in an open ballot. Quantitative and qualitative studies demonstrate that ecological condition in the group ranches steadily declined (even though they performed better than adjacent individual ranches). Scarcely fifteen years after their inception, the owners of group ranches started to subdivide their land into individual parcels to be distributed among their constituent members.

Much of the ecological decline over this long time period is associated with this process of individuation of land ownership. Individuals tend to increase livestock herds, wildlife populations are seen to decline, while forage options needed to sustain livestock and human nutrition are severely constrained. Land allocation and management decisions now fully reside with the individual parcel owner. During the post-colonial time, as in the times of the colonial rule (ca. 1890–1963), the robustness of traditional institutions of resource access were further undermined and eventually snuffed out. Statutory institutions gained prominence after 1963, but they were poorly adapted to the risk inherent in this ecological setting. Despite reducing livestock mortality through veterinary innovations and water provision, drought and rainfall continue to be limiting factors, severely impacting group ranches, and ecological degradation continues. Group ranch members continued to move their livestock outside the group ranch, exploiting mutual reciprocal arrangements across clan and age sets.

The newly introduced formal rules for resource access and decision making in the group ranch structure were not robust. Group ranches disintegrated. The new formal rules were unenforceable, as they contradicted cultural norms that underpin Maasai society. Livestock management is the preserve of each individual owner, who is under great pressure to maintain large herds for subsistence, to ensure against risk, and to meet cultural obligations.

In short, the earlier indigenous institutions prior to colonial rule appear to have been more robust, even though officials did not consider them to have formal status. Again, the indigenous institutions of the earlier times were nested at the group and higher levels and covered large spatial scales. Other indigenous institutions such as age-grades and clans are also cross-cutting institutions, found in all group ranch areas. In a post-subdivision setting, these norms of reciprocity and bonds of kinship and friendship now assume even greater importance. Most individual parcel owners continue to move their herds out of their parcels to other areas, even to Tanzania, during dry and drought spells. Other parcel owners do move their livestock, but also reconsolidate parcels for joint herding and pasturing at a very local level, often sharing with friends, neighbors, and family. Reconsolidated parcels have somewhat better ecological conditions than non-reconsolidated ones.

10.7 Conclusion

An important lesson to be learned from studying the relationships between institutions and ecology in the drylands of Kenya is that the "real" tragedy of the commons has been the lack of understanding shown by colonial and contemporary Kenyan government officials of the importance of a nested governance system for sustaining this Social-Ecological System over time. Many scholars and public officials presume that effective governance is possible only when a single, monocentric government makes all of the rules related to all policy issues within a national domain (see, for example, Miller, 1992). Garrett Hardin (1968) presumed that pastoralists involved in a tragedy of the commons dilemma could not extract themselves from it. He proposed that government should control access and use of a commons or that private property rights should be assigned. These are the two "solutions" that have been imposed on the Masaai over time. Neither of them have worked better than the nested system that the Masaai had themselves evolved over long periods of time, using trial-and-error methods to learn how to make better decisions. Neither of Hardin's preferred solutions were more effective in the short term, or more robust in the long term, than the nested layers of institutional rules that the Masaai had developed.

In our introduction to this chapter, we promised to examine three questions: (1) Which of the institutions that have existed during these time periods are more robust and why? (2) How does institutional robustness influence ecosystem resilience? and (3) What assumptions can be made about human behavior and incentives in light of this sweep of human history? Given the substantial evidence summarized above, we must conclude that the answer to the first question is quite clear. The traditional rules and norms evolved before colonial times were more robust than the formal, imposed rules made by officials who applied simplified panaceas regarding how to manage land. The officials are delinked from, and poorly adapted to, the risk inherent in the existing environmental setting and have largely served to create conditions that are associated with land degradation. The Maasai themselves continuously face risk. The traditional norms of herd redistribution and reciprocity assume more importance for them than for government officials, since the exposure to risk is not only more severe for the Maasai, but is also felt among a broader segment of society.

The evidence also provides some insight into our second question: How does institutional robustness influence ecosystem resilience? The robust institutional arrangements exhibited in this history were the set of nested arrangements ranging in size from a family, to localities, to the sections, and finally to alliances among the twelve sections. Each of these levels was able to make rules and norms related to terrains about which the participants in decision making at each level knew well. Thus, decisions could be and were tailored to the specific conditions of a particular locality. When drought hit one location, Maasai decision makers could search out other regions where rainfall was adequate and negotiate movement of the herds from the dry patch to wetter patches. Moving the cattle off of the range suffering from overly dry weather protected that patch and enabled it to regenerate when the next rains came. This rotation over a very large space was conducive to sustaining these drylands over time.

Unfortunately, the traditional nested governance system of the Maasai was not recognized by outsiders and officials who repeatedly tried to impose a centralized governance system to correct presumed management errors. A broad range of studies has demonstrated similar outcomes, yet very few have adopted frameworks that explicitly link robustness and resilience. Sporrong (1998), for example, demonstrates a degree of social and ecological resilience in Central Sweden prior to the enclosures of the 1820s, while Niamir-Fuller (1998), Alcorn and Toledo (1998), and Jodha (1998) all speak to the importance of nested institutions in enhancing the resilience of local resource management in pastoral, forest, and mountain ecosystems in Sahelian West Africa, Mexico, and the Hindukush-Himalaya, respectively.

Currently, however, the capabilities of a nested governance system for more effective management of natural resources and for mitigating risk are being recognized in other parts of the world, because of the promise that nested systems hold of perhaps being more effective and robust than centralized systems. Marshall (2008), for example, is exploring what can be learned from nested community-based governance systems for Australian ecologies that are very large but composed of meaningful units at multiple spatial scales. As more and more ecologists are recognizing that ecological systems exist at multiple scales, policy analysts need to recognize this fact and learn how to think about and encourage nested systems that facilitate decision making at multiple scales (Cash et al., 2006; Gibson, Ostrom, & Ahn, 2000). Problem solving related to complex SESs is best done under diverse institutions at multiple scales with sufficient autonomy and flexibility to make and change rules, depending on the nature of the ecology and the human organization at that scale.

Our third question relates to the appropriate assumptions that could be made about human behavior and incentives in light of this sweep of human history. In our introduction, we laid out our basic assumptions related to fallible humans who make decisions at multiple tiers of action intended to increase net benefits to themselves and potentially to others. We found that, when the Maasai made decisions within their evolved norms and rules, their decisions benefited not only themselves and their immediate families, but also generated benefits for a larger group. When government officials tried to replace the indigenous system, many of these norms of reciprocity and trust were destroyed in the process. Individual decisions became more self-centered on family survival rather than the survival of a larger group. We did find that human choice has been interdependent within tiers of decision making and across time and space, with the impacts of decisions being horizontal, upward, and downward. The change in governance shortened the time horizon of individual Maasai, because government officials no longer recognized the Maasai system for taking long-term effects into account.

Thus, from this effort to understand more than a century of the interrelationships among the components of an SES, we urge scholars and practitioners to recognize the advantage of nested governance systems organized at diverse levels. And, in particular, to be conscious that top-down changes may disrupt institutional adaptations that enable resource users to utilize the spatial and temporal distribution of resources to avoid excessive pressure on particular locations within larger ecosystems (Janssen et al., 2007). In our modern era of communications and market exchanges, relying strictly on small-scale common-property institutions for effective and robust management of ecosystems is not sufficient. Nor, is it sufficient to try to impose uniform rules on large, patchy environments when officials have little information about variations in rainfall, regrowth of key plants, soil nutrition, and water availability and suffer little harm from making decisions that can bring major damage to the citizens on the ground, trying to find ways of surviving over the long run. We continue to need nested governance systems that range from the very small to the global in scale.

Acknowledgments

Esther Mwangi gratefully acknowledges support from the Giorgio Ruffalo and Zif fellowship programs at Harvard University. Elinor Ostrom gratefully acknowledges support from the National Science Foundation (subaward No. 06-653) for the project "Dynamics of Rules in Commons Dilemmas". We appreciate the suggestions of Pauline Peters, Martina Padmanabhan, and Volker Beckmann, and the excellent editing of Patty Lezotte and Christopher Hank.

References

Alcorn, J. B., & Toledo, V. M. (1998). Resilient resource management in Mexico's forest ecosystems: The contribution of property rights. In F. Berkes & C. Folke (Eds.), *Linking social and ecological systems: Management practices and social mechanisms for building resilience* (pp. 216–249). Cambridge: Cambridge University Press.

Anderies, J. M., Janssen, M., & Ostrom, E. (2004). A framework to analyze the robustness of social-ecological systems from an institutional perspective. *Ecology and Society, 9*, article 18, from: http://www.ecologyandsociety.org/vol9/iss1/art18.

Anderson, J., Bryceson, D., Campbell, B., Chitundu, D., Clarke, J., Drinkwater, M., et al. (2004). *Chance, change and choice in African drylands: A new perspective on policy priorities.* (Paper presented at the workshop on development assistance in the African drylands, Durban, 2003), from: http://www.cifor.cgiar.org/publications/pdf_files /research/livelihood/Dryland.pdf.

Axinn, G. H., Birkhead, J. W., & Sudholt, A. W. (1979). *Evaluation of the Kenya national range and ranch development project.* AID Project No. 615–0157. Prepared for the U.S. Agency for International Development, Kenya Mission, Nairobi, Kenya, September 10, 1979.

Baxter, P. T. W., & Almagor, U. (1978). *Age, generation, and time: Some features of East African age organizations.* London: C. Hurst.

Berkes, F., & Folke, C. (1998). Linking social and ecological systems for resilience and sustainability. In F. Berkes & C. Folke (Eds.), *Linking social and ecological systems: Management practices and social mechanisms for building resilience* (pp. 1–26). Cambridge: Cambridge University Press.

Bernardi, I. M. C. (1952). The age-system of the Nilo-Hamitic peoples: A critical evaluation. *Africa, 22,* 316–332.

Berntsen, J. L. (1979). Maasai age-sets and prophetic leadership, 1850–1910. *Africa, 49,* 134–146.

Boone, R. B, Burnsilver, S., Thornton, P. K., Worden, J. S., & Galvin, K. A. (2005). Quantifying declines in livestock due to land subdivision. *Rangeland Ecology and Management, 58,* 523–532.

Bridges, R. C. (1991). Official perceptions during the colonial period of problems facing pastoral societies in Kenya. In J. C. Stone (Ed.), *Pastoral economies in Africa and long-term responses to drought.*(pp. 57–72). (Proceedings of a colloquium at the University of Aberdeen, April 1990). Aberdeen: University of Aberdeen, African Studies Group.

Burnsilver, S., & Mwangi, E. (2006). *Beyond group ranch subdivision: Collective action for livestock mobility, ecological viability and livelihoods.* Paper presented at the conference on pastoralism and poverty reduction in East Africa: A policy research conference, Nairobi.

Campbell, D. J. (1991). The impact of development upon strategies for coping with drought among the Maasai of Kajiado District, Kenya. In J. C. Stone (Ed.), *Pastoral economies in Africa and long-term responses to drought* (pp. 35–56). (Proceedings of a colloquium at the University of Aberdeen). Aberdeen: University of Aberdeen, African Studies Group.

Campbell, D. J. (1993). Land as ours, land as mine: Economic, political and ecological marginalization in Kajiado District. In T. Spear & R. Waller (Eds.), *Being Maasai: Ethnicity and identity in East Africa* (pp. 258–272). London: James Curry.

Carlson, J. M., & Doyle, J. (2002). Complexity and robustness. *Proceedings of the National Academy of Sciences, 9,* 2499–2545.

Cash, D. W., Adger, W. N., Berkes, F., Garden, P., Lebel, L., Olsson, P., et al. (2006). Scale and cross-scale dynamics: Governance and information in a multilevel world. *Ecology and Society,* 11, article 8, from: http://www.ecologyandsociety.org/vol11/ iss2/art8.

Davis, R. K. (1970). *Some issues in the evolution, organization and operation of group ranches in Kenya* (Discussion Paper No. 93). Nairobi: University College, Institute for Development Studies.

Davis, R. K. (2000). *The Kajiado group ranches: A perspective.* Unpublished report. Boulder: Institute of Behavioral Science.

Dietz, T., Ostrom, E., & Stern, P. (2003). The struggle to govern the commons. *Science, 302,* 1907–1912.

Doherty, D. A. (1987). Maasai pastoral potential: A study of ranching in Narok District, Kenya. Ph.D. dissertation, McGill University.

Eliot, C. (1905). *The East Africa protecorate*. London: Frank Cass and Co.

Evangelou, P. (1984). *Livestock development in Kenya's Maasailand: Pastoralists' transition to a market economy*. Boulder: Westview Press.

Fallon, L. E. (1962). *Masai range resources, Kajiado District*. Nairobi: USAID Mission to East Africa.

FAO (Food and Agriculture Organization of the United Nations). (2001). *Pastoralism in the new millennium* (Animal Production and Health Paper No. 150). Rome: FAO.

Fratkin, E., & Smith, K. (1994). Labor, livestock and land: The organization of pastoral production. In E. Fratkin, K. A. Galvin, & E. A. Roth (Eds.), *African pastoralist systems: An integrated approach* (pp. 69–89). Boulder: Lynne Rienner.

Galaty, J. G. (1989). *Seniority and cyclicity in Maasai age organization* (Discussion paper No. 6). Montreal, Quebec, Canada: McGill University.

Galaty, J. G. (1992). The land is yours: Social and economic factors in the privatization, subdivision and sale of Maasai ranches. *Nomadic Peoples, 30*, 26–40.

Galaty, J. G. (1994a). Ha(l)ving land in common: The subdivision of Maasai group ranches in Kenya. *Nomadic Peoples, 34/35*, 109–121.

Galaty, J. G. (1994b). The pastoralist's dilemma: Common property and enclosure in Kenya's rangeland. In R. Vernooy & K. M. Kealey (Eds.), *Food systems under stress in Africa: Proceedings of a workshop held in Ottawa, Ontario, Canada, November 7–8, 1993*. Ottawa: IDRC.

Gibson, C. C., Ostrom, E., & Ahn, T. K. (2000). The concept of scale and the human dimensions of global change. *Ecological Economics, 32*, 217–239.

GoK/ILRI/WORLD BANK/WRI/Rockefeller Foundation. 2003. *Geographic dimensions of well-being in Kenya: Where are the poor?* Volume 1. Ministry of Planning and National Development of the Government of Kenya, International Livestock Research Institute, The World Bank, World Resources Institute and the Rockefeller Foundation.

Goldschmidt, W. (1980, August). The failure of pastoral economic development programs in Africa. In G. Galaty, D. Aronson, & P. C. Salzman (Eds.), *The future of pastoral peoples* (pp. 110–128). (Proceedings of a conference held in Nairobi, Kenya, August 4–8, 1980). Ottawa, Ontario: International Development Research Center).

Grandin, B. E. (1987). Pastoral culture and range management: Recent lessons from Maasailand. ILCA Bulletin 28. International Livestock Center for Africa, Addis Ababa, Ethiopia, September 1987.

Halderman, J. M. (1972). *An analysis of continued semi-nomadism on the Kaputiei Maasai group ranches: Sociological and ecological factors* (Discussion Paper No. 152). Institute for Development Studies, University of Nairobi.

Halderman, J. M. (1985). Problems of pastoral development in Eastern Africa. *Agricultural Administration, 18*, 199–216.

Halderman, J. M. (1989). Development and famine risk in Kenya Maasailand. Ph.D. dissertation, University of California, Berkeley.

Hardin, G. (1968). The tragedy of the commons. *Science, 162*, 1243–1248.

Hedlund, H. (1971). *The impact of group ranches on a pastoral society* (Staff Paper No. 100). Institute for Development Studies, University of Nairobi.

Helland, J. (1980). *Some issues in the study of pastoralists and the development of pastoralism*. Addis Ababa: International Livestock Center for Africa (ILCA).

Herskovits, M. J. (1926). The cattle complex in East Africa. *American Anthropologist, 28*, 230–272.

Holling, C. S. (1973). Resilience and stability of ecological systems. *Annual Review of Ecology and Systematics, 4*, 2–23.

Hopcraft, P. N. (1980). Economic institutions and pastoral resource management: Consideration for a development strategy. In G. Galaty, D. Aronson, & P. C. Salzman (Eds.),

The future of pastoral peoples (pp. 224–243). (Proceedings of a conference held in Nairobi, Kenya, August 4–8, 1980). Ottawa, Ontario: International Development Research Center.

IFAD (International Fund for Agricultural Development) (2000). *Sustainable livelihoods in the drylands.* (Discussion paper for the 8th session of the Commission on sustainable development). Rome: IFAD, from: http://www.ifad.org/lrkm/theme/range/sustainable.pdf

Ingule, F. O. (1980). Cultural change and communication among the pastoral Maasai of Kajiado District of Kenya. MA thesis, Daystar International Institute, Wheaton College Graduate School.

Jacobs, A. (1965). The traditional political organization of the pastoral Maasai. Ph.D. dissertation, Oxford University, Nuffield College.

Jacobs, A. (1980). The pastoral Maasai and tropical rural development. In R. H. Bates & M. Lofchie (Eds.), *Agricultural development in Africa: Issues of public policy* (pp. 275–300). New York: Praeger.

Jahnke, H. (1978). *A historical view of range development in Kenya.* Nairobi: International Livestock Center for Africa.

Jahnke, H., Ruthenberg, H., & Thimm, H. U. (1972). *Range development in Kenya: The Kenya livestock development project and its impact on rural development.* Washington, DC: IBRD Consultation.

James, L. (1939). The Kenya Masa: A nomadic people under modern administration. *Africa, 12,* 49–73.

Janssen, M., Anderies, J. M., & Ostrom, E. (2007). Robustness of social-ecological systems to spatial and temporal variability. *Society and Natural Resources, 20,* 307–322.

Jodha, N. (1998). Reviving the social system – ecosystem links in the Himalayas. In F. Berkes & C. Folke (Eds.), *Linking social and ecological systems: Management practices and social mechanisms for building resilience* (pp. 285–310). Cambridge: Cambridge University Press.

Kenya Republic. (1966). Report of the mission on land consolidation and registration in Kenya, 1965–1966. Nairobi: Government Printer.

Kenya Republic. (1990). *Kajiado District Atlas.* Kajiado: Ministry of Reclamation and Development of Arid, Semi-Arid Areas and Wastelands.

Kimani, K., & Pickard, J. (1998). Recent trends and implications of group ranch subdivision and fragmentation in Kajiado District, Kenya. *Geographic Journal, 164,* 202–213.

Kipuri, N. (1989). Maasai women in transition: Class and gender in the transformation of a pastoral society. Ph.D. dissertation, Temple University.

Kituyi, M. (1990). *Becoming Kenyans: Socio-economic transformation of the pastoral Maasai.* Nairobi: African Center for Technology Studies Press.

Lewis, R. W. (1934). *A plan for the development of Maasailand.* Kabete: Department of Veterinary Services.

Livingstone, I. (1977). *Economic irrationality among the pastoral people in East Africa: Myth or reality?* Discussion Paper No. 25. Institute for Development Studies, University of Nairobi.

Livingstone, I. (1986). The common property problem and pastoral behavior. *Journal of Development Studies, 23,* 5–19.

Lybbert, T. J., Barrett, C. B., Desta, S., & Coppock, D. L. (2004). Stochastic wealth dynamics and risk management among a poor population. *The Economic Journal, 114,* 750–777.

Macharia, P. N., & Ekaya, W. N. (2005). The impact of rangeland condition and trend to the grazing resources of a semi-arid environment in Kenya. *Journal of Human Ecology, 17,* 143–147.

Marshall, G. R. (2008). Nesting, subsidiarity, and community-based environmental governance beyond the local level. *International Journal of the Commons, 2,* 75–97, from: http://www.thecomonsjournal.org/index.php/ijc/article/vie/50.

McCay, B. J., & Acheson, J. M. (1987). *The question of the commons: The culture and ecology of communal resources*. Tucson: University of Arizona Press.

Migot-Adholla, S. E., & Little, P. D. (1980). Evolution of policy toward the development of pastoral areas in Kenya. In G. Galaty, D. Aronson, & P. C. Salzman (Eds.), *The future of pastoral peoples* (pp. 144–156). (Proceedings of a conference held in Nairobi, Kenya, August 4–8, 1980). Ottawa, Ontario: International Development Research Center.

Miller, G. J. (1992). *Managerial dilemmas: The political economy of hierarchy*. Cambridge: Cambridge University Press.

Mol, F. (1996). *Maasai language and culture: Dictionary*. Limuru: Kolbe Press.

Munei, K. (1987). Grazing schemes and group ranches as models for developing pastoral lands in Kenya. In P. T. W. Baxter & R. Hogg (Eds.), *Property, poverty and people: Changing rights in property and problems of pastoral development*. Manchester: Department of Social Anthropology and International Development.

Mwangi, E. (2007a). *Socioeconomic change and land use in Africa: The transformation of property rights in Maasailand*. New York: Palgrave Macmillan.

Mwangi, E. (2007b). Subdividing the commons: Distributional conflict in the transition from collective to individual property rights in Kenya's Maasailand. *World Development, 35*, 815–834.

Mwangi, E. (2007c). The puzzle of group ranch subdivision in Kenya's Maasailand. *Development and Change, 38*, 889–910.

Niamir-Fuller, M. (1998). The resilience of pastoral herding in Sub-Saharan Africa. In F. Berkes & C. Folke (Eds.), *Linking social and ecological systems: Management practices and social mechanisms for building resilience* (pp. 250–284). Cambridge: Cambridge University Press.

Njoka, T. J. (1979). Ecological and socio-cultural trends of Kaputiei group ranches in Kenya. Ph.D. dissertation, University of California, Berkeley.

NRC (National Research Council). (1986). *Proceedings of the conference on common property resource management*. Washington, DC: National Academy Press.

NRC (National Research Council). (2002). *The drama of the commons*. Committee on the human dimensions of global change. E. Ostrom, T. Dietz, N. Dolšak, P. Stern, S. Stonich, & E. Weber (Eds.). Washington, DC: National Academy Press.

Ostrom, E. (1990). *Governing the commons*. New York: Cambridge University Press.

Ostrom, V. (1997). *The meaning of democracy and the vulnerability of democracies: A response to Tocqueville's challenge*. Ann Arbor: University of Michigan Press.

Ostrom, V. (2008). *The intellectual crisis in American public administration*. 3rd ed. Tuscaloosa: University of Alabama Press.

Reid, R., Gichohi, H., Said, M., Nkedianye, D., Ogutu, J., Kshatriya, M., et al. (2007). Fragmentation of a peri-urban Savanna, Athi-Kaputiei Plains, Kenya. In K. A. Galvin, R. S. Reid, R. H. Behnke, & N. T. Hobbs (Eds.), *Fragmentation in semi-arid and arid landscapes: Consequences for human and natural systems* (pp. 195–224). New York: Springer.

Rutten, M. M. E. M. (1992). *Selling wealth to buy poverty: The process of the individualization of landownership among the Maasai pastoralists of Kajiado District, Kenya, 1890–1900: Vol. 10. Nijmegen studies in development and cultural change*. Breitenbach: Saarbrucken.

Sandford, G. F. (1919). *An administrative and political history of the Masai reserve*. London: Waterlow and Sons.

Scholes, R. J., & Walker, B. H. (1993). *An African savanna: Synthesis of the Nylsvley study*. Cambridge: Cambridge University Press.

Simel, O. J. (1999). Premature land subdivision, encroachment of rights and manipulation in Maasailand – the Keekonyokie clan section. Arid Lands and Resource Management Network in Eastern Africa (AlARM). Working Paper No. 8. Center for Basic Research, Kampala.

Simpson, M. C. (1973). *Alternative strategies for range development in Kenya.* Rural Development Study No. 2. Department of Agricultural Economics, University of Leeds, Leeds.

Spencer, P. (1997). *The pastoral continuum: The marginalization of tradition in East Africa.* Oxford: Clarendon Press.

Sporrong, U. (1998). Dalecarlia in Central Sweden before 1800: A society of social stability and ecological resilience. In F. Berkes & C. Folke (Eds.), *Linking social and ecological systems: Management practices and social mechanisms for building resilience* (pp. 67–94). Cambridge: Cambridge University Press.

Talbot, L. M. (1972). Ecological consequences of rangeland development in East Africa. In M. T. Farvar & J. P. Milton (Eds.), *The careless technology: Ecology and international development* (pp. 694–711). Garden City: Natural History Press.

Thomas, D., Twyman, C., & Harris, F. (2002). Sustainable development in drylands: Geographical contributions to a better understanding of people-environment relationships. *The Geographical Journal, 168*, 193–194.

Thomson, J. T. (1885). *Through Masai land: A journey of exploration among the Snowclad Volcanic Mountains and strange tribes of Eastern Equatorial Africa.* London: Frank Cass and Co.

Thornton, P. K., Boone, R. B. Galvin, K. A., Burnsilver, S. B., Waithaka, M. M., Kuyiah, J., et al. (2007). Coping strategies in livestock-dependent households in East and Southern Africa: A synthesis of four case studies. *Human Ecology, 35*, 461–476.

Tignor, R. T. (1976). *The colonial transformation of Kenya: The Kamba, Kikuyu and Maasai from 1900 to 1939.* Princeton: Princeton University Press.

Waller, R. D. (1993). Acceptees and aliens: Kikuyu settlement in Maasailand. In T. T. Spear & R. Waller (Eds.), *Being Maasai: Ethnicity and identity in East Africa* (pp. 226–257). London: J. Currey; Dar es Salaam: Mkuki na Nyota; Nairobi: EAEP; Athens: Ohio University Press.

11 The Downgrading Effect of Abuse of Power on Trust and Collective Action in Bulgaria's Irrigation Sector

Insa Theesfeld

Leibniz Institute of Agricultural Development in Central and Eastern Europe (IAMO), Theodor-Lieser-Str.2, 06120 Halle (Saale), Germany, E-mail: theesfeld@iamo.de

Abstract. Bulgaria's irrigation facilities have largely deteriorated, property rights over the infrastructure are ambiguous and water loss in the system at present amounts to 70%. Thus, the Bulgarian government is currently attempting to formally reform the sector by implementing collective action management schemes. In analyzing the possible success of this envisaged local cooperation, I draw on Ostrom's (2007) development of collective action theory. In her theoretical framework, Ostrom posits variables affecting the likelihood of undertaking diverse forms of collective action leading to positive or negative results for others. The core relationships affecting cooperation are between reputation, trust, and reciprocity. In turn, eight structural variables influence these core relationships: one of them being the "heterogeneity of participants". In the following, empirical evidence from Bulgaria's irrigation sector is provided to explain how incongruity of rules helps to maintain opportunistic strategies, how various transactions in the foundation of a water user association are affected by abuse of power, and how low the level of trust in formal actors actually is. Based on that, I examine one detailed link in Ostrom's theory, namely between heterogeneity of participants and trust, showing in particular that the interdependency between abuse of power and decrease in trust produces a downgrading effect on collective action.

Keywords: Bulgaria, Collective action theory, Heterogeneity of participants, Irrigation, Trust

11.1 Introduction

In Bulgaria's irrigation sector, the Irrigation System Company (ISC), a state firm, has a monopoly on the irrigated water supply. Irrigation systems based on market coordination, such as trading water rights or quotas, do not exist. Irrigation sector management is centralized. Decisions are implemented top-down, and there are no opportunities for the agricultural water users to participate. The ISC is responsible for the management, operation and maintenance of all state-owned irrigation and drainage systems in Bulgaria. Twenty-three regional branches operate semi-autonomously, but answer to the head office in Sofia, especially for financial control. Water guards are the village representatives of the ISC. From the viewpoint of the water users, especially the small ones, the water guards are often the only visible ISC personnel.

In order to find solutions for Bulgaria's deteriorated irrigation infrastructure and the rising demand of farmers for better, more reliable water provision, an irrigation sector reform was initiated in the late 1990s. Collective action management solutions have been propagated for more sustainable resource use by the Bulgarian government and the World Bank. One outcome was that the Bulgarian government enacted two laws: the Bulgarian Water Law, implemented in January 2000, and the Water User Association Act, which came into force in March 2001. Their aim was to cope with unreliable irrigation water provision and appropriation and to incorporate local self-governance and collective action, which should be accomplished by reforming and decentralizing the centrally planned water sector and increasing the involvement of local actors. Most of the established water user associations, however, were only formally created. In practice, they were neither functioning nor familiar to the farmers in the respective villages. Regardless of these formal efforts, little collective action in the irrigation sector has been observed in Bulgarian villages, and present formal attempts do not seem to have found common ground where collective action can grow. Instead, ongoing deterioration of the facilities is observed, and only a small percentage of the fields equipped with irrigation devices are actually irrigated. Chaotic water appropriation rules and insecure and ineffective property rights prevail (Penov, Theesfeld, & Gatzweiler, 2003).

Irrigated water and irrigation infrastructure are common-pool resources. Common-pool resource scholars have advocated taking distributional aspects and power relations into account when analyzing institutional change in common-pool resource management (Meinzen-Dick, Raju, & Gulati, 2002, p. 652; Agrawal, 2001, pp. 1650–1656). The way benefits are distributed among various actors is decisive, and the respective political weight of the latter can influence the likelihood of institutional change (Baland & Platteau, 1998, p. 649). When social dilemmas are solved and new rules implemented, some people benefit more than others. Indeed, some may even benefit at the expense of others. Empirical evidence from Bulgaria supports the view that local actors use power asymmetries to maintain their benefits. Ostrom (2007, p. 190) points out that, in contrast to the early stages in a process of collective action, inequalities in distribution of benefits may, however, reduce trust and cooperation later in the process.

In this contribution, I will unpack the link between the structurally variable heterogeneity of participants and one of the core variables that influence the likelihood of collective action, namely trust. First, the incongruity between formal and effective rules is highlighted as a transition-typical feature. Empirical material shows that the incongruity of rules enables heterogeneous participants to misuse power asymmetries and, thus, maintain opportunistic strategies. Second, I will outline various transactions in the irrigation sector, particularly the foundation of a water user association, and describe related decisions affected by abuse of power. Third, I will present direct empirical evidence for low levels of trust in formal actors and perceptions of corruption. Finally, based on the observed aggravating process between abuse of power and decreased trust that constrains the development of collective action, policy-relevant conclusions are drawn regarding constraints in implementing blueprints for collective action management schemes in the irrigation sector.

11.2 Downward Cascade Between Opportunistic Behavior and Trust

Ostrom (2007) presents in her theoretical explanation of successful or unsuccessful collective action the links between (1) the trust that each participant has in the others involved in a collective action situation, (2) the investment others make in establishing and maintaining a trustworthy reputation, and (3) the probability of all participants using reciprocity norms. On the one hand, levels of trust, reputations for being trustworthy, and reciprocity are positively reinforcing. For instance, someone with a good reputation is regarded as trustworthy and the norm of reciprocity leads actors to stick to their promises, that is, behaving in a trustworthy manner. This reminds us of the frequently stated positive correlation between cooperation and trust towards strangers and beliefs about the fairness and helpfulness of others, as underlined by Gächter, Herrmann, and Thöni (2004, p. 523). Trust lowers the cost of working together (Putnam, 1993; Pretty & Ward, 2001; Baland & Platteau, 1998). A characteristic of actor groups fostering collective action solutions is that most appropriators must share generalized norms of reciprocity and trust. Collective action needs credible commitment, and one decisive requirement for that is trust among actors. On the other hand, the core links described by Ostrom mean that a decrease in trust, reputation or reciprocity can generate a "downward cascade", leading to little or no cooperation (Ostrom, 2007, p. 201). When a society is pervaded by distrust, cooperative arrangements are unlikely to emerge. Transition economists argue that experiences from the socialist era and the transition process following it have resulted in low and deteriorating trust as well as specific actor characteristics that constrain opportunities for collective action and the provision of public goods (Danchev, 2005; Gächter et al,. 2004; Paldam & Svendsen, 2000; Rose-Ackermann, 2001). In the remaining, the focus will be on this negative feedback loop whereby distrust hinders the emergence of collective action, looking in particular at how bad reputation may lead to distrust and to reciprocal opportunism, which further diminishes a reputation.[1]

Ostrom presents eight external structural variables that influence the inner core links between trust, reputation and reciprocity: (1) the number of participants involved, (2) whether benefits are subtractive or fully shared, (3) the heterogeneity of participants, (4) face-to-face communication, and (5) the shape of the production function. Additional structural variables that can have an impact in repeated situations are: (6) information about past actions, (7) how individuals are linked, and (8) whether individuals can enter or exit voluntarily. These external variables are interlinked, for instance, a small group with extreme heterogeneity in terms of the benefits to be obtained from a collective action is an entirely different group than a small group of relatively homogenous players. Equally, in a small group with extreme heterogeneity, face-to-face communication may lead to exacerbated conflicts rather than reduction in conflict and agreements (Ostrom, 2007, p. 202). Thus, it is only possible to analyze specific causal directions, as I do in the following, zooming in to a linkage and explaining the relationship of causality between one of these external structural variables, "the heterogeneity of participants" – here expressed in terms of its negative consequences with regard to abuse of power and opportunistic behavior – and decrease in trust.

In general, heterogeneity of participants can facilitate or constrain the process of cooperation, for which there is the need to differentiate between its early and later stages. The presence of wealthy and knowledgeable participants early in the process may encourage trust. Hurrelmann, Murray, and Beckmann (2006) stress the role of appropriate mediating agencies involved, finding that, particularly in transition countries with low social capital, well-educated and well-connected local leaders can initiate and maintain local cooperation. Moreover, trust without the role of leaders does not necessarily lead to collective action. In turn, inequality in distribution of benefits in the later stages of cooperation may reduce trust and reputation and constrain the emergence of further cooperation (Ostrom, 2007, p. 190).

The broad analytical framework in Fig. 11.1 shows that there are four dimensions influencing the emergence of collective action as well as transition-specific features that hinder the emergence of collective action in the irrigation sector. The dimensions are grouped into: formal political settings; effective institutional settings; characteristics of the resource, infrastructure settings and, the transactions involved; and characteristics of actor groups and their interactions (Theesfeld, 2004). The special characteristics described within these four dimensions determine whether actor heterogeneity leads to the persistence of abusing individual power for private benefits.

---

[1] Korf (this volume) describes civil war situations, where opportunistic behavior and reduced trust may also lead to a form of reciprocal opportunism, described as seeking strategic cooperation; due to the particular characteristics of civil war, actors follow rules out of fear instead of conceiving them as fair.

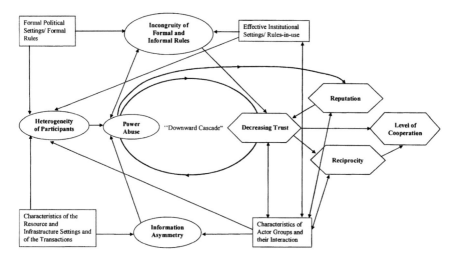

Fig. 11.1: Variables influencing cooperation for an irrigation sector in transition
Source: Adapted from Ostrom (2007, p. 200) and Theesfeld (2004)

The incongruity of formal and informal rules and information asymmetry are typical for a transition economy and facilitate the cultivation of a milieu in which opportunistic behavior can persist. Opportunistic behavior, or abuse of power, leads to decreasing trust. The interdependency between abuse of power and decrease in trust represent a mutually reinforcing process – a downward cascade – that constrains collective action. Ostrom draws a connection between the decreasing trust variable and her framework, showing the core relationships between trust, reputations and reciprocity affecting levels of cooperation in a social dilemma (Ostrom, 2007, p. 200). Abuse of power also leads to development of a bad reputation, which leads to further distrust, and may even lead to reciprocal opportunism, diminishing trust and reputations on both sides even more.

In other contexts, the impact of institutional reform on collective action can be more direct, as in the case of Kenya's dryland ecosystems described by Mwangi and Ostrom (this volume). External actors impose management systems that formally replace indigenous systems of resource management, resulting in a direct, negative influence on local norms of reciprocity and trust.

11.3 Methods and Research Site

The empirical material supporting the argument presented here was collected in six months of empirical fieldwork, subdivided into three phases spanning two and a half years from 2000 until 2002. In addition to interviews with experts in Sofia and with representatives of the regional administration, two kinds of case studies were conducted: (1) In the first research phase, 17 village case studies were conducted in three regions of Bulgaria exemplary for their natural water conditions, farm and crop structures, and size of irrigation devices (for details see Theesfeld, 2005). They provided an overview of the irrigation situation in the villages and allowed for a rough analysis of the main hypotheses. (2) In the two following research phases, four contrasting in-depth case studies were chosen out of the 17 original case studies, according to three main criteria: location in the irrigation command area[2], variation in farm structures, and a locality's state of establishing water user associations. The selections, especially as regards the state of establishing water user associations, had to be made according to preliminary information, which was specified and verified during the case studies. Two irrigation command areas were selected in the Haskovo region in South East Bulgaria. In each area, two villages were chosen, with one village located directly behind the water dam (top-ender) and the other further back – at the middle or tail-end of the canal and river system. In order to guarantee the anonymity of the individuals involved, abstract abbreviations for the villages were set up.

Village A is a top-end village in the first irrigation command area. As in all other villages, subsistence producers cultivate vegetable and forage crops on their small plots of less than 0.5 hectares. Besides them, the majority of agricultural land is cultivated by two agricultural cooperatives, one socialist-successor cooperative, or a red cooperative, and one newly founded reformer cooperative, or a blue cooperative. In Village A, the production specificity regarding irrigation water needs is defined by a large group of Turks, almost 40 families, producing tobacco on small plots. Tobacco is a crop which does not need many irrigation turns, but the crucial turns have to happen within a certain time slot. According to the official documents of the ISC head office in Sofia, one water user association (WUA) has been established.

Village B is a middle-end village in the first irrigation command area. Its agricultural structure consists of a socialist-successor cooperative, a big tenant and midsized family farms. The existence of one WUA has been reported.

Village C is a top-end village in the second irrigation command area. A socialist-successor cooperative and one newly established cooperative farm the land. Its

---

[2] An irrigation command area is a superior spatial unit, defined as an area where one main water source, such as a dam, provides the water to irrigate most of the surrounding arable area. In such irrigation command areas, at least one main distribution canal runs from the water dam through a number of villages. Water storage basins along the main canal serve as reservoirs to secure water for the next village. A network of side-canals and ditches divert water from the main canal. The water consumption of villages located at the tail-end of such irrigation command areas depends on the preceding villages' water use. There are irrigation command areas in which tail-end villages have minor alternative water sources. Such sources, for instance additional microdams, are independent from water use of the village located at the top-end position in such a command area. An irrigation command area is the spatial unit used when analyzing irrigation-water interrelationships among various villages.

production specificity is that seasonal workers come into the village to produce pickles, which need a comparatively large amount of irrigation water.

Village D is a tail-end village in the second irrigation command area. It has three big agricultural producers competing for lease contracts: one successor co-operative, one newly established cooperative and one big tenant.

With the help of explorative and qualitative methods in the first two research phases, I analyzed the institutional changes taking place in Bulgaria's irrigation sector. Among other aspects, the rules-in-use which govern the daily practices of irrigation were investigated and examples given. In the third research phase, more standardized quantitative methods were conducted to elucidate selected relationships.

11.4 Incongruity of Rules, Information Asymmetry and Abuse of Power

In transition countries, a large discrepancy can be observed between formal political intentions and informal, effective institutional change at the local level. This incongruity represents a transition-specific feature.[3] The simultaneous change from a centrally planned to a market-oriented economy and from a communist-determined to a democratic political system created an institutional vacuum in Bulgaria, among other countries. In Bulgaria, this was the result of numerous economic, political, and institutional constraints, such as the unpredicted fall in output, unsuccessful attempts to stabilize the economy, limited law enforcement mechanisms, limited implementation capacities for formal rules, and weak public administration capacities (Roland, 2000; Nenovsky & Koleva, 2002, p. 49). Chavdarova (2002, p. 68) contradicts the argument of mainstream economists, arguing that informal institutions have filled up the formal institutional vacuum. In fact, informal institutions form the core of present Bulgarian society. Compared to other Eastern European transition countries, in which formal institutions provide more orientation for their people, the Bulgarian state could not provide a vision for its people and, to a large extent, formal actors lost their reputations and trustworthiness (Theesfeld, 2005; Dobrinsky, 2000).

Korf (2004) also refers to the gap between formal and informal rules but, due to his focus on civil wars, he develops a more nuanced view. Korf starts from the definition that rules are constantly made and remade through people's practices. Formal institutions may be "re-interpreted, re-negotiated and re-practiced in the

---

[3] Yet, this incongruity of rules can also be observed in other parts of the world, such as in the case described by Mwangi and Ostrom (this volume) regarding institutional reform in Kenya's dryland ecosystem, where newly established formal rules for resource access and decision making have contradicted the cultural norms that otherwise underpin Maasai society, whose members rely on the ecosystem for their livelihoods.

local action arenas" (Korf, 2004, p. 172). Korf (this volume) develops the concept of hybrid institutions, among other aspects, expressing that a pure distinction between formal and informal institutions in the practices of social interaction would be artificial. There are, rather, multiple and contesting rules for governing. This hybridity of rules and structures may also hold true for Bulgaria's transition period, characterized by the coexistence of multiple and incongruent formal and informal rules.

The incompatibility of formal rules and everyday practices creates a no-man's-land, which lays the groundwork for illegitimate redistribution of power and wealth (Chavdarova, 2002, p. 72). The high degree of incongruity between formal and effective rules provides conditions under which opportunistic behavior is able to expand and persist. Likewise, the dynamic nature of effective rules and the ambiguity of multiple rules, as described by Korf (this volume), bears the risk that rules can become resources manipulated by powerful actors.

Abuse of power is understood here as the individual expression of opportunistic behavior and, thus, is almost synonymous with opportunistic behavior[4]. According to Ostrom, Gardner, and Walker (1994, pp. 37–50), an institutional analysis relevant to field settings requires an understanding of the effective rules, or rules-in-use, used by individuals. All rules are the result of implicit or explicit efforts to achieve order and predictability among humans. Rules-in-use govern the patterns of interaction among the different actors in a system and represent the set of rules to which participants would refer if asked to explain or justify their actions to fellow participants. The rules-in-use and opportunistic strategies develop and change interdependently. On the one hand, effective local rules provide a basis for opportunistic strategies. On the other hand, because of opportunistic strategies certain rules-in-use are manifested, so that those effective rules reflect previously existing opportunistic strategies. The latter situation is illustrated by Hagedorn (2004), who points out how the laws and property rights that came about through agricultural land reforms in Central and Eastern Europe reflect the relative bargaining power of the actors involved. The incongruity between formal and rules-in-use also applies to Bulgaria's irrigation sector. Together with information asymmetry, this incongruity has paved the ground on which opportunistic behavior and abuse of power has been able to grow and thrive.

---

[4] Opportunistic behavior is defined by various expressions of self-interest-seeking relying on guile, including calculated efforts to mislead, deceive, obfuscate, and otherwise confuse (Williamson 1996, p. 378).

11.4.1 Incongruity of formal and effective rules in the irrigation sector

In this section, the incongruity of formal and effective rules for one of the studied tail-end villages is analyzed with the help of empirical material. Similar signs of incongruity were observed in all case study villages. The examples can therefore be regarded as typical ones. As will be shown, limited sanctioning and enforcement mechanisms as well as practically non-existent monitoring mechanisms provide favorable conditions for opportunistic behavior, which is observable in both actual water appropriation practices and maintenance work.

Water ordering and appropriation rules

Water users have to put in an advance order with the local water guard if they want to irrigate. The formal rule stipulates that the guard must collect a certain amount of orders before he can open the barrage and fill the canal with water. Nevertheless, compliance with this rule varies. Informally, no farmer can rely on irrigation water via canal being delivered when needed, even if he orders it well in advance.

Another issue is that usage rights to the canal system and the water dam belong to different people. The dams are often rented to private individuals who farm fish in the reservoir behind the dam. Formally, the stock of fish should not reach a level that would initiate competition for water between irrigation and fish farming. Normally, farmers in the respective village want to irrigate and order water, but the tenant of the water dam does not divert water into either the canal or the river. Based on this situation, the informal rule appears to be: when the canal is filled, irrigate to be on the safe side, whether you have ordered water or not. The water guard tries to collect the fees afterwards. The first formal rule – a farmer who orders water and pays in advance has the right to irrigate – does not work in practice.

If water is scarce and farmers, despite their orders, do not receive water via canal, some may join forces and engage in a so-called rebellion: a group of them goes to the barrage and opens it. This generally leads to fights between them and other water users.

In addition, the ISC regional branch offers verbal advice to the water guards in ranking the crops for irrigation. For instance, only the pickles should be irrigated from 5 p.m. until 8 p.m. During the day, priority should be given to eggplants, tomatoes, and peppers. Corn ranks third as it needs a lot of water. It should mainly be irrigated late at night. Most cases of irrigation practice, however, do not reflect these regulations. A statement taken from an interview summarizes the second rule-in-use regulating the irrigation sequence: "Whoever is ahead of you at the canal is the first to irrigate. That is the [unofficial] law." This is a common situation:

farmers who extract water from the head of an irrigation system can obtain more water than those located at the tail-end (Ostrom, 1990). Most of the interviewees described the situation as chaotic. The problems of water allocation among neighboring villages are the same as those for small-scale water users sharing one canal. A typical situation involves a tail-ender ordering water. When the canal is filled, everyone ahead of him irrigates, and the tail-ender faces a water shortage, even though he ordered the water and may have even already paid for it.

The third rule of irrigation from one canal is specified by sheer physical force. Physical violence among the users of an irrigation system is symptomatic of inadequate assignment of spatial or temporal irrigation slots to appropriators.

Monitoring rules

There is almost no monitoring system for water appropriation. This situation leads to farmers guarding their fields around the clock. First, farmers wait for the water in the canal to reach their plot so that they can immediately start irrigating before another farmer begins. Second, they must supervise while irrigating, otherwise another farmer diverting water from a top-end position can start irrigating, leaving them insufficient water to complete their irrigation turn.

Water storage basins are filled overnight to secure the availability of water in all villages belonging to one irrigation command area. If water flows into the canal system at night, it immediately motivates farmers to irrigate at night too, often in an attempt to avoid payment. Such illegal irrigation is usually discovered by daylight, but farmers simply claim that neighboring farmers flooded their fields, which cannot be proven to the contrary.

Excludability and sanctioning rules

Water users who have not paid the water fee cannot technically be excluded from water diversion from a canal. There is no graduated and credible sanction mechanism of the kind described by Ostrom (1990, 1992) in the design principles for enduring, self-governing, common-pool resource institutions. Formal sanctioning power is generally lacking. For instance, the one water guard that worked in the village during the irrigation season 2000–2001 carried no authority. Nonetheless, he made use of social sanctioning measures to force people to pay the water fees, shouting in front of their houses - loud enough for the neighbors to hear – as a way of embarrassing the water users into paying.

Another event serves as illustration. During the summer of 2002, a group of irrigators refused to pay in advance. Consequently, the water guard stopped the water flow into the distribution canal. A group of farmers then went to the barrage, where the water is distributed between the river and the distribution canal, and opened it on their own. During this violation, they broke the mechanism of the barrage. Technicians were needed to repair it. Although the ISC caught some of the violators, they were not sanctioned, much to the regret of the water guard.

Operation and maintenance rules

Maintenance practices are largely affected by the ambiguity of ownership rights to the irrigation infrastructure and lack of clarity regarding responsibilities. Problems resulting from the transformation of the irrigation infrastructure stem from ambiguous property rights on the medium-scale infrastructure, including midsized canals, pump stations, and microdams. Maintenance duties are not clearly assigned among the various entities, such as successor agricultural cooperatives, municipalities, the ISC, WUAs, and water users. No distinct formal rules for operation and maintenance work have been laid down. The maintenance guidelines for WUAs are particularly fuzzy, even though they form the basis for granting the use rights to the infrastructure. These guidelines are not followed, however, and neither the ISC nor the water users control the maintenance work done by a WUA's management. Accordingly, there is a discrepancy between the need for maintenance to secure long-term system operation and the actual work conducted.

Routine maintenance is generally delayed until the system's complete deterioration. Holes and cracks in the concrete canal linings are not repaired, stolen concrete plates are not restored, and broken devices to regulate the water flow are very rarely replaced. Additional water outlets are largely missing, and their installation is not planned. They would help serve the growing number of individual water users that have resulted from an increasingly scattered crop production structure. Maintenance work is dominated by (1) urgent and temporary repairs carried out provisionally and (2) freeing the canals from dirt, trash, weeds, and brushwood for the upcoming season only, rather than when it's needed.

Further explanations of farmer reluctance to take on responsibilities and maintenance duties include prevailing free-rider behavior and the mental model of superordinate authorities as being responsible. The ISC regional branch occasionally cleans the canals to be able to serve its clients. Likewise, several of the WUAs conduct minimal, short-sighted maintenance work to justify their collection of water fees.

The following observation was made regarding the few cases in which water users have cleaned the canals themselves. Only a minor share of those who promised to participate actually did. Instead of working as a cooperating group and cleaning the whole canal, they cleaned on their own in front of their own plots. Furthermore, upon closer examination, it is striking that most of them started to clean the canal at the beginning of their plot, but only as far as the water outlet serves it. The outlets are usually located at the centre of the plots and, in most cases, consist of illegal holes made in the concrete linings. The remaining canal line of the farmer's plot would be left untouched, overgrown with weeds and brushwood. Once the farmer cleaned the canal up to the outlet, he had no private benefit to clean further, even though this would serve the collective benefit. This observation indicates not only the individualistic behavior of those who participated and their lack of ability and willingness to cooperate, but also the free-riding behavior of those who did not participate.

11.4.2 Abuse of power in the irrigation sector

Different ways in which actors exercise of power inappropriately can be conceptualized as abuse of power, that is, the intentional exercise of power to pursue private benefits. Hence, abuse of power is the individual expression of the opportunistic behavior of different actors. The aforementioned examples of actual water appropriation practice and maintenance work indicate that incongruity of formal and effective rules facilitates and, in turn, is a result of abuse of power in the irrigation sector. Table 11.1 summarizes examples of transactions in the irrigation sector that are affected by abuse of power. Transactions are understood here as not being restricted to situations in which resources are actually transferred in the physical sense of delivery (Furubotn & Richter, 2000), but also seen as social transactions necessary to establish, maintain, or change social relationships. Social transactions are necessary for the formation and maintenance of the institutional framework in which economic activities occur. Transactions are also formulated with reference to Hagedorn, Arzt, and Peters (2002, pp. 4–6), who give an example of the "leaching of nitrates into the groundwater on sandy soils" as a transaction related not only to nature, but also to the farmer and the public or community concerned. Based on these definitions, renting in a plot from a cooperative refers to a transfer of property rights. Likewise, with the formal recognition of a founded WUA or of a Constituent Committee for a WUA, certain property rights are transferred to the respective actors, such as the right to decide on the territory to be served and, therewith, which clients to exclude. Finally, one party's withholding of documents that are needed by another is a social transaction, hindering the formation of a new institutional framework.

The following section elaborates a bit more on the last example of Table 11.1, founding a WUA, and questions concerning who is in the management and how certain water users can be excluded. In 2000, in case study Village B, non-villagers founded a WUA according to the Cooperative Law. The only precondition was that the founders had to be landowners of plots located alongside the main distribution canal, which serves a number of villages. The way in which this WUA was founded was inscrutable for the population of the respective village. For instance, the head of this association refused to name the other six founders and members. Most of the villagers were in fact unaware of the possibility of establishing a WUA, much less knew about the formal existence of a WUA in their village. The villagers, rather, spoke of this organization either as a private water firm or as a tenant renting the canal system. They were only aware that the water guard was from their village, without knowing the other parties involved. As it turns out, however, the water guard was the father of the head of the association. Since there was at least one connection to one of the villagers, an uncertainty and uneasiness in discussing this topic was evident during the study. Information asymmetry was striking, as villagers knew hardly anything about the formal existence of the WUA. Thus, the situation resembled one of open access, with efforts by a formal institution to exert some authority – but largely, as we will see, for its own benefit. The effective water ordering and appropriation rules in the village show that the WUA was not an effective company. During spring of 2001, the water guard employed five pensioners for five days to clean the canals, which was the only maintenance work for the season completed by the WUA.

Table 11.1: Transactions in the irrigation sector affected by abuse of power

Transactions in the irrigation sector	Actors involved actor I ↔ actor II	Specific decisions affected by abuse of power
Renting in plots from the cooperative	Water users ↔ cooperative	Who gets plots at top-end position along the canal?
Starting an irrigation turn	Water users ↔ neighboring water users at the canal	Who irrigates first, and who violates the water appropriation rules?
Paying for irrigation water	Minor water users ↔ water guard Major water users ↔ ISC regional office	Who refrains from paying, or who pays less?
Releasing water into the canal	Water users ↔ water guard Water users ↔ ISC regional office	When is the water released, i.e. favoring whom?
Closing the barrage of a microdam	Fish farmers ↔ water users	For how long is water not released into the irrigation canal?
Providing uncleaned irrigation canals to the water users	ISC ↔ water users WUA ↔ water users	How can maintenance work be reduced to a minimum?
Establishing a constituent committee to found a WUA	Initiators ↔ water users	Who is involved in the initiative, and how are operational rules set?
Withholding necessary documents needed to transfer water dam use rights to a WUA	ISC ↔ constituent committee	When should necessary documents be provided, and how can the procedure be prolonged?
Founding a WUA	Management of WUA ↔ water users	Who is in the management, and how can certain water users be excluded?

The head of the WUA took advantage of the information asymmetry that existed between him and the villagers. Even prior to his involvement with the WUA, he held a leadership position in the Youth Organization of the Peasant Party, which had held governmental power in coalition with the Union of Democratic Forces (UDF) from 1997 until 2001. The UDF aimed to increase its political influence in the rural areas by supporting political adherents to found WUAs in rural areas. Due to his political engagement, this future manager of the WUA had access to various kinds of information and could participate in a course offered by the World Bank, in which he was trained in establishing WUAs under the Cooperative Law. He used his powerful position, good contacts, and supplementary knowledge to establish the WUA. The prestige he had earned by establishing a WUA in fact furthered him in his political career. He gained extra income for the collection of water fees and made an additional profit by not spending adequate funds for maintenance work.

It became evident that the mere implementation of new formal rules – such as those under the Cooperative Law for founding WUAs – without respecting local power structures could again lead to an abuse of power by those individuals already occupying advantageous positions. Certain characteristics of irrigation transactions which also reflect the resource characteristics and infrastructure settings can provide support for the abuse of power strategies of participants.

11.5 Decreasing Trust and Reputation

This section provides selected empirical evidence for decreasing trust and the development of bad reputations, expressed as perception of corruption in Bulgaria's irrigation sector.

11.5.1 Distrust in formal actors

Standardized questions were included in the questionnaires used in the third phase of field research to assess *special trust* in formal actors. One question was: *Whom do you trust?* A list of organizations was presented, starting with national formal organizations and ending with local authorities.

Figure 11.2 shows the aggregated results of a sample of 52 interviewees representing all four villages. The generally low level of trust in formal actors is astonishing. There is almost no trust in the parliament, the government, the court (0%), or the district administration. The average trust in local authorities is higher than in any of the formal authorities at the national level; nonetheless it is low. Interestingly, trust in the mayor is even lower than trust in the police, both being the only two authorities representing the national government at village level. This gives an indication of the weak trustworthiness of mayors in their villages, although they are elected representatives. In addition, the data in sum show that a share of 46%

of the interviewees does not trust any formal authority at the national level and a share of 19% does not trust any local actor.

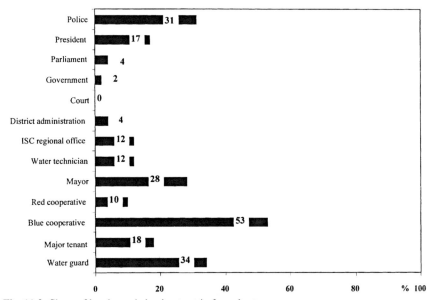

Fig. 11.2: Share of local people having trust in formal actors

11.5.2 Bad reputation

An aspect of interest to the present analysis is the reputation of an actor, in particular, the correlation between considering someone corrupt and not trusting him, as shown in Fig. 11.3. Paldam explains this correlation as follows: "When people do not trust institutions, it is for good reasons. The best existing proxy for low trust I have been able to find is corruption" (2001, p. 3). This underlines why corruption should be considered in an investigation on trust.

Thus, inquiries were made about the villagers' perceptions of the corruption of various formal actors: *In your opinion, how many members of the following organizations are corrupt?* The scale ranged from "none," "a few," "many," "the majority," to "everyone," and "I do not know", or "no answer." The same list of formal organizations and authorities was presented. The all-village distribution of relative frequencies of a sample of 42 interviewees revealed that the majority of members of the parliament, and especially of court members, are considered to be corrupt. With regard to the corruption of individual local authorities, 26% identified the mayor, 33% the water guard, and 43% the red cooperative manager as corrupt.

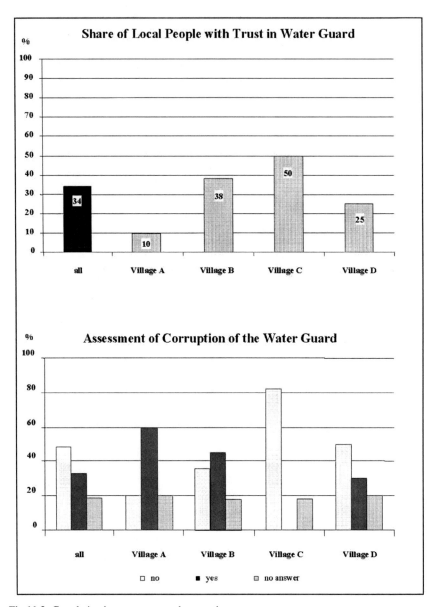

Fig.11.3: Correlation between trust and corruption

Processing the analysis of individual local authorities, we have chosen to focus on the assessment of the water guard among the four single-village distributions along with the all-village distribution, as shown in Fig. 11.3. With the corruption assessment of the water guard, a major difference becomes noticeable between the all-village distribution and the four single-village distributions. The differences among the four single-village distributions of relative frequencies are explained according to the heterogeneity of the local communities. In Village A, the water guard is known for accepting side-payments, which is reflected by the survey result of 60% of interviewees assessing him as being corrupt. In contrast, as the figure indicates, nobody perceived the Village C water guard to be corrupt. He is a poor Russian immigrant and not in a powerful position to ask for bribe money. This shows that, at the local level, survey data may vary noticeable depending on the individual case.

Another consideration shall be added at this stage: the fact that an interviewee is not sure whether a formal actor is corrupt implies that this actor can hardly be trusted. As shown in Fig. 11.3, the Village A water guard is the least trusted compared to the other villages' water guards and is considered to be the most corrupt. The Village C water guard, on the other hand, is the most trusted; none of the interviewees perceives him as corrupt. Although there are variances among the four single-village distributions, the maximum share of 50% of local people with trust in the water guard is low. As described above, the water guards are the people who best understand the system, and most of them have long-term experience. Their involvement in collective action solutions for the irrigation management is crucial, but constrained, as they do not enjoy the confidence of local actors.

11.6 Conclusions

Empirical material from Bulgaria's irrigation sector has shown that there is an aggravating process between abuse of power, on the one side, and decreased trust and reputation, on the other, that constrains the development of collective action. Powerful actors misuse their positions and resource endowments for personal benefits. This, in turn, further reduces the level of trust, a prerequisite for cooperation, contributing to its further deterioration.

With every new rule, the distribution of benefits and duties among various actors change. Distributional patterns and power relations have to be taken into account, as actors in fear of losing their favorable powerful positions will oppose new rules (Dobrinsky, 2000, p. 598). Extreme asymmetries in resource endowments among actors can imperil the success of decentralization efforts (Blomquist, Dinar, & Kemper, 2005, p. 9). But this general statement has to be qualified in one respect. When scrutinizing the influence of heterogeneity of participants, one has to differentiate between the early stage in a process of collective action and its later stages (Ostrom, 2007). Some inequality of resource endowments is necessary to facilitate initiatives, by enabling some actors to bear the costs of taking a leadership role. Those with greater endowments are willing to bear a disproportionate share of the initial costs of organizing institutional arrangements in order to stimulate movement.

Concerning the transplantation of blueprints for collective action, I draw on Pistor (2002), who argues that the incongruity of formal and informal rules, which has described at length at the outset of this paper concerning Bulgaria's irrigation sector, are a consequence of the laws imported into transition countries. Pistor (2002, p. 75) concludes that the observed weak law enforcement in transition countries is not due to inadequate institutions, but rather to a missing demand for legal rules and institutions that enforce them, and proposes three premises for effective legal transplants: First, in order to be effective, formal legal systems and imposed organizational forms and institutions must respond to and foster demand. Every formal legal system relies heavily on voluntary compliance, because state-controlled resources are insufficient to ensure legal compliance by means of coercion only. Second, there must be an alignment of formal norms with underlying social norms and beliefs. Third, the law or institution must, in particular, provide solutions for actual conflicts and take into account the various interests of actors behind them; otherwise, the formal institution will be ignored.

Pistor's description of legal transplants can be applied to Bulgaria's institutional transplant, namely the water user associations (WUAs). Disseminating organizational blueprints for WUAs throughout the world is generally inadequate for changing people's incentives and behaviors. State officials frequently design the basic structure for farmer organizations that are formally accepted. Such designs are conceived as predetermined blueprints for farmers' self-organization, but without considering farmers' incentives and capabilities (Tang, 1992, p. 8). Chambers (1988, p. 90), for instance, concludes that farmers cannot be organized through persuasion or fiat, but will only participate if they perceive an advantage. In particular, the success of transferring these blueprints to transition countries in South East Europe to facilitate rehabilitation of deteriorated irrigation systems is questionable. Transition societies have experienced over 40 years of socialist systems and two decades of transition, which have distinctly shaped their mental models and action patterns, as exemplified in their low level of trust in formal actors.

Empirical material proves that the attempts of the World Bank and the Bulgarian government to establish WUAs has not been effective up to now at the local level in terms of successful collective action. One reason is that the heterogeneity of both participants' interests and endowment with power resources has been disregarded. People may ignore, oppose or take advantage for private benefit these institutional transplants.

Instead of a predetermined blueprint, specific policy measures could have a major impact, especially by addressing the main obstacles that hamper collective action, particularly the transition-specific features. To limit the prospects for opportunism and reduce information asymmetry, governance structures should increase the extent of common knowledge and facilitate information exchange. As shown by Hurrelmann et al. (2006), the appearance of well-educated and connected leaders is necessary for starting a process of local cooperation. One way to overcome the cycle of opportunism and reciprocal distrust in Bulgaria's irrigation sector reform might be a careful selection of the leader of WUAs. If people are selected who are well respected within the village community and who have a high reputation, this may lead to norms of reciprocity that foster cooperation. The chances of finding such leaders would be higher if information asymmetry could be reduced, with more people having access to the necessary information needed for WUA foundations. The remaining question is in how far these leaders would start to behave in a self-interested manner, once they are in power.

References

Agrawal, A. (2001). Common property institutions and sustainable governance of re-sources. *World Development, 29*, 1649–1672.

Baland, J. -M., & Platteau, J. -P. (1998). Division of the commons: A partial assessment of the new institutional economics of land rights. *American Journal of Agricultural Economics, 80*, 644–650.

Blomquist, W., Dinar, A., & Kemper, K. (2005) *Comparison of institutional arrangements for river basin management in eight basins* (Working Paper No 3636). Washington, D.C.: World Bank Policy Research.

Chambers, R. (1988). *Managing canal irrigation: Practical analysis from South Asia.* Cambridge: Cambridge University Press.

Chavdarova, T. (2002). The informal economy in Bulgaria: Historical background and present situation. In R. Neef & M. Stanculescu (Eds.), *The social impact of informal economics in Eastern Europe* (pp. 56–76). Aldershot: Ashgate.

Danchev, A. (2005). Social capital influence on sustainability of development. Case study of Bulgaria. *Sustainable Development, 13*, 25–37.

Dobrinsky, R. (2000). The transition crisis in Bulgaria. *Cambridge Journal of Economics, 24*, 581–602.

Furubotn, E., & Richter, R. (2000). *Institutions and economic theory: The contribution of the new institutional economics.* Ann Arbor: The University of Michigan Press.

Gächter, S., Herrmann, B., & Thöni, C. (2004). Trust, voluntary cooperation, and socio-economic background: Survey and experimental evidence. *Journal of Economic Behavior & Organization, 55*, 505–531.

Hagedorn, K. (2004). Property rights reform on agricultural land in Central and Eastern Europe. *Quarterly Journal of International Agriculture, 43*, 409–438.

Hagedorn, K., Arzt, K., & Peters, U. (2002). Institutional arrangements for environmental co-operatives: A conceptual framework. In K. Hagedorn (Ed.), *Environmental co-operation and institutional change: Theories and policies for European agriculture* (pp. 3–25). Cheltenham and Northampton: Edward Elgar.

Hurrelmann, A., Murray, C., & Beckmann, V. (2006). Social capital and leadership: Rural cooperation in Central and Eastern Europe. *Society and Economy, 28*, 219–243.

Korf, B. (2004). *Conflict, space and institutions: Property rights and the political economy of war in Sri Lanka.* Institutional Change in Agriculture and Natural Resources, Vol. 19. Aachen: Shaker.

Meinzen-Dick, R. Raju, K. V., & Gulati, A. (2002). What affects organization and collective action for managing resources? Evidence from canal irrigation systems in India. *World Development, 30*, 649–666.

Nenovsky, N., & Koleva, D. (2002). Bulgaria. In R. Neef & M. Stanculescu (Eds.), *The social impact of informal economics in Eastern Europe* (pp. 49–55). Aldershot: Ashgate.

Ostrom, E. (1992). *Crafting institutions for self-governance irrigation systems.* San Francisco: Institute for Contemporary Studies Press.

Ostrom, E. (1990). *Governing the commons: The evolution of institutions for collective action.* Cambridge: Cambridge University Press.

Ostrom, E. (2007). Collective action theory. In C. Boix & S. C. Stokes (Eds.), *The Oxford handbook of comparative politics* (pp. 186–208). Oxford: Oxford University Press.

Ostrom, E., Gardner, R., & Walker, J. (1994). *Rules, games and common-pool resources.* Ann Arbor: University of Michigan Press.

Paldam, M. (2001, July). *Social capital and sustainability.* Paper presented at the DSE forum Berlin on "Sustainable development with a dynamic economy", Berlin.

Paldam, M., & Svendsen, G. T. (2000). *Missing social capital and the transition in Eastern Europe.* Aarhus: University of Aarhus.

Penov, I., Theesfeld, I. & Gatzweiler, F. (2003). Irrigation and water regulation systems in transition: The case of Bulgaria in comparison with Latvia, East Germany and Romania. In F. Gatzweiler & K. Hagedorn (Eds.), *Institutional change in Central and Eastern European agriculture and environment,* Vol. 3, Budapest and Berlin: Food and Agriculture Organization of the United Nations (FAO) and Humboldt University of Berlin.

Pistor, K. (2002). The demand for constitutional law. *Constitutional Political Economy, 13,* 73–87.

Pretty, J., & Ward, H. (2001). Social capital and the environment. *World Development, 29,* 209–227.

Putnam, R.. D. (1993). *Making democracy work: Civic traditions in modern Italy.* Princeton: Princeton University Press.

Roland, G. (2000). *Transition and economic: Politics, markets, and firms.* Cambridge: The MIT Press.

Rose-Ackermann, S. (2001). Trust and honesty in post-socialist societies. *Kyklos, 54,* 415–444.

Tang, S. Y. (1992). *Institutions and collective action: Self-governance in irrigation.* San Francisco: Institute for Contemporary Studies Press.

Theesfeld, I. (2004). Constraints on collective action in a transitional economy: The case of Bulgaria's irrigation sector. *World Development, 32,* 251–271.

Theesfeld, I. (2005). *A common-pool resource in transition. Determinants of institutional change in Bulgaria's postsocialist irrigation sector:* Vol. 23. Institutional change in agriculture and natural resources. Aachen: Shaker

Williamson, O. E. (1996). Efficiency, power, authority and economic organization. In J. Groenewegen (Ed.), *Transaction cost economics and beyond* (pp. 11–42). Dordrecht: Kluwer.

12 Payment for Environmental Services: Interactions with Property Rights and Collective Action

Brent Swallow[1] and Ruth Meinzen-Dick[2]

[1] World Agroforestry Centre (ICRAF), United Nations Avenue, Gigiri, PO Box 30677-00100 GPO, Nairobi, Kenya, E-mail: B.Swallow@cgiar.org
[2] International Food Policy Research Institute, 2033 K Street, NW Washington, DC 20006-1002, USA, E-mail: R.Meinzen-Dick@cgiar.org

Abstract: Global climate change and environmental degradation highlight the need for institutions of sustainability. In particular, there is increased interest in the potential of payments for environmental services (PES) to improve incentives for sustainable land management. Although smallholder land users can be efficient producers of environmental services of value to larger communities and societies, experience shows that the international and national institutions that govern PES are often designed in ways that entail transaction costs that cannot be feasibly met by individual smallholders. This chapter presents a conceptual framework to examine the inter-linkages between property rights, collective action, payment for environmental services, and the welfare of smallholder land users, examining how these play out in the contexts of carbon sequestration, biodiversity, and watershed functions. Greater consideration of the linkages between PES and other rural institutions can lead to more equitable outcomes, particularly by (1) suggesting how collective action can be used to overcome transaction costs and barriers to participation by smallholders and (2) identifying mechanisms through which managers of small private parcels or areas of common property can be rewarded for environmental stewardship through PES.

Keywords: Biodiversity, Carbon sequestration, Collective action, Payment for environmental services, Property rights

12.1 Introduction

Prof. Konrad Hagedorn's work on "institutions of sustainability" is gaining increasing relevance as global climate change and environmental degradation highlight the need for sustainable management of natural resources. As the limitations of command and control regulatory approaches to many environmental problems

V. Beckmann, M. Padmanabhan (eds.), *Institutions and Sustainability*,
DOI 10.1007/978-1-4020-9690-7_12, © Springer Science+Business Media B.V. 2009

become apparent, there is growing attention being paid to other institutional mechanisms to protect or enhance the delivery of environmental services. In particular, a range of payments for environmental services (PES) are being explored to match the demand for services with the incentives of land users whose actions modify the supply of those environmental services. A range of such programs have been set up for carbon sequestration, biodiversity conservation, and watershed functions. But while there has been considerable attention given to the formal institutional mechanisms for PES programs themselves, there has been relatively less interest shown in understanding the interrelationships between PES and other rural institutions. In this paper we present a conceptual framework to examine how the function and welfare effects of PES depend on the institutions of collective action and property rights. We then examine how these play out in the contexts of carbon sequestration, biodiversity, and watershed functions, with particular emphasis on the involvement of poor smallholders in developing countries.

There is considerable academic and policy enthusiasm for PES programs as potential "win–win" arrangements for the farmers or other land managers and others who benefit from such services. The potential benefits of market-based approaches often referred to include improved resource conservation, more sustainable sources of conservation financing, greater environmental justice in the distribution of conservation benefits and costs, and new and sustainable sources of income for resource-dependent communities. Because the majority of the world's poor are smallholder farmers, there is further interest in the potential of such programs to reduce poverty and create sustainable livelihoods. Smallholder land users can be efficient producers of environmental services of value to larger communities and societies; consequently, the European Union, Japan, and the United States have set up numerous payment schemes that supplement farm incomes while improving incentives for smallholders to increase the supply of these services (Engel, Pagiola, & Wunder, 2008). But experience in developing countries reveals that the international and national institutions that govern PES are often designed in ways that entail transaction costs or other restrictions that cannot be feasibly met by individual smallholders.

PES include a range of voluntary transactions in which farmers or other land managers are rewarded – directly or indirectly – for practices that will continue or increase the provision of environmental services.[1] The practical and theoretical case for PES in developing countries is laid out in several recent works (see Engel et al., 2008; FAO, 2007; Landell-Mills & Porras, 2002; Pagiola, Arcenas, & Platais, 2005). Van Noordwijk, Chandler, and Tomich (2004) discuss the conceptual basis of rewards for environmental services from various perspectives, concluding that a location-specific blending of rights, obligations and rewards is needed as long as the essential "preconditions" for market-based payments are not met in large parts of the developing world.

---

[1] This definition is consistent with FAO 2007, which is somewhat broader than the definition followed by Wunder, Engel, and Pagiola, (2008).

   While the largest PES programs are government-initiated (e.g., the large Sloping Lands Conversion program in China), there are also a growing number of private transactions, many with startup financing from private foundations (e.g., Shell Foundation, FACE Foundation, Mercedes-Benz, Dow Company Foundation) and support from multilateral or bilateral development agencies such as the UK Department for International Development, the International Fund for Agricultural Development, and the United States Agency for International Development. Some programs are also funded directly by the users of the services, especially for biodiversity conservation or watershed functions that benefit downstream water systems.

   There also has been considerable interest in PES to address global environmental challenges. The Clean Development Mechanism (CDM) of the United Nations Framework Convention on Climate Change (UNFCCC) is a PES mechanism in which greenhouse gas emitters in Annex A countries can meet part of their emission reduction targets through projects that reduce net emissions in developing countries, including Agriculture, Forestry and Other Land Use (AFOLU) projects. Currently, there is considerable global interest in an international mechanism for Reduced Emissions from Deforestation and Forest Degradation (REDD) (e.g., Miles & Kapos, 2008). The World Bank has established a number of funds to support experimental programs for carbon PES, including the BioCarbon Fund, the Community Carbon Fund, and most recently the Forest Carbon Partnership Facility.

   While high-profile PES programs have emerged in Costa Rica and other Latin American countries (Pagiola et al., 2005), other developing countries, especially in Africa, have relatively few PES programs, particularly as a share of the global carbon trade (Jindal, Swallow, & Kerr, 2008). Nonetheless, there is a growing number and variety of other forms of compensation or rewards for environmental services being explored. Direct monetary payments can be considered an extreme form of market development, bringing together the supply and demand for specific environmental services. Other less direct and less specific reward mechanisms can also usefully be analyzed in terms of their supply and demand characteristics. In this paper, we analyze markets for environmental services from the perspective of the new institutional economics (Hagedorn, 1993, 1996; North, 1990; Ruttan & Hayami, 1984), focusing particular attention on institutions of collective action and property rights.

   The framework we present is centered on concerns about the function and welfare effects of PES. The functional perspective helps to clarify the effects of collective action and property rights institutions on the supply of environmental services. The welfare perspective considers smallholders as one of several potential sources of supply. Using this conceptual framework can help us to postulate conditions under which smallholders are likely to be able to participate in PES schemes. Greater consideration of the linkages between PES and other rural institutions can lead to more equitable outcomes, particularly by

1. suggesting how collective action can be used to overcome transaction costs and barriers to participation by smallholders and
2. identifying mechanisms through which managers of small private parcels, and even common property managers, can be rewarded for environmental stewardship through PES.

Section 12.2 below presents a brief description of the particular environmental services considered in this paper: watershed protection, biodiversity conservation and carbon sequestration. We then develop a conceptual framework for linking factors affecting the development of markets for environmental services with the institutions of property rights and collective action, and the likelihood of smallholder involvement. Section 12.4 describes some of these relationships in more detail, with reference to experience that has been accumulated with PES in the developing world. Section 12.5 applies this framework to watershed protection, biodiversity conservation and carbon sequestration, and the final section draws implications for PES mechanisms to contribute towards poverty reduction among smallholders.

12.2 Environmental Services, Land Use and Smallholder Farmers

The paper focuses on three environmental services: watershed protection and rehabilitation, biodiversity conservation and landscape restoration, and carbon sequestration and protection of existing carbon stocks. All three services have aspects of "conservation" and "rehabilitation" that have consequences for the institutional context of reward mechanisms, leading to six different service-reward situations. Most of the PES schemes currently in operation cover one or more of these three groups of services (Miranda, Porres, & Luz Moreno, 2003). This section presents a brief description of these services, with an emphasis on the nature of each service and how land use might affect it. The following sections highlight differences between the services that affect the function and welfare implications of PES mechanisms.

Watershed protection refers to a set of land uses that preserves the integrity of a watershed to yield water that is relatively free of pollutants, low in sediment, and buffered against flash floods, relative to the pattern of rainfall and without large fluctuations in dry-season and groundwater flows. Watershed rehabilitation aims at returning a landscape to a condition where it can again provide these services after a period of degradation. Watershed protection is often equated with forest protection, based on the simple understanding that forested landscapes act as sponges and filters that reduce runoff, store water, and remove sediment and pollutants. Many forest protection, resettlement and afforestation programs are based on this premise. The empirical evidence suggests, however, that the relationships between tree cover and watershed function are more complex. Land use types other than natural forest may be able to provide these "forest functions", while planting fast-growing trees in the foresters' approach to reforestation is unlikely to return a landscape to the original forest condition. Indeed, South Africa's Working for Water is a PES program for clearing alien species to restore hydrologic functions (Turpie, Marais, & Blignaut, 2008). At the plot scale, runoff and erosion depend on ground cover, soil structure, and topography, while at the landscape scale, runoff and sedimentation depend upon the relative location of sources, lateral flows and sinks of water, soil and nutrients (Swallow, Garrity, & van Noordwijk, 2002; Ranieri et al., 2004; Bruijnzeel, 2004; van Noordwijk et al., 2004). Land use has large impact on watershed function in certain locations within the landscape, particularly in riparian areas, wetlands and hillside areas. Strategically located vegetative filters and conservation structures will often be more effective than general reforestation. In drier climates, water harvesting structures may have a positive impact in situations where general re- or afforestation programs may be counterproductive.

PES schemes for watershed protection have emerged in all regions of the world. Supported by government regulations and public investments, suppliers of domestic and industrial water and hydropower provide incentives to land users in the catchment areas to adopt practices that are expected to minimize chemical pollutants and sediment loads.

Appleton (2004) and Pires (2004) describe the famous case in which New York City negotiated with farmers in the 8,300 square kilometer Catskills-Delaware catchment area to maintain the quality of water supplied to residents of New York City. After a series of negotiations and shared vision exercises, New York City agreed to provide finances for the human resource and capital inputs required to develop whole farm plans for reducing pollution. The resulting program was voluntary at the individual farm level, but required that at least 85% of farmers participate. Within five years, 93% of farmers in the catchment enrolled in the program.

Biodiversity conservation refers to the preservation of valuable ecosystems, plant and animal communities, and individual plant and animal species. Land use affects biodiversity at all of these scales. It is well known that agricultural land use shapes agrobiodiversity – the diversity of plants, insects and soil biota that sustains agricultural production and the resilience of agricultural systems. Agricultural land use and farming practices also affects wild biodiversity at the landscape level. Relative to monocrop agriculture, positive effects on biological diversity have been noted for a variety of farming practices including integrated pest management, organic agriculture, agroforestry, conservation farming and pastoralism (McNeely & Scherr, 2001). Specific types of agroforestry systems, for example, have potential to foster wild biodiversity by providing corridors between protected areas, providing habitat conducive to wild fauna and flora, and reducing human pressure on protected areas (Schroth et al., 2004; Donald, 2004). Multi-strata damar and rubber agroforestry systems in Sumatra, Indonesia, foster plot-level levels of plant diversity that rival the levels found in nearby primary rainforests (Tomich et al., 2001). At landscape scale, however, there are both qualitative and quantitative differences in the biodiversity supported by these agroforests and the former natural forest (Beukema & van Noordwijk, 2004). In Africa, there are several examples in which smallholder farmers have been compensated for adopting land uses that foster conservation of wildlife with high tourism value. Perhaps best known are the CAMPFIRE program in Zimbabwe (Frost & Bond, 2008), group ranches in Kenya, or community conservancies in Namibia (Yatich, 2007).

Carbon sequestration is the absorption and long-term storage of atmospheric carbon in woody biomass and soils against some baseline situation, often restocking after earlier degradation. To reduce emissions, efforts have focused on preventing the degradation of carbon stocks in above-ground vegetation or peat soils, as carbon stocks in mineral soils tend to be more resilient.

The Clean Development Mechanism (CDM) of the Kyoto Protocol creates opportunities for industrialized countries with high CO_2 emissions to meet part of their emission reduction targets by supporting "clean development" in developing countries that have ratified the protocol. After protracted international negotiations, CDM also covers carbon sequestration through reforestation and afforestation, with many safeguards against misuse of the mechanisms. These safeguards, however, tend to substantially increase the transaction costs (Climate, Community and Biodiversity Alliance, 2004).

Because of cumbersome transactions and reporting requirements, payments for afforestation under CDM have been limited. However, pilot carbon sequestration projects with smallholder farmers outside of current CDM rules have been promoted in several developing countries, including Mexico, India, Indonesia, Uganda, Tanzania and Mozambique. The Ecosystem Marketplace (cited in Jindal et al., 2008) estimates that over 880,000 ha have been brought under carbon sequestration programs, with the majority of these under voluntary programs rather than the CDM. The Edinburgh Centre for Carbon Management promotes the Plan Vivo approach developed in Mexico for linking individual farmers with voluntary purchasers of carbon emission reductions (DTZ Pieda Consulting, 2000). In Indonesia pilot schemes in carbon-rich peat swamps have provided micro-credit for agricultural development with repayment of the loan via demonstrated success in survival of trees planted.

Relative to watershed functions and biodiversity, the carbon market is the most global and has most resemblance to commodity markets. Even so, the carbon "market" shows that "demand" for emission reduction certificates strongly depends on the institutional framework of (voluntary, negotiated) obligations. The "supply" of these credits requires national institutions that guard against a predominance of external benefits, but that run the risk of pricing a country out of the market.

In all the above we need to distinguish between the local demand for a demonstrable service (e.g., clean water), concern for the public image of countries or companies, and the more "global" concepts of reducing overall impacts via the concept of "offsets". Such offsets involve a linkage between environmental damage in one location and improvement or protection against demonstrable threats elsewhere. Offsets depend on the supply and demand for rules in the slow process of institutional development. The public image depends on the highly volatile market of supply and demand for "feel-good" factors of affluent consumers.

12.3 A Framework of Function and Welfare Effects of PES

Current PES projects and pilot schemes seek to foster the creation or expansion of markets for environmental services. That those markets did not exist before necessarily means that there have previously been some obstacles to the operation and efficiency of those markets. We first describe ten factors that have been postulated as factors constraining the development and function of ES markets – using the term in a broad sense of a mechanism to match supply and demand for environmental services by adjustment of the level of rewards.

1. *Legal basis and restrictions / fixed costs of market development:* Most of the demand for carbon sequestration offset is based on legally binding commitments to reduce environmental problems of development. The supply of marketable services depends upon legal baselines of "acceptable" levels of environmental damage, as only provision above such baseline is marketable. In many cases, national laws and local institutions that affect environmental governance constrain ES markets by lack of clarity of obligations for the buyers, lack of realistic baselines of acceptable levels of environmental damage, and high regulations on transactions. Such constraints are found in laws related to environment, agriculture, water, or local government institutions. International agreements, bilateral contracts, international donors, and international experience may create new opportunities for ES markets, but these do not immediately override national and local restrictions.

2. *Costs of excluding free-riders from benefit streams:* Compared to conventional marketed goods, environmental services have a higher cost of excluding outsiders from ES benefit streams. For example, some of the benefits of biodiversity conservation accrue to people who place a value on the existence of threatened species and ecosystems, whether or not they have paid for the conservation. Global warming and ozone layer depletion are global phenomena: mitigation of greenhouse gas emissions thus generates benefits across the global community. This public good nature of ES has been used as a justification for inter-governmental collective action, resource management by government agencies, and regulation of resource use through government environment agencies. Mobilizing more individualized sources of finance for PES often requires legal and organizational frameworks that can assign and enforce private responsibility for environmental damage (e.g., following the polluter pays principle), as well as more individualized rights to the benefits of ES (although not necessarily to the partner resources that generate those services). The buyers of environmental services may not be interested in the environmental services, per se, but in certification that they are adhering to government regulations, or in a positive public image.

3. *Small demand for ES:* Many environmental services have been characterized by small effective demand from the beneficiary populations. Early studies of the Environmental Kuznets Curve supported a hypothesis that demand for a safe

environment was very low for countries with low to middle income, but much higher for middle-to-higher income countries. This implies that ES are luxury goods and that economic growth is perhaps the most important solution to environmental degradation. More recent analysis of disaggregated data suggests that even low-income people demand environmental services, that changes in environmental awareness are important, and that the structure and function of environmental management institutions have major effects on demand for ES (Dasgupta, Laplante, Wang, & Wheeler, 2002; Stern, 2004; Kuuluvainen, 2002). Population growth and concentration also increases demand for clean water, and settlement of people in areas affected by floods can increase demand for watershed services. In some cases, people may express these demands through political processes that favor tighter environmental laws.

4. *Transaction costs of market function / market entry and validation of ES:* Two major categories of transaction costs can pose major obstacles to functional markets for environmental services: negotiation costs and enforcement costs. Negotiation costs include the time, social and financial costs of organizing buyers and sellers into operating units, as well as the costs of establishing contact, preparing necessary documentation, and negotiation between buyers and sellers. Enforcement costs include the costs of certification, monitoring and enforcement of contracts between buyers and sellers, and among groups of buyers and sellers. Krey (2005) has measured the transaction costs associated with CDM projects in India, and found very clear evidence of declining transaction costs per unit of carbon dioxide emission reduction, with costs ranging from 0.47 to 0.07 $US / tonne of carbon dioxide. These costs of validating transactions limit market entry, especially for smallholders.

5. *Small number of ES buyers or sellers with large share of the market:* Concentration in the supply or demand for environmental services could hinder or enhance markets for environmental services. On the positive side, single firms that stand to benefit from the supply or demand of environmental services may have greater incentive to incur the negotiation and enforcement costs associated with new contractual arrangements with widely-dispersed farming communities. This seems to have contributed to the development of the innovative approach to watershed management instigated by New York City. On the negative side, a high concentration among supplies of environmental services limits the possibility for smallholders to participate effectively.

6. *Functional relation between effort and ES supply:* There is large variation among environmental services, and the knowledge base on what factors affect ES supplies is limited and context specific. This is particularly the case where there are important threshold effects and non-linear cause-effect relations. Among the three environmental services considered in this paper, carbon sequestration has the most certain and linear functional relationships with resource use.

Table 12.1: Links between ES market constraints, property rights, collective action and smallholder welfare

Constraint to function and participation in ES market	Link to security and distribution of property rights (PR)	Link to collective action among smallholders (CA)	Link to conditions of smallholders
1. Legal restrictions/ fixed costs of market development	Institutions for secure rights are pre-condition for ES market; Changing legal restrictions often involves the de facto creation of a new property right	CA to lobby for / against institutional change	Entry costs may be prohibitive for smallholders; PR changes may benefit smallholders
2. Costs of excluding free-riders from benefit streams	Case for public ownership & or management	Public ownership / regulation may spur collective opposition or negotiation with government	Many smallholders reside in public land
3. Small demand for ES	Little direct link	Little direct link	ES demand likely to increase with income and population
4. Transaction costs of market function / entry	Secure rights as precondition for entry into ES market	CA to reduce average costs of transactions and validation	Variable costs may be prohibitive for smallholders
5. Small number of ES buyers or sellers with large share of the market	Largeholders more likely to have secure rights	CA to compete with largeholders or counter power of single buyer	Difficult for smallholders to compete
6. Functional relation between effort and supply of ES	Tenants and sharecroppers may have little incentive to adopt land uses that produce ES; Common property may facilitate the achievement of thresholds and scale economies	CA in supply to achieve thresholds & scale economies	Increasing returns to ES supply may exclude smallholders
7. Spatial specificity in ES supply	PR to high impact spaces may be most contested; High specificity to places with weak PR may foster PR change	Challenge to organize around high impact spaces	Smallholders often located in high impact spaces
8. Time path of ES production as a result of land use choices	Returns far into future make secure PR more important	CA facilitates pooling and temporal evening of returns	Smallholders may have shorter investment horizons
9. Time path of ES payments	One-off payments may finance changes in PR but not recurrent costs of secure PR	One-off payments may finance CA organization but not operations	Smallholders may discount future payments highly
10. Key partner resources for ES supply	Determines what resources PR are needed for; Potential for secure PR as a PES	Little direct link	Smallholders may have more secure rights to some resources than to others

7. Spatial specificity in ES supply: Some environmental services (e.g., carbon sequestration) have many alternative sources, while others (e.g., preservation of particular habitats) are highly specific to particular sites. These differences determine the size of the market of ES, the spatial specificity of markets, and the extent of competition to meet ES demand.

8. *Time path of ES production as a result of land use choices:* Some environmental services are produced through one-off actions, while others are produced through actions which must be kept in place or renewed indefinitely. For example, replacing a non-renewable energy source with a renewable energy source (such as from diesel to wind generation of electricity) produces a permanent net reduction in greenhouse gas emissions, while trees planted to sequester carbon as wood do so only as long as the wood is not burned.

9. *Time path of ES payments:* Payments that regularly reward ES supply have different implications than one-off payments, with one-off payments better suited for financing fixed costs and achievement of thresholds. Of course, on their own, one-off payments do not address the challenge of long-term compliance or the possibility of reversion to previous land use. Reward mechanisms – both one-off payments and regular rewards – are most likely to have sustained impact on farmers' behavior if they change the overall incentive structure in favor of land uses consistent with ES supply.

10. *Key partner resources for ES supply:* ES normally require "partner resources" that are necessary for supply. Resources that are most essential and tangible, such as land, will tend to be given special focus by the potential demanders of environmental services. Other partner resources are less tangible, such as appropriate skills, knowledge and capacity to enter the market.

Table 12.1 presents a summary of how those factors relate to property rights to environmental services and partner resources, collective action among smallholders, and the welfare of smallholders. The following section gives more details and illustrations.

12.4. Institutions and the Function of PES Mechanisms

12.4.1 Property rights and PES

Property rights as a necessary condition for ES markets – Environmental service mechanisms that link private purchasers with private or collective suppliers of those services are usually supported by an explicit contract that increases the accountability of the suppliers to the performance of agreed-upon actions. Contracts usually require that the ES providers have clear and secure rights to perform the agreed-upon actions on that land, because this is seen as necessary to generate a credible commitment (Climate, Community and Biodiversity Alliance, 2004).

Property rights do not need to be individual in order to allow environmental service mechanisms to proceed. Contracts with individual farmers require individual property rights, while contracts with groups of farmers may be more effectively secured with group rights. The latter have an advantage for environmental services that have minimum scale and threshold effects such as biodiversity conservation.

The requirement of secure property rights, as commonly stated in terms of land ownership, has the effect of excluding groups of people and even countries from environmental service mechanisms. For example, the constitution of Ethiopia prohibits individual freehold title to land, and the majority of land in sub-Saharan Africa is under customary tenure, without clear titles – a factor that restricts carbon sequestration projects (Jindal et al., 2008). In northern Costa Rica, smallholders who had received their land under the Agrarian Development Institute program for small farmers were not entitled to receive PES for watershed management. There are increasing instances where environmental service mechanisms even threaten the property rights of poor and marginalized populations, as in Bualeba Reserve in Uganda, where commercial plantations to generate carbon offsets threatens to evict local people from their customary rights for farming, grazing, fishing, and timber collection (Jindal et al., 2008). Grieg-Gran and Bann (2003, p. 37) caution that if communities do not have secure rights in an area suited for PES mechanism, then it is possible that other people with better connections will take over from the communities.

On the other hand, the necessity to have secure property rights has encouraged some agencies involved in the formulation of the schemes to secure property rights as an early part of the program. For example, the PAMB (Protected Area Management Board) program in the Philippines recognizes the need for farmers to be provided secure tenure in order for them to be effective partners in the co-management of protected areas. It is issuing "tenurial instruments" to all migrants who have occupied the land for at least 5 years before the program was initiated. This covers a huge part of the Philippines (Rosales, 2003, pp. 35–45).

Property rights and the time path of ES production and payments – ES demands that are satisfied through one-off purchases of services already rendered or to be rendered in the near future, such as energy projects that replace non-renewable with renewable energy sources, do not require secure property rights as much as ES demands that must be met through periodic and indefinite payments, such as carbon sequestration projects.

Secure property rights to partner resources as a payment for ES production – In situations where the production of environmental services requires long-term commitment of land resources, land tenure security may be a very important determinant of the production of environmental services. In such cases, stronger and more secure rights over land and other partner resources can be used, instead of or in addition to other payments, as a reward for environmental services. There are instances of this where the state claims rights over the land, and has not recognized the rights of "squatters" (even those who have been using the land for generations). In Indonesia, new social forestry agreements (Hutan ke-masyarakatan in Bahasa Indonesia or HKm) increase security of tenure for poor upland farmers in exchange for their commitment to land management agreements (Suyanto,

Khususiyah, & Leimona, 2007). In the Maasin watershed in the Philippines, farmers participating in the CADT / CALT scheme (Certificates of Ancestoral Domain Title / Certificates of Ancestoral Domain) were given 25 year tenure under the terms of a community based forest management program (Rosales, 2003; Tecsen, 2004). Even where farmers have some recognized rights, participating in an ES program offers a way to strengthen their property rights. In the Virilla watershed in Costa Rica, people who enrolled in the program experienced more secure land tenure because they are protected against land incursions. Thirteen percent of participants said that the main benefit of being involved is the reduced threat of land invasions (Miranda et al., 2003, p. 36).

Functional relation between effort and supply of ES – The form of property rights can shape the opportunities for different types of ES and ES mechanisms. For example, communal tenure in Maasai group ranches is consistent with community tourism, as in Olagasali in Kenya, whereas community tourism is more difficult where land has been privatized (Horan, Shogren, & Gramig, 2008).

Property rights to key resources – Some environmental services, particularly watershed function and biodiversity conservation, are heavily dependent upon key resources such as wetlands, riparian areas, corridors and buffer zones. One of the dilemmas of ES supply is that this high environmental value also justifies public ownership of those resources. If public resources are well managed, and regulations enforced, then public ownership may lead to high levels of ES supply. On the other hand, where such public resources are poorly managed, resources tend to be overused and poor levels of ES produced. In such circumstances, it becomes very important that the public sector concentrates on key resources where it has comparative advantage and encourages collective and private management of other resources. In the uplands of Sumatra, for example, large tracts of gazetted forest lands no longer have any tree cover because they have been burned and cleared by farmers. Farmers operating on plots without secure tenure tend to practice extractive short-duration agriculture, while farmers operating on plots with secure private title tend to practice complex multi-strata agroforestry systems. In those areas, the agroforestry systems are associated with higher levels of profit, greater carbon stocks, and higher levels of biological diversity than short-duration agriculture (Tomich et al., 2001).

PES and the creation of new property rights to environmental services – The creation of PES institutions itself represents the creation of new forms of property, with all of the tensions and tradeoffs that are entailed. As Hagedorn, Arzt, and Peters (2002) note, changes in institutional arrangements regarding agri-environmental coordination entail differentiated property rights on nature components – those cost and benefit streams that can be attributed to natural capital. For example, watershed protection payments create a new benefit stream related to land use. In a few cases ES property rights have been formally created through legislation, such as 1998 legislation in New South Wales, Australia that established property rights to forest carbon services, which are defined as tradable interests in the carbon sequestration potential of forests. Forestry covenants are used to guarantee that landholders will maintain land in forest cover in exchange for carbon sequestration payments (Rosenbaum, Schoene, & Mekouar, 2004). In 1996, the Government of Namibia legally granted local communities rights of ownership over huntable game, revenues from sale of game products, and rights to tourism (Yatich, 2007). In most cases (as with most property), the rights are evolving, but careful attention needs to be given to who receives the property rights over each benefit stream, as that will affect the equity as well as effectiveness of the programs.

The experience from other types of property rights offers important lessons for ES property rights. Even if laws are passed to define property rights over ES, the rights will not be effective property rights unless they are accompanied by effective governance structures for supervision and sanctioning (Hagedorn et al., 2002). Governance can come from a range of international, state, local or customary institutions. However, international bodies are unlikely to have a strong presence on the ground in many of the places where ES provision is most critical. Experience with forest, water, and rangeland management indicates that neither state nor local bodies are likely to be able to enforce such property rights alone, and that some type of co-management regime will be most effective. Cultural or religious norms can also come into play as enforcement institutions. For example, "sanctifying" a forest by dedicating it to the local deity in India invokes divine oversight, and enhances people's respect for the rules or fear of punishment (Aggarwal, 2001). Similarly, Maasai cultural taboos on eating wild animals strengthen biodiversity conservation.

Property rights are found to be most valuable, and create the strongest incentives for resource management, when they are secure. But how would tenure security of rights over environmental services be defined? Definitions provided by Place, Roth, and Hazell (1994) highlight the importance of breadth (the number of bundles of rights one holds), duration (time frame), and assurance (robustness of rights in the face of competing claims). Applying this to environmental service rights implies the need to look carefully at who holds not only rights over benefit streams from the resource and payment for the resource, but also who holds decision-making rights, and the extent to which right-holders can exclude others. Duration implies the need to look at long-term assignment of rights, and assurance requires attention to enforcement institutions, as discussed above.

12.4.2 Collective action and PES

Collective action and the functional relation between effort and ES supply – The functional relation between effort and supply of environmental services affects the potential benefits of collective action in supply (Hagedorn et al., 2002). Services with a proportional or more-than-proportional observable relationship with effort require less collective action than services that require landscape-scale efforts or involve non-negligible thresholds before they emerge. Carbon sequestration benefits are approximately proportional to the amount of land involved; the contribution of one farmer growing trees on one hectare is approximately the same, whether or not neighboring farmers grow trees. By contrast, species counts have often been observed to increase at an increasing rate as the area targeted in an ecosystem grows larger. When this is true, biodiversity protection involves more-than-proportional benefits. Other biodiversity functions have important threshold effects, meaning that if not adopted on a large enough area, the benefits are not realized at all (Landell-Mills & Porras, 2002). For example, landscape corridors only play a function if they are sufficiently connected with centers of biodiversity. Such situations require coordination among neighbors. Water quality is a strong example of the necessity of full compliance and collective action, as a single source of pollution can make the efforts of a large number of actors meaningless. Collective action provides a mechanism for farmers to coordinate their actions over a large area to provide environmental services such as biodiversity and water services.

Collective action and the costs of PES mechanisms – Even where the provision of the ES is not "lumpy" due to critical thresholds in supply, collective action offers an important means to reduce the transaction costs of verification and payment for PES systems (FAO, 2007). Experience from around the developing world has shown that smallholder land users often are both important and efficient producers of the environmental services of value to larger social groups (Tomich et al., 2001; Schroth et al., 2004; McNeely & Scherr, 2003). But experience also shows that the international and national institutions that govern PES are often designed in ways that entail transaction costs that cannot be feasibly met by individual smallholders. Economies of scale in contracting, monitoring, and making payments favor larger suppliers such as plantations over many individual smallholders. However, when smallholders group together in cooperatives or other forms of user groups, they can achieve some of these economies of scale. Effectively, the cooperatives assume the transaction costs of developing and enforcing contracts with individuals, so that the PES implementing agency does not have to. In some cases, the PES may even be channeled through producer cooperatives as a premium price of output for "certified" producers. For example, the premium price paid for fair trade, shade-grown, organic coffee provides smallholders in Mexico an incentive for biodiversity conservation, which is compatible with shade-grown coffee. The cooperatives negotiating with purchasers also undertake the costs of certification.

Collective action and bargaining power in PES mechanisms – Collective action potentially strengthens the bargaining power of smallholders relative to other producers of environmental services and buyers of environmental services. In the Sumber Jaya area of Sumatra, farmers' groups have been very important for providing voice to upland farmers previously considered to be squatters on public land. In negotiations for new HKm social forestry agreements, the farmer groups have been effective in convincing local officials that they are concerned about the environment and are willing to adopt land use practices that have been documented to produce high levels of environmental services. Farmers' groups often need assistance with such negotiations, however, since they normally are formed for other purposes and are unfamiliar with the concept of producing environmental services through their farming activities.

PES schemes affecting collective action – The nature of environmental service payments also influences collective action. Conventional regulatory approaches stress enforcement and negative penalties. Demanders have a feeling of entitlement, and expect public agencies to assume the responsibility to deliver services or protect against negative impacts. Under a regulatory regime, collective action among suppliers is often to evade the rules and enforcement, rather than collective action to enforce the rules, especially if the rules do not have local legitimacy. By contrast, PES offers positive economic and other incentives for ES provision. These offer greater potential for collective action to enforce the rules and provide the service.

Despite these potential advantages – even necessity – of collective action for many PES programs, especially involving smallholders, it is not a panacea. In many cases, the cooperation does not emerge or sustain, due to a host of factors related to the resource or the users (see Hagedorn et al., 2002). As van Huylenbroeck et al. (this volume) note, the costs of coordination are often higher where the advantages of coordination are also greatest, because of the need for increased governance mechanisms. In many cases, outside groups such as governments or NGOs have borne a large share of the initial transactions costs to enable people to come together, but there is a risk of dependency or elite capture of the benefits of PES that needs to be guarded against.

12.4.3 PES and the potential for poverty reduction

As with many other "new" resources (i.e. those which have suddenly become more valuable, and do not yet have clearly established claims), PES has generated considerable enthusiasm on the part of those who hope that it might provide income streams or other benefits to poor people. Yet experience to date indicates that this is far from assured (Landell-Mills & Porras, 2002). In general the poverty impact of PES will depend on whether poor people are potential suppliers of ES and whether they can take advantage of PES mechanisms (FAO, 2007).

Spatial patterns of ES supply and poverty – The spatial pattern of supply – demand interaction will determine how specific or general are the pools of potential suppliers and potential demanders for the service. The consumers of some environmental services demand ones that can only be provided by potential suppliers living in specific locations, while consumers of other environmental services demand ones that could be provided by suppliers from almost anywhere in the world. Potential demanders are more likely to be willing to incur the higher transaction costs of working with smallholders for services that are specific to locations where smallholders form a majority of the population. In many parts of southeast Asia and Latin America, the areas with highest value for biodiversity conservation and watershed protection tend to populated by relatively poor people. Traditional approaches to conservation and land classification may be partially responsible for these situations. Escobal and Torero (1999) show that the high levels of poverty that exist in the highlands of Peru are largely explained by their low levels of private and public assets. In Indonesia, Thailand and the Philippines, most upland areas have been designated as forest domain that should be reserved for the generation of environmental services and not settled for farm production (Fay & Michon, 2003). The tens of millions of people who have settled (illegally in some cases) in such areas have deliberately not been provided with public infrastructure or services.

Viewing the upland poor as providers of environmental services thus requires a significant paradigm shift away from traditional approaches to environmental regulation. Traditional approaches generally try to enforce the approach of segregation: exclude people from areas important for environmental services, and do not expect areas with high numbers of people to produce environmental services. While in some instances certain environmental services are indeed provided efficiently through the segregation of people and protected areas, other environmental services are provided by the integration of agricultural and non-agricultural land uses (van Noordwijk, Tomich, de Foresta, & Michon, 1997). For example, flooded rice fields provide habitats for migratory waterfowl, and natural vegetative strips in the Philippines create habitats for wild flora and fauna (McNeely & Scherr, 2003). On the other hand, conservation of mega-fauna, like tigers, gorillas and elephants, often requires designating certain protected areas and working with farmers in the buffer zones to provide connectivity and reduce pressure on the protected area.

Resources of the poor to participate in ES mechanisms – One factor that constrains the ability of the poor to participate in environmental service mechanisms is lack of access to sufficient resources to devote to environmental service provision. Smallholders facing subsistence constraints face high opportunity costs in setting aside substantial portions of their land, which they need to live on. For example, in the Virella watershed in Costa Rica, Miranda et al. (2003) found that only people with large land holdings were willing to dedicate part of their holdings to conservation. Large disparities in land holdings and security of tenure are likely to exacerbate the bias against smallholders. Wherever effective control over land is the basis of environmental services, very specific agrarian interventions will be needed to achieve "pro poor" impacts. However, where labor or effort is involved, pro-poor mechanisms are more easily envisaged. For example, South Africa's Working for Water program produces improved hydrologic functions by contracting with unemployed people (rather than with the land owners) to restore public or private lands (Turpie et al., 2008).

Empowerment or exclusion of the poor through PES mechanisms – Environmental service reward mechanisms generally entail some shift in attitude toward rural people whose resource uses affect the environment. Traditionally, rural people living in or near protected areas have been viewed as troublesome squatters; evicting them or sharply curtailing their land use activities (through "fines and fences" approaches) were seen as the best way to improve land management. Rewards for environmental services represent a fundamental shift in perspective, with rural land users treated as land stewards who should be compensated for providing positive externalities. Giving rewards for environmental services builds on the idea of creating goodwill with residents of environmentally sensitive areas and takes the additional step of providing those residents with incentives to protect the landscape. However, there is also the very real possibility that, if PES mechanisms are very remunerative, they will create an incentive for elites to take over the land (FAO, 2007, Grieg-Gran & Bann, 2003). Thus, for PES mechanisms to address poverty, safeguards need to be included to guard against elite capture.

12.5 Characterization of Environmental Services

The interactions of PES with property rights, collective action, and poverty reduction differ between types of environmental services. The nature of the environmental services will influence the scale and type of collective action needed, the bargaining power of smallholders, and the investment or reinvestment requirements, which in turn affect the ability of the poor to invest. Table 12.2 presents a characterization of watershed protection, biodiversity conservation and carbon sequestration services according to key factors related to property rights and collective action.

While there will clearly be differences from site to site even within a broad category of ES, this analysis helps to identify key tendencies.

Because of the long time frame of carbon sequestration and the preference for one-time payments, secure property rights over land resources are likely to be very important for carbon PES mechanisms. However, this is a two-way relationship: land rights being required as a condition for participating in PES, but secure tenure also being a potential incentive mechanism for ES in itself. Because both land and tree resources are relatively immobile, defining property rights is easier than is the case when the key resources are mobile or fluctuating. The linear and observable nature of carbon sequestration means that collective action is not necessary for provision, though it can reduce transaction costs for payment. Although smallholders are very appropriate suppliers of carbon sequestration, the lack of differentiation among suppliers means that any purchaser can go to many alternative suppliers; hence the bargaining power of any particular smallholder or group is likely to be low.

Table 12.2: Characterization of environmental services by the ten factors affecting reward mechanisms

Factor	Carbon sequestration	Biodiversity	Watershed function
1. Legal restric-tions/ fixed costs of market development	Countries that have ratified the Kyoto protocol are eligible for CDM, but need to harmonize with other domestic policies	Highly variable across countries, depending on conservation and wildlife policies and programs	Many countries are experimenting and enacting new water laws to facilitate
2. Costs of excluding freeriders from benefit streams	The CDM facilitates this	Very problematic, except for tourism	Moderate
3. Small demand for ES	Demand for carbon sequestration under Kyoto protocol amounts to about $1 billion per year in 2004/5, likely to grow in the future	In developing countries there is more concern with functional and ecotourism value of biodiversity than the existence value of particular species	Growing due to water shortages and changes in settlement patterns
4. Small number of ES buyers or sellers with large share of the market	Many buyers and inter-mediaries at global scale, segmented by concerns for small-holders; Normally a single buyer at local scale	Large number of tourists, but otherwise limited	Generally mediated through hydro-electric or municipal water supply agencies
5. Transaction costs of market function/ market entry /validation	High but clear under CDM at present time	High but clear for tourism; Uncertain otherwise	Uncertain
6. Thresholds & increasing returns to effort in ES supply	Linear, relatively observable, with risks associated with permanence	Non-linear, with important thresholds, uncertainty about the function of complex ecosystems	Non-linear with important scale effects and high uncertainty in cause – effect relations
7. Spatial specificity in ES supply	Source matters little in competitive markets, but more in voluntary markets, where demanders are seeking good public image through the mechanism; Small-holders manage the largest areas appropriate for Kyoto afforestation, with little differentiation among smallholders	Smallholders seen as major threat to wild biodiversity; Poor small-holders often reside in buffer zones; Some types of biodiversity conservation are more site specific than others; Higher value for sites that are more visible and accessible;	Supply limited to certain areas, but may be other more cost-effective ways to achieve the same service; Public agencies are major alternative sources of supply, particularly in hotspot areas such as riparian areas, hillsides and wetlands
8. Time path of ES production as a result of land use choices	Produced slowly over time and needs to be maintained indefinitely	Produces current and future values, which depend on relative scarcity	Produces current and future values, which depend upon downstream exposure to risks
9. Time path of ES rewards	Buyers prefer one-time payments with long-term assurance	Mixture of one-time and recurrent payments	Mostly recurrent payments associated with water use
10. Key partner resources for ES supply	Land, trees	Land in areas with high value for biodiversity conservation.	Land in riverine areas, water, vegetation in riverine and hillside areas, wetlands

As complex as creating PES for carbon sequestration may be, the challenges are even greater for biodiversity. The fluctuating nature of the genetic resources (particularly animals, but also plants), the generation of current and future values (Balmford et al., 2002), and the need for recurrent investment leads to a combination of one-time and recurrent payments, so long-term property rights over land are not as essential; rewarding tenants might be just as important as rewarding land owners. On the other hand, because of important threshold effects, collective action is much more important for provision than in the case of carbon. Smallholders occupy many of the global biodiversity hotspots, but this does not automatically give them bargaining power. In many cases smallholders' livelihoods are perceived as being in conflict with biodiversity, and public agencies are seen as an alternative supplier. Thus, in some cases, for example the CAMPFIRE program in Zimbabwe, poor people have been able to benefit from biodiversity conservation, but in many other cases they have lost access to land and livelihoods through eviction and creation of protected areas.

Like biodiversity, watershed functions produce current and fluctuating future values. While land is certainly a key resource, vegetation and water play key roles, and these fluctuate considerably. This combination of factors often leads to recurrent payments, which means that long-term property rights over land may not be as essential as decision-making rights over the land, vegetation, and water flows. The supply of watershed ES is non-linear; there are important scale effects, but also differentiation in the importance of different types of land within a watershed. Thus collective action is important, but not all land or farmers are equally important. Certain areas, like streambanks, steep hillsides, and wetlands, may be more important than others. Nor do all watersheds generate equal value; those upstream of major cities, industries, hydroelectric facilities or other critical water users are more likely to receive attention. Smallholders may be able to benefit from watershed PES if they live in such critical areas, but public agencies are important alternative sources of supply, and regulation is more common than rewards.

12.6 Conclusions

Demand for environmental services will continue to grow, especially for carbon sequestration and water quality services in highly populated catchments. Attempts by the state to meet this demand through regulatory approaches and excluding users from upland watersheds, forests, and biodiversity hotspots have demonstrated their limitations, both in terms of effectiveness in delivering the resource and the high human welfare costs of the "fines and fences" approaches. Whether this increasing demand will be met by increasing supply from smallholders depends largely on the design of appropriate institutions.

Rewarding land users for delivering environmental services off-site is a promising approach for protecting natural resources. It offers improvements over past command and control systems, which created enmity between local people and the authorities without achieving great success. There is also a great deal of interest in such mechanisms as a way of supplementing the incomes or enhancing the welfare of poor land users. However, emerging experience suggests that there are several major challenges that limit the ability of smallholders to benefit from PES mechanisms.

Our conceptual framework helps to identify the conditions under which smallholders are likely to be able to participate in environmental service reward schemes. In particular, we maintain that greater consideration of the linkages between environmental service mechanisms and other rural institutions can lead to more equitable outcomes.

One important area of linkage relates to how collective action can be used to overcome transaction costs and barriers to participation in environmental service reward schemes by smallholders. Environmental service rewards will be viable as a significant source of income for smallholders only if smallholders can be proven to be a large, effective and credible supplier of services. Currently, millions of smallholders sequester carbon, shelter biodiversity, and manage landscapes in ways that benefit downstream water users, but the costs of identifying such users and developing and enforcing contracts for specific environmental services means that they do not receive payments to maintain or enhance those services. Realizing this potential requires successful pilot projects, generalizable design principles, cost-effective monitoring, and multi-disciplinary approaches to assessment.

Environmental service mechanisms in themselves represent the development of a new form of benefit stream, and the allocation of that benefit stream represents the emergence of a new kind of property rights. The vital question is whether this new form of rights will bypass the poor or enhance their livelihoods.

Linkages between environmental service reward mechanisms and property rights over the partner resources (especially land, water, and biodiversity), offer both constraints and opportunities for poor resource users to participate, depending on the institutional design. Identifying mechanisms through which managers of small private parcels, common property managers, and even resource users without state-recognized title to resources can be rewarded for environmental stewardship through environmental service rewards is critical for these reward mechanisms to enhance the welfare of poor resource-dependent communities. Although current mechanisms tend to require land ownership as a prerequisite for participating in reward schemes, the creation of new mechanisms for smallholder environmental services has the potential to generate more secure property rights and effective collective action for environmental services and partner resources (land, water, and genetic resources). These new approaches also allow the expansion of carbon sequestration or other environmental benefit programs, especially in Africa, where much land is not titled.

One of the greatest benefits of environmental service reward systems may lie not so much in the payments themselves, but in stimulating a change in attitude toward poor smallholders in environmentally sensitive areas: a shift from the state as protector to the smallholder as steward. An environmental services perspective requires the understanding of spatial inter-relations, property rights over key resources, and a degree of consistency with social relations. A deeper understanding of the underlying differences in institutional, economic and social contexts between the various parts of the world is urgently needed, as direct extrapolation has not been successful.

Acknowledgments

Earlier versions of this paper were presented at the biennial meeting of the International Association for the Study of Common Property in Oaxaca, Mexico, 9–13 August 2004 and published in a book edited by Merino and Robson (2006) (Swallow, Meinzen-Dick, & van Noordwijk, 2006). Our ideas on this have benefited from substantial discussions with colleagues, particularly John Kerr, Fiona Chandler, Nancy McCarthy, S. Suyanto and John Pender.

References

Aggarwal, S. (2001). *Supernatural sanctions in commons management: Panchayat forest conservation in the Central Himalayas.*Honolulu: Dissertation, University of Hawaii.

Appleton, A. (2004, November). *How New York City used an ecosystem services strategy carried out through urban-rural partnership to preserve the pristine quality of its drinking water and save billions of dollars.* Paper presented at the World Conservation Forum, Bangkok.

Balmford, A., Bruner, A., Cooper, P., Costanza, R., Farber, S., Green, R. E., et al. (2002). Economic reasons for conserving wild nature. *Science, 297*, 950–953.

Beukema, H. J., & van Noordwijk. M. (2004). Terrestrial pteridophytes as indicators of a forest-like environment in rubber production systems in the lowlands of Jambi, Sumatra. *Agriculture, Ecosystems and Environment, 104*, 63–73.

Bruijnzeel, L. A. (2004). Hydrological functions of tropical forests: Not seeing the soil for the trees? *Agriculture, Ecosystems and Environment, 104*, 185–228.

Climate, Community and Biodiversity Alliance. (2004) *Climate, community and biodiversity design standards (Draft 1.0)*, CCBA, Washington DC, from: http://www.climate-standards.org.

Dasgupta, S., Laplante, B., Wang, H., & Wheeler, D. (2002). Confronting the environmental Kuznets curve. *Journal of Economic Perspectives, 16*, 147–168.

Donald, P. F. (2004). Biodiversity impacts of some agricultural commodity production systems. *Conservation Biology, 18*, 17–37.

DTZ Pieda Consulting. (2000). *An evaluation of FRP's carbon sequestration project in Southern Mexico.* (Consultancy report for DfID).

Engel, S., Pagiola, S., & Wunder, S. (2008). Designing payments for environmental services in theory and practice: An overview of the issues. *Ecological Economics, 65*, 663–674.

Escobal, J., & Torero, M. (1999). *How to face an adverse geography? The role of private and public assets.* Lima, Peru: UNU-WIDER and Grupo de Análisis para el Desarrollo (GRADE), from: http://www.wider.unu.edu/conference/conference-2002-2/papers /escobal%20&%20torero.pdf.

FAO (Food and Agriculture Organization of the United Nations). (2007). *The state of food and agriculture 2007: Paying farmers for environmental services.* Rome: FAO.

Fay, C., & Michon, G. (2003, May). *Redressing forestry hegemony: When a forestry regulatory framework is best replaced by an agrarian one.* Paper presented at the International Conference on Rural Livelihoods, Forests and Biodiversity, Bonn.

Frost, P. G. H., & Bond, I. (2008). The CAMPFIRE programme in Zimbabwe: Payments for wildlife services. *Ecological Economics, 65,* 777–787.

Grieg-Gran, M., & Bann, C. (2003). A closer look at payments and markets for environmental services. In P. Gutnam (Ed.), *From goodwill to payments for environmental services: A survey of financing options for sustainable natural resource management in developing countries* (pp. 27–40). Washington, DC: WWF.

Hagedorn, K. (1993). Institutions and agricultural economics. *Journal of Economic Issues, 27,* 849–886.

Hagedorn, K. (1996). *Das Institutionenproblem in der agrarökonomischen Politikforschung.* Tübingen: J. C. B. Mohr (Paul Siebeck).

Hagedorn, K, Arzt, K., & Peters, U. (2002). Institutional arrangements for environmental cooperatives: A conceptual framework. In K. Hagedorn (Ed.), *Environmental cooperation for institutional change: Theories and policies for European agriculture* (pp. 3–25). Cheltenham and Northampton: Edward Elgar.

Horan, R. D., Shogren, J. F., & Gramig, B. M. (2008). Wildlife conservation payments to address habitat fragmentation and disease risks. *Environment and Development Economics, 13,* 414–439.

Jindal, R, Swallow, B., & Kerr, J. M. (2008). Forestry-based carbon sequestration projects in Africa: Potential benefits and challenges. *Natural Resources Forum, 32,* 116–130.

Krey, M. (2005). Transaction costs of unilateral CDM projects in India: Results of an empirical survey. *Energy Policy, 33,* 2385–2397.

Kuuluvainen, J. (2002). Value of nature conservation: The good or the context? *Journal of Forest Economics, 2,* 101–103.

Landell-Mills, N., & Porras, I. T. (2002). *Silver bullet or fool's gold? A global review of markets for forest environmental services and their impact on the poor.* London: International Institute for Environment and Development.

McNeely, J. A., & Scherr, S. J. (2001). Common Ground Common Future. How Ecoagriculture Can Help Feed the World and Save Wild Biodiversity. Gland, Switzerland: IUCN and Future Harvest.

McNeely, J. A., & Scherr, S. J. (2003). *Ecoagriculture.* Washington, DC: Island Press.

Merino, L., & Robson, J. (Eds.). (2006). *Managing the commons: Payment for environmental services.* Mexico City: Instituto Nacional De Ecologia (INE).

Miles, L., & Kapos, V. (2008). Reducing greenhouse gas emissions from deforestation and forest degradation: Global land-use implications. *Science, 320,* 1454–1455.

Miranda, M., Porres, I., & Luz Moreno, M. (2003). The social impacts of payments for environmental services in Costa Rica. Environmental Economics Programme, International Institute for Environment and Development, London.

North, D. C. (1990). *Institutions, institutional change and economic performance.* Cambridge: Cambridge University Press.

Pagiola, S., Arcenas, A., & Platais, G. (2005). Can payments for environmental services help reduce poverty? An exploration of the issues and evidence to date from Latin America. *World Development, 33,* 237–253.

Pires, M. (2004). Watershed protection for a world city: The case of New York. *Land Use Policy, 21,* 161–175.

Place, F., Roth, M., & Hazell, P. (1994). Land tenure security and agricultural performance in Africa: Overview of research methodology. In J. W. Bruce, & S. Migot-Adholla (Eds.), *Searching for land tenure security in Africa* (pp. 15–39). Washington, DC: The World Bank.

Ranieri, S. B. L., Stirzaker, R., Suprayogo, D., Purwanto, E., de Willigen, P., & van Noordwijk, M. (2004). Managing movements of water, solutes and soil: From plot to landscape scale. In M. van Noordwijk, G. Cadisch, & C. K. Ong (Eds.), *Belowground interactions in tropical agroecosystems* (pp. 329–347). Wallingford: CAB International.

Rosales, R. M. P. (2003). *Developing pro-poor markets for environmental services in the Philippines.* London: International Institute for Environment and Development.

Rosenbaum, K. L., Schoene, D., & Mekouar, A. (2004). *Climate change and the forest sector: Possible national and subnational legislation.* FAO Forestry Paper 144. Rome: Food and Agriculture Organization of the United Nations.

Ruttan, V.W., & Hayami, Y. (1984). Toward a theory of induced institutional innovation. Journal of Development Studies 20, 203–233.

Schroth, G., Da Fonseca, A. B. G., Harvey, C. A., Gascon, C., Vasconcelos, H. L., & Izac, A. M. N. (2004). *Agroforestry and biodiversity conservation in tropical landscapes.* Washington, DC: Island Press.

Stern, D. (2004). The rise and fall of the environmental Kuznets curve. *World Development, 32,* 1419–1439.

Suyanto, S., Khususiyah, N., & Leimona, B. (2007). Poverty and environmental services: case study in Way Besai watershed, Lampung Province, Indonesia. *Ecology and Society,* 12, from: http://www.ecologyandsociety.org/vol12/iss2/art13/

Swallow, B., Garrity, D. P., & van Noordwijk, M. (2002). The effects of scales, flows and filters on property rights and collective action in catchment management. *Water Policy, 4,* 449–455.

Swallow, B., Meinzen-Dick, R., & van Noordwijk, M. (2006). Localizing demand and supply of environmental services: Interactions with property rights, collective action and the welfare of the poor. In L. Merino & J. Robson (Eds.), *Managing the commons: Payment for environmental services* (pp. 35–49). Mexico: Instituto Nacional de Ecologia (INE).

Tecsen, E. (2004). Indigenous peoples amidst clashing cultures and conflicting laws. *Farm News and Views,* second quarter 2004, from: http://www.ppi.org.ph/ publications /fnv/current_issues/fnv_5.htm.

Tomich, T. P., van Noordwijk M, Budidarsono, S., Gillison, A., Kusumanto, T., Murdiyarso, D., et al. (2001). Agricultural intensification, deforestation and the environment: Assessing tradeoffs in Sumatra, Indonesia. In D. R. Lee & C. B. Barrett (Eds.), *Tradeoffs or synergies? Agricultural intensification, economic development and the environment* (pp. 221–244). Wallingford: CABI Publishing.

Turpie, J. K., Marais, C., & Blignaut, J. N. (2008). The working for water programme: Evolution of a payments for ecosystem services mechanism that addresses both poverty and ecosystem service delivery in South Africa. *Ecological Economics, 65,* 788–798.

Van Noordwijk, M., Chandler, F., & Tomich, T. P. (2004). An introduction to the conceptual basis of RUPES: Rewarding upland poor for the environmental services they provide. ICRAF-Southeast Asia, Bogor, from: http://www.worldagroforestry.org /sea/ Networks/RUPES/abs_13.htm

Van Noordwijk, M., Tomich, T. P., de Foresta, H., & Michon, G. (1997). To segregate or to integrate? The question of balance between production and biodiversity conservation in complex agroforestry systems. *Agroforestry Today, 9,* 6–9.

Wunder, S., Engel, S., & Pagiola, S. (2008). Taking stock: A comparative analysis of payments for environmental services programs in developed and developing countries. *Ecological Economics, 65,* 834–852.

Yatich, T. (2007). Status and potential of payments schemes for wildlife conservation in Africa. In F. Waswa, S. Otor, G. Olukoye, & D. Mugendi (Eds.), *Environment and sustainable development: A guide for higher education in Kenya* (pp. 224–246). Nairobi: Kenyatta University School of Environmental and Human Studies.

13 An Institutional Economics Analysis of Land Use Contracting: The Case of the Netherlands

Nico B. P. Polman[1] and Louis H. G. Slangen[2]

[1] Agricultural Economics Research Institute (LEI), Spatial and Regional Policy, Postbus 29703, 2502 LS Den Haag, The Netherlands, E-mail: Nico.Polman@wur.nl
[2] Wageningen University, Agricultural Economics and Rural Policy Group, Hollandseweg 1, 6706 KN Wageningen, The Netherlands, E-mail: Louis.Slangen@wur.nl

Abstract. The area of leased land in The Netherlands has decreased from roughly 50% of all agricultural land in 1966 to about 27% in 2005. In 1995, the Dutch government introduced two new types of lease contracts in order to prevent the decline from continuing. The new types of lease contracts implied the possibility of transferring a smaller part of the bundle of property rights from landowner to tenant. However, the trend towards decreasing lease area did not stop. In 2007, a new reform was introduced implying, again, less restrictions on formal leasing (the so-called liberalised lease). According to contract theory, transferring fewer property rights from a landowner to a tenant-farmer will lead to an institutional change for land leasing. For policies regulating land leasing, it is therefore important to recognise the characteristics of contractual arrangements and the parties involved. In this paper we analyse contract choice using a Trivariate probit model and taking into account the type of landowner and farmer characteristics. Results show that an official contract is more likely to be chosen if public organisations are involved. In contrast, when farmers exchange land among themselves, they are more likely to use less explicit contracts in which trust and reputation play an important role for coordination.

Keywords: Contract choice, Formal rules, Land use, Lease contracts, Trust and reputation

13.1 Introduction

Leasing land implies that a landowner transfers a part of or almost his entire bundle of property rights to the tenant on a contractual basis, for a given period of time. The bundle of property rights transferred by means of a lease transaction varies with the type of contractual arrangement. Lease contracts belong to a larger category of land transactions, including selling and buying land. Land transactions take place when a set of rights to land is transferred from one individual to another (see also Hurrelmann, 2002, p. 43). This paper focuses on situations in which only a part of the bundle is transferred.

The area of leased land in The Netherlands has decreased from roughly 50% of all agricultural land in 1966 to about 27% in 2005. Explanations for the decrease in area rented until 1997 are mostly couched in terms of relatively low returns for the landowner and the oppressive nature of the totality of the tenant's rights due to the Lease Law. These rights consist, for example, of priority rights for the tenant in case of sale and continuation rights, meaning an almost automatic lease renewal. Moreover, the Land Tenure Board exerts considerable influence over the official lease contracts. For example, the Board has the right to intervene directly in the private contractual arrangements. The Lease Law of 1995 introduced two new forms of contract for land leasing which can be characterised as short-term lease contracts (maximum of 12 years) and imply the transfer of fewer property rights from the landowner to the tenant when compared to the traditional lease contract. In the beginning of this new period (1995–1999), the total area leased remained about 30% of all agricultural land due to these new contract types. However, at the beginning of the present century the total leased area decreased further. After a discussion lasting about seven years, the Lease regulation of 2007 – coming into force in September 2007 – adopting a more liberalised form of lease. However, during the policy debates very little attention was given to the institutional economic aspects of the lease reform.

Land leasing has attracted the interest of researchers for the past several years (see for instance Dasgupta, Knight, & Love, 1999 or Allen & Lueck, 2002). The literature on contract choice is often focused on the choice between cropshare contracts and cash leases, examples being studies of Datta, O'Hara, and Nugent (1986); Eswaran and Kotwal (1985); Allen and Lueck (1992); and Janssen et al. (2002). Factors explaining contract choice include risk preferences and risk characteristics, differences in transaction costs (e.g. Allen & Lueck, 1993), farming experience, property rights (Barry, Escalante, & Moss, 2002, p. 2), soil characteristics, and financial security (Patterson, Hanson, & Robison, 1998, p. 8). Several studies conclude that risk is of secondary importance in leasing arrangements relative to transaction costs and property rights (Barry et al., 2002, p. 1). Related to our study is the work of Hurrelmann (2005), who investigated the role of the institutional environment and the properties of transactions on land lease contract design in Poland. Contract type is important for adopting soil conservation measures (Lichtenberg, 2007, p. 294 and Soule, Tegene, & Wiebe, 2000, p. 993), which also provide public benefits in terms of water quality and other environmental characteristics (Soule et al., 2000, p. 1004). It is also suggested in the literature that land use should contribute to the maintenance of landed estates of cultural, historical and landscape interest as well as the quality of land and wildlife (Slangen, Polman, & Oskam, 2003, p. 8).

The first question this paper addresses is what determines the choices made between different contract types with respect to differences in farm characteristics. Understanding the factors behind contract choice is not only relevant for both tenants and landowners, because they can certainly use this knowledge when making contracts, but also for policy makers. Contract choice linked to contract design is important for the policy maker because, in many countries, land leasing is regulated by the government. The second question of this paper refers to what is the role of the type of landowner for contract choice. In this paper, we focus on differences between public landowners – including the Service of Public Lands[1], National Forestry Service and other nature conservation organisations – and other farmers.

Our study contributes to the existing literature by paying attention to the choices available among different cash lease contracts and the role of specific investments. In order to investigate this problem, a formal model focusing on contract choice is developed. Insights about the relation between contract design and contract choice is relevant for both farmers and landowners in order to sign a suitable contract. Furthermore, government views on contract design and contract choice are important because of the role the government plays in regulating land leasing. Moreover, unadapted regulations and their blind implementation, motivated more by ideological prejudices than by sound comparative analysis, may seriously endanger structures that have emerged as adequate answers to the organisations involved and their transactions (Ménard, 1998, p. 417). The result of such maladaptations can be a shift toward less efficient institutional arrangements for land leasing.

The paper is arranged in the following manner: Section 13.2 gives an overview of the use of different types of leases in the period 1995–2005. Next, it analyses the characteristics of lease contracts in the Netherlands. Section 13.3 theoretically examines contractual arrangements and different contract types as well as the role institutional factors play concerning the choices made between different contract types. Section 13.4 discusses the empirical model and gives an overview of the data. Section 13.5 assesses the results concerning the analysis of contractual arrangements, the estimated results and their interpretation. The paper finishes with a summary and conclusions in Section 13.6.

13.2 Land Lease Contracts in the Netherlands

The total area of leased land in the Netherlands has sharply declined over the course of time. Table 13.1 provides an overview of the developments during the period 1950–2005. In the period 1995–2005 the percentage of regular land leasing is still on the decline. Even with the one-cultivation-cycle lease and the single-

---

[1] The Service of Public Lands is an important organization for leasing out public land to farmers.

term lease introduced with the Lease Law of 1995, the total area of leasing has been further decreasing since 1999. The hereditary lease – which is not included in Table 13.1 – decreased from about 4% in 1995 to 2% of the total agricultural area in 2005 (LEI/CBS, 2007, p. 35). However, the hereditary lease does not fall under the Lease Law Regulation.

Table 13.1: Distribution of land use (excluding hereditary lease and grey lease)

Year	% Owner-ship	% lease Total	Regular lease	One-cultivation-cycle lease	Single-term lease
1950	44.1	55.9			
1959	47.6	52.4			
1970	51.9	48.1			
1979	59.9	40.1			
1983	61.4	38.6			
1985	63.0	37.0			
1990	67.5	32.5			
1995	70.3	29.7			
1997	71.0	29.0	22.7	1.6	4.4
1998	70.7	29.3	21.7	1.8	5.4
1999	70.1	29.9	21.5	1.8	6.1
2003	72.7	27.3	21.5	1.7	4.0
2005	73.3	26.7	20.9	1.9	3.9

Source: LEI/CBS 2007 and other volumes (figures between 1999 and 2003 are not available)

After the modification of the Lease Law in 1995, the following three types of legal lease existed in the Netherlands:

1. Regular lease contracts
   These contracts have a term of 12 years for farmsteads and 6 years for plots of land. Important characteristics of these contracts include: price control by lease rent-standards, continuation rights for the tenant, and priority rights for the tenants for sale and purchase of land. In the period 1997–2005 the area of regular lease contracts was on average about 22% of total agricultural area.
2. One-cultivation-cycle lease
   These contracts for a plot of land have a term of 1 or 2 years, with no price controls, no continuation rights and no priority rights for the tenants. In the period 1997–2005 the area of one-cultivation-cycle lease contracts was on average about 2% of total agricultural area.
3. Single-term lease
   These one-time only (non-repeatable) contracts for plots of land range between a minimum of 1 and a maximum of 12 years, with no price controls, no

continuation rights and no priority rights for the tenants. In the period 1997–2005, the area of single lease contracts was, according to Table 13.1, on average about 5% of the total agricultural area.

These three types of lease contracts were regulated by the 1995 Lease Law. This implied that they had to be approved and registered by the *Grondkamer* (Land Tenure Board), which checked whether the contracts adhered to the Dutch regulations. However, for the one-cultivation-cycle lease, only registration by the Land Tenure Board was required.

In addition to these formal lease contracts (i.e. based on the Lease Law regulation), there is also the grey lease: one which not approved and not registered by the Land Tenure Board and is often used as an alternative to single-term and cultivation-cycle leases. In the period 1995–2005, the total area under grey lease has increased from about 150,000 ha (= 8% of the total agricultural area in the Netherlands), to about 190,000 ha, or almost 10% of the total (Berkhout & van Bruchem, 2007, p. 128). In terms of area, the three most important of types of land lease were – in descending order – regular, grey and single term.

The 2007 Lease Regulation introduced two types of liberalised leases for plots of land (Ministry of Agriculture, Nature and Food Quality, LNV, 2007, pp. 9–10). Both replace the single-term lease. The remainder of the Lease Regulation has not been changed. One important difference between the two types of liberalised leases is their duration: less than 6 years or longer than 6 years. For land lease agreements of 6 years or less, the regulation requires:

1. no continuation or priority rights for the tenant; and
2. registration and approval by the Land Tenure Board is compulsory.

For a liberalised land lease longer than 6 years, the regulation requires:

1. no continuation or priority rights for the tenant;
2. registration, approval by the Land Tenure Board is compulsory; and
3. price control by the Land Tenure Board is compulsory.

Table 13.2 summarises the characteristics of the land lease contracts. From Table 13.2 it follows that liberalised lease of 6 years or shorter is comparable to single term lease. Liberalised lease longer than 6 years can institutionally be located between regular lease and single term lease.

Farmers and landowners are free to choose any of the possible institutional arrangements or not to lease at all. In other words, the closing of a lease contract is a *voluntary exchange*. Because it is voluntary, it is only accepted if the expected result of the agreement appears to be individually and mutually advantageous for both parties (Milgrom & Roberts, 1992, p. 127). Second, contracts contain a coordination mechanism, an important part of the contract governance structure. In this section we analyse the coordination mechanisms used in Dutch land lease contracts, especially those types which will be empirically investigated in Section 13.3. The coordination mechanism determines what needs to be coordinated and how it is achieved. In other words, the type of coordination mechanism will make some contract types more likely and others less likely to be adopted.

Table 13.2: Summary of the characteristics of Dutch lease contracts

Characteristic	Regular lease	One-cultivation lease	Single-term lease	Liberalised lease > 6 year	Liberalised lease ≤ 6 year	Grey lease
Continuation rights	yes	no	no	no	no	no
Priority rights	yes	no	no	no	no	no
Price controls	yes	no	no	yes	no	no
Approval by Land Tenure Board required	yes	yes	yes	yes	yes	no
Registration with Land Tenure Board required	Yes	yes	yes	yes	yes	no
Duration in years	12 or 6	1–2	1–12	> 6	≤ 6	open
Operational in 2008	Yes	yes	no	yes	yes	yes

Figure 13.1 gives an overview of four coordination mechanism groups. Coordination can take place via one of the four groups or a mix of them. On the left side, we have the 'invisible hand' group. The coordination mechanism here is price, which coordinates the governance structure 'spot market'. As explained above, in a land lease contract, purchase and delivery (*quid* and *quo*) do not take place at the same moment. For that reason the *pure spot market* can not be the sole coordination mechanism for lease contracts.

At the bottom of Fig. 13.1, we have the so-called handbook group. The handbook – as a coordination mechanism – is often applied in the 'contracts' governance structure, particularly for detailed contracts. Contracts often also contain price as a coordination mechanism. In such cases, contracts consist of a mix of the 'handbook' and 'invisible hand' coordination mechanisms. In general, the type of contract determines which coordination mechanism will prevail and what the role of price will be in the relationship *quid pro quo*.

For regular land lease contracts, the coordination mechanism consists of rules, directives and safeguards based on the Lease Law regulations. This means that the coordination mechanism for regular lease contracts emphasises the 'handbook', as provided by the regulations. Important characteristics of these contracts include: fixed duration – 12 years for farmsteads and a term of 6 years for plots of land; price controls through lease price standards; continuation and priority rights for tenants. Because of price controls by regional lease price standards – monitored by the Land Tenure Board – price plays a minor role as a coordination mechanism. The lease price is limited by these lease price standards, reducing its influence as a coordination function. It should be pointed out that the lease price standard is a fixed monetary price per ha.

The modest role of price as a coordination mechanism also holds for liberalised lease contracts of longer than 6 years, because of the price testing to lease price standards by the Land Tenure Board. However, continuation and priority rights for the tenants are lacking. This is an important difference compared to a regular lease contract. Consequently, such contracts rely less on the handbook as compared with regular leases.

The single-term and the one-cultivation-cycle lease have no price controls and no continuation or priority rights for the tenant. However, single-term leases have to be approved – whereas one-cultivation-cycle leases need only be registered – by the Land Tenure Board. While both make use of the handbook approach, they do so to a lesser degree than regular lease contracts. The absence of price controls increases the role of price as a coordination mechanism. The lease price is therefore also higher than for regular lease contracts. For liberalised leases of 6 years or less, we may expect the same mix of coordination mechanisms as for single-term leases. The mix of coordination mechanisms of these contracts differs from regular lease contracts and liberalised lease contracts of longer than 6 years.

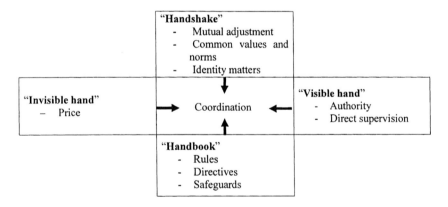

Fig. 13.1: Coordination mechanisms (adapted from Borgen & Hegrenes, 2005, p.12)

At the right side of Fig. 13.1, we have the 'visible hand' group used in firms and organisations that are based on a hierarchy, by which we mean that the positions in a firm are ranked: higher order levels command lower ones. In this case, coordination will be carried out by authority or direct supervision. The 'visible hand' group of coordination mechanisms is not relevant for contracts in general, and especially not for lease contracts. After all, landowners have their own businesses and are not vertically integrated with the tenant-farmers. Both parties – the land-owner and farmer-tenant – retain their separate external identities.

At the top of Fig. 13.1, we have the 'handshake' as a coordination mechanism, important elements of which are common values and norms, mutual adjustment, and the identities of the involved persons. Common values and norms (based on repeated interaction promoting solidarity, consensus and trust) and codes of conduct can serve as a co-ordination mechanism among groups of people. *Mutual adjustment* refers to the co-ordination achieved by informal, horizontal communication.

As explained above, the grey lease also involves a certain amount of continuity in the relationship between tenant and landowner, meaning that the identities of the parties matter. The 'handshake' is often used as a coordination mechanism for such types of lease contracts, complemented by price. The coordination mechanism for the grey lease is, thus, a mix of the 'handshake' and the 'invisible hand'. Grey lease contracts can be verbal or written, the content is open and not officially regulated or disclosed. This is an important difference from the regular lease contract. A liberalised lease with a duration of 6 years or less also means a shift to the 'handshake' as a coordination mechanism, because price testing to lease rent standards is not required. This can imply a shift to the invisible hand as coordination mechanism. However, for a liberalised lease of longer than 6 years, price testing is compulsory.

The third property of contracts is that they contain a *motivation element* (Milgrom & Roberts, 1992, pp. 126–127). The motivation elements are not the same for regular, single-term, one-cultivation-cycle and grey leases. Motivation can be driven by external motives, such as lease regulation or financial incentives, and by internal motives, like the pressure or feeling to do one's work well, trustworthiness and having or building up a good reputation. However, there can be a trade-off between these two kinds of motivation, such that too much emphasis on external motivation can drive out internal motivation (Le Grand, 2003, pp. 53–55)[2].

The fourth characteristic of lease contracts is that the set of agreements made therein are explicit. This especially holds for regular leases. For the single-term lease, liberalised lease with a duration of 6 years or less and one-cultivation-cycle lease, contacts are less explicit. They have no price controls and no continuation or priority rights for the tenants, but the single-term lease and the liberalised lease of 6 years or less have to be approved by the Land Tenure Board. One-cultivation-cycle lease contracts only need to be registered. Liberalised leases of longer than 6 years lie between regular lease contracts and single-term leases.

Grey lease contracts have often the character of implicit contracts: no formal record of the terms and conditions agreed upon by the parties. Such contracts are enforceable by the *reputation-mechanism* (Milgrom & Roberts, 1992, pp. 139, 259).

---

[2] A more detailed analysis of the role of motivation is available upon request from the authors)

However, a party with a short-term horizon is less willing to invest in a reputation than a party with a longer-term horizon. Similarly, investing in a reputation at the beginning of a game is more attractive than at the end. However, in order to build a reputation, the game has to be played several times. As indicated above, for grey lease contracts a certain degree of continuity needs to exist in the relationship between tenant and landowner.

The fifth characteristic of lease contracts is that – given the definition of a contract – the relationship between parties involved is often more important than in a market transaction (Milgrom & Roberts, 1992, p. 131). However, lease contracts are incomplete contracts. To limit the consequences of this implication, regulation principles are required. In the current leasing system in the Netherlands, the lease regulations, the Land Tenure Board and the Agricultural Land Tribunal determine these principles. However, these regulation principles reduce the flexibility of lease contacts. Especially in regular lease contracts, flexibility is hardly present or is greatly limited. Legal principles also limit the opportunistic behaviour of tenant and landowner, while hold-up and lock-in problems. Single-term leases and one-cultivation-cycle lease contracts have more flexibility. However, both together are less important than grey lease contracts, which contribute significantly to flexible land-use. Apparently, parties prefer the grey lease above the single-term or one-cultivation-cycle lease. It is expected that the two types of liberalised lease will also contribute to flexible land use.

Based on the arguments above, it can be concluded that one of the most important characteristics of regular lease contracts is the 'handbook' as a primary coordination mechanism and the restricted role of prices as a factor of adjustment. The use of the handbook as coordination mechanism is a result of Dutch leasing regulations. The legal principles underlying the leasing regulations and related governmental services are meant to limit the consequences of the asset-specificity of land, buildings (barns and sheds) and land-bound investments, such as drainage and soil improvement.

13.3 Contract Choice for Land Leasing

Parties to a contractual arrangement will choose to contract or to renew a contract if the expected gains from doing so are greater than those of organising the transaction in some other way (Masten, 1996, p. 47; Masten & Saussier, 2002, p. 274), or formally,

$$G^* = G^i, \text{ if } V^i > V^j, \text{ and}$$
$$= G^j, \text{ if } V^i \leq V^j \tag{13.1}$$

where G^i represents contract type i, G^j an alternative contract type j, V^i and V^j (the farmers beliefs about) the corresponding values of contract type i and alternative j, and G^* represents the contract type actually chosen.

For this paper we focus on three different contracts types:

1. regular lease contracts (G^1);
2. single-term lease contracts (G^2); and
3. grey leases (G^3).

Because the returns farmers expect from governing their land lease transactions in different ways are difficult to observe, a testable theory of contracting requires that the theory relate the benefits and costs of contract types to observable features of the transaction (Masten & Saussier, 2002, p. 275). Therefore, the following relations are added to Equation (13.1)

$$V^i = V^i(x, e_i) \tag{13.2}$$

$$V^j = V^j(x, e_j) \tag{13.3}$$

where x represents a vector of observable attributes affecting the gains from using a contract type[3]. In Equation (13.2), e_i and e_j represent error terms that may reflect either variables omitted or misperceptions on the part of the contracting parties about the true values of V^i and V^j. This means for the case of land use that contracting parties choose a specific lease contract type if the gains from doing so appear to be greater than those from another contract type. Besides the choice of an institutional arrangement for land use (organisational mode), it also needs to be decided whether a transaction should be carried out based upon the characteristics of the farm (technology mode). The technology and organisational modes ought to be treated symmetrically within modelling; they are decision variables whose values are determined simultaneously (Williamson, 1985, p. 89). Factors used as indicators for production motives are: farm type; farm size, age of farmer, agricultural education, and the presence/lack of a successor.

The observable attributes of a land lease transaction (vector x in Equation 13.2) will be derived from transaction costs economics, according to which there are three key transaction dimensions that are directly involved in determining transaction costs: asset specificity, uncertainty and frequency (Williamson, 1985, p. 52, 1996, p. 45; Ménard, 1996, p. 173; Williamson, 1998, p. 36; Saussier, 2000a, p. 381). Asset specificity refers to the degree to which an asset can be redeployed for

---

[3] The choice for concluding land-leasing contracts on a farm is a revealed preference that can be observed. However, alternative contract types (institutional arrangements) that are not chosen are not observable, as are the transaction costs of alternative institutional arrangements. Thus, even if the transaction costs could be adequately measured, the costs that would occur if the same transaction were governed under an alternative arrangement cannot be observed (Masten, 1996, p. 45). Therefore the choice for managing farmland has to be related to observable dimensions of a (potential) transaction.

alternative uses, and by alternative users, without sacrifice of productive value (Williamson, 1996, p. 105). The basic logic is that higher levels of uncertainty and higher degrees of asset specificity, particularly when they occur in combination, result in a more complex contracting environment and a greater need for adjustments after a relationship has begun and commitments have been made (Hölmstrom & Roberts, 1998, p. 76). The frequency of a transaction matters because, the more often a transaction takes place, the more widely the fixed transaction costs of establishing a non-market governance structure are spread (over different transactions). The following three key dimensions will be analysed in more detail.

13.3.1 Specific investments

Depending on the level of specific investments (or sunk costs) made by the different parties to institutional arrangements, parties become to varying degrees 'locked-in' after concluding the contract. Specific investments cannot easily be transferred to service alternative partners, so they are less valuable if the relationship is discontinued. Depending on the degree of asset specificity, the expropriation of the residual income of one party by the other is quite conceivable (hold-up problems). The question is whether the contractual safeguards protecting specific investments of tenants are large enough to protect these investments against potential ex post expropriation of the residual income. The same is relevant for farmer-tenants: protecting investments against expropriation of residual income by landowners.

According to transaction costs economics, the benefits of a contracting arrangement are expected to increase with the value of relationship-specific investments. Higher levels of asset specificity make the market less attractive as an institutional arrangement. This means that the design of a contractual arrangement (contract type) should be tailored to the transaction the landowner and farmer-tenant want to conclude. Asset specificity is difficult to measure and proxy variables are often used in empirical research (Shelanski & Klein, 1995, p. 338). For this paper we use specific investments of farmers in leased land as the attribute of the transaction explaining contract choice.

13.3.2 Uncertainty and incompleteness

Contingent on the set of transactions to be affected, the basic proposition following from transaction costs economics is that institutional arrangements differ in their capacities to respond effectively to uncertainties (Williamson, 1985, p. 56). Greater uncertainty could take either of two forms (Williamson, 1996, p. 116). One is that the probability distribution of disturbances remains unchanged, but more numerous disturbances occur. The other is that disturbances become more consequential: due, for example, to an increase in their variance. Uncertainty of a strategic kind is attributable to opportunism; Williamson (1985, p. 58) refers to this kind of uncertainty as behavioural uncertainty. An example of uncertainty with respect to the choice of a type of land lease contract is the way a contract partner will behave during the contractual relationship.

It is expected that farmers are more likely to use a grey contract when they are more familiar with their contracting partner, because they are less uncertain about the way the partner will behave within the relationship. They will take the reputation and the trustworthiness of the contracting partner into account. On the other hand, it is less likely that farmers will be able to conclude a grey contract with a public agency, but for different reasons: (i) public agencies are required to conclude a formal contract and (ii) they often seek to regulate land use, sometimes via detailed contracts.

Most contracts are more or less incomplete, in that they usually do not try to take into account all future contingencies. Since we have incomplete foresight about what the future may bring, that makes it impossible to take all future possibilities into account when writing a contract. Writing and accepting incomplete contracts means that the costs and benefits are equal at the margin, because there is a trade-off between the marginal cost of writing a more complete contract, and writing a more incomplete contract. The advantages for the contract partners of writing more complete contracts for land leasing include given the involvement of specific investments, a reduced exposure to the opportunism of the other party and savings on repeated renegotiating costs (Saussier, 2000b, p. 193). This implies that the parties to a contract are exposed to more opportunism in contracts involving more specific investments, compared to contracts with less specific investments, assuming a contract with the same institutional design. The more the contract specifies the transaction, the smaller the probability that the contract will be renegotiated (Saussier, 2000b, p. 193).

According to Saussier (2000b, p. 192) in his definition of feasible completeness, one contract is more complete than another if it gives a more precise and complete definition of the transaction and of the means to carry it out. An upper limit can be imagined as a complete contract that specifies how to perform the transaction in every conceivable case. The degree of incompleteness for lease contracts depends on the contract type. Regular contracts are more complete as compared to single-term contracts, for example, because more contingencies of the transaction are prescribed:

1. the contract price is bound to a maximum;
2. the way contracts are renewed is regulated;
3. what to do when one party wishes to terminate the contract is regulated;
4. conflict resolving mechanisms are given by the government; and
5. how landowners can sell their land it is partly regulated.

In this sense, single-term contracts are more complete than grey contracts, because they have to be approved and registered by the Tenure Law, and the enforcement mechanism is – just like with regular contracts – the Agricultural Land Tribunal. This means that parties with a regular lease or a single-term lease can always fall back on the lease regulations.

In contrast, the grey lease contracts have no formal lease regulations. The motivation to comply with such agreements comes from elements such as reputation and trustworthiness. Parties with a grey contract can not, for example, make use of the enforcement mechanisms of the Agricultural Land Tribunal. Therefore, the reputation mechanism and the quality of trustworthiness are very important for the enforcement and renewing of such contracts (compare Theesfeld in this volume).

Private enforcement is normally considered to require 'hands tying' through the posting of a 'hostage', that is, the creation of an offsetting vulnerability affecting the party who would otherwise be tempted to practice hold up and capture appropriate quasi rents (Dnes, 2003, p. 318). If it is not possible to rely on the court to enforce the original terms, or if it is desirable to avoid court costs, the hostage may be an alternative enforcement mechanism, which works by ensuring that the promissor has more to lose by cheating than by sticking with the original terms, thus deterring opportunistic renegotiations (Dnes, 2003, p. 319). The penalty for cheating needs to be at least as large as the benefit that could be derived thereby. Allen and Lueck (1992, p. 422) show that the variation in contracts is largely determined by the costs of enforcing the contracts in various situations. In order to assess incompleteness of contracts we analyse the use of standard contracts, negotiations and reasons for contracting in more detail.

13.3.3 Frequency

The third dimension, frequency, involves repetition of the same transaction. The frequency of a transaction can be recurrent, occasional or one time (Williamson, 1985, p. 72). The frequency of repeated contracting is important, both because it is repetition which generates transaction-specific knowledge and because infrequent contracting would not warrant the development of an expensive institutional arrangement (Ricketts, 2002, p. 49). The costs of specialised institutional arrangements are easier to recover for large transactions of a recurring kind (Williamson, 1985, p. 60). In the case of specific investments, recurrent transactions result in the building-up of reputation capital, which serves as a safeguard against *ex post* opportunism.

The regular lease contracts offered by landowners have a fixed duration that is known to both parties when the contract is concluded. Furthermore, the lease regulation for regular lease contracts gives the farmer the opportunity to put his successor in place. This is not the case for the single-term lease. The duration of a contractual relation can be analysed as an optimisation process in which costs and benefits of additional length are traded-off at the margin (Saussier, 1999, p. 5). On the one hand, a long-term contract involving investments in specific assets by one party leads to reduced exposure to the opportunism of the other party. On the other hand, a tenant-farmer would have no incentive to avoid degradation of soil, natural features, or landscape characteristics that have effects on the quality of the attributes of a parcel of land beyond the lifetime of the lease. As a result, he supplies the optimal amount of his own inputs, but overutilises any inputs supplied by the landowner (Allen & Lueck, 1992, p. 401). This means that the tenant-farmer has an incentive to overuse the unpriced attributes of the land (Allen & Lueck, 1992, p. 409).

Many farming practices that cause long-term degradation of soil, natural features, or landscape characteristics cannot be monitored at reasonable cost. However, such degradation may also be caused by unobservable random factors, such as locally severe downpours, so that tenants' use of degrading farming methods cannot be inferred from the condition of the land at the end of the lease period (Lichtenberg, 2002, p. 1). Further, a long-term contract leads to savings on negotiation costs. On the other hand, long-term contracts lead to a greater risk of being trapped in a bad contract. This problem is more serious the greater the uncertainty concerning the transaction. Short-term contracts can create more flexibility, but hold-up problems concerning investments in the quality of land and buildings are more likely to occur. Furthermore they do not solve the incentive problem in terms of overuse of the unpriced attributes of the land. Frequency will be analysed below by focusing on contract duration and contract renewal.

13.4 Empirical Model and Data

We use a trivariate probit model that allows the three decision equations jointly estimated. (Cappellari & Jenkins, 2003; Greene, 2003). Since the outcomes are treated as binary variables, any combination of contracts is possible, and the contracts can be complements rather than just substitutes. The multivariate model applies when several decisions may be interdependent or may depend on a common set of explanatory variables:

$$v_1^* = \begin{cases} 1 \text{ if } X_1\beta_1 + \varepsilon_1 > 0 \\ 0 \text{ otherwise} \end{cases} \qquad v_2^* = \begin{cases} 1 \text{ if } X_2\beta_2 + \varepsilon_2 > 0 \\ 0 \text{ otherwise} \end{cases}$$

$$v_3^* = \begin{cases} 1 \text{ if } X_3\beta_3 + \varepsilon_3 > 0 \\ 0 \text{ otherwise} \end{cases} \qquad (13.4)$$

Where v_1, v_2 and v_3 are binary variables; X_1, X_2 and X_3 are explanatory variables; β_1, β_2 and β_3 are regression coefficients; and ε_1, ε_2 and ε_3 are error terms.

This three-equation model is featured by correlated disturbances, which (for identification reasons) are assumed to follow a normal distribution (variance is normalised to unity). That is:

$$E[\varepsilon_1] = E[\varepsilon_2] = E[\varepsilon_3] = 0$$
$$\mathrm{cov}[\varepsilon_1, \varepsilon_2, \varepsilon_3] = \rho = \{\rho_{1,2}, \rho_{1,3}, \rho_{2,3}\} \qquad (13.5)$$
$$\mathrm{var}[\varepsilon_1] = \mathrm{var}[\varepsilon_2] = \mathrm{var}[\varepsilon_3] = 1$$

where ρ is a vector of correlation parameters denoting the extent to which the error terms co-vary. Should covariation be the case, we need to estimate the three equations jointly, following a trivariate normal distribution:

$$\{\varepsilon_1, \varepsilon_2, \varepsilon_3\} = \phi_3\left(0, 0, 0, 1, 1, 1, \rho\right). \qquad (13.6)$$

As long as we are interested in simultaneous decisions, we need to define their joint probability. For example, the probability of observing the three decisions taking place at the same time, $v_1 = 1$, $v_2 = 1$, $v_2 = 1$, would be:

$$\Pr(v_1 = 1, v_2 = 1, v_3 = 1) = \int_{-\infty}^{u_1} \int_{-\infty}^{u_2} \int_{-\infty}^{u_3} \phi_3(X_{1i}\beta_{1'}, X_{2i}\beta_{2'}, X_{3i}\beta_{3'}, \rho) \mathrm{d}\varepsilon_1 \mathrm{d}\varepsilon_2 \mathrm{d}\varepsilon_3 =$$
$$\phi_3(X_{1i}\beta_{1'}, X_{2i}\beta_{2'}, X_{3i}\beta_{3'}, \rho) \mathrm{d}\varepsilon_1 \mathrm{d}\varepsilon_2 \mathrm{d}\varepsilon_3 \qquad (13.7)$$

As in the standard probit model, observations contribute some combination of $\Pr(v_k = 1)$ for k{1,2,3}, depending on their specific values for those variables. The log-likelihood is then just a sum across the eight possible contracting variables, that is, eight possible combinations of successes ($v_k = 1$) and failures ($v_k = 0$) times their associated probabilities (Greene, 2003). These probabilities may be drawn from Equation (13.7) as well. The most relevant coefficients estimated in the model are β_1, β_2, β_3 and $\rho(\rho_{1,2}, \rho_{1,3}, \rho_{2,3})$. The latter, if significantly different from 0, will evaluate to which extent each pair of decisions is interrelated. The Geweke-Hajivassiliou-Keane simulator (GHK) is used to approximate those integrals[4].

Lease level data are often difficult to collect because lease agreements are determined by private negotiation between tenants and landowners in localised markets, which are often unique (Rainey, Dixon, Ahrendsen, Parsch, & Bierlen, 2001, p. 1). Especially data at the transaction level are often not available. For this paper, two sources for data are used: (1) from the Dutch Farm Accountancy Data network (FADN) and (2) a mail survey among tenants. The survey was developed to deepen and complement the findings from the FADN data in a more qualitative way.

---

[4] See Cappellari and Jenkins (2003) and Greene (2003) for a brief description of the GHK.

Table 13.3: Data for the average farm in period 1995/96–1999/2000 (number of observations = 782)

Variable	Description	Mean	Std. Err.
Dependent variable			
Regular lease	Dummy indicating a regular lease contract	0.53	
Single-term lease	Dummy indicating a single-term contract	0.33	
Grey lease	Dummy indicating a grey lease contract	0.61	
Independent variables			
Contracting partners			
Farmers	Dummy landowner is farmer =1, else 0	0.38	
Public agencies	Dummy landowner is public agency =1, else 0	0.64	
Specific investments			
Specific investments in land	Dummy if investments in leased farmland = 1, else = 0	0.16	
Farmer characteristics			
Economic size of farms	Economic farm size (Dutch Size Units[5])	120	72
Intensity of farms	Economic farm size per ha	3.29	3.91
Farmland owned	Farmland owned (ha)	26	26
Year of birth	Year of birth farmer	1947	11.0
Agricultural education	Dummy if agricultural education = 1, else = 0	0.92	
Successor present	Dummy if successor present or uncertain = 1, else = 0	0.87	

Source: FADN data

For the trivariate probit model, data on farm structure was available from FADN and is used for estimating the multivariate probit model. The FADN data on Dutch farmers covering the period 1995/96–1999/00 are from a stratified sample of farms keeping accounts on behalf of the Dutch Agricultural Economics Research Institute (LEI) farm accounting system. The stratification is based on economic farm size, age of the farmer, region, and type of farming. In the sample (very) small farms are not represented. The data set used for estimation is built up of farms that leased land in the period 1995/96–1999/2000. Table 13.2 gives an overview of the data used for estimation.

---

[5] The size of the farm ('business size') is measured by the Dutch Size Units (DSU). The DSU is roughly comparable to the European Size Unit. The DSU is based on the standard gross margins (SGM), which are calculated by deducting related specific costs from the gross returns per hectare or per animal. The SGM is expressed in Euro (current prices). On the EU level, the size of farms is not measured in SGM, but in the more workable European Size Units (ESU). The DSU is recalculated frequently in such a way that the average farm size in DSU corresponds to the development of the volume of the added value of the average farm (Berkhout & Bruchem, 2003, p. 24). Some examples (on the basis of the DSU, 2004): 1 ha winter wheat = 0.84 DSU; 1 ha sugar beet = 1.72 DSU; 1 dairy cow = 1.27 DSU; 1 sow = 0.25 DSU.

Table 13.3 shows that farmers' tenants use more than one type of contract simultaneously. Public landowners include the Service of Public Lands and nature conservation organisations, like the State Forest Commission. Investments cover investments made by the farmer. The farming type 'grazing animals' is the most important farming type in the set. Farms own on average about 26 ha. The average farm size is about 47 ha. On average the percentage of the farm leased is about 45%. The average age of the farmer was about 53. The majority of the farmers did have a successor as well as an agricultural education.

Another data source for this research is the mail survey among tenants in the Netherlands, carried out in the second half of 2002. In the middle of 2002, the addresses of 1,200 farmers were traced by using information from the government and farmers' organisations. By using several sources and by consulting experts, the non-coverage error was reduced. The survey was sent to the selected tenants at the beginning of October 2002. A small financial compensation (lottery) was promised to encourage tenants to fill out the questionnaire. A letter reminding the tenants of the questionnaire was sent in mid-November 2002. The response-rate was 29% (number of completed interviews from responding tenants/number of mailed tenants mailed to). The survey will be referred to as 'questionnaire data'.

13.5. Results

The results of the multivariate Probit model are reported in Table 13.4, based upon the theoretical considerations given in Section 13.3.

If the landowner is a public organisation, this has a positive impact on the probability of having a regular or single-term contract. An explanation is that the Service of Public Lands mostly used regular lease contracts for leasing land to farmers, whereas if the landowner is another farmer, regular contracts are not likely.

From the survey results, it follows that the most frequently mentioned reason for using regular contracts is that they have already used the contract type for several years (about 62%). This reason is less important for the other two contract types. For a single-term contact this can be explained by the fact that these contracts have only existed from 1995 on. For the single-term contracts, often the landowner takes the initiative for the contractual relation (about 40%). The quality of the land and farm practices play a minor role as reasons for concluding a regular or single-term contract. Looking at contracting parties for farmers, several categories of landowners can be distinguished: family, farmers (non-family), other private persons, public organisations, private legal organisations, and wildlife and landscape preservation organisations. These categories are given in Table 13.5.

Table 13.4: Results of multivariate Probit model for choice of lease contract

Independent variable	Regular lease		Single-term lease		Grey lease	
Constant	−2.09		−2.57		5.2	
Contracting partner						
Farmers	−0.48	**	0.27	**	1.08	***
Public agencies	0.34	***	0.93	***	−0.20	*
Specific investments						
Specific investments in land	0.61	***	−0.43	***	−0.55	***
Farm characteristics						
Economic size of farm	0.0024	***	−0.00082	***	0.0032	***
Intensity of farm	−0.033	*	−0.12	***	−0.017	
Farmland owned	−0.010	***	0.0043		−0.0061	**
Year of birth	0.00098		0.00094		−0.0027	
Agricultural education	0.16		0.11		−0.078	
Successor present	0.13		−0.090		0.10	

Log likelihood = −1263.34; Wald-test of the model χ^2 (27) = 324.15, p = 0.0000.

* variable significant at .10 level, ** variable significant at 0.5 level *** variable significant at 0.01 level.

Table 13.5: Institutional arrangements for the oldest and most recent contract, categorised by contracting party (%), 2002

	Contract type		
Contracting partner	Regular	Single-term	Grey
Family	12	5	18
Farmers (non-family)	4	10	29
Other private persons	29	24	30
Public organisations	20	27	9
Private organisations	22	11	5
Wildlife and landscape preservation organisations	8	13	4
Other	5	9	5
Total	100	100	100

Source: Questionnaire data

From Table 13.5, it follows that grey contacts are relatively more frequent between farmers and family, other farmers and private persons. This confirms the model that the contracting partner plays a role in selecting an institutional arrangement.

The official term of the (formal) contract does not give information about the length of the relationship between the landowner and tenant. The average duration of the contractual relation differs for the distinguished contract types. Table 13.6 gives an overview of average contract duration, area contracted and number of landowners.

Table 13.6: Duration of contractual relation or the time elapsed between contract conclusion and the day of the mail survey, 2002

Contract type		Average duration (years)	Average area con- tracted (ha)	Average number of landowners
Regular	Oldest	30	24	2
	Newest	10	40	
Single-term	Oldest	7	7	2
	Newest	2	10	
Grey	Oldest	10	6	2
	Newest	2	6	

Source: Questionnaire data

The oldest regular contractual relations have existed on average 30 years, which implies a long-term relationship. Given the official term of 6 years for farmland, it means that these contracts have been renewed several times. Single-term regular and grey contracts were on average concluded for, respectively, 3 years (standard deviation: 3.3) and about 2 years (standard deviation: 4.7). These contracts were renewed several times. However, in contrast to regular contracts where the lease regulations coordinate the renewal of contracts; the partners could have faced re-negotiations, given the average duration of the contractual relation. The plots contracted with regular contracts were on average larger compared to the plots contracted with single-term or grey contracts. On average, tenants have had contractual relations with two landowners. Contracts could be drawn by the farmer, the landowner or jointly. Table 13.7 highlights this aspect of the contractual relation between farmer and landowner.

Table 13.7: Responsibility for drawing the most recent land lease contract (%), 2002

Formulated	Contract type		
	Regular	Single-term	Grey
Landowner	69	67	21
Negotiations and drawing together	13	18	37
Not known because relation has lasted a long time	10	3	13
Other	8	12	30
Total	100	100	100

Source: Questionnaire data

Based on our survey it was the landowner who wrote down most of the official contracts. Often standard contracts were used (about 80% of the respondents mention the use of a standard contract). In the Netherlands, a few types of 'standard contracts' are used which can reduce transaction costs. As Table 13.7 shows, negotiations are more frequent for grey contracts, compared to single-term and regular contracts.

Many farmers were involved in contractual relations with more that one landowner (about 40%) in addition to using multiple contract types simultaneously. This implies that, within cash leasing, different contract types are chosen for land use. Table 13.8 gives an overview of the reasons for concluding contracts.

Table 13.8: Reasons for concluding a contract in percentage, with more than one reason being possible per farmer, 2002

Contract type	Contract		
	Regular	Single-term	Grey
I have already leased this land for years	62	23	34
Quality of land	1	2	9
Location of land	14	26	29
The land was offered to me by the land-owner	19	42	34
Land is needed for expansion of my farm	9	9	20
Land is needed to fulfil manure regulations	8	28	27
Crop rotation	2	4	13
Other	12	12	7

Source: Questionnaire data

From Table 13.4, it follows that economic size has a negative sign for the single-term lease and a positive sign for the grey lease. Farmers who owned more land were also more often involved in a single-term lease contract. If farmers leased a large share of their farm, it is likely that they would use regular or single-term contracts and the coefficient would not be significant for grey leases. More intensive farms were less likely to use the contracts mentioned in Table 13.4, but rather used other types of contracts for flexible land use.

From the estimations, it follows that if farmers wanted to make investments they were less likely to choose a grey lease contract. This is in line with hold-up theory. Concerning physical asset specificity the main question is whether farmers need to buy special equipment for land leasing that cannot be used for other purposes. The assets can be distinguished with respect to the degree of asset specificity. For instance, fencing posts and wire can only be removed at a certain cost. About 40% of the tenant-farmers invested in farmland that was leased. Important categories of investments in the survey were draining (about 40%); levelling out land (about 10%); fencing off, maintenance of paths and renewing grassland (about 5%). Table 13.9 gives an overview of the level of investments by tenant-farmers in farmland.

Table 13.9: Investments (€) in farmland under lease contract (%), 2002

Category	Percentage of farms	
	Percentage	Cumulative percentage
0	61	61
0–500	27	88
500–1,000	5	93
1,000–1,500	3	96
1,500 and more	4	100

Source: Questionnaire data

Many of these investments were sunk in the contractual relation, because they could not be moved to another plot. This means that these investments are location-specific and that the farmers would have been vulnerable to possible opportunistic behaviour by the landowner if their investments had not been secured through a contract that guaranteed the tenants could recapture the residual income from their investments. Landowners invested less often in farmland (about 6% of the landowners) compared to tenant-farmers. This means that tenant-farmers would be relatively more dependent on the continuation of contractual relations due to the level of specific investments.

We find evidence of correlations between the contracting decisions: the error terms between regular leases and single-term leases ρ_{12} are positively correlated and the error terms between regular leases and grey leases ρ_{13} are positively correlated. Also, the error terms between single-term leases and grey leases are positively correlated (ρ_{23}). The correlation coefficients are, respectively, –0.65, –0.33 and –0.39, with all coefficients being statistically significant at the 0.01 level. The likelihood ratio test statistics suggest that $\rho_{12} = \rho_{13} = \rho_{23}$ can be rejected at the 1 percent significance level (LR–χ^2 = 214.32).

13.6 Summary and Conclusions

The results of this study provide insight into land lease transactions and the factors that influence the choice of contract type, particularly with regard to the Netherlands from 1995 to 2005. The results indicate that land leasing is not a standard transaction within a fixed format. Tenants can be partners in a number of contract types simultaneously. The reasons for leasing land are different, thereby affecting choice of contract type. For instance, tenants often use single-term contracts in order to fulfil the manure regulation. Larger plots are leased using regular contracts, whereas smaller plots are more frequently leased with grey contracts. This means that tenants and landowners tailor the contract type to the reasons for leasing land. Renegotiation of contracts is likely, because contractual relations tend to last longer than the official duration of each written contract. Contracts for regular leases can be renewed automatically. However, tenants indicated that negotiation about the institutional content of written contracts were not common. In practice, parties to official land lease relations choose from a number of standard contracts, with the landowner often taking the initiative in selecting a contract type.

Tenant-farmers conclude contract types for different purposes with several landowners. The results of a multivariate probit model show that the contracting partner and farm characteristics were important for the probability of using specific contract types. The results also showed that the choice of a contract type is dependent on the contracting partner. Contracting decisions among different contract types are not taken independently. Farmers who own more land make more use of liberalised lease contract types for increasing their land area.

Specific investments were also important for contract choice. Contracting partners want to protect these investments through long-term contracts, because short-term contracts can lead to hold-up problems related to investments like drainage. With a shift in lease regulations allowing more short-term contracts with less regulation (the so-called liberalised lease), specific investments by farmers are less likely. These developments could be negative for sustainable land use. Parties use different coordination mechanisms for different contracting relations.

For contracting with other farmers, farmers use the handshake as the main coordination mechanism (grey leases). Public organisations are more in favour of using the 'handbook' as the coordination mechanism (regular or single-term leases). The introduction of a more liberalised lease system is less relevant for farmers leasing land to other farmers, because they prefer the grey lease, for which trust and reputation are most important. This is expressed by the handshake as the coordination mechanism.

The foregoing analysis is subject to some qualifications. First, we only modelled a limited number of different contract types and contracting partners. In addition, the contracts consist of groups of similar contracts which have different characteristics. This could have led to aggregation errors. Second, other factors not included in the model, for example preferences about contract terms like contract duration and payment levels, might play a role in contract choice.

Despite these qualifications, the approach discussed above contributes to the existing literature because it makes it possible to determine farmers' choices between different contract types. Given farm-specific/contract-specific outcomes, the survey and model can help to better understand some reasons why farms use different contract types. This information is relevant for understanding the results of the recent changes in land lease regulation in the Netherlands.

References

Allen, D. W., & Lueck, D. (1992.) Contract choice in modern agriculture. *Journal of Law and Economics, 35*, 397–426.

Allen, D. W., & Lueck, D. (1993). Transaction costs and the design of cropshare contracts. *Journal of Law and Economics, 35*, 397–426.

Allen, D. W., & Lueck, D. (2002). *The nature of the farm: Contracts, risk, and organisation in agriculture.* Cambridge: The MIT Press.

Barry, P. J., Escalante, C .L., & Moss, L. E. (2002, July). *Rental premiums for share versus cash leases.* Paper presented at annual meeting of the American Agricultural Economics Association, Long Beach.

Berkhout, P. & van Bruchem, C. (Eds.). Landbouw-economisch Bericht 2007. Den Haag, Periodiek repport 07.01

Borgen, S. O., & Helgreness, A. (2005). *How can transaction costs economics add to the understanding of new contractual formats in the Norwegian agri-food system.* Working paper 2005–7, Centre for Food Policy, Norwegian Economics Agricultural Economic Research Institute.

Cappellari, L., &. Jenkins, S. P (2003). Multivariate probit regression using simulated maximum likelihood. *The Stata Journal, 3*, 278–294.

Dasgupta, S., Knight, T. O., & Love, H. A. (1999). Evolution of agrictultural land leasing models: A survey of the literature. *Review of Agricultural Economics, 21*, 14–176.

Datta, S. K., O'Hara, D. J., & Nugent, J. B. (1986). Choice of agricultural tenancy in the presence of transaction costs. *Land Economics, 62*, 145–158.

Dnes, A. W. (2003). Hostages, marginal deterrence and franchise contracts. *Journal of Corporate Finance, 9*, 317–331.

Eswaran, M., & Kotwal, A. (1985). A theory of contractual structure in agriculture. *American Economic Review, 75*, 352–367.

Greene, W. H. (2003). *Econometric Analysis.* Upper Saddle River: Prentice Hall.

Hölmstrom, B., & Roberts, R. J. (1998). The boundaries of the firm revisited. *Journal of Economic Perspectives, 12*, 73–94.

Hurrelmann, A. (2002) *Land markets in economic theory: A review of the literature and proposals for further research: Vol. 7. Institutional change in agriculture and natural resources.* Aachen: Shaker.

Hurrelmann, A. (2005) Institutions and properties of transactions: Influences on rental contract design in Polen. *Agrarwirtschaft, 54*, 284 –291.

Janssen, L., Cole, J, Xu, X., & Johnson, B. (2002, July). *Economic evaluation of cropshare and cash lease contracts in South Dakota and Nebraska.* Selected paper presented at the 2002 Annual meeting of the Western Agricultural Economics Association held jointly with the American Agricultural Economics Association, Long Beach.

Le Grand, J. (2003). *Motivation, agency and public policy: Of knights and knaves, pawns and queens.* Oxford: Oxford University Press.

LEI/CBS (2007 and older volumes). Land- en tuinbouwcijfers 2006. Landbouw-Economisch Instituut Den Haag.

Lichtenberg, E. (2002, July). *Tenancy and soil conservation revisited.* Paper presented at the Second annual workshop on the economics of contracts in agriculture, Annapolis.

Lichtenberg, E. (2007). Tenants, landlords, and soil conservation. *American Journal of Agricultural Economics, 89*, 294–307.

Masten, S. E. (1996). Introduction. In S. E. Masten. (Ed.), *Case studies in contracting and organization.* Oxford: Oxford University Press.

Masten, S. E., & Saussier, S. (2002). Econometric of contracts: An assessment of developments in the empirical literature on contracting. In E. Brousseau & J. M. Glachant, *The economics of contracts: Theories and applications* (pp. 273–292). Cambridge: Cambridge University Press.

Ménard, C. (1996). On cluster, hybrids, and other strange forms: The case of the French poultry industry. Journal of Institutional and Theoretical Economics (JITE), 152, 154–183.

Ménard, C. (1998). Maladaptation of regulation to hybrid organizational forms. *Interational Review of Law and Econmics, 18*, 403–417.

Milgrom, P., & Roberts, J. (1992). *Economics, organization and management.* Englewood Cliffs: Prentice Hall International.

Ministry of Agriculture, Nature and Food Quality (LNV) (2007). Pacht, nieuwe regels en prijzen 2007, 1 augustus 2007.

Patterson, B., Hanson, S. D., & Robison, L. J. (1998). *Characteristics of farmland leasing in the North Central United States.* Michigan State University, Staff Paper 98–31.

Rainey, R. L., Dixon, B. L., Ahrendsen, B. L., Parsch, L. D., & Bierlen, R. W. (2001, August). *Contract choice selection with land-leasing agreements.* Selected paper annual meeting American Agricultural Economics Association, Chicago.

Ricketts, M. (2002). *The economics of business enterprise: An introduction to economic organisation and the theory of the firm.* Cheltenham and Northampton: Edward Elgar.

Saussier, S. (1999). Transaction cost eocnomics and contract duration: An empirical analysis of EDF coal contracts. *Louvain Economic Review, 65*, 3–21.

Saussier, S. (2000a). When incomplete contract theory meets transaction cost economics: A test. In C. Ménard (Ed.), *Institutions, contracts and organizations: Perspectives from new institutional economics* (pp. 376–398). Cheltenham and Northampton: Edward Elgar.

Saussier, S. (2000b). Transaction costs and contractual incompleteness: The case of Electricité de France. *Journal of Economic Behavior & Organization, 42*, 189–206.

Shelanski, H., & Klein, P. (1995). Empirical research in transaction cost economics: A review and assessment. *Journal of Law, Economics & Organization, 11*, 335–361.

Slangen, L. H. G., Polman, N. B. P., & Oskam, A. J. (2003). *Grondgebruik, pachtcontracten en pachtprijszettingsmechanismen.* Report for Ministry of Agriculture (LNV), Nature and Food Quality, Wageningen University.

Soule, M .J., Tegene, A., & Wiebe, K. D. (2000). Land tenure and the adoption of conservation practices. *American Journal of Agricultural Economics, 82*, 993–1005.

Williamson, O. E. (1985). *The economic institutions of capitalism.* New York: The Free Press.

Williamson, O. E. (1996). *The mechanisms of governance.* Oxford: Oxford University Press.

Williamson, O. E. (1998). Transaction cost economics: How it works; where it headed. *De Economist, 146*, 23–58.

Part IV

Challenges of Institutional Analysis
for Sustainability

14 Sustainability, Institutions and Behavior

Arild Vatn

Department of International Environment and Development Studies (Noragric), Norwegian University of Life Sciences, P.O. Box 5003, 1432 Aas, Norway, E-mail: arild.vatn@umb.no

Abstract. This paper is about how to facilitate sustainability, arguing that it is important to undertake changes in the institutional structures governing economic activity. The basic question concerns which logic or rationality is fostered by prevailing institutions and which changes in these should be facilitated. Two integrated arguments are put forward: Sustainability demands a shift from separating to integrating institutions and away from institutions exclusively fostering individual rationality towards those supporting cooperative rationality. The necessity for such a move is argued on the basis of the characteristics of the problems humanity are facing. Concerning the possibilities for making the proposed institutional changes, a wide variety of literatures from different fields looking at human motivation and the relationship between motivation and institutions is evaluated. The paper also sketches some alternative ways through which an increased emphasis on integration and cooperative rationality could be facilitated.

Keywords: Integrative institutions, Individual rationality, Separating institutions, Social rationality, Rationality contexts, Resource regimes

14.1 Introduction

The present paper develops the argument that the problems humanity faces from environmental degradation to poverty alleviation seem very hard to solve without undertaking substantial institutional changes. I will especially emphasize the need for achieving some basic transformations of the existing motivation structures of the economy. In relation to that, I offer some concrete ideas concerning how this could be done, the main suggestion being to build institutional structures which facilitate integration and cooperative behavior, hence reducing the contemporary emphasis on competition and economic growth as the driving forces of economic and social development.

Current trends are worrying. Global warming is challenging the present functioning of our environmental base. The same goes for biodiversity loss, as the two processes are strongly interlinked. These trends seem, moreover, to restrict our

V. Beckmann, M. Padmanabhan (eds.), *Institutions and Sustainability,*
DOI 10.1007/978-1-4020-9690-7_14, © Springer Science+Business Media B.V. 2009

options for future poverty alleviation. It is both the scale and form of our activities that is causing these problems. Our economic system is characterized by its capacity to expand. Moreover, as long as growth demands expanded use of material resources – matter and/or energy – human impact on our environmental resource base will increase. Ecological footprint measurements (Rees & Wackernagel, 1996) indicate that we already consume more resources than can be sustained. Analyses made of net human appropriation of biological primary production (Heberl, Krausmann, & Gingrich, 2006) point in the same direction. Certainly, there are many problems related to the accuracy and ultimate meaning of these kinds of estimates. Nevertheless, they emphasize the need for concern about present developments.

Many argue, however, that growth is the cure, not the problem. Growth is just the result of human ingenuity, and the more intelligent we are, the more the economy will grow, even with less use of resources. Certainly, the basic problem is not growth per se, but resource use. So far, however, growth has implied increased material use, despite the observation that the use of material resources per unit of GDP is declining. The 'rebound effect' has been pervasive. Moreover, we live in times where we must evaluate very critically any expansion of the economy. The use of natural resources should most probably be reduced, not increased, to maintain the integrity and vitality of natural systems and their dynamics. Instead, we have presently been on a path implying that the world economy will grow more than ten times in the coming hundred years. While the present financial crisis has created some uncertainty concerning future trends, the growth so far in the 21st century has been above the average of the previous one. This is, if we measure in relative terms, and it is an order of magnitude higher measured in absolute terms. It is very hard to see how this can actually come about parallel to a reduction in physical impact.

There are certainly also some grounds for hope. As an example, several recent studies show that beyond a certain level of economic development well-being does not seem to increase. People do not seem to get much happier as GDP per capita increases beyond $10–15,000 (Layard, 2005). Hence, directing development in rich countries towards other aims than increased consumption of goods does not seem problematic, even concerning immediate well-being. Given present economic institutions, however, it is not advisable. Low growth levels tend to provoke crises. Hence, while continued growth in poor countries is socially and economically very important, the importance of growth in rich countries seems rather related to keeping the system functioning well. It is a lubricant, securing positive expectations concerning future revenues and, hence, a consistent will to invest. The reactions to the present financial crisis is a vivid illustration of this. So while governments, bankers and representatives of corporations on the bridge of collapse are dependent on recreating the belief in future growth, the long-run effect of this on sustainability is, if successful, highly problematic.

Hence, we reach the conclusion that sustainable futures demand some fundamental institutional change. While the present institutional changes seem to point in other directions, there are also some cause for hope. Research over the last few decades indicates very strongly that motivation structures are flexible. They are not given once and for all, but are rather influenced by prevailing institutional structures. Hence people can act both egoistically and other-regardingly. They can both compete and cooperate. What is happening at a given moment rests very much with the kinds of institutions available.

In building my argument, the paper is divided into three main parts. First, I define more specifically the characteristics of the sustainability problem and how it relates to present institutional structures. In the next section, I present a series of empirical findings concerning the relationship between institutions and rationality. Different interpretations of the findings are discussed and the 'institutions-as-rationality-context' hypothesis is put forward. In the final section I develop a set of ideas concerning institutional changes that should have the capacity to foster sustainability.

14.2 The Sustainability Problem

The sustainability problem concerns providing the necessary conditions for human wellbeing in the long run. Normally, definitions of sustainable development include three dimensions: environmental, social and economic. My argument is that, under present conditions, it is impossible to secure sustainability along all of these dimensions. There is a fundamental inconsistency between our economic institutions demanding growth and the demands for sustaining environmental and even to some extent social opportunities.

14.2.1 Weak and strong sustainability

The various existing perspectives regarding sustainable development depart concerning the views on the substitutability between natural and human-made capital. Hence, the distinction between of weak as opposed to strong sustainability prevails (Toman, Pezzey, & Krautkraemer, 1995). Taken as extreme positions, the former is based on the assumption that natural capital and human capital are substitutable along all their dimensions. The latter implies that there is no opportunity for substitution between the two.

None of these extremes offer a reasonable understanding of the actual capacities of the two groups of resources or capitals. Another way is to focus on the concept of critical natural capital (Nöel & O'Connor, 1998), which implies that, while there are options available for substitution, they are restricted. Examples of non-substitutable resources include those that are necessary for biological growth, such as oxygen, nitrogen, carbon dioxide, phosphorous and water. Lack of substitution possibilities may not create problems if the actual resources are all abundant. Of the above-mentioned, the greatest future restrictions have to do with phosphorous and fresh water. In the case of phosphorous, production is estimated to peak at about 2040 (European Fertilizer Manufacturers Association, 2000). This represents a very serious problem, as phosphorous is so fundamental to all food production, and it cannot be substituted for in the process of photosynthesis. Certainly, as matter can only be degraded, not lost, scarcity at this level can be seen as relative only to the availability of energy. As an example, phosphorous can be extracted from sea water, but then at a very high energy cost.

Moreover, the most fundamental type of critical natural capital does not consist so much of the various compounds themselves, but rather the functioning of the biosphere and its various life support systems. The biosphere is a very complex system in which matter cycles and various life forms are interlinked through a high number of processes. While the biosphere is a variable system, it is still characterized by a large set of negative feedback loops that keeps it within certain bounds. While these bounds change over time – as species go extinct, new ones appear, the climate changes etc. – there is also a remarkable degree of stability if we look at the system from the perspective of single species survival.

Concerning the human species, our ingenuity has given us the power to alter ecosystems tremendously. Due to system's resilience, this seems not to have very much influenced the macro-adaptability of the system until recently. Though local collapses have certainly been experienced over and over again (e.g., Diamond, 2005), at the global scale it is perhaps only over the last 200 years that humankind seems to have set in motion processes which have the capacity to change the motion of the system. Given 'full information' – that is, complete knowledge about the laws of motion of the natural system – we could be able to impact the system in ways increasing opportunities in the short run, without running the risk of future backlashes. Under such assumptions, substitution possibilities would be more abundant. Hence, part of the problem is also our inability to fully understand the complexities of interlinked natural processes – the biogeochemical underpinning of the productivity of the biosphere.

14.2.2 Separation or integration?

The basic problem, from the perspective of human behavior and governance, is that, while the environmental system we depend on is a system of *interlinked processes*, we have over the years become dependent upon an institutional system where *delinking* or *separation* – that is, dividing up decisions and responsibilities – are the dominant characteristics. This has been very productive for the economy and a main driver behind the rapid growth we have observed over the last couple of centuries. Evaluated against the dynamics of the system, however, these separations are fundamentally arbitrary. Hence, a system has evolved that is ill fitted to the dynamics of the environment on which the economy so fundamentally rests. This was perhaps a minor problem when economic activity was at a low level compared to the scale of environmental processes. But humanity now impacts several natural cycles, not only at measurable levels. In fact, some cycles have doubled in magnitude due to human activity: the N cycle being a prominent example.

As emphasized by Hagedorn (2005), to find a balance between 'segregative' and 'integrative' institutions is the greatest challenge for future institutional development. The historical process has so far weakened the integrative capacity relative to the forces of segregation or separation, which have of course been an important impetus to economic growth. Dividing up resources, by establishing a formal identity between the extent of a certain (piece of a) resource and the execution of decision power over it, established a motivational situation whereby investing in the productivity of the specific resource became more interesting. While individual property has not been the only mechanism behind growth – we must also add the importance of, for example, markets, the money institution, state power, welfare state programs, education and research – it has played an important role, as emphasized by the work of North (1981, 1990). Linking decision power to clearly separated units with legally defined and protected rights to act on their own behalf has been an important factor behind establishing the security necessary to foster investment and, hence, growth.

This unity between resource delineation and resource use can, however, only be nominal. As nature is foremost a set of interlinked processes, it is clear that the flow of influences across the 'fictitious' borders established can become tremendous as each resource is more intensively used. Given that institution-building is focused on separation, our power to coordinate human influence on natural processes is weak. Rather, the fundamental structures established create an environment where deciding about these influences – building integrative institutions – becomes very difficult, as such processes must operate in opposition to the fundamental dynamics created by separation.

There are three important issues involved here. First, we have *separation in space* creating high transaction costs – that is, the costs of integrating across separated units. These costs have, in a sense, been maximized by splitting up available resources into pieces. The more units, the more borders between units and, hence, the more costly it becomes to transact over the matter flows (= flows of uncompensated costs) across borders of decision units as they operate (Kapp, 1971; Bromley, 1991).

Surely, state regulations like environmental taxes may be a way to reduce transaction costs as compared to individual bargains between separate entities. Hence, more externalities can become Pareto relevant. Nevertheless, holders of individual properties may have good reasons to oppose such policies. This takes us to my second point. Separation also represents a *separation of interests*, or rather *the creation of separated interests*. The common interest in conserving the dynamics of the integrated resource system is weakened by the asymmetry established between the costs and gains of integration from the perspective of each unit.

The costs of integration hit each agent directly, while the gains are more thinly distributed across many/all agents, due to the common-pool characteristics of most natural resources.

These difficulties are finally compounded by the time lags of the system. Subsequently, the third point is *separation in time* between when the physical interferences across the nominal borders take place and when their consequences become visible. This is also a great obstacle. The capacity of the natural system to counteract the effects of changed matter or energy flows is in many senses a good thing, creating a more stable environment. The negative side of that coin is that the stability of such systems operates within thresholds, and when some of these are finally passed, returning to the previous stability domain is very difficult, if at all possible.

Moreover, the cost of doing anything with the 'externality' will – due to the time lags between acts and consequences – be defined by investments etc. undertaken under the presumption that no future harm would be caused. When, in the end, harm is still observed and proven, the system may be locked into a path from which it is very costly to deviate. The present 'carbon lock-in' is a good illustration. The future costs of CO_2 emissions have not been a factor considered when making investments in energy use and transport systems until maybe recently. Such emissions have, however, been generated for a couple of centuries now. The important point is that the cost of 'path dependency' is very much a systems' feature (Vatn, 2002). Other systems where stronger focus on potential long-run side effects of economic activity is included into the institutions of the economy could create less dependency on unsustainable paths.

The most powerful unit of separated decision making of the modern world is the corporation. Its history – its emergence, fall and later rise 'to the skies' – can be read not only as a tale of how separation won out over integration (Veblen, 1904; Commons, 1924; Polanyi, 1944/1957; Bakan, 2004), but also as a reminder that the corporation's presently strong position is neither a necessity nor a natural outcome of the rationalization of society. It illustrates rather how difficult it has been to stick to integrative solutions when the short term gains from separation and exclusion have been so readily available.

Parallel to the separation of the power to act is the separation of interest. As indicated above, this separation relates both to time and space. Some would argue that this is not a question about institutional structure, but one of what humans are like: We are fundamentally egoistic, and what institutional systems do is simply to canalize these external forces.

Over the last the last two to three decades, a tremendous amount of research has been undertaken that heavily challenges this presumption. The alternative hypothesis is evolving that preferences are endogenous to the system. Actually, there is evidence that institutions may best be understood as rationality contexts. While separating decisions fosters individual rationality, social rationality may be supported by integrative institutions. So, while separation promotes individual rationality and increases transaction costs, integration may not only reduce transaction costs, but also favor social rationality or consciousness.

14.3 Institutions and Rationality

The ability and willingness of people to cooperate has been documented across a wide variety of disciplines. We see this in many anthropological studies (e.g., Murdoch, 1967), it forms a whole tradition in sociology (e.g., Etzioni, 1988) and it is evident in very much of the research on common pool resource management (e.g., Ostrom, 1990, 2005). Certainly, this literature does not say that cooperation or social rationality is the only capacity in the human repertoire. What it does is to emphasize that this capacity exists and is evident in very many situations.

A large amount of supplementary insights are now available from the experimental literature in economics and psychology. While one should be careful and remember the limitations of experiments, they are interesting as they offer control over many variables that no real life observations can give. The value of the research is enhanced by the fact that it seems to strongly support conclusions obtained in the field (e.g., Gintis, Bowles, Boyd, & Fehr, 2003; Ostrom, 1998).

14.3.1 There is not only selfishness

The experimental literature shows that human motivation is much more complex than that described by the standard model of rational choice – the rationality as maximizing individual utility (RMIU) model. People are willing to share in many situations. They may choose to cooperate even though defecting is the individually rational to do, or they may retaliate against non-cooperators even in settings where that this is not offering any gains to the retaliator.

The literature on this issue is now quite large, including the findings observed in the ultimatum and dictator games, in public goods games and various wage experiments. The presentation here will have to be brief. Encompassing overviews are found in Gintis (2000a), Ostrom (1998, 2000), Fehr and Falk (2002), Gintis et al. (2003), Bowles (2004), and Vatn (2005).

In the *ultimatum game* a proposer is given a sum of money, which she must divide between herself and an unknown respondent. If the respondent accepts the split, both players get the money as divided by the proposer. If the respondent turns the offer down, the two participants get nothing. Over the years a large series of studies have been published within this area (see, for example, Roth, Prasnikar, Okuna-Fujiwara, & Zamir, 1991; Hoffman, McCabe, Shachat, & Smith, 1994; Camerer & Thaler, 1995; Henrich et al., 2001). Gintis (2000a) concludes that the dominant split is 50–50, while respondents often turn down offers of less than

30%. These refusals are difficult to explain on the basis of the traditional RMIU hypothesis. Offering more than the minimum might, however, be individually rational if the proposer fears refusals of low bids.[1]

The related *dictator game* looks into this. Here the respondent must accept the bid. Proposers now make reduced offers when compared to the ultimatum format. Nevertheless, a large fraction of the proposers still makes positive offers. In a pioneering study, Forsythe, Horowitz, Savin, & Sefton (1994) found that 80% of the participants in their game wanted to share. In this case the modal offer was a split 70–30. Compared with findings from the ultimatum game, this suggests that a fraction of what is given in this game follows from the fear of being punished. Nevertheless, average offers do not fall to zero. Later studies accentuate among other issues the effect of variations in context (e.g., Hoffman, McCabe, Shachat, & Smith,. 1996; Frohlich, Oppenheimer, & Kurki, 2004).

In *public goods games* cooperation pays for the group as a whole, while defection is individually rational. Nevertheless, substantial levels of cooperation are observed. After reviewing the literature, Biel and Thøgersen (2007) conclude that even in one-shot public goods games 40–60% of participants cooperate. It should, however, also be noted that, in repeated games without opportunities to communicate or punish, cooperation tends to gradually break down, whereas if the option to communicate and/or punish is available, the level of cooperation is substantially increased (e.g., Ostrom, Gardner, & Walker, 1994). Moreover, opportunities to punish non-cooperators are often utilized even though the retaliators may not gain from doing so – for example in games where groups are recomposed (Fehr & Gächter, 2000).

Moving to the *wage experiments*, these typically include employers and employees contracting over wages and expected efforts. Of special interest here are experiments where delivered effort is not monitored by the employer. Nevertheless, employees deliver an effort that on average is a large fraction of what was contracted (Fehr, Kirchsteiger, & Riedl, 1993; Fehr, Gächter, & Kirchsteiger, 1997; Fehr, Kirchsteiger, & Riedl, 1998; Fehr & Falk, 2002). Fehr and Falk (ibid.) characterize this kind of behavior as 'reciprocity-driven voluntary cooperation'.

Having observed this, we must also acknowledge that many experiments exist that support the RMIU model (for example, Holt, Langan, & Villamil, 1986; Davis & Holt, 1993). While behavioral 'errors' have been observed,[2] many experiments confirm the individual rationality assumption quite nicely. Typically, market settings are created and participants are asked to trade a certain good. As a case in point, in a study by Holt et al. (1986) a market was set up for selling and

---

[1] Which s/he should not, though, given the RMIU model.

[2] This is especially the case when risk is involved, e.g., preference reversal (Grether & Plott, 1979; Tversky & Kahneman, 1986). It is of course emphasized by many that humans do not have the capacity to (always) calculate what is best; see, for example, the work of Herbert Simon on bounded rationality. This position has many merits. The point here is, however, not the issue of lacking capacities, but what motivates the individual when choosing, whether boundedly or not.

buying chips. The market was constructed such that there was partly excess supply and partly excess demand. The results of this experiment followed the expectations of the RMIU model quite well. After a few rounds, people found the equilibrium price and quantities of their own accord.

An interesting development within this line of research is based on the idea that by constructing favorable institutions, one can help people avoid making 'behavioral errors'. By forming the right kind of institutions, people can be enabled to act 'rationally'. Shogren (2006) emphasizes that markets create rationality in the population by putting a cost on irrational behavior. He offers a series of examples showing this and emphasizes that through intelligent institutional design – making the cost of what he terms irrational behavior large enough – we can make people act rationally in the RMIU sense.

This idea could, however, be generalized to also explain the very different observations presented above. Institutions not only help people to act 'in accordance with' the RMIU model. They may also have the capacity to help people distinguish between different rationalities and help people operate 'within' these different logics. Before I engage in discussing this hypothesis, I will, however, present briefly a set of models explaining also non-selfish acts on the basis of individual utility considerations.

14.3.2 Interpretations based on maximization of individual utility

There are three dominant types of explanations in the literature that are of interest to us: the Folk Theorem, the various models of expanded utility functions, and finally the theory of individual types. Concerning the *Folk Theorem*, it is based on standard RMIU and formulated within non-cooperative game theory. If games are repeated infinitely (or with an unknown stopping point), cooperation within for example public goods games may be sustained if people are sufficiently patient (Romp, 1997). While the Folk Theorem may explain cooperation in some games, it is unable to explain cooperation in one-shot games and games with a known stopping point, positive offers in dictator games and offers beyond a minimum in ultimatum games.

Another type of explanation is based on *expanding the utility function*. An other-regarding act is interpreted as rational in the RMIU sense if the act itself produces a 'feeling of being good' that is greater than the cost of acting nicely. The model of the 'warm glow of giving' (Andreoni, 1990) is typical of this class of explanations, as are the 'intrinsic motivation' (Frey, 1997) and 'self-image' (Brekke, Kverndokk, & Nyborg, 2003) models.

A third category of explanations concerns the idea that *people are of different types*. Gintis (2000b) distinguishes between *homo economicus* (the standard RMIU type), *homo reciprocans* (acts reciprocally), *homo egualis* (prefers equality) and *homo parochius* (distinguishes between insiders and outsiders). Gintis puts most of his effort into developing the type *homo reciprocans*, which 'exhibits a propensity to cooperate and share with others that are similarly disposed, even at personal cost, and a willingness to punish those who violate cooperative and other social norms, even when punishing is personally costly' (Gintis, 2000b, p. 262). He includes institutions into his understanding by emphasizing that reciprocity is a type of norm. He does, however, seem to understand the effect of norms in utility terms.

Ostrom has also pursued the idea that variations in observed behavior can be explained by variations in individual types, distinguishing between 'norm-using' players, 'conditional cooperators' and 'willing punishers.' In her work together with James Walker, she has been especially engaged in the study of trust as an important factor explaining cooperation in games where the Nash equilibrium is defection (e.g., Ostrom & Walker, 2003; Walker & Ostrom, 2003). They observe that many are willing to forego the gains of defection if there is enough trust established concerning the participants' willingness to cooperate, emphasizing moreover that some people – some types – are more trustworthy than others. Variations in the level of cooperation can then be explained by differences in how easy it is to build trust.

While Ostrom and Walker put much emphasis on how institutions may help people to establish insights both concerning the issues at stake and the character of other agents, they still seem to see agents' behavior as being based on a utility calculus. Ostrom's work on 'second-generation models of (bounded) rationality' is prominent here. This model includes norms and assumes that they are effective only through influencing the perceived costs and benefits of the different acts. In Crawford and Ostrom (1995), a delta parameter is included in the individual's utility function reflecting the influence of the norm. Depending on the act, an extra cost (shame) or benefit (pride) is added to the utility calculation, making the model analogous to Andreoni's in this specific sense. Andreoni does, however, not see a warm glow (= pride) as being institutionally influenced.

Actually, the explanations of both Gintis and Ostrom are different from Andreoni's. The former authors involve two kinds of factors when explaining variation across types. One is genetic/personal and the other is institutional or cultural. The genetic explanation refers to differences in capacities to, for example, be observant or build trustworthiness. The cultural aspect refers to variations in how we are raised, covering variation both within and between cultures.

14.3.3 The institutions-as-rationality-contexts (IRC) hypothesis

One may ask, is the only capacity of institutions to form individual types? As already indicated, an alternative or supplementary role is to see institutions as also influencing the logic or rationale of a certain setting. The basis for the institutions-as-rationality-contexts (IRC) hypothesis is that people have the capacity to be both individually and socially rational. Individual rationality is understood along much the same lines as the RMIU model: it is 'I' rationality. Certainly, information and transaction costs make it impossible to define optimal solutions (Knudsen, 1993), and hence individual (as social) rationality must in some way be bounded. Nevertheless, individual rationality is about what is best for the individual.

Social rationality is about what is best for the group or for 'the other'. It is, respectively, 'We' rationality (Etzioni, 1988) and 'They' rationality. The We form is expected to appear where behavior is understood as interdependent: when the behavior of one is seen as influencing the opportunities for others. Interdependencies can take the form of prisoners' dilemma situations or public goods games. In such situations, cooperation achieves the best result for the group, while the individually rational logic – the Nash strategy – results in lower pay-offs, even for each individual to the extent that everybody follow this logic. The idea is that norms may have the capacity to cut through this dilemma and establish the cooperative solution as the expected one. Of course, if no retaliation options exist, free-riding might be tempting for the more individualistically inclined types involved. Hence, the development of reciprocity norms including that of retaliation against non-cooperators should be expected given the existence of so many interdependencies in human lives.

'They' rationality concerns only the needs or interests of 'the other'. In principle it can, furthermore, encompass the whole of humanity and even animals. Certainly, 'the other' may also be part of a group that one defines oneself to belong to. Thus, it may be very difficult to draw a strict line between We and They rationality. If it can be brought back to the symmetry 'if I help you today, you will help me tomorrow', it is rather a form of We rationality.[3]

The above reasoning is based on the idea that there is a plurality of rationalities fitting well the distinction between separation and integration. Moreover, the idea is that institutions define which rationality is expected. Certainly, as the issues vary, what We rationality implies may also vary substantially. The group involved will differ, and the structure of the problem will vary, demanding variations in the structure of norms and the like.

14.3.4 Empirical support for the institutions-as-rationality-contexts (IRC) hypothesis

To prove which model is best – that of expanded individual utility functions, different individual types or institutions-as-rationality-contexts – is not a simple task. As Sober and Wilson (1998) have emphasized, as soon as a model includes an 'in-

---

[3] While the Andreoni and also Ostrom type models of 'warm glow' and 'delta parameters' could be termed selfish altruism, We and They rationality could be labeled solidarity and pure altruism, respectively. See also Crowards (1997).

trinsic' reward, it can in principle be reformulated to fit whatever observation one wishes. Moreover, existing research has not been focused on comparing and testing the different models outlined above. Each model refers by and large to its own 'type cases'. It is also true that, to date, few studies have varied institutional frames so as to test the IRC hypothesis. Hence, my argument here will have to be built on a reinterpretation of already existing analyses undertaken predominantly for other purposes. There are three different types of analyses helpful in assessing the IRC hypothesis:

1. experiments where institutions shift, while pay-offs are kept unaltered;
2. simultaneous shifts in payoffs and institutional context, where the change in pay-offs is very small; and
3. the existence of incommensurable values.

Examples of experiments where institutions shift and pay-offs/external rewards are kept constant are fairly few. Ross and Ward (1996) document a public goods game with identical pay-offs, but with different naming of the games, alluding to different institutional contexts. Calling the game the 'Wall Street Game' as opposed to the 'Community Game' resulted in significantly lower levels of cooperation. A similar result was found in Hoffman et al. (1994), where in an ultimatum game the proposers were asked to 'divide', respectively 'exchange', when splitting the offered sum. Again it was only the naming of the setting that was different, resulting in significantly different splits.

Experiments with varying opportunities to communicate (e.g., Ostrom et al., 1994; Cardenas, 2000; Cardenas & Ostrom, 2004) also belong to this group with changed institutions, but unaltered rewards. These experiments are typically formed as repeated public goods games, where communication is included after a certain number of rounds. Opportunity for face-to-face communication may be included once or, for example, after each consecutive round. The findings are quite consistent. Communication results in substantially increased cooperation. This is the case even for series where only one communication opportunity is offered. While pay-offs are constant throughout the series of games, one could argue that communication offers an opportunity to 'punish' others, in the form of stating that those cooperating dislike non-cooperative behavior. This could be seen as a way to change the pay-offs by making people feel bad. In the experiments referred to, there was, however, no opportunity to mete out external punishments or to identify who were defecting. Moreover, analyzing the arguments used during the communication phase and the behavior following it, Ostrom et al. (1994, p. 168) conclude by stating: '1. Communication did provide an opportunity for individuals to offer and extract promises of cooperation for non-enforceable contracts. 2. Communication did facilitate the boosting of prior normative orientations.'

What then about experiments where institutions are changed simultaneously with small changes in pay-offs? The expected consequences given the RMIU model would be minor changes in peoples' behavior. The IRC hypothesis would imply, however, that more substantial changes may appear. It could even imply that just small changes in external rewards – such as including low payments or fees – could shift behavior substantially. This would not happen because of the amount of money received or paid, but rather because a shift from a We to an I rationality is established by including a payment. The implication would be a shift from norm-following to calculating what is individually best.

Examples of such behavioral shifts are among others found in Titmuss (1971) and Gneezy and Rustichini (2000a, 2000b). I also include Frey's (1997) research on crowding-out as an example of this effect. The Titmuss case is about blood donation: going from a situation where blood was donated without compensation to one including some pay reduced the amount of blood donated. Gneezy and Rustichini (2000a) refer to a case where including a small fine for coming late when picking up one's children from a day care center resulted in a doubling of instances of lateness. They also document (2000b) an experiment where high-school students were engaged in a donation experiment. Collecting donations without reward resulted in the highest effort by students. Paying 1% of the obtained donation as compensation for the students' effort reduced the amount of collected money substantially. Increasing payments to 10% of what was collected increased the total amount gathered relative to the 1% reward structure, but not to the level of the 'non-incentive' case.

The above examples all show that shifting from a setting without pay to one with pay results in lower supply. In the case where higher levels of pay are also involved, delivery is increased again. This is exactly what would be expected, as we now are in a situation where individual rationality is supported. Certainly, one should expect that if pay was high enough, supply could be brought above the 'no incentive' situation. Hence Gneezy and Rustichini (2000b) name their paper 'Pay enough or don't pay at all'.

From the IRC hypothesis perspective, what happens in all the above cases is a shift from the logic of doing the right thing – supporting community values, following a norm of voluntary cooperation etc. – to calculating what is best for the individual. By including incentive payments, the logic is shifted, and if payments are low, the calculation comes out in favor of doing less.

Certainly, other explanations could be established. In the literature these typically refer to 'intrinsic motivation'. This is the solution offered by Frey (1997) discussing Titmuss' and his own findings. Gneezy and Rustichini, on their hand, emphasize that in the daycare example contracts between parents and owners are incomplete; parents may wonder, for example, whether the owner is soft or though. In the case studied by the authors, the small fine could help reveal that the owner is soft. Hence, the expected cost to the parents of coming late to pick up their children is reduced by acquiring new information. The authors do, however, also offer an institutional type explanation which is based on norms and is quite congruent with the IRC hypothesis.

While I do find much support for the IRC hypothesis in the above references, none of them offer conclusive backing. Additional evidence for IRC comes, however, from the literature on plural or incommensurable value dimensions and the related observations of blocked trade-offs. Both philosophical and empirical analyses offer strong support for the existence of incommensurable values (e.g., Walzer, 1983; Sagoff, 1988; O'Neill, 1993; Fiske & Tetlock, 1997; Spash, 2000; Aldred, 2006). Walzer generalizes by emphasizing that across societies there exist several 'spheres of justice' which are characterized by different rules concerning which issues should be prioritized and how they should be treated.

Such an observation goes against RMIU both in its standard and expanded forms. It goes against the continuity axiom and supports the fact that human decisions are not based on a single type of reasoning. A similar argument comes from a very different source: modern brain science. The main finding in this literature is that the brain is a compartmentalized structure and that different types of activities or decisions involve different parts of the brain (e.g., Tancredi, 2005). Similar arguments are found among evolutionary psychologists (e.g., Clark & Karmiloff-Smith, 1991; Manktelow & Over, 1991; Oaksford & Chater, 1994). They emphasize that the human brain is characterized by a domain-specific capacity for reasoning. When undertaking deontic reasoning, people check for violations, cheaters and so on, whereas when reasoning about the truth of empirical information, they tend to use a confirmation strategy.

The final piece of argument for plurality I present here is delivered by Sober and Wilson (1998). Their work is related to understanding why people may act altruistically. They observe that Andreoni type explanations with an expanded utility function may have explanatory power. Using an evolutionary argument, however, they propose that true altruism is the most plausible explanation. If the ability to cooperate has been important for the survival of the human species – a premise they find very reasonable – it would be better if care for others was a goal in and of itself. This is the most secure way of establishing cooperative behavior. In short, their argument is that in this way helping others/the group is not dependent on the exactness of an intermediate variable, like the feeling of pleasure or pain.

From the above, the fact that people are able to take the interests of others into account seems hard to deny. It also seems hard to defend the idea that decisions are based on a uniform type of utility calculation (i.e. the expanded RMIU). I agree with Sober and Wilson that as soon as intrinsic motivation of the Andreoni type is included in the utility function, a final proof for either model is hard to deliver. Nevertheless, the sum of the above pieces of evidence points strongly towards the existence of a plurality of preferences and of rationalities.

14.4 Resource Regimes for Sustainability

I started this paper by emphasizing that separation, while supporting economic expansion, is a problematic strategy when the issue of sustainable development is taken into account. Separation is built on the idea that humans maximize individual utility and that, by doing so, the highest social gain should also be attained. This is a sensible conclusion only if both choices and forms of wellbeing across individuals are independent. The old formula of Adam Smith does not hold when interdependencies dominate – when 'externalities' are pervasive. In the present situation, handling various 'externalities' well may be more important than expanding 'internalities'. Hence, one may need to start thinking about how to build institutions where the basis is to treat interdependencies between human action, rather than to continue creating nominal independencies to foster economic growth.

Developing the principles for integrative institutions at the level we are talking about here is no easy task. Surely we can recognize that humanity has created many cooperative institutions. Common property regimes are of this kind and have proven successful. They exist, however, mainly for management of local resources and involve rather small groups of people (National Research Council, 2002). Expanding solidarity beyond the local level is a great challenge. I find it nevertheless urgent to start thinking along these lines, since some kind of integrative cooperation must be established to secure the future of our civilization. We must change structures to preserve dignity and wellbeing.

I propose consideration of two fundamental changes of the economic system. First, we should consider changing the operating principles of the basic unit of the economy: 'the firm'. Second, we must consider building a 2nd order governance structure that is able to communicate between these reorganized economic units in ways that both facilitate their pursuing of sustainability and link decisions at different levels of impact. Some issues can be decided upon locally, while in cases where higher-scale processes are influenced significantly, higher level involvement is necessary.

Concerning principles for linking decisions at different levels, a core aspect is to create complementarity between actions. Recently, there is increased attention to this issue (e.g., Berkes, 2002; Young, 2002a, 2002b). In some of the literature, the state is seen more as part of the problem than as a part of the solution. There are certainly many occasions where states are corrupt and where state property has had very negative influences on resource use. Local interests and needs may be overridden. I do not disagree with this claim. Nevertheless, I support Paavola (2007) in that the state must constitute a core level in the hierarchy, and what is needed is not simply to move decisions down to the lowest level possible. The very structure of the hierarchy is just as important. Instead of viewing the state as something different from other cooperative structures, we should utilize its potentials to coordinate activities at lower levels. The state is a public body, and state property could be viewed, hence governed, as a form of common property, especially regarding which rules and rationales are to be instituted at this level. While local users have much better capacities to evaluate consequences of various use and preservation strategies at the local level, coordinating between different local and sub-national decision-making units is also a very important task. Here we need to involve structures like the state. The challenges for the future are twofold.

First, the accountability of states towards its citizens must be strengthened. Second, finding ways of linking state decisions through facilitating cooperation is paramount. One way forward here is to expand the ideas of common property management to the level of the global commons with states as primary actors (Vatn, 2007).

Turning next to the way we organize economic activity, we observe that these activities take place within various structures: from the family firm, non-profit organizations, and locally owned stock holding companies to large, multi-national corporations. At present, it is the corporate organization that represents the greatest challenge for sustainability, because it has accumulated great power and is led by principles that are quite contradictory to those that are demanded by sustainable development. It is therefore hard to envision sustainability without a reform process aimed at including integration, social rationality and responsibility also at this level.

What could a reform of the corporate sector look like? Two different ways in which social rationality and multi-dimensionality could be instituted at the heart of economic life could be envisioned. First, one could reduce the direct power of the corporation by embedding it within socio-political structures built on social rationality. Secondly, one could institute social rationality within the firms themselves. While the latter would in effect remove the corporation as an economic entity from the scene, the former would imply changing its power and dynamics.

The first option could imply reinventing some of the contexts in which the corporation operated in its youth, such as, reverting the rule of restricted responsibility, limit the geographic domain of the corporation to secure community ties, and restrict its existence in time (Bakan, 2004). The latter point would be a core element here, possibly involving for instance a contract between the firm and society including goals to be attained concerning social and environmental standards. A full public assessment of the corporation could take place every ten years demanding the firm to demonstrate how it had met the terms set by society. While its bottom line would still be that of maximizing profits, the firm would have to abide by a wider set of explicit demands to survive such a check. There is a danger for opportunistic behavior. To avoid this, corporations could be held legally responsible for setting aside funds to take care of contracted responsibilities including supporting its employees for a defined period of time if the contract with society was not renewed.

The second option, that of instituting social rationality within the firm, could take several directions. One alternative is to institutionalize a triple bottom line along the three dimensions of sustainability: one including market revenues and costs, one including social goals and finally one related to environmental impacts. Ownership would be distributed along these three dimensions, implying that individuals could still hold shares, but that proceeds would depend not only on market revenues and costs, but the ability to fulfill social and environmental goals as well. Actors representing the social and environmental interests could, as an example, be empowered with the right to block remuneration of shareholders if the delivery of social and environmental output was not acceptable. Certainly, many details need to be worked out to make such a system functionable. A core issue to be decided upon would be who should represent the social and environmental interests. Another would be whether they should have the right to block the shareholders. Similarly, this change would have to be reflected in the role of the board, which in the end would be responsible for balancing the different values and interests involved.

Finally, one could envision that beyond a certain size, and within certain sectors like water and energy, the public should own the firms. The dominant form of ownership would be either state or community based, the latter making it potentially more like a co-operative or common property regime. Public or community ownership offers an interesting alternative to the solution of a corporate triple-bottom-line-firm because it also offers more flexibility. An aspect standing out when looking at the operation of common property regimes is their ability to adapt as new challenges or problems appear, without getting 'stuck' in all types of formally protected rights that must be compensated for. Because of the large influence of human activity on the dynamics of ecosystems, the future is highly uncertain. This demands establishing institutional structures securing very high levels of flexibility. Common property systems can offer this capacity. Certainly, the adaptability implied can be a source of abuse. This does not seem to be a great problem for these regimes, though. Rather they seem to foster community values like fairness and reciprocity, most probably because they would otherwise collapse. Hence, while common property regimes have a rather substantial flexibility to change rules and responsibilities as new challenges appear, they can do so also in ways accepted as fair.

None of the above structures depend on institutionalizing social rationality as the only principle. Rather, they are combinations of individual and social rationality. Moreover, none of the above changes would demand abolishing markets. Some markets would, however, disappear, like the stock market in some proposals. Furthermore, the role of markets would partly be changed, as broader evaluations than monetary assessments and exchange would increase in importance as compared with the situation of today.

14.5 Conclusion

This paper has acknowledged the interdependencies of human choice in a world of pervasive physical interconnections. Moreover, it has emphasized a range of problems that have resulted from instituting separation and individual rationality as the fundamental principle of organizing human decision making. The subsequent creation of disjointed interests and the separation of choices in time and space are seen as creating severe problems. So, while on the one hand fostering economic growth, our institutions have simultaneously been found to constitute a severe obstacle against fostering sustainable development on the other.

As the solution to this problem must be found in changing existing institutional structures, the paper has proposed to institute social rationality at the operative level of the economy – the firm – and to establish a hierarchical decision structure above this level that is able to coordinate decisions in time and space. While the first change is a way towards creating or strengthening common interests within the basis of the economy, the latter is to be founded in order to ensure coordination between these still disjointed entities.

The above ideas have been laid out in the form of rough sketches. They are built on the idea that institutions act as rationality contexts and that instituting social or cooperative rationality is a viable option. The idea has been to illustrate possible directions to go. Institutional changes cannot, however, be made in the drawing-room. Ideas can be developed there, and they can be taken further through cooperative efforts among scholars. The process will, nevertheless, depend on interaction with practical life, implying experimentation and reflexive learning. It will have to be a step-by-step process where theory and practice interact.

It is a problem that we have until now rarely seriously engaged these issues. Yet, the growing understanding of the interrelation between institutions and motivation – the existence not only of individual and myopic interests, but also of cooperative will and social engagement – offers a chance to rethink the way forward. While demanding, it also opens up a whole new area of opportunity, not only for academic research, but for the future of our civilization.

Acknowledgments

Parts of this paper draw on analyses in Vatn (2008a, 2008b). The author would like to thank Achim Schlüter and Elinor Ostrom for comments to an earlier version of the paper.

References

Aldred, J. (2006). Incommensurability and monetary valuation. *Land Economics, 82*, 141–161.

Andreoni, J. (1990). Impure altruism and the donations to public goods: A theory of warm glow giving. *The Economic Journal, 100*, 467–477.

Bakan, J. (2004). *The corporation: The pathological pursuit of profit and power*. New York: Free Press.

Berkes, F. (2002). Cross-scale institutional linkages: Perspectives from the bottom up. In National Research Council (Eds.), *The drama of the commons* (pp. 293–321). Washington DC: National Academy Press.

Biel, A., & Thøgersen J. (2007). Activation of social norms in social dilemmas: A review of the evidence and reflections on the implications for environmental behavior. *Journal of Economic Psychology, 28*, 93–112.

Bowles, S. (2004). *Microeconomics. behavior, institutions and evolution.* Princeton: Princeton University Press.

Brekke, K. A., Kverndokk, S., & Nyborg, K. (2003). An economic model of moral motivation, *Journal of Public Economics, 87*, 1967–1983.

Bromley, D. W. (1991). *Environment and economy: Property rights and public policy.* Oxford: Basil Blackwell.

Camerer, C., & Thaler, R. H. (1995). Anomalies. Ultimatums, dictators and manners. *Journal of Economic Perspectives, 9*, 209–219.

Cardenas, J. -C. (2000). How do groups solve local commons dilemmas: Lessons form experimental economics in the field. *Environment, Development and Sustainability, 2*, 305–322.

Cardenas, J. -C., & Ostrom, E. (2004). What do people bring into the game? Experiments in the field about cooperation in the commons. *Agricultural Systems, 82*, 307–326.

Clark, A., & Karmiloff-Smith, A. (1991). The cognizer's innards: A psychological and philosophical perspective on the development of thought. *Mind and Language, 8*, 487–519.

Commons, J. R. (1924/1974). *Legal foundations of capitalism.* Clifton: Augustus M. Kelley Publishers.

Crawford, S. E. S., & Ostrom, E. (1995). The grammar of institutions. *American Political Science Review, 89*, 582–600.

Crowards, T. (1997). Nonuse values and the environment: Economic and ethical motivations. *Environmental Values, 6*, 143–167.

Davis, D. D., & Holt, C. A. (1993). *Experimental economics.* Princeton: Princeton University Press.

Diamond, J. M. (2005). *Collapse: How societies choose to fail or succeed.* New York: Viking Books.

European Fertilizer Manufacturers Association. (2000). *Phosphorous: Essential element for food production.* Brussels: European Fertilizer Manufacturers Association.

Etzioni, A. (1988). *The moral dimension: Toward a new economics.* New York: The Free Press.

Fehr, E., & Falk, A. (2002). Psychological foundations of incentives. Joseph Schumpeter lecture. *European Economic Review, 46*, 687–724.

Fehr, E., & Gächter, S. (2000). Cooperation and punishment in public goods experiments. *American Economic Review, 90*, 980–994.

Fehr, E., Gächter, S., & Kirchsteiger, G. (1997). Reciprocity as a contract enforcement device: Experimental evidence. *Econometrica, 65*, 833–860.

Fehr, E., Kirchsteiger, G., & Riedl, A. (1993). Does fairness prevent market clearing? *Quarterly Journal of Economics, 108*, 437–459.

Fehr, E., Kirchsteiger, G., & Riedl, A. (1998). Gift exchange and reciprocity in competitive experimental markets. *European Economic Review, 42*, 1–34.

Fiske, A. P., & Tetlock, P. E. (1997). Taboo trade-offs: Reactions to transactions that transgress the spheres of justice. *Political Psychology, 18*, 255–297.

Forsythe, R., Horowitz, J. L., Savin, N. E., & Sefton, M. (1994). Fairness in simple bargaining experiments. *Games and Economic Behavior, 6*, 347–369.

Frey, B. S. (1997). *Not just for the money: An economic theory of personal motivation.* Cheltenham: Edward Elgar Publishing Limited.

Frohlich, N., Oppenheimer, J., & Kurki, A. (2004). Modeling other-regarding preferences and an experimental test. *Public Choice, 119*, 91–117.

Gintis, H. (2000a). Beyond *Homo economicus*: Evidence from experimental economics. *Ecological Economics, 35*, 311–322.

Gintis, H. (2000b). *Game theory evolving: A problem-centered introduction to modeling strategic interaction*. Princeton: Princeton University Press.

Gintis, H., Bowles, S., Boyd, R., & Fehr, E. (2003). Explaining altruistic behavior in humans. *Evolution and Human Behavior, 24*, 153–172.

Gneezy, U., & Rustichini, A. (2000a). A fine is a price. *The Journal of Legal Studies, 29*, 1–17.

Gneezy, U., & Rustichini, A. (2000b). Pay enough or don't pay at all. *Quarterly Journal of Economics, 115*, 791–810.

Grether, D., & Plott, C. (1979). Economic theory of choice and the preference reversal phenomenon. *American Economic Review, 69*, 623–638.

Hagedorn, K. (2005, October). *The dichotomy of segregative and integrative institutions and its particular importance for sustainable resource use and rural development*. Paper presented at the workshop in political theory and policy analysis colloquium, Mini Series, Bloomington.

Heberl H., Krausmann, F., & Gingrich, S. (2006). Ecological embeddedness of the economy: A socioecological perspective on humanity's economic activities 1700–2000. *Economic and Political Weekly, 25*, 4896–4904.

Henrich, J. R., Bowles, B. S., Camerer, C., Fehr, E., Gintis, H., & McElrath, R. (2001). In search of Homo economicus: Behavioral experiments in 15 small-scale societies. *American Economic Review Papers and Proceedings, 91*, 73–78.

Hoffman, E., McCabe, K., Shachat, K., & Smith, V. (1994). Preferences, property rights, and anonymity in bargaining games. *Games and Economic Behavior, 7*, 346–380.

Hoffman, E., McCabe, K., Shachat, K., & Smith, V. (1996). Social distance and other regarding behavior in dictator games. *American Economic Review, 86*, 653–660.

Holt, C. A., Langan, L., & Villamil, A. P. (1986). Market power in oral double auctions. *Economic Inquiry, 24*, 107–123.

Kapp, K. W. (1971). *The social costs of private enterprise*. New York: Schoken Books.

Knudsen, C. (1993). Equilibrium, perfect rationality and the problem of self-reference in economics. In U. Mäki, B. Gustafsson, & C. Knudsen (Eds.), *Rationality, institutions and "economic methodology"* (pp. 133–170). London: Routledge.

Layard, R. (2005). *Happiness. Lessons from a new science*. New York: The Penguin Press.

Manktelow, K. I., & Over, D. E. (1991). Social roles and utilities in reasoning with deontic conditionals. *Cognition, 39*, 85–105.

Murdoch, G. P. (1967). *Ethnographic atlas*. Pittsburg: University of Pittsburg Press.

National Research Council. (2002). The drama of the commons. Committee on the Human Dimensions of Global Change. In E. Ostrom, T. Dietz, N. Dolsak, P. C. Stern, S. Stovich, & E. U Walker (Eds.), *Division of Behavioral and Social Sciences and Education*. Washington DC: National Academy Press.

North, D. C. (1981). *Structure and change in economic history*. New York: W.W. Norton & Company.

North, D. C. (1990). *Institutions, institutional change and economic performance*. Cambridge: Cambridge University Press.

Nöel. J. F., & O'Connor, M. (1998). Strong sustainability and critical natural capital. In S. Faucheux & M. O'Connor (Eds.), *Valuation for Sustainable Development* (pp. 75–98). Cheltenham: Edward Elgar.

Oaksford, M., & Chater, N. (1994). A rational analysis of the selection tasks as optimal data selection. *Psychological Review, 101*, 608–631.

O'Neill, J. (1993). *Ecology, policy and politics: Human well-being and the natural world*. London: Routledge.

Ostrom, E. (1990). *Governing the commons: The evolution of for collective action*. Cambridge: Cambridge University Press.

Ostrom, E. (1998). A behavioral approach to the rational choice theory of collective action. Presidential address, American Political Science Association, 1997. *American Political Science Review*, 92, 1–22.

Ostrom, E., (2000). Collective Action and the Evolution of Social Norms. *Journal of Economic Perspectives*, 14, 137–158.

Ostrom, E. (2005). *Understanding institutional diversity*. Princeton: Princeton University Press.

Ostrom, E., Gardner, R., & Walker, J. (1994). *Rules, games, and common-pool resources*. Ann Arbor: University of Michigan Press.

Ostrom, E., & Walker, J. (Eds.) (2003). *Trust & reciprocity: Interdisciplinary lessons from experimental research*. New York: Russell Sage Foundation.

Paavola, J. (2007). Institutions and environmental governance: A reconceptualization. *Ecological Economics, 63*, 93–103.

Polanyi, K. (1944/1957). *The great transformation: The political and economic origins of our time*. Boston: Beacon Press.

Romp, G. (1997). *Game theory: Introduction and application*. Oxford: Oxford University Press.

Ross, L., &. Ward, A. (1996). Naïve realism: Implications for social conflict and misunderstanding. In E. S. Reed, E. Turiel, & T. Brown (Eds.), *Values and knowledge*. Mahwah: Lawrence Erlbaum Associates.

Roth, A. E., Prasnikar, V., Okuna-Fujiwara, M., & Zamir, S. (1991). Bargaining and market behavior in Jerusalem, Ljubljana, Pittsburg and Tokyo: an experimental study. *American Economic Review, 81*, 1068–1095.

Sagoff, M. (1988). *The economy of the earth: Philosophy, law and environment*. Cambridge: Cambridge University Press.

Shogren, J. (2006). A rule of one. *American Journal of Agricultural Economics, 88*, 1147–1159.

Sober, E., & Wilson, D. S. (1998). *Onto others. The evolution and psychology of unselfish behavior*. Cambridge: Harvard University Press.

Spash, C. L. (2000). Multiple value expression in contingent valuation: Economics and ethics. *Environmental Science Technology, 34*, 1433–1438.

Tancredi, L. R. (2005). *Hardwired behavior: What neuroscience reveals about morality*. Cambridge: Cambridge University Press.

Titmuss, R. M. (1971). *The gift of relationship: From human blood to social policy*. New York: Pantheon Books.

Toman, M. A., Pezzey, J., & Krautkraemer, J. (1995). Neoclassical economic growth theory and "sustainability". In D. W. Bromley (Ed.), *The handbook of environmental economics* (pp.139–165). Oxford: Blackwell.

Tversky, A., & Kahneman, D. (1986). Rational choice and the framing of decisions. In R. M. Hogarth, & M. W. Reder (Eds.), *Rational choice: The contrast between economics and psychology*. Chicago: University of Chicago Press.

Vatn, A. (2002). Efficient or fair: Ethical paradoxes in environmental policy. In D. W. Bromley & J. Paavola (Eds.), *Economics, ethics and environmental policy: Contested choices* (pp 148–163). Oxford: Blackwell.

Vatn, A. (2005). *Institutions and the environment*. Cheltenham: Edward Elgar.

Vatn, A. (2007). Resource regimes and cooperation. *Land Use Policy, 24*, 624–632.

Vatn, A. (2008a). Sustainability: The need for institutional change. In P. Utting, & J. Clapp (Eds.), *Corporate accountability and sustainable development* (pp. 61–91). Delhi: Oxford University Press.

Vatn, A. (2008b). Rationality and institutions. In S. Batie & N. Mercuro (Eds.), *Assessing the evolution and impact of alternative institutional structures* (pp. 113–139). London: Routledge Press.

Veblen, T. (1904/1958). *The theory of business enterprise.* New York: The new American library.

Wackernagel, M., & Rees. W. (1996). *Our ecological footprint: Reducing human impact on the earth.* British Colombia: New Society Publishers.

Walker, J., & Ostrom, E. (2003). Conclusion. In E. Ostrom & J. Walker (Eds.), *Trust & reciprocity. Interdisciplinary lessons from experimental research* (pp. 381–387). New York: Russell Sage Foundation.

Walzer, M. (1983). *Spheres of justice: A defense of pluralism and equality.* New York: Basic Books Inc. Publishers.

Young, O. R. (2002a). *The institutional dimension of environmental change: Fit, interplay, and scale.* Cambridge: The MIT Press.

Young, O. R. (2002b). Institutional interplay: The environmental consequences of cross-scale interactions. In National Research Council (Eds.), *The drama of the commons* (pp. 263–291). Washington DC: National Academy Press.

15 Institutional Change and Ecological Economics: The Role of Mental Models and Sufficient Reason

Achim Schlüter

Faculty of Forestry and Environmental Sciences, Albert-Ludwigs-Universität Freiburg, Institute of Forestry Economics, Tennenbacher Str. 4, D-79085 Freiburg, Germany, E-mail: a.schlueter@ife.uni-freiburg.de

Abstract. Paavola and Adger (2005) claim that ecological economics could benefit from institutional economics when analysing environmental governance. One aspect they focus on is the discussion about motivational and cognitive assumptions in institutional economics. This paper deepens this focus, explaining in theoretical terms what it means to include cognition in our institutional analysis and presenting the main theoretical approaches on this topic within institutional economics. A short comparison is made between two approaches, one by Douglass North and the other by Daniel Bromley. The paper argues that, even if traditionally the differences between the old and the new institutionalisms have been substantial, in relation to recent developments they are becoming a lot closer. Especially if we compare the role of mental models as seen by Douglass North with the arguments made by Daniel Bromley about sufficient reason, the two approaches can be seen as complementary and could fructify each other. Particularly if we draw the methodological implications of these two theoretical approaches, we see that both require the use of qualitative data in order to understand mental models or forms of sufficient reason. Some qualitative data is used to demonstrate what it means to apply the approaches empirically.

Keywords: Cognition, Ecological economics, Institutional economics, Mental models, Sufficient reasons

15.1 Introduction

During the early years of ecological economics, only a few links were made between ecological and institutional economics (e.g., Constanza, 1991). Ecological economics as an interdisciplinary science was linked more closely to the natural than the social sciences (Siebenhühner, 2001, p. 7). However, the links between the two have grown stronger over the years. The person linking the two traditions for the longest amount of time is Daniel Bromley (e.g., Bromley, 1991). Within the last few years, the amount of publications linking the two fields has risen constantly. Vatn (2005a) even recently wrote a textbook, Institutions and the environment, which links the two perspectives. Institutional economics is itself divided into two different traditions (Hodgson, 1998), the old and the new, each with its own distinct features. Traditionally, scholars within ecological economics have been associated much more with the old institutionalists (Kant & Berry, 2005; Vatn, 2005a; Bromley, 2006a), however, there are also many works now emerging oriented towards the New Institutional Economics (NIE) (Bleischwitz, 2003; Dedeurwaerdere, 2005; Paavola & Adger, 2005). According to Berkes and Folke (1994), this closeness is also a result of work emerging in the field of common property, which is, in part, closely linked to NIE (Johnson, 2004) while, at the same time, dealing with issues at the centre of interest of ecological economics.

There are many reasons why institutional economics are used more and more within ecological economics and why this seems to be appropriate. Ecological economics is based on the normative claim of wanting to help build a more sustainable society (Common & Stagl, 2005). If this is one of the central goals of an inter-discipline, then it is obvious that the question about (sustainable) institutions is of great importance. Paavola and Adger (2005) see essentially three reasons why institutional economics should become more important for ecological economics and, particularly, why institutional economics is better suited than mainstream economics as a tool for ecological economics. First of all, there is the joint understanding between ecological and institutional economics that the problems emerging in economic exchange are not well described as being due to externalities, but are rather a problem of interdependence (p. 354)[1]. Interdependence as a guiding concept understands economic exchange according to its systemic properties and does not allow for atomisation and disintegration, which occur if we understand most environmental problems as arising from externalities (raise the optimal Pigouvian tax and we can let the economic process develop with rational utility-maximising individuals). According to Paavola and Adger, the second important issue which institutional economics can elucidate for ecological economics is that of transaction costs, which was already raised very early by Coase in 1937 (p. 357). They rightly claim that policy-oriented ecological economics is well advised to take the issue of transaction costs for policy alternatives seriously. It otherwise risks giving recommendations which are far from any realistic applicability.

The third reason mentioned by Paavola and Adger why ecological economics should incorporate more insights from institutional economics is the latter's preoccupation with cognitive aspects of the economic choice process (p. 358). Since neoclassical economics has taken over and become a synonym for economics as such, the choice process of the individual has been black-boxed (Lindenberg,

[1] See also Vatn's contribution in this volume.

1985, p. 75). Individuals and their preferences have been taken as given and are outside the interest of the economist (Hodgson, 1993b). It was institutional economists who realised that for understanding choice processes in economics, it does not make sense to take the individual and its preferences as given, thus understanding it as a mechanistic utility maximiser which does not actually choose anything (Siebenhühner, 2001, p. 124)[2]. It is necessary to have a closer look at the choice process, they argued, something which is now taking place. Obviously we can see various rationalities at work at the same time: people, for example, use different behavioural heuristics in families or in markets (Vatn, 2005a). These aspects are addressed when we look at cognition and its implications for the choice process. Elucidation of the choice process is of particular importance when we look at non-trivial choices, such as new institutional arrangements (Denzau & North, 1994)[3].

This different view on the economic process will be explored a little bit further on in this paper, which is itself structured in the five following steps. First, I explain, why it is wise, particularly from the perspective of ecological economics, to go into more detail about the cognitive process of human beings when they make economic decisions. This holds especially true when economic decisions on the rules of the game are made. Therefore, it seems obvious that ecological and institutional economics have a common interest in cognition. Second, I explain the understanding of institutional economics on the cognitive process and its importance for institutional choice, looking mainly at two different approaches, one more associated with the new institutionalism and the other more associated with the old institutionalism, arising out of the works of Douglass North and Daniel Bromley, respectively. I have chosen those two approaches for a variety of reasons. One has the impression reading the literature that ecological economics would need to decide which approach to adhere to (Vatn, 2005b). On the one side, we have the more famous "mental model" approach of Douglass North, probably being more famous simply because of its belonging to the "mainstream" institutional economics approach (Hodgson, 2007, p. 12). Meanwhile, on the other side we have the "sufficient reason" approach, which comes from Daniel Bromley, obviously more closely related to ecological economics. These two different world views have been central in much work coming out of Konrad Hagedorn's "workshop", and I am myself puzzled as to how far one needs to be either on the one or the other side. Is there a fundamental non-compatibility between the two approaches? In a third step various aspects of the approaches are compared as I argue that they are "getting closer" to each other and that their differences might result from their epistemological starting points as well as their main foci of interest, therefore

---

[2] Choosing means having alternatives; the neoclassical human does not choose, due to the assumption that the alternative that must be taken is already determined (Bromley, 2006, p. 69).

[3] See also the contribution of Blomquist in this volume, where he points out the importance of complexity and uncertainty when dealing with institutions regulating eco-systems.

making the two approaches complementary rather than substitutable. Additionally, it is argued that, if one takes a "pragmatic" approach – here the word pragmatic is used in a colloquial sense and not in the sense of philosophical pragmatists (as Daniel Bromley would describe himself) – and is interested from an empirical perspective in the questions of emergence and change of rules governing the environment, then "on the ground" the two different understandings of cognition would make no difference.

We want to know what a greater emphasis on cognition would signify for our way of doing scientific, applied empirical research – the main field of work by scholars associated with Konrad Hagedorn. Therefore, in a fourth step I explore the methodological implications of focusing more on cognitive aspects of institutional change in the field of the environment. After a methodological discussion, I explore what it would mean to investigate the role of mental models and sufficient reason in an explorative empirical study, using data from a study about institutional change in the forestry sector that was accomplished recently. Due to its great uncertainly and long time horizons, forestry provides a good example where mental models are of particular importance for the understanding of institutional change (Schlüter, 2007). However, due to space restrictions, the empirical examples are only used for illustration purposes about the significance of mental models and not for an entire analysis of institutional change. In a fifth step some conclusions are drawn.

15.2 Cognition Within Institutional Economics and Its Relevance for Ecological Economics

One of the main reasons why ecological economics should focus on the cognitive process is linked to the argument of complexity. There seems to be a more or less unanimous opinion that the easier the choice process is, the more we can rely on a simple actor model: the rational person, which is used basically in neoclassical economics. When we deal with simple choice processes, where the relevant payoffs are clear; the system dynamics are understood simply, or do not exist (as with trivial choice); and there is no interdependence, then we might be able to work with the simple model of the rational actor (Denzau & North, 1994; Ostrom, 1998, p. 3; Ostrom, 2005).

But, the more complex the choice situation is, the more we use heuristics, cognitive frames, institutions, positive and normative models on how we believe the world is and how it should be, to help us in the choice process (Wilson, 2002). Most of the decision processes humans face in day-to-day life are of the latter type. Wilson (2002, p. 337), for example, makes clear how even games that are relatively simple in comparison to reality (the number of rules is relatively small and therefore easily remembered) largely exceed our "rational" abilities and we must consequently rely on patterns and rules of behaviour when playing them[4]. The same is true when looking at choice situations, either in our institutional settings when they need to be altered, or in terms of dealing with the ecological environment, which, with all its system dynamics, is very complex[5]. Therefore, understanding the cognitive models people use for making decisions in this field is necessary if we want to understand their choice processes.

In addition, much experimental and empirical research has discovered that human beings employ different rationalities, depending on the context, or even within one context; they do not employ one or the other rationality in its pure form (Ostrom, 2005, p. 69; Vatn, 2005a, p. 113). The institutional setting, the context of choice, to which an individual is exposed, determines, at least partially, its behaviour. Placing an agent into an extremely competitive neoclassical-like market environment will lead to a behaviour (not in its purest form, but close to it), which is very similar to the behaviour of neoclassical rational ideal (Ostrom, 2005)[6]. As many environmental goods cannot, and in the eyes of many citizens should not, be regulated by the market, we can expect that in the field of the environment many other forms of rationality[7] than the homo oeconomicus, will be relevant for our understanding. Homo reciprocans, homo sustinens (Siebenhühner, 2001), homo behaviouralis (Vanberg, 1994, p. 35) – a rule-and patterns-guided individual – will all be of importance. If the assumption of such diversified modes of behaviour is justified, then a deeper understanding of the individual, group and context surrounding the choice process is needed (Holland, 2002). The understanding that human beings behave differently than rational individual utility maximising actors is central for ecological economics (Beckenbach, 2001, p. 22).

One of the important questions in ecological economics is how to properly regulate the environment via the provision of (normative) policy advice to decision makers. But how can we give such advice without knowing how the actors we regulate behave with regard to particular incentives given through our recommended regulations? Paavola (2002) points out how important it is for the regulator to understand the reasons (the mental models) of the regulated, to be able to predict their behaviour after a certain rule has been changed. He exemplifies this with the help of an imagined scenario concerned with change in legislation on animal welfare. If, for example, we try to influence vegetarianism, we need to know the reasons why people would choose to be vegetarian: do they not eat meat due to faith reasons; do they not eat meat because its expensive; do they not eat

---

[4] See also Vanberg (1994) for a discussion on where we should use rational and where rule-following behavior.

[5] See the fascinating description of institutional emergence in East Africa's rangeland by Mwangi and Ostrom in this volume.

[6] However, game-theoretic experiments have shown that even in a game under the rules of a competitive neoclassical market, people often behave differently than the models predict (Siebenhühner, 2001, p. 131)

[7] See Schlüter and Phillimore (2005), where the various rationalities employed by the people living in a petrochemical town are shown.

meat due to animal welfare considerations; or do they not eat meat due to considerations concerning their own health? If we have not understood the underlying reasons behind the range of actions of different people, we will not be able to give policy advice. Or, even worse, if we unjustifiably assume a neoclassical rational human being, we might destroy a significant potential for self-regulating environmental governance (Spash, 1995, p. 275; Frey, 1997; Bowles, 1998; Vatn, 2002, p. 154)[8].

Considering the above-mentioned aspects, it seems clear that ecological economics and institutional economics need to consider the process of cognition more carefully, in order to develop a more comprehensive picture of the human choice process (Söderbaum, 1999, p. 164)[9].

15.3 Cognition, Mental Models and Sufficient Reason

The basic idea of looking at the cognitive process is that the human choice processes will never be understood if we don't consider the processes taking place inside the brain. If we define economics as the theory of choice (Samuelson & Nordhaus, 1998), then we need to understand how humans make decisions and, therefore, need a cognitive theory (Hodgson, 1993b). This is even more so if we look at institutions (particularly in the field of the environment) where non-monetary aspects play such a crucial role (Loasby, 2002). It is obvious that institutional theory needs to think about cognition because the two aspects are so closely linked: mental models as "internal routines of the brain appear to perform similar functions to the external phenomena of institutions" (Loasby, 2002, p. 12).

In most choice processes, human beings are not able to understand the data they observe as such; rather, the data needs to be interpreted and understood. Thus, heuristics are needed to help us make decisions in a complex world. Many of our choice situations cannot be characterised by a cost-benefit analysis, or the cost-benefit analysis cannot be understood as a simple process of summing up, for example, monetary values. Holland (1996) has described this process as a process of induction which every individual goes through while the brain and mental abilities develop. The void individual – similar to the optimal researcher described in inductive research/grounded theory (Glaser & Strauss, 1967) – makes empirical observations and is able, due to those observations, to develop certain mental

---

[8] A similar understanding can be found in North (1992, p. 46), where he writes that an important effect of ideology is to reduce the free-riding problem in a society and has, therefore, a positive, transaction-cost-reducing role to play. Ideologies make people think differently than the neoclassical model of individual utility maximisation would predict.

[9] Konrad Hagedorn has long ago pointed out that "Interpretationssysteme", which would translate into something in between North's terminology of ideologies and mental models, are crucial for an understanding of policy choice in the field of agriculture in Germany (Hagedorn, 1992, 1996, p. 429–449).

structures. These structures and patterns enable the individual to detect regularities and start to make predictions, which then help the individual to make choices. Whenever an individual as a "pattern matcher" (North, 2005, p. 27) observes something which does not match an expected pattern, she then corrects her model, thereby improving it (Handlbauer, 2000). It is these models that allow the individual to act (Holland, 1996, p. 281). We do not need to develop our models and patterns on our own – as a true inductive learner would, because they always start from an "empty" unbiased brain; rather, we take the patterns, routines and models from others who surround us. These are the mental models we acquire through our culture (North, 2005). From this perspective, one would probably replace the idea of an inductive learner by an abductive learner (Hodgson, 1993a). We have our models and half-baked theories in our mind, and we constantly feed them with empirical information. If a particular pattern is not matched by new data, we search for the reasons why they conflict and we might adapt our model to be more in accord with this specific situation[10].

This influence of the past shows that the starting point of the cognitive process cannot be the individual alone, but the individual which is formed and shaped by the society in which it grew up. The recognition of path dependencies (North, 1990) in the more individual-oriented approaches within institutional economics seem, to my understanding, to also recognise the fact that no individual exists outside of a society (Hodgson, 2007, p. 14). Knight and North (1997, p. 217) reject the presently dominant approaches within economics, which use individual psychological approaches for understanding the importance of cognition. According to them, "rational decisions are the product of beliefs that are instantiated in social institutions and in other cultural symbols" (p. 218). An approach from cultural anthropology is therefore needed.

According to North, mental models do not only consist of positive elements, which try to understand on how the world works, but also involve a normative element on how the world should be (North, 1994, p. 363)[11]. From North's description, I find it unclear whether the normative aspect enters into the model of cognition because of the complexity of reality, which makes it unavoidable to make normative decisions and value judgments, or if it's because he believes human beings are volitional creatures (similar to Bromley, 2006a). However, on practical grounds it does not make any difference whether (normative) mental models are used, because one does not know what would be, for example, utility maximising or because there is a volition, an ethic to be considered. In both interpretations, we need to consider those models if we want to understand institutional change.

---

[10] See Mwangi and Ostrom in this volume, describing such a process of learning, based on culture and new experiences.

[11] This distinction is similarly made by Bromley (2006, p. 14), where he distinguishes between volitional and epistemic premises.

The cognitive process heavily influences the institutional choice process taking place. According to Denzau and North (1994), we do not immediately perform a cost-benefit analysis and then choose the institutional solution that maximises our individual pay-off. We need our models, our beliefs[12], and our filters, in order to interpret the data and be able to then adopt the solution the individual considers to be the wisest at that particular moment in time (in Bromley's words, there are sufficient reasons). This circle, as described in Fig. 15.1, is gone through a number of times during an institutional learning process.

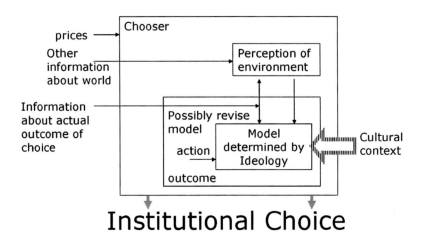

Fig. 15.1: Mental models and institutional change
Source: Adapted from Denzau and North (1994, p. 18)

The process of selecting one of the various institutional solutions proposed is unclear in North's explanations. It is a spontaneous order of selection, in which competition plays an important role (North, 2005, 59). However, if ideologies ("incorrect"[13] representations of reality; normative aspects) play an important role in this process, which they always will, the selection mechanism does not allow for any predictive theory.

Bromley (2006a, 2006b) describes a conceptual scheme (see Fig. 15.2) which is, on a first view, similar to that of North. Human beings have certain beliefs (in North's words a mental model) about how the world works and how they want it

---

[12] Bromley explicitly uses the word "beliefs", indicating that although there in an understanding of many social phenomena, there is no ultimate truth. Knight and North (1997, p. 212) also think that "beliefs determine the strategic choice of the actors".

[13] Incorrect is in quotation marks to indicate that there is no correct representation, or at least nobody would be able to identify one, when thinking of institutional phenomena (Searle, 2005).

to work. However, the important situations for institutional change are when the "irritation of doubt" arrives, so important for the process of abduction.

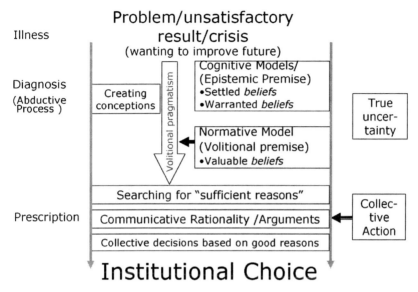

Fig. 15.2: Sufficient reason and institutional change
Source: Own drawing

A particular phenomenon occurs which the current models either cannot explain or the current arrangement delivers an unsatisfactory result for, and therefore we want a change. Consequently, we start searching, similar to a doctor who detects a disease in his patient, for a diagnosis (Bromley, 2006a, p. 96) and a possible medication we could prescribe. This is the cognitive process of changing our beliefs, during which we use the "toolbox" of all our old patterns (settled beliefs) and try do adapt them. It is a creative, abductive process of recombination of old beliefs, which results in the creation of new beliefs and reasons. We may use the knowledge and opinions of experts – warranted beliefs (Bromley, 2006a), in other words scientific theories[14] – to underpin our arguments for a particular position. As volitional creatures, having our own will and not just being "rational" machine like maximisers, we use normative statements (valuable beliefs) in formulating our arguments. At this point it seems necessary to indicate that the distinction between warranted beliefs and valuable beliefs (positive and normative elements of mental models in North's terms) is somehow impossible to draw if we deal with social phenomena. What is important in Bromley's argument is that in this process, launched by the "irritation of doubt", we try in discussion with others to accumulate

---

[14] Denzau and North (1994, p. 25) also ascribe an important role to science as being a particularly approved mental model.

"sufficient reasons" for a particular change, which we then propose and attempt to negotiate on. Similar to the case of North (see above), the bargaining process (Bromley, 1989), or the collective action process (Bromley, 2006a), which leads to the selection of a particular institutional solution is not explained in detail by Bromley. But, to a certain degree like a deus ex machina, the most reasonable solution for which there is "sufficient reason" is selected in a collective action process (Bromley, 2006a, p. 75). However, this shortcoming of the two approaches should not concern us too much here, because our focus is on the description and understanding of the cognitive process and not the selection process of the particular medication (Bromley) or the selection of the mental model, which then becomes the shared mental model (North).

15.4 Mental Models and Sufficient Reason: What is Different?

Some authors find it important to draw a clear line between the old and the new institutionalists (Hodgson, 1993b; Vatn, 2005a). In other contributions, the demarcation line between the two does not seem to play a particular role (Söderbaum, 1999; Bleischwitz, 2003; Paavola & Adger, 2005). Daniel Bromley gave a guest lecture in Freiburg in 2006 (Bromley, 2006a), where the question was raised concerning what the differences are between his approach and the approach developed over the years by Douglass North, who deals extensively with the issue of cognition. I did not find the answer given at the seminar to be satisfactory, which acted as another motivation for the present paper[15]. The rejection of the approach of new institutional economics, particularly those aspects of it represented through the ideas of North, has been one of the most important issues in Daniel Bromley's writings for a long time. The main arguments against the new institutionalism are the tautology (Bromley, 1989) or the infinite institutional regress (Vatn, 2005a), which cannot be solved if we do not give up as the final reason for any institution the rational individual, which remains – according to the new institutionalism – as the basis for any institution-building process. In the beginning there is a rational individual, who, after making a cost-benefit analysis, thinks that establishing an institution is more useful. This idea is most clear when looking at the early North and his theory of the state (1988, p. 20). Bromley and others continue to stress the point that making this cost-benefit analysis cannot be done in an institutional vacuum because costs and benefits are always tied to a particular institutional setting

---

[15] In Schlüter (2001), the theories I applied to the privatization process in Czech agriculture were mainly those of Douglass North. Daniel Bromley commented on my work at that time, rejecting a good part of my argumentation with the justification that it was based on the tautological arguments of North. Parts of this criticism have been understood by me, other parts have not. However, this is certainly one of the other reasons (apart from the seminar experience mentioned) why I would like to further explore the fundamental differences between the two approaches.

(Vatn refers to this as the chicken and the egg problem)[16]. Knight, who is no doubt a new institutionalist and has often published with North, writes "that culture's place in the cognitive process is to provide the substantive content of individual thoughts" (2000, p. 18). With this understanding, there cannot be a culturally-contextually "unbiased" choice. Therefore, starting then from the rational calculus is a solution of the chicken and egg problem, but does not negate the problem of infinite regress, which is unsolvable. "This recognition of social influences on individuals places North very close to the old institutionalist tradition", says Hodgson (2007, p. 14).

North, following Holland, Holyoak, Nisbett, and Thagard (1986), Holland (1996), describes our learning process as more of an inductive process[17]. Bromley's (2006a, p. 96) and Hodgson's (1993) descriptions of it favours an abductive process, in which the already existing models and theories we have from society play a larger role. This might be explained by the fact that the former came from a strongly methodological individualist tradition and the latter, being old institutionalists, have a more nuanced understanding However, North recognises in many ways that culture, the inheritance of the past, is crucial for the understanding of the choices made by the individual (North, 2005, p. 33)[18]. Holland (1996, p. 282), on whom North bases his explanation of learning, clearly indicates that the experience-based process of induction unavoidably requires the context, history, and past[19]. From an epistemological perspective, there is an important distinction to be made between an inductive and an abductive process (Reichertz, 2003; Bromley, 2006a), and what is described by North might be better put with the term abduction. However, if it comes to the description of how individuals come to adopt their mental models or beliefs, the word seems to be different but the process of adaptation seems to be the same. Individuals see a mismatch between their current model and the empirical result and, depending on their previous models/beliefs,

---

[16] Reading Denzau and North (1994), one gets the impression that for them the question of chicken or egg is not of central importance; rather, they are interested in finding out what different degrees of rationality do to our cognitive process.

[17] The methodological discussion regarding grounded theory, which strongly emphasizes induction, clearly showed that it is impossible to do inductive research without any theoretical understanding prior to the research (e.g. Siebenhühner, 2001, p. 41). This is not only true for scientific reasoning, but also for everyday reasoning, which is not possible without existing cognitive concepts (Lakatos, 1982).

[18] There, North rejects a pure methodological individualism in favour of a certain form of constructivism, quoting Hutchins (1995, p. 354): "culture, context, and history ... are fundamental aspects of human cognition and cannot be comfortably integrated into a perspective that privileges abstract properties of isolated individual minds." Also see Dequech (2006), who makes the same argument about Knight and North.

[19] Inductivism (and having a theoretical void) was one of the main criticisms directed towards the historical school within the Methodenstreit. The historical school can be seen as the predecessor of the old institutionalists. Perhaps this connection leads the old institutionalists to try to avoid any proximity to inductivism. To my understanding, taking a pragmatic position, the difference between what Holland and Bromley describes is not fundamental.

they might come up with different solutions. The only difference might then be that the one focuses slightly more on the individual and the other more on the context.

This difference might result from the fact that the main empirical foci of the two authors are quite different. Daniel Bromley looks, nearly exclusively, at institutions and property rights dealing with the environment (Bromley, 1992, 1996). They are always at the intersection between the environmental and the economic sphere. Due to the complexity argument mentioned above, one cannot rely on a "simple" utility maximising logic; instead, reasons, beliefs and mental models shaped by culture must be more prominent. It is obvious that in this field a non-market logic, one which does not place the individual in the centre of interest, plays an important role. It has been always the society which has had to decide how we deal with and treat our environment (Bromley, 2001).

North, on the other hand, mainly emphasises institutions governing economic exchange less influenced by interdependencies with the environment. Looking at more directly market-influenced institutional change, it is apparent that one puts the individual and the expected benefits of his actions into the centre of the analysis. Markets favour this rationality (Vatn, 2005b, p. 126).

In both explanations there is insufficient description of how the selection of a mental model or a belief takes place on its way to becoming either a shared mental model or being perceived as providing "sufficient reason", as being relevant for institutional choice. Nevertheless, there is in fact a difference in the two selection processes that seems to be relevant. North believes that competition plays the central role in selection. Different institutional designs compete with each other, and the more successful (efficient) one survives in the long run. Obviously, Bromley is strongly opposed to the idea that the efficient solution exists (Bromley, 1989). He sees a process of collective action as being crucial for selection. Differently opinionated groups try to persuade each other with what they consider to be the most reasonable suggestion[20]. This difference in the selection mechanisms might also be explained by the kinds of institutions that they have focused on. Environmental legislation is, at least in some areas, exposed to economic competition, for example between various nation states. However, the predicted outcomes of this institutional change would often not be very desirable, if a competitive process for economic advantages is always assumed. Additionally, complexity is often too high to indicate either one or the other alternative as being clearly superior (and superior for whom?). The competitive pressure, when looking at institutions closer to business actions, is probably higher and the role of competition therefore more central.

This may at least partly explain the greater emphasis on volition in Bromley's account. North comes from a neoclassical and evolutionary background, where the will of the individual human being does not play an important role. In the neoclassical

---

[20] See Hotimsky, Cobb, and Bond (2006) for a classification according to selection mechanism.

world, human beings behave in a mechanistic way (Bromley, 2006a, p. 24). In an evolutionary world, human beings do not behave like machines, but their elbow room is considerably reduced due to the selective pressures they face (Alchian, 1950). However, there is no doubt that North recognises the considerable room for choice which remains. There are complex areas in the economy where cognitive differences will endlessly persist and, therefore, selection of the most "efficient" set of institutions will probably never take place (Denzau & North, 1994).

One gets the impression that North and Bromley understand the malleability of mental models or reasons differently. One gets the idea when reading North that mental models are, at least in the short run, rather static. Changing a model takes time. They are rooted in our culture (Denzau & North, 1994; North, 2005)[21]. It is more a process of a spontaneous order type, which cannot be influenced by the volitional individual. Reading Bromley, one thinks that many of the problems we face are new and, therefore, we need to adapt and change our models substantially. There is then, in his world, more scope for change in finding the appropriate reasons. Therefore, the difference might also be due to the different processes primarily focused on.

This paper does not want to argue that there are no fundamental differences between old and new institutional economics; otherwise the different authors would not try to distance themselves from each other. The same applies to a comparison between Bromley and North. There are differences in their assumptions on how human beings behave. But one could imagine a continuum of all the various assumptions, and neither author would place himself at one or the other extreme. Assumptions are, at least in this field of social science, more a question of belief or faith: we find, for example, much evidence of selfish behaviour, but also of altruistic behaviour (see e.g., Chapter 3 in Ostrom, 2005). The arguments regarding assumptions are therefore as old as the social sciences, and a definite answer to them will never be found.

What is very similar indeed in the two understandings compared here is the central role they put on cognition for understanding processes of institutional change. For the one this is called mental models, for the other "sufficient reason". Both imply that in order to understand institutional change and the processes which lead to it, we need to understand the reasoning (others would call this discourses) of people. Therefore, one should not be dogmatic and argue about the differences, but rather step ahead, join interests, and try to better understand the cognitive processes of human beings. Institutional economists might then learn jointly from other sciences.

---

[21] O'Neill (2004) sees an incompatibility between evolutionary approaches based on Hayek, who does not believe in humankind's ability to steer development, and ecological economics, which traditionally has a strong faith in the possibility of volitional human beings guiding economic processes. Lenger (2005) sees no fundamental incompatibilities, but rather suggests mutual fertilization.

To demonstrate the central similarity of the two approaches in their understanding of cognition, here a quote from North, which could likewise have been written by Bromley:

A bare-bones description of the process of economic change is straightforward. The "reality" of a political-economic system is never known to anyone, but humans do construct elaborate beliefs about the nature of that "reality" – beliefs that are both a positive model of the way the system works and a normative model of how it should work. The belief system may be broadly held within the society, reflecting a consensus of beliefs; or widely disparate beliefs may be held, reflecting fundamental divisions in perception about the society. The dominant beliefs-those of political and economic entrepreneurs in a position to make polices-over time result in the accretion of an elaborate structure of institutions that determine economic and political performance. (North, 2005, p. 2).

If there is a consensus on the central role of cognition for understanding institutional change, then this has clear methodological consequences, which are the same for the two approaches. We cannot black-box the individual anymore; we need to understand her reasoning, we need to understand the mental models she employs. For getting at those mental models, we need qualitative data. We need to understand how actors involved frame phenomena relevant for institutional change. These methodological questions are of particular importance, if we want to apply both of those theories to empirical situations. Therefore, a possible empirical approach is laid out in the following section.

15. 5 Methodological Implications: Investigating Mental Models and Sufficient Reason

If we take the above seriously, that cognition plays an important part in understanding institutional change in the field of the environment, we must get at the mental models used by people to give sufficient reasons for their planned actions. According to Holland (2002, p. 18), Loasby (2002, p. 8) or Knight (2000, p. 21), using an experimental setting for analysing cognition and institutional change has not been getting us far, because a context-free environment will not lead to an appropriate understanding of institutional change. There is certainly no scope for any methodological fundamentalism, because reality is often so complex that it is wise to also observe the situation from the opposite angle: a relatively simple experimental setting in the lab can give us further insights into human rationality (Ostrom, 1998, 2005). A similar argument as between "cognition in the wild" (Hutchins, 1995) and cognition in an experiment could be made in relation to the qualitative/open versus the quantitative/standardised divide. In an explorative phase of research, where the emphasis is on understanding the relevant mental models existing, certainly a qualitative approach would need to dominate (see below). In other phases of research, where the emphasis is on determining what is the "shared" (Denzau & North, 1994), and therefore most relevant, mental model for institutional change, a more standardised approach is adequate. The argument here would be in favour of a methodological pluralism (Poteete & Ostrom, 2004, 2005; Hotimsky et al., 2006). However, here I make an argument in favour of a qualitative approach, as in (agricultural) economics this approach has been long neglected.

Knight (2000, p. 21), referring to Hutchins (1995), believes it necessary to investigate "cognition in the wild" in order to understand the cognitive process which leads to institutional change. We need sufficient contextual information and "thick description" (Geertz, 1987), as can only be delivered by case studies (Hiedanpää & Bromley, 2002). We need the reasoning of individuals and groups, as can be delivered by "open" (Lamnek, 1995) interviews and participatory observation. Adger et al. (2003) make this argument for ecological economics, stating the need for "'thick' analysis" to understand environmental decision making.

For understanding the mental models/reasons of people who are making an institutional choice, and thereby promoting institutional change, we need to have qualitative data, the discourses of people: how they argue in favour of one or the other institutional proposition. In-depth analysis of the verbal statements of individual actors will help us to understand the mental models and reasons that then lead to institutional choices being made. Which type of data analysis technique we use, for example, content analysis or grounded theory, depends on the particular question we are focusing on. Obvious is that we need to consider qualitative data, which is not very common either in ecological or in institutional economics.

Bromley argues that it is a process of discussion, a gathering of sufficient reason for a proposed change, making clear that we are dealing with a group process, and the analysis of an individual discourse is not enough. Also with North, it is not the mental model, but the shared mental model that ultimately drives institutional change. Above it was argued that both approaches do not fully explain how we pass from the individual mental model or reason to the shared mental model or the sufficient reason, which finally attains conviction about the necessity of a change. However, on methodological grounds, it would be participatory observation which allows us to observe how a joint understanding of a particular choice situation is formed, how the individual mental models are influenced by each other. So, the method of choice for understanding cognition in a process of institutional change would actually be the case study approach.

In the following, I use some qualitative data from a project which I am part of that analyses institutional change in the forestry sector[22]. It is not about political change; rather, we analyse contractual and organisational changes on the local level. With the help of new contracts or new forms of organisation, property rights

---

[22] Over a period of a year and a half, 46 schedule-based interviews were conducted with the various actors involved in a region of Germany (Allgäu) and participant observation was undertaken. The data was transcribed and analysed with the help of MaxQDA, a qualitative data analysis software. For more information see: www.zufo.de.

are distributed differently. One can imagine that such processes of redistribution are of great significance for the way in which the resource is managed and, therefore, the subject is germane to ecological economics. Examples of these changes are contracts for standing timber instead of harvesting through the owners, or the question of who gets the right to determine when and how much is actually harvested. All involved parties (saw mills, forest owners, forest associations) have realised that a change seems to be needed and, therefore, have an interest in this change. For the purpose here, where I just want to show what it would mean to analyse mental models and the reasoning of actors involved in a process of institutional change, the details of the process and the arguments are not important, offering only some snapshots about the process. Important to remember is that these actors are promoting and determining the institutional change currently under way through the mental models and reasons described below.

I underline the role of mental models or sufficient reason with the help of two sets of quotes, the first of which shows what a singular mental model would be and what it means to observe such mental models "in the wild". The second set of quotes, where I present two lines of argument, shows how a bundle of mental models provides sufficient reason for arguing in favour of the one or the other institutional choice. The first argument is in favour of a contractual choice, which leaves all responsibilities and work with the forest owner, even if from an efficiency point of view a contracting of service providers would be more reasonable. The second argument supports the choosing of a new contracting partner. It is against new service providers which are associated with the big saw mill industry.

The following, first, set of quotes show a few "competing" mental models in relation to the question of whether small saw mills, and therewith their contractual arrangements, should still be supported or not. Only if we consider these mental models will we be able to understand why a particular institutional choice is taken. Many forest owners, as the first quote below indicates, say that they would sacrifice a few of Euros without difficulty, in order to secure the survival of the small and medium-sized saw mills. They speak like volitional, wilful beings (Bromley, 2006a). Supporting regional development and small businesses, which create employment in the region, is a prominent discourse. Others (2, 3) seem to argue in favour of the survival of the small and medium-sized saw mills because it secures a condition of long-term competition instead of a cartel, demonstrating the use of "warranted beliefs" (Bromley, 2006a)[23]. The cognitive models of quotes two and three resemble a type of rudimentary economic theory of competition[24]. A managing director of a forest association (4) has a neoclassical understanding of the

---

[23] The role of warranted beliefs can also be perceived when looking at another module within the project referred to in this paper. Its aim is to give advice towards improving the actors' network-building process. Views from scientific community representatives are used to back up and underline the opinions formed in the module.

[24] One could distinguish even further: quote two represents a structure-based understanding of competition, found in old theories of competition, whereas quote three seems to have a more modern and dynamic understanding of it.

process. If the price is lower, then it will obviously be selected – the invisible hand will do its job. The last two forest owners have a view similar to spontaneous order/evolutionary approaches. The first combines it with a value judgment, saying he dislikes this selection process, while the second sees it as a natural process.

1. *Forest Owner:* No, to me that's not worth it, because I agree with the traditional way of doing things. I think that it's more reasonable to have several of them, some smaller and medium-sized ones – they don't have to be really small – but I like the medium-sized and small ones better. I could do without a few Euros so that these people could continue to exist.
2. *Forest Association Manager:* All in all, it's not a bad thing when the structures can be kept the way they are, that we keep small, medium and large ones, and not just large ones that eventually destroy all the small ones. That's always the problem. The resulting competitive situation is probably what has been responsible for the price increase.
3. *Forest regulator:* Naturally, it's definitely going to lead to an acceleration of the dying out of medium-sized saw mills, this is clear – it's certainly tough competition. But I mean, then that's the way it is, just like it is elsewhere too. There are some big ones, a few niche providers, a couple of family businesses and the rest. The rest is gone now and so this development is going to proceed faster than it would have before. Altogether though, it's clearly keeping the timber demand in this area alive. But how long this is going to last, and to what extent price arrangements and contacts might eventually lead to some kind of oligopsony, remains to be seen. But it's not going to be easy [for the firms to maintain the oligopsony], because such a plant is there to treat timber, not to not treat timber, so I'm therefore rather confident.
4. *Forest Association Manager:* This is bad. I believe that we want the small ones to stay, but we don't have the timber[25], so when the market price is 80 Euros, I can't just tell the one sawyer that, because of his significantly higher break-even point, he can get it from me for 70 Euros – that just doesn't work. Either he comes through, because he's found some kind of niche, or he's gone. ... Because the local carpenter, who always bought the wood from him, he says to the sawyer that he needs to offer his goods for a good price too, so he needs the wood as cheap as possible, it doesn't matter how well they know each other when the wood is more expensive. And the consumer doesn't care, he just wants it cheap.
5. *Forest Owner:* That's how, in principle, the whole economic system works. Whether it's the sawyers or the farmers, it's the same principle. Always more of the bigger ones and the smaller ones disappear, whether that's in agriculture or, like we used to say, "Aunt Emily's Shop" – they aren't around anymore. The big discounters built on the green field, and yeah, that's how it is with the sawyers too. Actually, I don't agree with this principle. Neither in agriculture,

---

[25] A member of the forest association is not obliged to sell her timber to the association. She can also look for better opportunities.

nor with the discounters, nor with the saw mills, because so much is being realised in one concentrated area, and the machines are so optimised that more and
more jobs are disappearing. And with the high unemployment rate, it would actually be much more logical to have better smaller ones with more jobs, instead
of a lot of unemployed workers.

6. *Forest Owner:* No, because that's the way it always is. It was already like that
50 years ago. I know, because my father was also affected by it, he was a
miller. There used to be a mill in every village, but it's not like that anymore –
we can't even imagine it. I think that the small sawmill – the kind you think of
in the country, to which the farmer directly brings his logs – it just can't work
economically. I also think that there's only one market, maybe even one world
market. And timber is simply a commodity. It's clear to me, that it has to be industrialised and profoundly automated. And there's absolutely no reason to
make this [seem like] a bad thing.

The excerpted quotes from above can certainly not be understood as providing
"sufficient reason" for one or the other institutional solution. They are rather
fragments of larger arguments, which would need to be joined together in order to
see the whole chain of arguments that finally result in sufficient reasons. They are
rather various (competing) mental models which argue either in favour of or
against a certain choice, for example: choosing small saw mills as contractors will
secure competition, which in the long run will favour the position of forest owners.

The second set of quotes below links a chain of mental models, providing a
first idea of what could be a sufficient reason for an institutional choice. Obviously providing "sufficient reason" needs a long thread of arguments, which
would make a paper in its own right[26]. Therefore, I just want to present two short
chains of arguments which indicate what type of analysis would be needed for understanding the process of change. The first example is a narrative of a forest
owner, who explains why he sticks with the old form of contract he has with his
forest association, under which he is now doing all the work in the forest on his
own or better said with his sons, even if from a transaction cost or efficiency perspective there is no doubt that a more integrated form of contract would be a lot
more advisable.

> *Forest Owner:* Yes, I know that [a kind of service contract] exists, but I've never
> considered it. It might be because I find this relatively small forest still kind of nice.
> Where you can sort of saw a bit of wood here and there, and take out your firewood.
> Only doing a really little bit, on a really small scale. We have a wetland in the
> middle, with a picturesque little creek that flows through there – we made more of a
> clearing in that area. So, what was it that I wanted to say – it has a really small
> recreational value and, perhaps when I go with my boys out into the forest, a
> somewhat larger pedagogical value. I've been doing that since they were little, we
> get wood in the summer when it's warm, for the winter when it's cold. Yeah, that
> kind of provisional thinking, I think you can really learn that in the forest. First you

---

[26] The entire study hopes to provide such an account (see Koch, 2008).

get the wood, then pile it up, then it has to be sawn down again, and finally it's piled up again. All in all it's a huge undertaking, but then we'll burn it here, and we'll be burning the wood that the kids have already had in their hands three times.

Looking at other literature on the motivations of small-scale forest owners, the above argument is certainly a typical line of reasoning (Madsen, 2003; Ziegenspeck, Härdter, & Schraml, 2004). However, it clearly shows that his decision to use a certain type of contract to service his forest is certainly not understandable on the basis of a narrowly economic rationale, calculating costs and benefits (or only if we declare everything as costs and benefits, which then renders the concept meaningless; see Holland, 2002, p. 20; Paavola, 2002). We need to understand the reasoning, the line of argument behind his decision. Harvesting or not harvesting the forest himself is much more than an economic decision – it is "pedagogical" one. In other words, it is about transferring cultural values to his sons, living in a certain relation to nature, and getting prepared in the summer for the cold winter days.

He then explains why he still continues to harvest the forest with his sons:

It also has something to do with the fact that I was actually in this forest with my father, I was as old as my kids are now, and I had to help him out. I remember too, that sometimes I didn't really feel like having to help anymore. And, after I got a little older, then it was ok again. And so now I experience this in the second generation from yet another perspective, and for me that's also one reason why I have it [the forest] at all.

Here the reasoning becomes even more complex. He seems to derive some utility from the fact that he can now see his sons, similar as his father once saw him, not enjoying having to accompany him to the forest. Policy instruments which wrongly assume a rational actor might never be able to realise their theoretically predicted power (Frey & Schneider, 1997). Therefore, such a statement also shows how important it is to know the cognitive models of the actors when designing policy.

Another excerpt below shows the reasoning of a forest association manager. If one would not consider his strategic interest in this line of argument, one could certainly see the sufficient reason for blocking this institutional change that he describes from the perspective of a forest owner or an environmentalist. From the perspective of many forest owners he makes a convincing argument, drawing on deeply rooted mental models about sustainability: the concept emerged in forestry, that sustainable forestry and a capitalist firm with only monetary interests are two incompatible antipodes. The excerpted text is about the role of his competitors in the field of forest services. His competitors are in most cases owned by the saw mill industry and have a strategic interest in changing the rules of timber harvesting, allowing them to better integrate forestry into their timber supply chain. This forest association manager is rather eloquent and his reasoning, his mental models, have a considerable influence on the emergence of shared mental models, as he proliferates his ideas in an endless series of forest association meetings and seminars for forest owners. His line of argument can be traced back, when analysing interviews or participant observation of forest owners.

> *Forest Association Manager:* Klenk [a big saw mill] has the TTW [a forest service provider owned by Klenk], he bought the forest operation – so far the forest operation has been part of the forestry sector, which means that the plans we're making consist of sustainable forestry, forest planning, and reasonable planning within the frame of what we've learned and what we understand. And now we have a paradigm shift. The TTW's assignment is to supply the Klenk lumberyard in the short term. He goes out and it doesn't interest him how the forest is or sustainability, he says supply, away with the trees. [...] PEFC [a certification scheme within forestry], they don't interest the TTW. ... There isn't any sort of optimalisation taking place, because they only remove as much as they need, but that doesn't mean that they're optimalising. ... They do not maximise the value added for the forest owner, that's rather bad. [...] He just [Klenk] goes out to cut down trees and sells them. Forest owners phone me up and say that they have a badger in the garage, a fox is digging around in my yard, there's a problem with one of my roads, I have a beetle, there's a caterpillar nibbling at my place, can you come over on the weekend? Klenk and TTW don't do that. That means that we take care of our forest owners, every boo-boo they have – he doesn't. And it simply isn't fair when someone says that you have to compete with each other on the economic market, but then please apples with apples and apples and pears. Then I'll just drop everything overnight, only do Hot-Logging, log, get rid of the wood, then I can do that too.

Normative statements/valued beliefs obviously play a large role in determining which institutional form is most preferred. However, these normative statements are strengthened by positive reasoning, a warranted belief, here about sustainable forestry. It shows how the positive and the normative part of mental models, as distinguished by North, is rather a matter of degree and, ultimately, a clear-cut distinction between the two parts is impossible. The two components are intertwined, together providing sufficient reason for change or not: in this case a rationale for keeping the old form of organisations with forest associations in comparison to saw-mill-owned completely private businesses.

15.6 Conclusions

The paper has shown on a theoretical basis that there is a need for ecological economics to integrate cognitive aspects, as they are increasingly being considered in institutional theory when analysing institutional change. There are some well known methodological and epistemological differences between the two main schools of institutional economics (old and new/ Bromley vs. North). However, the importance of cognition and the way it influences institutional change seems very similar for both. They seem complementary and do not imply an either/or decision. A special emphasis on one or the other might depend on the particular issue examined (emphasis on the market vs. environment-oriented processes).

If we just focus on cognitive processes (mental models and sufficient reasons) and not on a broader comparison, we realise that they are very similar indeed. Particularly if we ask what their theoretical insights signify for empirical investigation. For understanding the importance of mental models and sufficient reasons for institutional change, we need qualitative data, particularly narratives and discourses of actors involved in the process of change. The empirical snapshots provided in this paper have only given selected insights into peoples' modes of reasoning, showing the importance of those discourses for getting at the mental models and sufficient reasons of the actors. Similar to the theories themselves, such snapshots do not provide us with an explanation of the selection of one or the other mental model. If we ever – and here we again meet one of the differences between the approaches – find such a generally satisfying explanation, it might also be seen differently by the old and the new institutionalists: the latter being more in search of such a general theory and the former being more sceptical that such a general and relatively context-independent theory could exist [27]. Therefore, the reactions to the "stories" told here might be different. On the one hand, one can argue that the only thing we can learn from this account is that reasons matter, but nothing more. On the other hand, one can argue that this is one necessary way forward: generating more "thickness" of this kind, will finally lead to a more general and, therefore, theoretical understanding of those processes.

Acknowledgments

A special thanks to Konrad Hagedorn, who gave me the opportunity many years ago to start thinking about the problems described above. Thanks also to Daniel Bromley, who put a lot of academic enthusiasm into discussing an earlier draft of the paper with me. I am sure he will still not agree with some of my arguments; sorry about this, but I tried to do him justice. Thanks also to Alicia Woynowski, Chantal Ruppert, Markus Koch, Michael Schwarz and Sharif Ahmadiar, who helped to improve the paper, which draws on data collected by my colleague Markus Koch within our joint ZUFO Project (Future markets of the forest timber chain: www.zufo.de). This project is financed by the German Ministry of Research and Development and takes part in the project panel "Nachhaltige Waldwirtschaft" (www.nachhaltige-waldwirtschaft.de). This support is gratefully acknowledged. We also thank the interview partners who gave us their valuable time.

---

[27] See Vanberg (1994, p. 30), who, from an evolutionary perspective, also doubts that a general theory could ever be developed, considering that such choices are influenced by all kinds of theories and beliefs, which are then put into rules/institutions with the help of human creativity.

References

Adger, N. W., Brown, K., Fairbrass, J., Jordan, A., Paavola, J., Rosendo, S., et al. (2003). Governance for sustainability: Towards a 'thick' analysis of environmental decisionmaking. *Environmental Planning A, 35*, 1095–1110.

Alchian, A. A. (1950). Uncertainty, evolution and economic theory. *Journal of Political Economy, 58*, 211–221.

Beckenbach, F. (2001). *Beschränkte Rationalität und Systemkomplexität*. Marburg: Metropolis.

Berkes, F., & Folke, C. (1994). Investing in cultural capital for sustainable use of natural capital. In A. Jansson, M. Hammer, C. Folke, & R. Constanza (Eds.), *Investing in natural capital* (pp. 128–149). Washington: Island Press.

Bleischwitz, R. (2003). Cognitive and institutional perspectives of eco-efficiency. *Ecological Economics, 46*, 453–467.

Bowles, S. (1998). Endogenous preferences: The cultural consequences of markets on other economic institutions. *Journal of Economic Literature, 36*, 75–111.

Bromley, D. W. (1989). *Economic interests and institutions: The conceptual foundations of public policy*. Oxford: Basil Blackwell.

Bromley, D. W. (1991). *Environment and economy: Property rights and public policy*. Oxford: Blackwell.

Bromley, D. W. (1992). The commons, property, and common-property regimes. In D. W. Bromley (Ed.), *Making the commons work* (pp. 3–16). San Fransisco: ICS Press.

Bromley, D. W. (1996). The social construction of land. In K. Hagedorn (Ed.), *Institutioneller Wandel und Politische Ökonomie von Landwirtschaft und Agrarpolitik. Festschrift zum 65. Geburtstag von Günther Schmitt* (pp. 21–46). Frankfurt: Campus.

Bromley, D. W. (2001). Searching for sustainability: The poverty of spontaneous order. In C. J. Cleveland, D. I. Stern, & R. Constanza (Eds.), *The economic of nature and the nature of economics* (pp. 74–88). Cheltenham and Northampton: Edward Elgar.

Bromley, D. W. (2006a). *Sufficient reason: Volitional pragmatism and the meaning of economic institutions*. Princeton: University Press.

Bromley, D. W. (2006b, – Mai). *Towards an Ordnungstheorie: Volitional pragmatism and economic institutions*. Paper presented in the economic policy seminars of Albert-Ludwigs-University, Freiburg.

Common, M., & Stagl, S. (2005). *Ecological economics: An introduction*. Cambridge: University Press.

Constanza, R. (1991). *Ecological economics*. New York: Columbia University Press.

Dedeurwaerdere, T. (2005). From bioprospecting to reflexive governance. *Ecological Economics, 53*, 473–491.

Denzau, A. T., & North, D. C. (1994). Shared mental models, ideologies and institutions. *Kyklos, 47*, 1–31.

Dequech, D. (2006). The new institutional economics and the theory of behaviour under uncertainty. *Journal of Economic Behaviour & Organization, 59*, 109–131.

Frey, B. (1997). *Markt und Motivation: Wie ökonomische Anreize die (Arbeits-)Moral verdrängen*. München: Vahlen.

Frey, B., & Schneider, F. (1997). Warum wird die Umweltökonomik kaum angewendet? *Zeitschrift für Umweltpolitik und Umweltrecht, 2*, 153–170.

Geertz, C. (1987). *Dichte Beschreibung; Beiträge zum Verstehen kultureller Systeme*. Frankfurt: Suhrkamp.

Glaser, B., & Strauss, A. (1967). *The discovery of grounded theory: Strategies for qualitative research*. New York: Aldine de Gruyter.

Hagedorn, K. (1992). Das Leitbild des bäuerlichen Familienbetriebes in der Agrarpolitik der 1970er und 1980er Jahre. *Zeitschrift für Agrargeschichte und Agrarsoziologie, 40*, 53–86.

Hagedorn, K. (1996). *Das Institutionenproblem in der agrarökonomischen Politikforschung.* Tübingen: Mohr (Siebeck).

Handlbauer, G. (2000). Decision-making and institutionalised cognition. In M. Streit, U. Mummert, & D. Kiwit (Eds.), *Cognition, rationality and institutions* (pp. 161–180). Berlin: Springer.

Hiedanpää, J., & Bromley, D. W. (2002). Environmental policy as a process of reasonable valuing. In D. Bromley & J. Paavola (Eds.), *Economics, ethics, and environmental policy* (pp. 69–83). Oxford: Blackwell.

Hodgson, G. M. (1993a). *Economics and evolution.* Cambridge: Polity Press.

Hodgson, G. M. (1993b). Institutional economics: Surveying the 'old' and the 'new'. *Metroeconomica, 44*, 1–28.

Hodgson, G. M. (1998). The approach of institutional economics. *Journal of Economic Literature, 36*, 166–192.

Hodgson, G. M. (2007). Evolutionary and institutional economics as the new mainstream? *Evolutionary and Institutional Economics Review, 4*, 7–25.

Holland, J. H. (1996). The rationality of adaptive agents. In K. J. Arrow (Ed.), *The rational foundations of economic behaviour* (pp. 281–297). New York: St Martin's Press.

Holland, A. (2002). Are choices tradeoffs. In D. W. Bromley & J. Paavola (Eds.), *Economics, ethics, and environmental policy* (pp. 18–34). Oxford: Blackwell.

Holland, J. H., Holyoak, K. J., Nisbett, R. E., & Thagard, P. R. (1986). *Induction: Processes of inference, learning, and discovery.* Cambridge: MIT Press.

Hotimsky, S., Cobb, R., & Bond, A. (2006). Contracts or scripts? A critical review of the application of institutional theories to the study of environmental change. *Ecology and Society, 11*, 41.

Hutchins, E. (1995). *Cognition in the wild.* Cambridge: Cambridge University Press.

Johnson, C. (2004). Uncommon ground: The 'poverty of history' in common property discourse. *Development & Change, 35*, 407–433.

Kant, S., & Berry, A. R. (2005). Sustainability, institutions, and forest management. In S. Kant & A. R. Berry (Eds.), *Institutions, sustainability, and natural resources: Institutions for sustainable forest management* (pp. 1–20). Doordrecht: Springer.

Knight, J. (2000). Suboptimality and social institutions: The relationship between cognition and context. In M. Streit, U. Mummert, & D. Kiwit (Eds.), *Cognition, rationality and institutions* (pp. 11–26). Berlin: Springer.

Knight, J., & North, D. (1997). Explaining economic change: The interplay between cognition and institutions. *Legal Theory, 3*, 211–226.

Koch, M. (2008). Institutioneller Wandel in der Forstwirtschaft: Zur Bedeutung von mentalen Modellen, Vertrauen und Verhandlungsmacht – dargestellt am Fallbeispiel Allgäuer Kleinprivatwald. Dissertation der Fakultät für Forst- und Umweltwissenschaften, Freiburg.

Lakatos, I. (1982). *The methodology of scientific research programmes: Philosophical Papers.* Cambridge: Cambridge University Press.

Lamnek, S. (1995). *Qualitative Sozialforschung: Methodologie.* Weinheim: Psychologie Verlags Union.

Lenger, A. (2005). *Institutions, culture and history in environmental economics.* Freiburg: Albert-Ludwigs-Universität, Abteilung für Wirtschaftspolitik.

Lindenberg, S. (1985). Rational choice and sociological theory: New pressures on cconomics as a social science. *JITE, 141*, 244–255.

Loasby, B. J. (2002). Evolution and institutions: A cognitive perspective. *East-West Journal of Economics and Business, 5*, 27–45.

Madsen, L. M. (2003). New woodlands in Denmark: The role of private landowners. *Urban-Forestry-and-Urban-Greening, 1*, 185–195.

North, D. C. (1988). *Theorie des institutionellen Wandels*. Tübingen: J C B Mohr (Paul Siebeck).

North, D. C. (1990). *Institutions, institutional change and economic performance*. Cambridge: Cambridge University Press.

North, D. C. (1992). *Theorie des institutionellen Wandels*. Tübingen: J C B Mohr (Paul Siebeck).

North, D. C. (1994). Economic performance through time. *American Economic Review, 84*, 359–368.

North, D. C. (2005). *Understanding the process of economic change*. Princeton: Princeton University Press.

O'Neill, J. (2004). Ecological economics and the politics of knowledge: The debate between Hayek and Neurath. *Cambridge Journal of Economics, 28*, 431–447.

Ostrom, E. (1998). A behavioral approach to the rational choice theory of collective action: Presidential address, American Political Science Association. *The American Political Science Review, 92*, 1–22.

Ostrom, E. (2005). *Understanding institutional diversity*. Princeton: Princeton University Press.

Paavola, J. (2002). Rethinking the choice and performance of environmental policies. In D. W. Bromley & J. Paavola (Eds.), *Economics, ethics, and environmental policy* (pp. 88–102). Oxford: Blackwell.

Paavola, J., & Adger, W. N. (2005). Institutional ecological economics. *Ecological economics, 53*, 353–368.

Poteete, A. R., & Ostrom, E. (2004). Conceptual consistency and data comparability: Methodological challenges to empirical research on collective action. Paper prepared for the 100th Annual Meeting of the American Political Science Association, 2–5 September 2004, Chicago.

Poteete, A. R., & Ostrom, E. (2005). *Bridging the qualitative-quantitative divide: Strategies for building large-N databases based on qualitative research*. Paper prepared for the 101st Annual Meeting of the American Political Science Association, 1–4 September, Washington D.C.

Reichertz, J. (2003). *Die Abduktion in der qualitativen Sozialforschung*. Opladen: Leske & Buderich.

Samuelson, P. A., & Nordhaus, W. D. (1998). *Economics*. Boston: McGraw-Hill.

Schlüter, A. (2001). *Institutioneller Wandel und Transformation*. Institutioneller Wandel der Landwirtschaft und Ressourcennutzung, Bd. 4. Aachen: Shaker.

Schlüter, A. (2007). Institutional change in the forestry sector: The explanatory potential of new institutional economics. *Forest Policy and Economics, 9*, 1090–1099.

Schlüter, A., & Phillimore, P. (2005). Rationalising risk: arguing over safety on the Firth of Forth. *Focaal – European Journal of Anthropology, 46*, 79–90.

Searle, J. R. (2005). What is an institution? *Journal of Institutional Economics, 1*, 1–22.

Siebenhühner, B. (2001). *Homo sustinens*. Marburg: Metropolis.

Söderbaum, P. (1999). Values, ideology and politics in ecological economics. *Ecological economics, 28*, 161–170.

Spash, C. L. (1995). The political economy of nature. *Review of Poltical Economy, 7*, 279–293.

Vanberg, V. J. (1994). *Rules and choice in economics*. London: Routledge.

Vatn, A. (2002). Efficient or fair: Ethical paradoxes in environmental policy. In D. W. Bromley & J. Paavola (Eds.), *Economics, ethics, and environmental policy* (pp. 148–163). Oxford: Blackwell.

Vatn, A. (2005a). *Institutions and the environment*. Cheltenham: Edward Elgar.

Vatn, A. (2005b). Valuing forest ecosystems and institutional perspective. In S. Kant & A. R. Berry (Eds.), *Institutions, sustainability, and natural resources: Institutions for sustainable forest management* (pp. 115–134). Doordrecht: Springer.

Wilson, J. (2002). Scientific uncertainty, complex systems, and the design of common-pool institutions. In N. R. Council (Ed.), *The drama of the commons* (pp. 327–360). Washington: National Academic Press.

Ziegenspeck, S., Härdter, U., & Schraml, U. (2004). Lifestyles of private forest owners as an indication of social change. *Forest Policy and Economics, 6,* 447–458.

16 Analysing Institutions: What Method to Apply?

Volker Beckmann and Martina Padmanabhan

Division of Resource Economics, Institute of Agricultural Economics and Social Sciences, Faculty of Agriculture and Horticulture, Humboldt-Universität zu Berlin, Philippstr. 13, 10099 Berlin, Germany, E-mail: v.beckmann@agrar.hu-berlin.de, martina.padmanabhan@agrar.hu-berlin.de

Abstract. This paper seeks to contribute to the ongoing debate about methods of institutional analysis. How to empirically analyse institutions and institutional change? Is there a superior method when it comes to institutional questions? We discuss these issues for the most common methods in empirical institutional analysis, i.e. case studies, econometrics, experiments and agent-based modelling. Building on Alston (1996), with reference to Williamson's (2000) overview of institutional economics, we identify level of social analysis and research questions as two important dimensions that may guide methodological decision. Distinguishing between effects, causes and processes of institutional choice and change as the basic research questions in institutional analysis, and combining these with the four levels of social analysis (i.e., social embeddedness, institutional environment, governance structures, and resource allocation) helps to precisely distinguish between differently oriented investigations within a common theme. In addition, we discuss how the time horizon of a study, the observability and measurability of the institutions examined, and the roles that actors play therein significantly constrain possible choice sets among methods. In doing so, we identify trade-offs as well as important complementarities between applying different methods.

Keywords: Agent-based modelling, Case studies, Econometrics, Experiments, Methods, New institutional economics

16.1 Introduction

New institutional economics (NIE) has progressed significantly in the last three decades (Ménard & Shirley, 2005; Brousseau & Glachant, 2008). Based on a small number of powerful assumptions and key concepts – including incomplete and asymmetric information; bounded rationality and opportunism; methodological

V. Beckmann, M. Padmanabhan (eds.), *Institutions and Sustainability*, DOI 10.1007/978-1-4020-9690-7_16, © Springer Science+Business Media B.V. 2009

individualism; transaction costs; and institutions as "the rules of the game" – a great number of theories have been developed. Principal-agent theory, for instance, originating with papers by Ross (1973) and Stiglitz (1974), has grown over the years into a comprehensive theory of incentives (Laffont & Martimort, 2002). Transaction cost economics, pioneered by Coase (1937) and Williamson (1975), although still not fully formalised today, has spread the concept of transaction costs into many areas of social sciences (Dixt, 1996; Rao, 2003). Similar developments can be mentioned concerning other branches of NIE, such as property rights theory, contract theory, collective action theory or the new political economy. Theories of NIE are increasingly being applied in environmental and resource economics or ecological economics, leading to significant extensions and theoretical refinements, with the goal of capturing the complexity of human – nature interactions (Ostrom, 1990; Bromley, 1991; Challen, 2000; Hagedorn, 2002; Young, 2002; Ostrom, 2005b; Vatn, 2005; Hagedorn, 2008).

Theoretical developments within NIE have always been accompanied by a wealth of empirical research to develop, test or redefine theoretical propositions. For many years, case studies and econometric analysis have been the main tools for empirical research. In the last decade, however, other tools, such as experimental economics and agent-based models, have come to play an increasingly important role, thus prompting increasingly intense reflection on methodology within NIE. Whereas Alston (1996) only discussed the advantages and disadvantages of case studies and econometric analysis for investigating processes of institutional change, Menard (2001) already included the option of using experimental economics. Then Schmid (2004) treated methods in institutional economics as experiments, followed by case studies, econometrics and finally simulation models. In the recent "guidebook" to NIE (Brousseau & Glachant, 2008), Alston (2008) argues for the use of case studies in NIE, Sykuta (2008) considers the use of econometrics in contracting and organisation research and Robin and Staropoli (2008) reflect on the importance of experimental economics.

This paper seeks to contribute to the ongoing debate about methods of institutional analysis. How to empirically analyse institutions and institutional change? Is there a superior method when it comes to institutional questions? Our paper builds on the discussion of Alston (1996), with reference to Williamson's (2000) overview of institutional economics. We argue that, in the selection of methods for institutional analysis, level of analysis, research questions, time horizons, measurability and observability of institutions and the roles played by actors are, or should be, central concerns.

The paper is organised as follows. Firstly, we will briefly characterise the main tools used in empirical institutional analysis by introducing case studies, econometrics, experiments and agent-based modelling as the four key methods of contemporary NIE. These techniques are partly substitutes for each other, but can also be largely complementary in analysing complex issues in a social system. However, researchers need to make decisions about what methods should be applied to reach specific research goals. In order to guide such decision processes, we argue that a number of issues matter, identifying in Section 3 *level of social analysis* and *research questions* as two basic dimensions guiding method choice. Indeed, we observe regularities between methods selected, levels of analysis chosen and the kinds of research questions posed. In order to explore these regularities further, in Section 4 we discuss additional dimensions to be taken into account when making methodological decisions: time horizon, observability and measurability of institutions examined, and the roles that actors play in particular action arenas. In doing so, we identify certain limitations characteristic of the currently employed methods. In the last section, we draw conclusions regarding method choice.

16.2 The Tool-Set of Empirical Institutional Economics

As already mentioned above, contemporary NIE make use of a great diversity of empirical methods to analyse the development and performance of institutions and to test and develop theories (see e.g., Schmid, 2004, pp. 138–162; Brousseau & Glachant, 2008, pp. 103–180), with the most prominent methods being (1) case study analysis, (2) econometric analysis, (3) experimental economics and (4) agent-based modelling. These four tools and their application within NIE are briefly described in the following sections.

16.2.1 Case study analysis

A case study primarily investigates a small number of units of interest – purposefully selected out of a population of possible units – in a largely qualitative manner (Yin, 2003; Gerring, 2007). Such units could be countries, firms, households, groups, individuals, transactions, resources, regions, political parties, but also events such as revolutions, disasters, crises or wars. Although the number of units may be small, each unit may contain a large number of subunits that can be investigated using quantitative methods (Seawright & Gerring, 2008). Case studies rely on observable or recorded data and are capable of investigating historical as well as contemporary units or events. Information may be gathered in a variety of ways, such as analysing documents, conducting interviews and surveys or through participant observation. The main tool for verifying acquired data is triangulation, i.e. the simultaneous use of different sources of information. The main advantage of case study research is often considered being thick description and identification of causal mechanisms; its main disadvantages being the lack of representativeness of its results and the limited ability to estimate causal effects (Gerring, 2004). However, case studies could be used at different stages of theory development, such as generating, illustrating or testing (George & Bennett, 2005), and can also be replicated for additional units.

Case studies are widely used in NIE, and many of the most seminal contributions therein rely on the investigation of single or few cases (Alston, 2008). Demsetz (1967), for example, illustrates his theory of property rights via the case of property rights over wildlife among the Native Americans of Labrador Peninsula. North and Thomas (1973) developed their theory of institutional change based on the history of Western Europe and, within that general unit, purposefully compared the histories of France, Spain, the Netherlands and England. Klein, Crawford and Alchian (1978) illustrate the implications of specific investments for contracting and vertical integration with the case of the acquisition of Fisher Body by General Motors in the 1920s. All of these authors employ case studies for illustration of a general theoretical argument. Other prominent case studies in institutional economics use them to rebut competing theories and to develop new ideas, with prominent examples being Coase (1974), whose case study on the British lighthouse system shows that it has been possible to provide "pure public goods" privately and rebuts the general theory of public goods that argues that pure public goods need to be provided by the government, and Ostrom (1990), who rebuts the "tragedy of the commons" argument (Hardin, 1968) through a detailed examination of cases of successful community common pool resource management in many countries around the world.

In this volume, Schlüter as well as Birner and Wittmer use case studies to illustrate more general theoretical arguments, whereas Korf uses a case study from Sri Lanka to rebut some theoretical claims. Meanwhile, Rozelle and Swinnen conduct a comparative historical case study for the East Asian and former Soviet transition countries, Mehl presents a single case from German social policy and Mwangi and Ostrom provide a case study of ecological resilience in the Massailand.

16.2.2 Econometric analysis

"Econometrics", according to Verbeek (2004, p.1) "is the interaction between economic theory, observed data and statistical methods". As such, econometrics usually relies on a large number of observations and quantitative measurements of dependent and independent variables, with the main goal being the investigation of relationships between particular quantities of interest. The number units under observation are most commonly a random sample for a larger population of units. Econometrics usually uses contemporary or historical data sets of observable or recorded data and, in many cases, relies on survey data. Data is analysed through application of statistical procedures, using different techniques according to the characteristics of the dependent variable(s), the distribution of the error term and the characteristics of the data set (e.g., cross-section, time-series or panel data) (Greene, 2003). The main strengths of econometrics are identification of causal effects, probabilistic testing of theoretical propositions and being able to regard results as representative of a larger set of homogeneous units. Its disadvantages include an almost exclusive reliance on quantitative information, inability to identify causal mechanisms and a need for large data sets.

Econometric analysis has become a standard tool in NIE, in particular for research on contracting and organisation (Masten & Saussier, 2002; Sykuta, 2008). Since organisational structures and contracts are mostly of a discrete type, contracting and organisational research employs discrete-choice models – such as binomial, multi-nominal, ordered logit or probit – which try to estimate the probability that a specific organisational form will be chosen (Sykuta, 2008). Numerous cross-sectional econometric studies have been conducted, for example, to test the discriminate alignment hypotheses of transaction cost economics (Williamson, 1975, 1985, 1996). The results, largely supportive of the theoretical predictions, have been frequently summarised in the literature (e.g., Shelanski & Klein, 1995; Klein, 2005; Macher & Richman, 2008). More recently, the availability of new data at the international level (Beck, Clarke, Groff, Keefer, & Walsh, 2001) has led to econometric investigation of links between institutions and economic growth, begun with the pioneering research of Knack and Keefer (1995), or between the institutional environment and the development of financial or labour markets (La Porta, Lopez de Silanes, Shleifer, & Vishny, 1998, Botero et al., 2004). A fast-growing literature using cross-country econometric analysis is providing significant evidence regarding the effects of the institutional environment on economic performance (Acemoglu, Johnson, & Robinson, 2001; Easterly & Levine, 2003; Rodrik, Subramanian, & Trebbi, 2004). Similar approaches have been adopted to examine the effects of institutions on environmental performance (Saleth & Dinar, 2004).

In this volume, Polman and Slangen use a trivariate probit model to estimate choice of contractual arrangements concerning land in the Netherlands.

16.2.3 Experimental economics

Experimental economics studies the interaction of human subjects within a context specified by the researcher. According to Smith (1994, p. 113), each experiment is characterised by an environment, institutions and observed behaviour. The environment consists mainly of the endowments of the actors and the payoff-structure. Institutions govern the possible exchange of information, possible actions and their consequences: in terms of, for example, what is allowed to become a binding contract. The observed behaviour of participants is, then, a function of the environment and the institutions that constitute the controlled variables. As such, experiments can study the impact of environments and institutions on human behaviour. Experiments are conducted in the laboratory as well as in the field, and they can be replicated anytime, anywhere. Their main advantage is that many influencing factors are under strict control of the researcher and stylises theories about human behaviour could be tested in a straightforward way. The highly stylised setting of laboratory experiments leads also to one of the most pronounced disadvantage, i.e. the limited transferability to real world setting. Field experiments try to bridge this gap (List, 2008).

Experimental economics mainly developed outside the core of NIE by analysing different modes of market exchange, focusing in particular on auction design (Smith, 1994). Experimental economics has been very much influenced by game theory, testing the predictions for different games, such as prisoners' dilemma games, coordination games, public goods games, ultimatum games, and dictator games. All of these games differ in terms of their environments and institutional settings, and the effect of institutional variation among them has been studied, such as public good experiments with and without the possibility of sanctioning (Fehr & Gächter, 2000). Since experiments often reveal significant differences between rational-choice predictions and observed behaviour, it has been found that games can also be used to measure social preferences or informal institutions. In this way, experiments can provide insights concerning different dimensions of culture (Henrich et al., 2005). Experiments have also been conducted, among many others, to study the performance of different kinds of labour contracts (Fehr, Kirchler, Weichbold, & Gächter, 1998; Fehr, Klein, & Schmidt, 2007), the choice of property rights (Fehr, Kremhelmer, & Schmidt, 2008), bargaining under different property rights settings (Croson & Johnston, 2000), different decision or voting rules (Guarnaschelli, McKelvey, & Palfrey, 2000), or anarchy and the emergence of the state (Duffy & Kim, 2005).

In this volume, Theesfeld reveals the negative reinforcement of trust through stylised games for the irrigation sector in Bulgaria, while Vatn discusses the role of framing effects and the use of experiments to shed light on different concepts of rationality.

16.2.4 Agent-based modelling

Agent-based modelling studies the interaction of artificial actors in artificial environments, using computer simulations (Epstein & Axtell, 1996; Epstein, 2006; Tesfatsion & Judd, 2006). Researchers create complete artificial worlds, which are regarded as evolving complex systems consisting of environments, rules and agents. Based on a bottom-up philosophy, aggregate properties are modelled as the outcome of micro-dynamics involving basic entities. In contrast to other modelling approaches, the heterogeneity of agents, information asymmetry, bounded rationality, and learning among agents is explicitly modelled. Additionally, the models are dynamic in the sense that agents form adaptive expectations, and the system as a whole is non-reversible and path-dependent. Interaction between agents is direct and endogenous, which means that although actors usually interact within their socio-economic neighbourhood, the pattern of interaction may change over time. The data produced is purely generated, but has the great advantage that the behaviour of agents, their computational capacities and modes of decision making are controlled by the researcher. The most important disadvantages are that the institutions modelled consist of rather simple rules and the models are often not well adjusted to any real-world empirical setting. Furthermore, agent-based models can only prove primary theoretical concepts, but are difficult to verify by empirical observations.

Agent-based modelling has been largely developed outside the core of NIE, with early contributions investigating the phenomenon of social segregation (Schelling, 1971) and norms of reciprocity in prisoner's dilemma games (Axelrod & Hamilton, 1981; Axelrod, 1984, 1986, 1997). Currently agent-based models are being applied in many areas, including the management of common pool resources (Janssen, Walker, Langridge, & Abel, 2000; Schlüter & Pahl-Wostl, 2007), the emergence of civil wars (Epstein, 2002), the emergence of religion (Dow, 2008), the development of language and money (Howitt & Clower, 2000), structural change in agriculture (Balmann, 1997; Berger, 2001) and complex human-ecological systems (Janssen & Ostrom, 2006).

Within this volume, none of the authors make use of agent-based models, although many topics and problems addressed here could inspire the design of a number of multi-agent models.

All of the methods briefly characterised above contribute to the empirical analysis of institutions and provide important insights. As such, they have to be regarded more as complementary rather than substitutes for each other[1]. However, all of these approaches have advantages and disadvantages which need to be judged in consideration of the type of research to be conducted. In the following, we develop the argument that choice of methods depends on a number of criteria: foremost, the level of social analysis and the questions that guide the research.

[1] Sometimes these methods are even difficult to distinguish from each other. Econometrics, which is characterised in this section as the quantitative analysis of large-N observed data, indeed could be used for analysing subunit observations within case studies, the results of experiments and even the results of different runs in simulation models. Econometrics is mainly a technique for data analysis. In fact, many econometric studies are actually often case studies from a philosophy of science point of view; moreover, experiments and agent-based models may also have the characteristic of case studies if they are conducted only once or a few times. Thus, it would be better to distinguish between small and large N, generated and observed data and quantitative and qualitative data analysis. For the purposes of this paper we, however, stick to the common distinction between case studies, econometrics, experiments and agent-based models.

16.3 Levels of Analysis and Research Questions in Institutional Economics

In order to structure our discussion on choice of methods in institutional economics, we start by introducing the four-level scheme for social analysis developed by Williamson (2000), which we further expand to aid our understanding of methodological considerations by combining it with the typical research questions suggested by Alston (1996) regarding effects, causes and processes of institutional choice and change.

16.3.1 Levels of social analysis

Williamson's four levels of social analysis scheme (2000, p. 597, see Fig. 16.1) distinguishes between the different objects of social analysis with regard to particular types of institutions, the considered time frames for analysis of change, normative criteria concerning what needs to be economised and suggested theories for the analysis of institutions at each level.

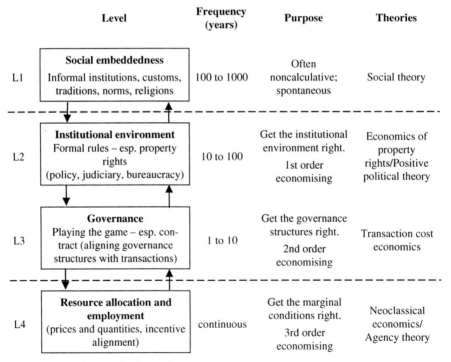

	Level	Frequency (years)	Purpose	Theories
L1	**Social embeddedness** Informal institutions, customs, traditions, norms, religions	100 to 1000	Often noncalculative; spontaneous	Social theory
L2	**Institutional environment** Formal rules – esp. property rights (policy, judiciary, bureaucracy)	10 to 100	Get the institutional environment right. 1st order economising	Economics of property rights/Positive political theory
L3	**Governance** Playing the game – esp. contract (aligning governance structures with transactions)	1 to 10	Get the governance structures right. 2nd order economising	Transaction cost economics
L4	**Resource allocation and employment** (prices and quantities, incentive alignment)	continuous	Get the marginal conditions right. 3rd order economising	Neoclassical economics/ Agency theory

Fig. 16.1: Four levels of social analysis
Source: Adapted from Williamson (2000: 597)

Williamson calls the first level of analysis "social embeddedness" (L1), which deals with informal institutions, such as norms, values, customs, and religion. Often (new institutional) economists do not treat informal institutions as variables in their analysis, since changes in norms and customs are supposed to take much longer than those in political institutions or organisational structures (Williamson, 2000, p. 596). Nevertheless, informal institutions may have profound impacts on the whole social system, since they influence all sublevel choices. The informal institutions at L1 are said to be mainly of spontaneous origin; thus, "deliberate choice of a calculative kind is minimally implicated" (Williamson, 1998, p. 27). This does not imply that different actors do not try to influence such institutions, but the effects are difficult to calculate. According to Williamson, this level is mainly analysed through social theory (Granovetter, 1985; Brinton & Nee, 2001). It should also be noted that the study of social capital has particularly attracted the attention of political scientists and economists.

Within the constraints imposed by the embeddedness level (L1), the "formal rules of the game" develop into the institutional environment (L2), consisting of basic legal rules, such as property rights, contracting rights, as well as political institutions, such as electoral rules, public regulations and so on. Even though formal institutions change more quickly than informal ones, change normally takes decades or even centuries, unless massive disruptions occur. Formal rules may stem from evolutionary processes, but design opportunities are also posed (Williamson, 2000, p. 598). This opens up the possibility to purposefully economise costs by shaping the basic rules of the game in the right way (first order economising). The suggested theoretical framework for analysing institutions and social outcomes at this level is positive political theory and theory of property rights. However, law and economics could be located at this level as well.

Within the realm of politics as well as the institutional embeddedness, the governance level (L3) deals with organisations and the appropriate choice of contractual relations. At this level markets, firms, public agencies, and contracts are located. Changes at L3 are supposed to occur over a period of one to ten years, thus again offering opportunities to economise, mainly by aligning the governance structures to transactions in a cost efficient way, that is, 2nd order economising. Williamson suggests the use of transaction cost economics at this level; however, alternative theories can also be drawn on, such as incomplete contracting theory or the resource based theory of the firm.

Finally, within constraints set by the upper levels, the continuous process of resource allocation occurs on the fourth level (L4), thus depending on the whole institutional environment set by its social embeddedness, the formal institutional environment and the governance structures in place. Within this structure, economising in the sense of maximising is assumed when the marginal conditions are met, that is, where marginal benefits equal marginal costs. This is the main research domain of neoclassical economics. Williamson locates agency theory at this level too, which deals with the problems of incentive alignments mainly within a given governance structure (see Birner & Wittmer, this volume). Alternatively, one may also locate ecological economics on this level, putting human activities explicitly in the context of the ecological system.

As represented in Fig. 16.1, the levels are linked by different kinds of arrows. The top-down arrows indicate the constraints that higher levels impose on lower levels, whereas the bottom-up arrows indicate feedback processes from lower to upper levels. Taken together, the arrows indicate that the whole social institutional system is completely interactive, which has to be taken into account when designing institutional analyses.

The framework developed by Williamson is widely recognised, not only because it distinguishes between different levels of analysis that correspond to different types of institutions, but also because it links the different levels with different frequencies of change in observable characteristics, different possibilities of purposeful institutional design as well as different theories to investigate institutions at the different levels. As will be shown subsequently, this holds important implications for choosing methods in institutional analysis. In addition, Williamson's framework precisely indicates that the options for economising are greatly reduced in moving from the lowest to the uppermost level. This, however, contrasts with the importance of institutions for the overall performance of a society, which increase in the same direction (i.e., the greatest influence at the highest levels).

16.3.2 Research questions in institutional analysis

Research questions, of course, depend on the subject matter under investigation. With regard to institutional analysis, three main types of empirical research questions may be distinguished (Alston, 1996). The first type is related to effects or consequences of institutions (and institutional change) at different levels. Questions in this vein include looking at how the institutional environment may affect governance structures (e.g., La Porta et al., 1998), how religion affects growth (e.g., Barro & McCleary, 2003) or how the organisational structure of farms may affect resource allocation (Mathijs & Swinnen, 2001). The second cluster of research questions is concerned with causes, reasons or determinants regulating the existence or change of institutions. Examples here include the determinants of democracy (Barro, 1999), the reasons for the development of modern corporations (e.g., Chandler, 1977; Williamson, 1981), the reasons for share-cropping contracts in agriculture (e.g., Stiglitz, 1974; Allen & Lueck, 1992; Polman & Slangen, this volume) or the causes of de-collectivisation in Central and Eastern European agriculture (Mathijs & Swinnen, 1998; Rozelle & Swinnen, this volume). Technically speaking, the difference between research questions concerning effects or causes is whether institutions appear at the left-hand side or at the right-hand side of an equation or an econometric model, which often assumes linear casual relationships between certain variables. The third type of research questions seek to discover processes of institutional development or change. Processes are cause-effect relationships that may not be solely linear in nature, but may also include non-linear relationships. Processes explicitly take feedback loops into account. Furthermore, process-oriented research questions explicitly pay attention to the timing and sequencing of events as well as to potential paths for further development. Examples of work guided by such questions include studies of property rights development in natural resources (e.g., Wang, 2001), the study of socio-ecological resilience (Mwangi & Ostrom, this volume), processes of privatisation and organisational change during transition (e.g., Schlüter, 2001; Hanisch, 2003), and processes of contract failure and public regulation (Libecap & Wiggins, 1985).

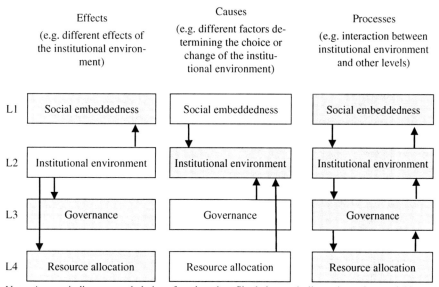

Note: Arrows indicate causal chains of explanation. Shaded areas indicate dependent variables.

Fig. 16.2: Effects, causes and processes combined with the four levels of social analysis

Source: Based on Williamson (2000: 597) and Alston (1996)

The different types of research questions proposed by Alston (1996) can be easily combined with the four-level scheme of Williamson (2000), as shown in Fig.16.2. Research on the effects of institutions take certain institutions or institutional changes as exogenous and ask how this choice or change affects higher or lower levels. Thus, a change in the institutional environment, for example, may affect the governance structures, the resource allocation and even the values and norms of a society (see Bowles, 1998; Alesina & Fuchs-Schuendeln, 2007). As a consequence, the effects could be multifold and the research has to specify the main effect under interest. In addition, the researcher needs to control for other possible influencing factors than the institution under investigation.

Analysing the causes of institutional choice or change defines institutions as the dependent variable and asked in how far factors at the other levels of social analysis determine the choice and change of institutions. The question is then, what kinds of determinants are taken systematically into account. For example, an examination of contract choice in agriculture may focus on resource allocation as a determinant of contract choice; simultaneously, contract choice may also be influenced by the formal institutional environment and social embeddedness (see Beckmann, 2000; Hurrelmann, 2005, 2008). Thus, the conditionedness of the results on the institutional environment specified has to be counterchecked by a comparative approach.

Investigations into causes and effects usually examine causality in a linear manner, thus often ignoring feedback loops. For example, in transaction cost economics feedback loops are largely ignored (Williamson, 2000). Incorporating feedback into the analysis leads to a process perspective that can look at, for example, the interaction between governance structures and the institutional environment, the interaction between governance structures and resource allocation, or between the formal institutional environment and the social embeddedness level. The most comprehensive analysis of the process of institutional change will take all four levels into account. As should now be evident from what has been said above, such an approach needs to take long time horizons into account and combine different theoretical approaches (see e.g., Eggertsson, 1996; Feeny, 1989; Wang, 2001; Mwangi & Ostrom, this volume)

Distinguishing between effects, causes and processes as the basic touchstones for research questions in institutional analysis and combining these with Williamson's four levels of social analysis enables us to more precisely distinguish between different investigations within a common theme; allows us to locate a particular research effort among the possible perspectives; and helps in the linking of this research to the existing body of literature, both theoretically and empirically. It also prepares the ground for our further discussion on the critical issues involved in selecting methodologies. Some regularity between the level of analysis, the research question and the method applied can already be observed (Hanisch, Beckmann, Boger, & Brem, 2007). Processes are mainly investigated by using case study approaches and to a very limited extent by other methods. Effects of different institutions on resource allocation are often investigated by econometric methods and experiments. Causes of institutional choice and change are frequently investigated by econometric tools at lower levels of social analysis (L3), while case studies are prominent at higher levels (L2, L1).

16.4 Critical Issues in Selecting Methods of Institutional Analysis

Based on Williamson's levels of social analysis and the typical research questions posed within NIE, this section investigates critical issues in selecting methods of institutional analysis. Although many issues may play a role of some sort, we focus on the three that we think are important and not very often reflected upon in the literature: the question of time, the observability and measurability of institutions and the role of actors. All of these issues are not only related to methods, but also to theoretical concepts. Therefore, we begin each section with a discussion of the theoretical concepts entailed by each topic before discussing its methodological implications.

16.4.1 The question of time

Institutions evolve and change over time (North, 1994). The four-level scheme from Williamson clearly underlines that time plays a significant role in institutional analysis. Although all theories of NIE address time within their theoretical concepts, reflection on the methodological implications of time is just emerging. Only recently have institutional sociologists and political scientists discussed the significance of time for methodological concerns (Abbott, 2001, Pierson, 2004). In the following, we first briefly investigate how different theories in NIE address time and discuss some theoretical implications of the four-level scheme, in combination with suggestions by Pierson (2004), to systematically distinguishing between the short- and long-term causes and effects of change. Then we consider how the different methods used within NIE deal with the problem of how institutions evolve over time.

All theories employed within NIE address the role of time theoretically, although in quite diverse ways. In principal-agent theory as well as in contract theory, time is approximated by the repeated interactions, sequences of moves and time horizons of decision makers. Transaction cost economics recognises time in the form of the frequency and uncertainty of transactions, by distinguishing between ex-ante and ex-post contractual problems and by arguing that adaptation is the central economic problem (Williamson, 1985). However, the main theoretical hypotheses therein are formulated in a comparatively static way. Game theoretic approaches to institutional analysis explicitly recognise time as the sequencing of moves, which can make a great difference for the outcome of a particular game (Aoki, 2001). Time plays an essential role in theories of institutional change (North, 1994; Eggertsson, 1996) and, in particular, in evolutionary economics (Nelson & Winter, 1982; Young, 1998). Feedback and learning are important features of evolutionary thinking. Within the latter, the concept of path-dependencies is prominent. Positive feedback processes stabilise informal and formal institutions and can lead not only to different developmental paths, but also to lock-in effects of "inefficient" institutions (David, 1994).

By their very nature, institutions oscillate between stability and change. In order to affect human behaviour, institutions need to be stable. Only then are actors able to form reliable expectations and take institutions as constraints into account. However, institutions also need to adapt to different circumstances. In general, this creates a tension between stability and change (North, 1990). Williamson's four-level scheme underlines the fact that institutions at different levels do not change at the same speed, consequently creating points of friction within the social system. Changes at a higher level will have long-term effects at lower levels. Changes in informal institutions, like traditions or religion, may take a long time to emerge and affect the economy over a long period. The same holds true for changes in the political system or legal system. Changes at the governance level more directly affect resource allocation, producing direct feedback. In the bottom-up direction, continuous changes within the resource allocation may lead to changes in the organisational structures, to changes in the institutional environment and also to changes within the social embeddedness. However, since institutions are often of a discrete nature, they are likely to change discontinuously, with threshold effects being significantly involved[2]. Pierson (2004) has developed an approach that allows us to systematically distinguish between short- and long-term causes and effects of change (see Fig. 16.3).

| | | Time Horizon of **Effect** | |
		Short	Long
		I	II
Time Horizon of **Cause**	Short	Direct feedbacks	Cumulative Effects
		(L4)	**(L3, L2)**
		III	IV
	Long	Thresholds effects	Cumulative Causes
		(L3, L2)	**(L1)**

Fig. 16.3: Time horizons of causes and effects in social sciences

Source: Adapted from Pierson (2004)

If the time horizon of the cause and effect is short, direct feedback occurs. This may apply to the majority of cases at Level 4, where changes in prices lead quite directly to changes in quantities. However, within the ecological system we observe other kinds of developments: long-lasting carbon dioxide emissions lead to long-lasting global climate change, for example. A flood or a tornado may have short-term causes, but long-term resource allocation effects. Meanwhile, regarding

---

[2] For a discussion of threshold effects in the case of externalities, see Tisdell this volume.

the economic system as a whole, the breakdown of financial markets is the accumulated result of long-term causes, culminating in short-term collapse. At Level 3 and, in particular, at Level 2 we observe both threshold effects as well as cumulative effects. Typically, organisational reforms as well as political reforms occur only after relatively long-term pressure; however, once they have occurred they may have cumulative effects in the long run (Rodrik, 1996). Finally, Level 1 is the domain of cumulative causes, where causes as well as the effects are long term. Given this background, we now turn to the empirical methods developed to analyse institutions either at a given point in time or over time.

Experimental and agent-based modelling both give consideration to the temporal dimension via the number of interactions between participants or agents. In experiments, the effect of time is controlled by contrasting the results gained in one-shot experiments with those in repeated experiments with the same subjects. The feedback process is almost always direct and the number of interactions quite limited to 20 or 30. Experiments are, therefore, mostly located in the first quadrant, I, of Fig. 16.3, with limited capacity to investigate cumulative effects, threshold effects or cumulative causes. Agent-based models usually work with a large number of iterations (from hundreds to thousands) and include indirect or lagged feedback. In this way, cumulative effects or cumulative causes and threshold effects can be modelled in a stylised way. Agent-based models are geared towards investigating the phenomenon that small differences or changes in rules may produce very different cumulative effects. Thus, agent-based models have a comparative advantage in studying the quadrants II, III and IV of Fig. 16.3.

In the real world, time is a continuous variable and, for a particular sequence of events, even minutes or seconds might make a difference. Case studies and econometrics work with real, observed data and can play a role in cross-section, time-series or panel-data settings. For a cross-section design, variables from the four levels could be correlated with each other at any point in time, with the strategy usually being to investigate the covariation of at least two levels. Thus, in a cross-section analysis resource allocation and governances structure may be investigated, as is commonly done in transaction cost economics. Here it is important to note that the institutional structure at any given point in time encompasses the accumulated effects of complex interactions between all four levels. Consequently, it is difficult to make positive and unassailable statements about relationships of causality. Democracy, for example, could affect GDP per capital, but conversely GDP per capital could affect democracy. Long-term contracts could facilitate specific investments, but specific investments could also demand long-term contracts. Thus, any cross-section analysis of effects faces the problem of the possible endogeneity of institutions, i.e. effects may be causes. There are at least two possible responses to that problem: first, sometimes econometric techniques could be used, like the instrumental variable (IV) approach, or the researcher could focus on identifying patterns instead of causalities. Transaction cost economics usually investigates covariation of L3 and L4 and relies on the discriminating alignment hypotheses: "transactions, which differ in their attributes, are aligned with governance structures, which differ in their costs and competence, so as to effect a (mainly) transaction-cost economising result" (Williamson, 1998, p. 75). Cross-section analysis could try to estimate the casual relationship between the attributes of the transaction, the choice of governance structure, and the related transaction costs, or it could just investigate if the observable alignment pattern matches the theoretically predicted one. At least the latter investigation is possible in a cross section design. However, cross-section analysis is unable to distinguish short-term and long-term effects and threshold effects or cumulative causes, because it does not pay explicit attention to time. In order to do so, the time needs to be taken explicitly into account.

The analysis of causes and effects of institutions at different levels could be much improved once time is taken explicitly into account. Case studies or econometrics then rely on time series or panel data sets. Econometric analysis work usually well if dependent and independent variables display significant variance over time and direct feedback occurs. Problems appear if variables change infrequently. Suppose a case where the institutional environment (L2) changes significantly at time t_0 and effects can be observed in the subsequent periods of time t_1, t_2, ... t_n at the level of governance (L3) and at the level of resource allocation (L4). Equally possible, causes could be investigated by studying changes at L1, L3, and L4 before change occurs at L2, that is, at times t_{-1}, t_{-2}, ... t_{-n}. Though only a single unit is under study, the time scale may provide many observations for drawing causal inferences, however options for econometric analysis are rather limited. Long term effects could be modelled as external shocks in vector auto regression (VAR) models and long-term causes may be estimated in Markov chain switching models. Although the options for econometric analysis are enlarged for panel datasets some significant shortcomings remain. Depending on the cases, relevant observations may differ greatly according to the time horizon and the timing interval. Distinguishing the long- and short-term causes and effects of institutional change requires differentiation between long-lasting and immediate determinants and relevant details that finally led to the occurrence of change. The case study approach usually is very flexible with regard to time intervals, whereas statistical time series or panel data analysis usually works with data on a fixed interval basis, mainly years, and needs a full data set on all dependent and independent variables. In many cases, data of this kind is either highly ambiguous or impossible to get one's hands on; moreover, the time interval of the data set might be too long for properly capturing the causal effects sought. Within a case study framework, qualitative methods of "process tracing" or "analytical narratives" could be used. By "process tracing" the researcher carefully traced the timing and sequencing of all intermediate steps that let to a specific outcome (George & Bennett, 2005, pp. 205–232). The data is presented as a historical narrative either in a more descriptive or more analytic way depending mainly on the role of theory within the analysis (Bates, Greif, Levi, Rosenthal, & Weingast, 1998; Greif, 2006). The detailed analysis of processes of institutional choice and change that may encompass short as well as long-term causes and effects may only be possible within a case study design.

16.4.2 Observability, measurability and data availability

Institutions are often difficult to observe and measure (Ostrom, 2005a, pp. 822–825). As bundles of rules, they shape human behaviour and structure social, political and economic interaction; however, these regulatory forces remain themselves invisible unless they are made explicit in written form. Human behaviour and structures of interaction – in the forms of markets, firms, households or bureaucracies – are relatively easily observed, but it is often difficult to infer their underlying rules. Actual behaviour may violate established rules, and seemingly similar structures may rely on quite different rules. Therefore, one important objective of empirical research into institutions is to identify, describe and classify rules. Without the proper identification and measurement of institutions, little further analysis is possible or could turn out to be largely misleading.

The task of identifying institutions requires theoretical conceptualisation of what institutions are and what important features characterise them. The four-level scheme from Williamson offers three broad categories of institutions: informal institutions (Level 1), formal institutional environment (Level 2) and governance structures (Level 3). However, he only offers intuitive ideas concerning what distinguishes them from each other. North (1990) uses a similar concept, dividing institutions into formal and informal and, further, into institutional environments and institutional arrangements. Based on their enforcement mechanisms, Ellickson (1991) distinguish between ethics, conventions, norms, private formal rules and public formal rules. Williamson (1985) categorises governance structures into markets, hybrids and hierarchies, based on the degree of independence or authority involved. Blomquist and Hanisch (both in this volume) distinguish between monocentric and polycentric governance structures, based on the number of decision-making units within a certain jurisdiction. Hagedorn (2005, 2008) proposes the concept of integrative and segregative institutions according to the degree to which actors have to consider the costs and benefits of their actions.

A fundamental concept for identifying institutions has been developed by Crawford and Ostrom (1995) within their "Grammar of Institutions" framework. According to them, the primary characteristics of all institutions can be expressed through the ADICO syntax: Attributes of actors; Deontic, for what actors are obliged, forbidden or permitted to do; AIm, describing particular actions or outcomes towards the achievement of which the deontic element has been assigned; Conditions under which the rule applies (where and when); and Or else, describing the consequences of breaking the rule. An example may be helpful in illustrating the use of the ADICO syntax: "All traffic participants must stop at an intersection if the traffic light is red or else they will be fined and will be responsible for all damages caused". This rule could be modified in very different ways by changing the attribute, the deontic, the aim, the condition or the or else formulation. With the ADICO syntax, formal or informal rules are made transparent using a common language. However, this format refers to single rules, whereas often the term "institution" is used for a set of rules (Furubotn & Richter, 2005, p. 560)[3]. Speaking of markets, firms, or ownership as institutions usually entails recognising the relatively large sets of rules defining them. For any type of interaction, Ostrom (2005b) takes into consideration at least seven relevant types of rules: those of position, boundary, choice, aggregation, information, payoff and scope. Thus, it is important during the formulation of an empirical strategy to acknowledge the differences in institutional concepts, especially whether they rely on individual rules or sets of rules, since individual rules are more difficult to identify than sets of rules or structures of interaction. In the following, we first discuss these issues for experiments and agent-based models and then for case and econometric studies.

Experiments as well as agent-based models share the feature that the institutions need to be described precisely in advance in order to run the experiment or the computer simulation, with the researcher specifying the principle mode of interaction (market exchange, public good provision, etc.) and the institutions that are exogenous or endogenous to the actors involved. It must be clearly stated or programmed what kind of information may, must or must not be exchanged, or whether participants may, must or not punish the behaviour of others (Fehr & Gächter, 2000). In this way, institutions are modified at the margin or in a discrete way, and effects can be observed. Actors have to make their decisions in scenarios with or without punishment or even revenge (Nikiforakis, 2008). Whereas experiments can be modified relatively easily, agent-based models need to reprogram behavioural algorithms or constraints, which may be more difficult to achieve. However, the logic of both approaches to institutions follows very much the ADICO syntax proposed by Crawford and Ostrom (1995), where the deontic, the condition or the or-else formula can be changed systematically. However, complex institutions that cannot be easily represented within an experimental setting or programmed into an agent-based model are difficult to study (e.g. the choice of the legal form of enterprises). This may limit the scope of applications significantly, limiting them to relatively simple forms of interaction and institutions, such as rules of market exchange or norms of reciprocity. Experiments and agent-based models, nevertheless, have the advantage that hypothetical institutions can be studied through them, with researchers being free to design any kind of institutions, even those not existing yet. Another advantage of experimental and agent-based modelling is their ability to extract the full data set of attributes, not only in terms of the environment, but also those regarding the interactions, the institutions, and, in agent-based modelling, the actors being studied. Actors are less

---

[3] "An institution is understood ... as a set of formal and informal rules, including their enforcement arrangements (the 'rules of the game', whose objective is to steer individual behavior in a particular direction" (Furubotn & Richter, 2005, p. 560).

controlled within an experimental setting than an agent-based one, though information on actors can be gathered systematically through survey techniques.

For analyses based on observed contemporary or historical data, questions concerning measurability, data availability and reliability arise, limiting in particular the application of econometric analysis significantly. Any econometric or statistical analysis of effects and causes of institutions relies on quantitative measurement, sufficient observations and variance within the dependent and independent variables. For data sets that are not reliable, which face missing observations or have little variance, statistical analysis does not yield any significant insights. Case studies have the advantage of combining different sources of information and use qualitative data to close information gaps. Since case studies are normally conducted on those cases where sufficient and reliable data is available, the following discussion focuses only on the limits of the application of econometric techniques. Based on Fig. 16.4, we first discuss the problem of quantitative measurement and then the problem of data availability.

	Complexity of Institutions	Quantitative Measurement	Data Sources	Variance in Space	Variance in Time
L1	Simple to complex	Nominal Ordinal Ratio Count	Historical records Official Statistics Surveys	Small to large (e.g.. 12 main religions; 6,800 main languages)	Small
L2	Complex	Nominal Ordinal	Historical records Documents Surveys	Small to Medium (e.g. 5 legal origins; 192 nations, 2005)	Small to Medium
L3	Simple to complex	Nominal Ordinal Ratio Count	Official Statistics Surveys Documents	Large (e.g. 2,915,482 firms in Germany, 2003)	Medium
L4	Simple	Interval Nominal Ordinal	Official Statistics Accounting Records Surveys	Very large (e.g. daily prices and quantities at the stock market)	Large

Fig. 16.4: Institutional complexity, quantitative measurement, data sources and variance among the four levels of social analysis

It is important to recognise that institutions at different levels may differ in respect to their complexity. An institution is simple if it only contains a single or a few rules; it is complex if it consists of a large number of interconnected rules. For example, simple institutions include the norm of reciprocity or the make or buy decision. Complex institutions, by contrast, contain a large number of often interrelated rules, examples being the Christian religion, democracy, joint-stock companies and sometimes even contracts. While institutions at L4 are often relatively simple, institutions at L3 and L1 range from simple to complex. Institutions at the level of the formal institutional environment, L2, are in particular complex.

As the ADICO syntax makes clear, institutions are usually coded into language (laws, statutes, or contracts). However, everything that can be named can, in principle, be coded in nominal terms. Other measurements – such as ordinal, ratio, count or interval – are often also possible. Take the example of measuring religion at L1, which can be done at the country or the individual level. A country is classified according to its main religion in nominal terms. However, it is also possible to collect ratio data, such as the share of Christians in the country, as well as count data, such as the number of religions present. At the individual level, people may be classified according to their main religion, but also a survey could ask for a self-assessment of the strength of religious beliefs as an ordinal measure. Similar possibilities exist at L2, where countries are classified as democracies or autocratic states, or whether a democracy is of a parliamentary of presidential type. Also, ratio or count indicators, such as the share of votes for left-wing parties or the number of governments within a given time period, are possible. An alternative measure relies on individual or expert assessment of different attributes of the political and legal system, such as freedom and accountability[4]. At L3, the type of contract, the make or buy decision, the type or organisation of the firm, all could be coded in nominal terms. Subjective ordinal measures are also quite common at this level. Count and ratio data, such as the number of firms in an industry, the concentration rate, and so on, are available as well. At L4, the level of resource allocation prices and quantities are often easy to measure on an interval scale[5]. As can be seen, there are many ways to measure institutions for statistical or econometric analysis.

Information on institutions and resource allocation are partly available from official statistics and historical records, in particular at L2 and L3 relevant information is only available through document analysis of, for example, laws, statutes and contracts. As Fig.16.4 shows, there is also a remarkable variance among institutions worldwide that are amenable to statistical analysis, although the number of observations is reduced in time and space once we move from L4 to L1. Official

---

[4] Such an approach is increasingly being applied; Freedom House, for example, has been providing annual assessments of the levels and types of political and economic freedom in different countries since 1974.

[5] However, this holds only for private goods and services; it is often difficult to measure resource allocation and prices for environmental goods or externalities produced. This puts an additional challenge in the way of empirical research on institutions of sustainability.

statistics or historical records allow for nominal, ratio or count measurement, while survey techniques may generate also ordinal and interval data at all levels. However, going back in time, more and more missing data and disruptions occur within official records. International surveys have only been conducted since 1974 by Freedom House, since 1981 by the World Values Survey, and since 2003 by the Doing Business group of the World Bank.

One of the crucial elements regarding measurement is to be able to adequately represent the institution in place. This is in particular problematic for complex institutions coded by nominal terms. Democracies may differ in many details; however, this differentiation vanishes when a nominal measurement is used. Complex institutions, such as the regulation of genetically modified organisms, contain many different and interlinked rules that are difficult to aggregate (Beckmann, Soregaroli, & Wesseler, 2006). Regulations are easily codified into language, but are only with difficulty translatable into quantitative measurements by simply stating whether a common sub-rule is in place or not. A survey approach can produce ordinal data via an assessment of the costs imposed by the regulation of different constraints. However, to capture the full meaning of particular institutions qualitative analysis is often necessary. The same is true for informal institutions: the more complex institutions are, the less they are suited for econometric techniques that rely on simple measurements. For complex institutions, the application of experimental and simulation modelling is difficult too, leaving case studies as the only reliable means of empirical research.

16.4.3 The role of actors and human behaviour

Institutions are developed, designed and maintained by human beings. And institutions are only effective if they exercise an influence on human behaviour. However, within Williamson's four-level scheme of social analysis actors are completely hidden, suggesting that we can analyse institutional structures without paying explicit attention to actors and that it is sufficient to correlate institutions among themselves or with resource allocations. Many econometric analyses, in particular at the macro level, but also in transaction cost economics, follow this strategy. In most case studies, experimental economics research and agent-based modelling, actors play a more prominent role and are often included in the analysis.

All theories within NIE pay much attention to actors, although they differ in terms of the ways in which actor attributes are important. Principal-agent theory, for example, starts from assumptions about the risk preferences of actors; in transaction costs economics, opportunism and bounded rationality of actors matter, although actors are seldom included explicitly in the analysis (Gazendam & Jorna, 2002; Sykuta, 2008). Theories of institutional change stress the power and bargaining resources of actors (Knight, 1992); new political economy the ability of actors groups to organise their common interests (Olson, 1965, 1982). Actors are of central importance in the Institutional Analysis and Development Framework of Ostrom (1990), the Institutions of Sustainability approach of Hagedorn (2002) and the Actor Cantered Institutionalism of Scharpf (1997). In all of these approaches, actors play the pivotal role for the performance of institutions, as institutions create effects through influencing human behaviour and actors create and change institutions to realise specific intentions.

Figure 16.5 categorises individuals and organisations as different kinds of actors at the four levels of social analysis, in addition to the institutions in place. With Scharpf (1997, pp. 51–68), we distinguish between individual and composite actors or, as with North (1990), between individuals and organisations. In line with methodological individualism, individuals may simultaneously occupy different positions, such as citizens, voters, consumers, or they may be members of social organisations, churches, political parties, interest groups, business associations or consumer clubs. Thus, at each level individual actors form collective actors that interact with each other in different ways. Consequently, the four-level scheme has been extended to include actors and distinguish between different types. The importance of actors for a particular empirical analysis of institutions cannot be gauged theoretically, but rather must be assessed based on the research context.

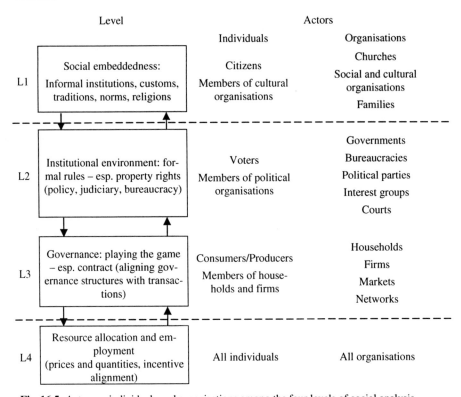

Fig. 16.5: Actors as individuals and organisations among the four levels of social analysis

Actors play a central role in agent-based modelling: the way they process information and the type of decision-making rules they apply are of central importance for model-generated outcomes. In experimental economics, conceptualisation of the actors involved is a necessary condition for running an experiment. As it turns out, since experimental economics studies reveal individual preferences, they are not only suitable for studying the effects of formal institutions, but also for gaining deeper insight into individual decision making and the role of informal institutions. Ultimatum or dictator games have been used to reveal social preferences and the notion of fairness. Thus, experimental economics has revealed detailed knowledge on human decision making in different situations and yields information on different types of behaviour, such as how actor attributes like fairness matter in making contracting decisions (Fehr & Fischbacher, 2002).

In econometric analysis, the characteristics of actors must be measured in order to be included in analyses of the causes or effects of institutions. Typical actors are included with their characteristics, and sometimes with their perceptions and expectations, which are measured through specific questions using surveys (see Slangen and Polman this volume). However, usually this approach leaves little room for actor deliberation and complex interactions among them. In this respect, case studies can offer a large degree of freedom for paying attention to the deliberations of actors, the ways in which they perceive both information and other actors, build perceptions about the future (see Vatn, this volume), or formulate arguments to convince others. Case studies – so far as they focus on a limited number of units – are very flexible with regard to the number of actors considered and the sources of information and data that can be utilised. The precise analysis of discourses, intentions, arguments of actors is only possible via a case study approach (Schlüter, this volume). A case study on the emergence of regulations for genetically modified organisms in Germany, for example, could be sparked by only one event, here the amendment of the Genetic Technology Law in 2004, but focus on the arguments and interactions of the different actors involved during this process of institution building. An econometric study, on the other hand, would have to measure all the differences in the coexisting regulations in the 27 member states of the EU, including specific indicators for the governments, the opinions of voters and the relative strengths of interest groups, in particular environmental groups.

16.5 Conclusions

This paper began with the observation that institutional economics has progressed significantly in theoretical and empirical research. The classical tool-box of institutional economics, consisting of case studies and econometric analysis, has been enriched significantly by experimental economics and, most recently, by agent-based modelling. Schmid (2004, p. 138) argues, "Institutional economics is not limited to any particular method of investigation. All of the tools usually available in economics are relevant". And we strongly agree with this pluralism. However, there are clear tradeoffs and the appropriate methodology depends on a great number of issues that need to be addressed, such as the level of analysis, the research questions posed, the time horizon addressed, the availability and measurability of data and the importance of actors within the process.

In general, experimental economics and agent-based modelling have the big advantages that they can control many relevant aspects and, therefore, isolate the effects of exogenously defined institutions on actor behaviour and resource allocation. Whereas experimental economics studies are run for a quite limited number of repeated interactions with a limited number of subjects, agent-based modelling is able to address long-term processes and include a large number of agents in their models. Agent-based models imitate the complexity of social processes, a complexity that increases once these models are linked with ecological models to study resilience. Where laboratory and field experiments can reveal information about human actors, their preferences and beliefs, feelings and modes of decision making, agent-based models need to make precise assumptions about the rationality and decision algorithms of agents. In this respect, experimental economics and agent-based models are clearly complementary tools. Currently, both methods are little used in studying the choice and change of institutions, meaning that some of the institutions under investigation are endogenous. However, recently experimental economics has started to examine contract choice (Fehr et al., 2007) and the property rights structures of firms (Fehr et al., 2008). There is much to expect from these methods in the future. While agent-based models promise insights into basic mechanisms, in combination with ecological modelling they promise to yield important insights into the dynamics of socio-ecological systems and the question of sustainability. However, the strict control that experiments and agent-based models offer comes at a cost: most types of interactions are highly stylised and only comparatively simple institutions are studied.

Although observed behaviour is often uncontrolled and poses problems of causal inference, the real world offers such a rich set of observations that should by no means be ignored and can be investigated using case-study and econometric techniques. Sometimes, cases offer natural experiments that are very difficult to imitate through artificial experiments or agent-based modelling. According to Eggertsson (2005, p. 99) case studies can have a "... role similar to that of formal mathematical models, which, when they are successful, bring transparency into complex issues and highlight important relationships that more opulent images would obscure." However, while the main challenge to econometric studies lies in the availability of sufficient data, the main issue for case studies is finding comparable concepts and approaches that allow for comparison. There are several research strategies to meet both challenges. One such approach is the creation of large panel data sets that allow for cross-section, time series analysis. At L1, such a data set can be found in the World Values Survey (www.worldvaluessurvey.org/), which has since 1981 presented worldwide data on values and norms; at L2, data on political systems is available from Freedom House (www.freedomhouse.org), provided since 1974, or the Worldwide Governance Indicators (WGI) from the World Bank, which provides governance indicators for 212 countries from 1996 to 2007 (www.worldbank.org/wbi/governance); at L3, the World Bank has been providing indicators for business regulations since 2003 (www.doingbusiness.org). Recently, the Ifo-Institute started to offer a database for institutional comparisons in Europe (DICE) (www.cesifo-group.de). Large data sets on environmental governance and environmental resource allocation are also increasingly available (www.earthtrends.wri.org), although not as complete as the others mentioned. All of these data sources offer rich opportunities to studies different effects and causes of institutional change with econometric methods. However, the general challenge remains concerning the quality of measurements, the problem of endogeneity and controlling for additional factors as well as limited time horizons. In this respect, case studies will always remain valuable sources of information, since they are more flexible in terms of data used and time horizons addressed. Complex institutions, long-term processes of institutional change and the deliberation of actors could probably only be studied by using qualitative case study approaches. Certain research strategies try to combine these advantages of case studies with large-N studies by repeating case studies on certain issues across many different cases, although this is not an easy undertaking (Poteete & Ostrom, 2004, 2008). Thus, the integration of case study analysis with econometric methods offers a promising way forward. Again, there is much to expect from them in the future. Ostrom and others also demonstrate that it is reasonable to go even one step further: integrating case-study analysis with experiments, econometric tools and agent-based modelling (Janssen & Ostrom, 2006). This shows once again that all methods have their strengths and weaknesses and, as the analysis of institutions at different levels requires the combination of different theories, a combination of different methods is needed to provide valuable insights into the links between institutions at different levels and time scales and sustainability.

This book contains theoretical and conceptual work as well as a wealth of empirical applications. Among the empirical papers, qualitative case-study methods dominate, with only two papers using quantitative methods. The case studies presented in this volume show that the tool can be very powerful, particularly if it is well-linked to common conceptual frameworks and theoretical approaches. As for the theoretical concepts outlined in this book, we need more empirical studies on polycentric governance, markets for public goods, environmental administration, integrative and segregative institutions and institutions as rationality contexts. To advance these concepts, focused case studies are needed that start to operationally them. The alignment hypotheses between complex, interrelated transactions and polycentric governance structures could be examined in cross-section settings using econometric methods, once measurement concepts have been developed and data is available. Integrative and segregative institutions could also be studied within experimental settings as well as through agent-based models to capture their long term consequences. With so many open possibilities, we can only concur with Ostrom's (1990, p. xvi) conviction "that knowledge accrues by the continual process of moving back and forth from empirical observation to serious efforts at theoretical formulation." Certainly, all methods can contribute their part to this endeavour.

Acknowledgments

We thank Insa Theesfeld and Renate Judis for valuable comments on an earlier draft of this paper.

References

Abbott, A. (2001). *Time matters: On theory and method*. Chicago: University of Chicago Press.

Acemoglu, D., Johnson, S. & Robinson, J. (2001). The colonial origins of comparative development: An empirical investigation. *Journal of Economic History, 61*, 517.

Alesina, A., & Fuchs-Schuendeln, N. (2007). Good-bye Lenin (or not?): The effect of communism on people's preferences. *American Economic Review, 97*, 1507–1528.

Allen, D., & Lueck, D. (1992). Contract choice in modern agriculture: Cash rent versus cropshare. *Journal of Law & Economics, 35*, 397–426.

Alston, L. J. (1996). Empirical work in institutional economics: An overview. In L. J. Alston, T. Eggertson & D. C. North (Eds.), *Empirical studies in institutional change* (pp. 25–30). Cambridge: Cambridge University Press.

Alston, L. J. (2008). The "case" for case studies in new institutional economics. In E. Brousseau & J.-M. Glachant (Eds.), *New institutional economics: A guidebook* (pp. 103–121). Cambridge: Cambridge University Press.

Aoki, M. (2001). *Toward a comparative institutional analysis*. Cambridge: MIT Press.

Axelrod, R. M. (1984). *The evolution of cooperation*. New York: Basic Books.

Axelrod, R. M. (1986). An evolutionary approach to norms. *American Political Science Review, 80*, 1095–1111.

Axelrod, R. M. (1997). *The complexity of cooperation: Agent-based models of competition and collaboration*. Princeton: Princeton University Press.

Axelrod, R. M., & Hamilton, W. D. (1981). The evolution of cooperation. *Science, 211*, 1390–1396.

Balmann, A. (1997). Farm-based modelling of regional structural change: A cellular automata approach. *European Review of Agricultural Economics, 24*, 85–108.

Barro, R. J. (1999). Determinants of democracy. *Journal of Political Economy, 107*, 158–183.

Barro, R. J., & McCleary, R. (2003). Religion and economic growth. NBER Working Paper No. W 9682, from: http://ssrn.com/abstract=406054.

Bates, R. H., Greif, A., Levi, M., Rosenthal, J. L., & Weingast, B. R. (1998). *Analytic narratives*. Princeton: Princeton University Press.

Beck, T., Clarke, G., Groff, A., Keefer, P., & Walsh, P. (2001). New tools in comparative political economy: The database of political institutions. *World Bank Economic Review, 15*, 165–176.

Beckmann, V. (2000). *Transaktionskosten und institutionelle Wahl in der Landwirtschaft: Zwischen Markt, Hierarchie und Kooperation.* Berlin: Ed. Sigma.

Beckmann, V., Soregaroli, C., & Wesseler, J. (2006). Coexistence rules and regulations in the European Union. *American Journal of Agicultural Economics, 88,* 1193–1199.

Berger, T. (2001). Agent-based spatial models applied to agriculture: A simulation tool for technology diffusion, resource use changes and policy analysis. *Agricultural Economics, 25,* 245–260.

Botero, J. C., Djankov, S., La Porta, R., Lopez de Silanes, F., & Shleifer, A. (2004). The regulation of labor. *Quarterly Journal of Economics, 119,* 1339–1382.

Bowles, S. (1998). Endogenous preferences: The cultural consequences of markets on other economic institutions. *Journal of Economic Literature, 36,* 75–111.

Brinton, M. C., & Nee, V. (2001). *The new institutionalism in sociology.* Stanford: Stanford University Press.

Bromley, D. W. (1991). *Environment and economy: Property rights and public policy.* Oxford and Cambridge: Blackwell.

Brousseau, E., & Glachant, J.-M. (Eds.). (2008). *New institutional economics: A guidebook.* Cambridge: Cambridge University Press.

Challen, R. (2000). *Institutions, transaction costs, and environmental policy: Institutional reform for water resources.* Cheltenham and Northampton: Edward Elgar.

Chandler, A. D. (1977). *The visible hand: The managerial revolution in American business.* Cambridge: Belknap Press.

Coase, R. H. (1937). The nature of the firm. *Economica, 4,* 386–405.

Coase, R. H. (1974). Lighthouse in economics. *Journal of Law & Economics, 17,* 357–376.

Crawford, S. E. S., & Ostrom, E. (1995). A grammar of institutions. *American Political Science Review, 89,* 582–600.

Croson, R., & Johnston, J. S. (2000). Experimental results on bargaining under alternative property rights regimes. *Journal of Law Economics & Organization, 16,* 50–73.

David, P. A. (1994). Why are institutions the 'carriers of history'? Path dependence and the evolution of conventions, organizations and institutions. *Structural Change and Economic Dynamics, 5,* 205–220.

Demsetz, H. (1967). Towards a theory of property rights. *American Economic Review, 57,* 347–359.

Dixt, A. K. (1996). *The making of economic policy: A transaction-cost politics perspective.* Cambridge: MIT Press.

Dow, J. (2008). Is religion an evolutionary adaptation? *Journal of Artificial Societies and Social Simulation, 11,* from: http://jasss.soc.surrey.ac.uk/11/2/2.html.

Duffy, J., & Kim, M. (2005). Anarchy in the laboratory (and the role of the state). *Journal of Economic Behavior & Organization, 56,* 297–329.

Easterly, W., & Levine, R. (2003). Tropics, germs, and crops: How endowments influence economic development. *Journal of Monetary Economics, 50,* 3–39.

Eggertsson, T. (1996). No experiments, monumental disasters: Why it took a thousand years to develop a specialized fishing industry in Iceland. *Journal of Economic Behavior & Organization, 30,* 1–23.

Eggertsson, T. (2005). *Imperfect institutions: Possibilities and limits of reform.* Ann Arbor: University of Michigan Press.

Ellickson, R. C. (1991). *Order without law: How neighbors settle disputes.* Cambridge: Harvard University Press.

Epstein, J. M. (2002). Modeling civil violence: An agent-based computational approach. *Proceedings of the National Academy of Sciences of the United States of America, 99,* 7243–7250.

Epstein, J. M. (2006). *Generative social science: Studies in agent-based computational modeling.* Princeton: Princeton University Press.

Epstein, J. M., & Axtell, R. (1996). *Growing artificial societies: Social science from the bottom up.* Washington, DC: Brookings Institution Press.

Feeny, D. (1989). The decline of property-rights in man in Thailand, 1800–1913. *Journal of Economic History, 49*, 285–296.

Fehr, E., & Fischbacher, U. (2002). Why social preferences matter: The impact of non-selfish motives on competition, cooperation and incentives. *Economic Journal, 112*, C1–C33.

Fehr, E. & Gächter, S. (2000). Cooperation and punishment in public goods experiments. *American Economic Review, 90*, 980–994.

Fehr, E., Klein, A., & Schmidt, K. M. (2007). Fairness and contract design. *Econometrica, 75*, 121–154.

Fehr, E., Kirchler, E., Weichbold, A., & Gächter, S. (1998). When social norms overpower competition: Gift exchange in experimental labor markets. *Journal of Labor Economics, 16*, 324–351.

Fehr, E., Kremhelmer, S., & Schmidt, K. M. (2008). Fairness and the optimal allocation of ownership rights. *Economic Journal, 118*, 1262–1284.

Furubotn, E. G., & Richter, R. (2005). *Institutions and economic theory: The contribution of the new institutional economics.* Ann Arbor: University of Michigan Press.

Gazendam, L., & Jorna, R. J. (2002). Transaction cost economics and plausible actors: A cognitive reappraisal. Faculty of Management & Organization, University of Groningen, from: http://www.semioticon.com/frontline/pdf/TrustLuit4.pdf.

George, A. L., & Bennett, A. (2005). *Case studies and theory development in the social sciences.* Cambridge: MIT Press.

Gerring, J. (2004). What is a case study and what is it good for? *American Political Science Review, 98*, 341–354.

Gerring, J. (2007). *Case study research: Principles and practices.* Cambridge: Cambridge University Press.

Granovetter, M. (1985). Economic-action and social-structure: The problem of embeddedness. *American Journal of Sociology, 91*, 481–510.

Greene, W. H. (2003). *Econometric analysis.* Upper Saddle River: Prentice Hall.

Greif, A. (2006). *Institutions and the path to the modern economy: Lessons from medieval trade.* Cambridge: Cambridge University Press.

Guarnaschelli, S., McKelvey, R. D., & Palfrey, T. R. (2000). An experimental study of jury decision rules. *American Political Science Review, 94*, 407–423.

Hagedorn, K. (Eds.). (2002). *Environmental co-operation and institutional change: Theories and policies for European agriculture.* Cheltenham and Northampton: Edward Elgar.

Hagedorn, K. (2005, June). *Integrative and segregative institutions.* (Paper presented at the TransCoop workshop "Problems of polycentric governance in the growing EU", Berlin).

Hagedorn, K. (2008). Particular requirements for institutional analysis in nature-related sectors. *European Review of Agricultural Economics, 35*, 357–384.

Hanisch, M. (2003). *Property reform and social conflict: A multi-level analysis of the change of agricultural property rights in post-socialist Bulgaria: Vol. 15. Institutional change in agriculture and natural resources.* Aachen: Shaker.

Hanisch, M., Beckmann, V., Boger, S., & Brem, M. (2007). In search of the market: Lessons from analysing agricultural transition. In V. Beckmann & K. Hagedorn (Eds.), *Understanding agricultural transition. Institutional change and economic performance in a comparative perspective: Vol. 26. Institutional change in agriculture and natural resources* (pp. 25–44). Aachen: Shaker.

Hardin, G. (1968). The tragedy of the commons. *Science, 162*, 1241–1248.

Henrich, J., Boyd, R., Bowles, S., Camerer, C., Fehr, E., Gintis, H., et al. (2005). "Economic man" in cross-cultural perspective: Behavioral experiments in 15 small-scale societies. *Behavioral and Brain Sciences, 28*, 795–815.

Howitt, P., & Clower, R. (2000). The emergence of economic organization. *Journal of Economic Behavior, and Organization, 41*, 55–84.

Hurrelmann, A. (2005). *Agricultural land markets: Organisation, institutions, costs and contracts in Poland: Vol. 24. Institutional change in agriculture and natural resources.* Aachen: Shaker.

Hurrelmann, A. (2008). Analysing agricultural land markets as organisations: An empirical study in Poland. *Journal of Economic Behavior & Organization, 67*, 338–349.

Janssen, M. A., & Ostrom, E. (2006). Empirically based, agent-based models. *Ecology and Society,* 11, article 37, from: http://www.ecologyandsociety.org/vol11/iss2/art37/.

Janssen, M. A., Walker, B. H., Langridge, J., & Abel, N. (2000). An adaptive agent model for analysing co-evolution of management and policies in a complex rangeland system. *Ecological Modelling, 131*, 249–268.

Klein, P. G. (2005). The make-or-buy decision: Lessons from empirical studies. In: C. Menard (Ed.), *Handbook of new institutional economics* (pp. 435–464). Dordrecht: Springer.

Klein, B., Crawford, R. G., & Alchian, A. A. (1978). Vertical integration, appropriable rents, and the competitive contracting process. *Journal of Law & Economics, 21*, 297–326.

Knack, S., & Keefer, P. (1995). Institutions and economic performance: Cross-country tests using alternative institutional measures. *Economics and Politics, 7*, 207–227.

Knight, J. (1992). *Institutions and social conflict.* Cambridge: Cambridge University Press.

La Porta, R., Lopez de Silanes, F., Shleifer, A., & Vishny, R. W. (1998). Law and finance. *Journal of Political Economy, 106*, 1113–1155.

Laffont, J. J., & Martimort, D. (2002). *The theory of incentives: The principal-agent model.* Princeton: Princeton University Press.

Libecap, G. D., & Wiggins, S. N. (1985). The influence of private contractual failure on regulation: The case of oil-field unitization. *Journal of Political Economy, 93*, 690–714.

List, J. A. (2008). Economics: Homo experimentalis evolves. *Science 321*, 207–208.

Macher, J. T., & Richman, B. D. (2008). Transaction cost economics: An assessment of empirical research in the social sciences. *Business and Politics,* 10, article 1, from http://www. bepress.com /bap/vol10/iss1/art1.

Masten, S. E., & Saussier, S. (2002). Econometrics of contracts: An assessment of developments in the empirical literature on contracting. In E. Brousseau & J. -M. Glachant (Eds.), *The economics of contracts. Theories and application* (pp. 273–292). Cambridge: Cambridge University Press.

Mathijs, E., & Swinnen, J. F. M. (1998). The economics of agricultural decollectivization in East Central Europe and the former Soviet Union. *Economic Development and Cultural Change, 47*, 1–26.

Mathijs, E., & Swinnen, J. F. M. (2001). Production organization and efficiency during transition: An empirical analysis of East German agriculture. *Review of Economics and Statistics, 83*, 100–107.

Ménard, C. (2001). Methodological issues in new institutional economics. *Journal of Economic Methodology, 8*, 85–92.

Ménard, C., & Shirley, M. M. (2005). *Handbook of new institutional economics.* Dordrecht: Springer.

Nikiforakis, N. (2008). Punishment and counter-punishment in public good games: Can we really govern ourselves? *Journal of Public Economics, 92*, 91–112.

Nelson, R., & Winter, S. (1982*). An evolutionary theory of economic change.* Cambridge: Cambridge University Press.

North, D. C. (1990). *Institutions, institutional change, and economic performance.* Cambridge: Cambridge University Press.

North, D. C. (1994). Economic performance through time. *American Economic Review,* 84, 359–368.

North, D. C., & Thomas, R. P. (1973). *The rise of the Western world: A new economic history*. Cambridge: Cambridge University Press.

Olson, M. (1965). *The logic of collective action: Public goods and the theory of groups*. Cambridge: Harvard University Press.

Olson, M. (1982). *The rise and decline of nations: Economic growth, stagflation, and social rigidities*. New Haven: Yale University Press.

Ostrom, E. (1990). *Governing the commons: The evolution of institutions for collective action*. Cambridge: Cambridge University Press.

Ostrom, E. (2005a). Doing institutional analysis: Digging deeper than markets and hierarchies. In C. Ménard & M. M. Shirley (Eds.), *Handbook of new institutional economics*. (pp. 819–848). Dordrecht: Springer.

Ostrom, E. (2005b). *Understanding institutional diversity*. Princeton: Princeton University Press.

Pierson, P. (2004). *Politics in time: History, institutions, and social analysis*. Princeton: Princeton University Press.

Poteete, A. R., & Ostrom, E. (2004). In pursuit of comparable concepts and data about collective action. *Agricultural Systems, 82*, 215–232.

Poteete, A. R., & Ostrom, E. (2008). Fifteen years of empirical research on collective action in natural resource management: Struggling to build large-N databases based on qualitative research. *World Development, 36*, 176–195.

Rao, P. K. (2003). *The economics of transaction costs: Theory, methods and applications*. Basingstoke: Palgrave Macmillan.

Robin S., & Staropoli, C. (2008). Experimental methodology to inform new institutional economics. In E. Brousseau & J.-M. Glachant (Eds.), *New institutional economics: A guidebook* (pp. 142–157). Cambridge: Cambridge University Press.

Rodrik, D. (1996). Understanding economic policy reform. *Journal of Economic Literature, 34*, 9–41.

Rodrik, D., Subramanian, A., & Trebbi, F. (2004). Institutions rule: The primacy of institutions over geography and integration in economic development. *Journal of Economic Growth, 9*, 131–165.

Ross S. A. (1973). Economic theory of agency: Principals problem. *American Economic Review, 63*, 134–139.

Saleth, R. M., & Dinar, A. (2004). *The institutional economics of water: A cross-country analysis of institutions and performance*. Cheltenham and Northampton: Edward Elgar.

Scharpf, F. W. (1997). *Games real actors play: Actor-centered institutionalism in policy research*. Boulder: Westview Press.

Schelling, T. C. (1971). Dynamic models of segregation. *Journal of Mathematical Sociology, 1*, 143–186.

Schlüter, A. (2001). *Institutioneller Wandel und Transformation: Restitution, Transformation und Privatisierung in der tschechischen Landwirtschaft*. Institutioneller Wandel der Landwirtschaft und Ressourcennutzung, Bd. 3. Aachen: Shaker.

Schlüter, M., & Pahl-Wostl, C. (2007). Mechanisms of resilience in common-pool resource management systems: An agent-based model of water use in a river basin. *Ecology and Society, 12*, article 4, from: http://www.ecologyandsociety.org/vol12/iss2/art4/.

Schmid, A. (2004). *Conflict and cooperation: Institutional and behavioral economics*. Oxford: Blackwell.

Seawright, J., & Gerring, J. (2008). Case selection techniques in case study research: A menu of qualitative and quantitative options. *Political Research Quarterly, 61*, 294–308.

Shelanski, H. A., & Klein, P. G. (1995). Empirical-research in transaction cost economics – A review and assessment. *Journal of Law Economics and Organization, 11*, 335–361.

Smith, V. L. (1994). Economics in the laboratory. *Journal of Economic Perspectives, 8*, 113–131.

Stiglitz, J. E. (1974). Incentives and risk sharing in sharecropping. *Review of Economic Studies, 41*, 219–255.

Sykuta, M. E. (2008). New institutional econometrics: The case of contracting and organization research. In E. Brousseau & J.-M. Glachant (Eds.), *New institutional economics: A guidebook* (pp. 122–141). Cambridge: Cambridge University Press.

Tesfatsion, L., & Judd, K. L. (Eds.). (2006). *Handbook of computational economics: Agent-based computational economics.* Oxford: Elsevier.

Vatn, A. (2005). *Institutions and the environment.* Cheltenham and Northampton: Edward Elgar.

Verbeek, M. (2004). *A guide to modern econometrics.* West Sussex: John Wiley & Sons.

Wang, N. (2001). The coevolution of institutions, organizations, and ideology: The Longlake experience of property rights transformation. *Politics & Society, 29*, 415–445.

Williamson, O. E. (1975). *Markets and hierarchies: Analysis and antitrust implications.* New York: Free Press.

Williamson, O. E. (1981). The modern corporation: Origins, evolution, attributes. *Journal of Economic Literature, 19*, 1537–1568.

Williamson, O. E. (1985). *The economic institutions of capitalism: Firms, markets, relational contracting.* New York: Free Press.

Williamson, O. E. (1996). *The mechanisms of governance.* New York: Oxford University Press.

Williamson, O. E. (1998). The institutions of governance. *American Economic Review, 88*, 75–79.

Williamson, O. E. (2000). The new institutional economics: Taking stock, looking ahead. *Journal of Economic Literature*, 38, 595–613.

Yin, R. K. (2003). *Case study research: Design and methods.* Thousand Oaks: Sage Publications.

Young, H. P. (1998). *Individual strategy and social structure: An evolutionary theory of institutions.* Princeton: Princeton University Press.

Young, O. R. (2002). *The institutional dimensions of environmental change: Fit, interplay, and scale.* Cambridge: MIT Press.

Index